"...quite a feat to integrate research articles from so many domains and turn them in a very readable, inspiring, useful often surprising and even stirring book... not only the problems, but also the solutions."
Daniel Blumberg, Principal and Investor, NY

"...everybody keeps complaining about a continuous input overload. Yet the real quandary is: while we are continuously flooded by the breakers of redundant signals we do suffer from a lack of relevant information. In his new book Theo Compernolle describes and analyzes this state of affairs and its impact on our daily life and our habitual and creative performance."
Gottlieb Guntern, President of Creando – International Foundation for Creativity & Leadership, Switzerland

"... blending his best knowledge in medical sciences and leadership development to give us a real eye opener on how our brain is working (or not) in our new environment"
Serge Zimmerlin. Group Vice President, Human Resources & Communication. SGD Group. France

"The book was a revelation for me and helped me better understand why people do what they do in a health & safety context. An essential and easy read for practical people, who want to know how people work and what can be practically done to maximize their efficiency and reduce human error"
Malc Staves, Global Health & Safety Director, L'Oréal

BRAINCHAINS

**DISCOVER YOUR BRAIN AND UNLEASH ITS FULL POTENTIAL
IN A HYPERCONNECTED MULTITASKING WORLD**

THEO COMPERNOLLE

COMPUBLICATIONS
SCIENCE MADE SIMPLE AND USEFUL

To my two most beloved successful brainworkers: my daughters
Phil and Lou.

BRAINCHAINS ONLINE
For free texts, related books, updates, discussions and comments
visit www.brainchains.info

ABOUT THE AUTHOR

Dr Theo Compernolle MD. PhD. Is an adjunct professor at the CEDEP European Centre for Executive Development (France) and teaches and coaches in the executive programs of business schools including INSEAD in France and TIAS in the Netherlands. He also consults, teaches and coaches professionals, managers and executives in a wide range of (multi)national companies, professional services firms and training institutions in many different cultures and countries. He holds these sessions in English, Dutch and French.

He has held the positions of Suez Chair in Leadership and Personal Development at the Solvay Business School, Adjunct Professor at INSEAD, visiting professor at several business schools and Professor at the Free University of Amsterdam.

As a medical doctor, neuropsychiatrist, psychotherapist and business consultant, Theo studies research from very different fields including medicine, biology, psychology, neurology, physiology and management. He then burns the midnight oil to integrate this information into a coherent whole and to find simple ways to pass on this knowledge, in a memorable way, to all kinds of professionals. His clients often call his sessions "Science made simple and useful".

Theo was first drawn into the world of business after the publication of his PhD about stress caused quite a stir in the media.

Since then he has become an expert on the emotional and relational aspects of leadership and enhancing the resilience of executives, executive teams, organizations and families with a business, especially in times of conflict, stress and change.

He has published several non-fiction books and more than a hundred scientific articles. Three of his books ao. "Stress: Friend and Foe. Vital Stress Management at work and in the family" became bestsellers and long-sellers.

He has also been the director of several inpatient and outpatient departments.

Theo gained a Ph.D on his research into stress from the University of Amsterdam (the Netherlands). He is certified as a psychotherapist and as medical specialist in neuropsychiatry and psychotherapy. He trained at the universities of Amsterdam (The Netherlands), Leiden (The Netherlands) and Pennsylvania (USA) where he was a fellow. He graduated as a Medical Doctor from the Catholic University of Leuven (Belgium).

Thanks to my late mother who tried to channel my many and diverse childhood interests and activities by endlessly repeating: "Do one thing, do your best, finish up and tidy up".

Thanks to the TIASNIMBAS business school which allowed me to keep using their electronic scientific databases, to Pierre Vermeulen who helped me out with the statistical analysis of my survey, to the 1,500 people who answered my survey, to Anna Jenkinson who turned my personal English into excellent English, Huw Aaron who did the illustrations, and Suzan Beijer and Hans Bosch who did the layout.

Many paragraphs in this book are inspired by the challenging questions and the willingness to try out new behaviors of my executive coachees, especially in the group coaching sessions we pioneered at INSEAD. I am also thankful for the more than enthusiastic and inspiring participation of the managers in Sam Abadir's great program "Leadership and Safety" that is organized six times a year at CEDEP. These Safety, Health and Environment (SHE) managers and plant managers are the quickest to realize the consequences for daily work of what they learn about the brain and BrainChains. They are also the most eager to collect the low hanging fruit in terms of productivity and safety.

Thanks also to David Strayer for permission to use his picture of the impact of using a phone on our vision while driving and to Shai Danziger for the graph of his research on decision fatigue.

Last but not least, thanks to Annemarie who has been there for me for more than 40 years and reminds me every day that there are more important things in life than writing a book, as fascinating as the subject may be.

Editor: Anna Jenkinson
Graphic design: Suzan Beijer
Illustrations: Huw Aaron

FEEDBACK
If you have any feedback, comments, criticism or suggestions to improve
this book, please contact me at: comments@brainchains.org
If you like the book, please leave a comment at Amazon.com or at
www.brainchains.org

ISBN: 978 90 822 0580 0
NUR: 771

THE BRAIN is wider than the sky,
For, put them side by side,
The one the other will include
With ease, and you beside.

The brain is deeper than the sea,
For, hold them, blue to blue,
The one the other will absorb,
As sponges, buckets do.

EMILY DICKINSON (1830–1886)

*

There is time enough for everything, in the course of the day,
if you do but one thing at once; but there is not time enough
in the year, if you will do two things at a time.
The steady and undissipated attention to one object is
a sure mark of a superior genius; as hurry, bustle and
agitation are the never-failing symptoms of a weak and frivo-
lous mind.

LORD CHESTERFIELD APRIL (1694-1773)

*

It's not that I'm so smart; it's just that I stay with
problems longer.

ALBERT EINSTEIN (1879-1955)

*

So a great intellect sinks to the level of an ordinary one,
as soon as it is interrupted and disturbed, its attention distracted and drawn off from the matter in hand; for its superi-
ority depends upon its power of concentration –
of bringing all its strength to bear upon one theme, in the
same way as a concave mirror collects into one point all
the rays of light that strike upon it.

ARTHUR SCHOPENHAUER: ON NOISE. 1851[1]

CONTENTS

IS THIS A BOOK FOR YOU?

1.1 ABOUT BRAINCHAINS AND BRAINGAINS

This is a book for you if you want to significantly improve your intellectual performance and take full advantage of the ICT (Information and Communication Technology) revolution – e-mail, texting, social media, the Internet, smartphones, tablets, computers etc. – to release the full potential of both your brain and your ICT tools.

This is certainly a book for you if you sometimes feel that your ICT use in general and e-mail in particular has a negative impact on your intellectual productivity, and even more so if you think you can multitask and that it is just fine to always be connected.

This is also a book for you if you would simply love to know how your thinking brain, your most important tool, works. Let there be no misunderstanding: Computers are unbelievably far from the sophistication of a human brain. The only thing computers do much better is massive number crunching, and analyzing data, big data. As I will describe later on, a computer that primitively mimics the working of a human brain would weigh a massive 40,000 tons and consume approximately all the megawatts of a nuclear power plant. You carry much more computing power than that around in your skull as only 3 pounds of wetware consuming a mere 30 Watt. Why not learn something more about your magnificent brain to unleash its full potential?

In this book you will not only learn about your fantastic brain, but also about the BrainChains that ruin too many people's intellectual performance and the countless BrainGains you can make individually, as a team and as a company to break those chains.

If you are also interested in knowing where I got the idea and the motivation to review more than 600 research articles and write this book, please turn to the afterword where I explain in more detail:
- how the managers, professionals and teams I coach, train and teach got me worried about how always being connected and multitasking is undermining their intellectual productivity and their problem-solving ability;
- why after reading several dozen research articles to prepare for a keynote presentation, I became so alarmed that I ended up postponing other projects and taking five years to review more than 600 research publications and write this easy-to-read book;
- why this research got me so upset that my working title became "How we unknowingly f*** up our intellectual productivity by always being connected and multitasking";
- why I think that many professionals get caught up in an inefficiency trap when they use gadgets made to privately consume information, to professionally process and produce information;
- and why I divided this book into three sections: the Brain, the BrainChains (the problems and challenges) and the BrainGains (the solutions).

1.2 THIS IS A BOOK FOR YOU IF YOU WANT TO SIGNIFICANTLY IMPROVE YOUR INTELLECTUAL PERFORMANCE

Intellectual performance is the most important contributor to progress in general and economic growth in particular. Your own intellectual performance, based on your IQ and EQ, is the most significant contributor to your personal development as well as to your career. In the working world you increasingly deal with non-routine and complex matters because the routine and simple work is gradually being taken over by computers. The only work left is that which only a human brain can do.

We can all therefore be considered as "brainworkers". I prefer this term to "knowledge workers" because knowledge worker is understood too much as professionals who only use very sophisticated knowledge: IT specialists, managers, consultants, engineers, lawyers etc... But people on the front lines like management assistants, bank tellers, office workers and most people who do manual work have become brainworkers too. Pure "brainless" work has all but disappeared; we are all brainworkers now. The words brainwork and brainworker also put the emphasis on the only place where knowledge resides and where in the end intellectual productivity happens: the human brain.

In today's world, where information technology is increasingly taking over more complex work, knowing how your brain works and how you can increase your intellectual performance is more important than ever before. And yet, astonishingly, the majority of brainworkers don't have a clue about the workings of their most important tool: their amazing brain.

▶ **Professional success depends on our brainwork, but professionals don't know how their brain works.**

We are living through an ICT revolution where if you make good use of ICT you can increase your intellectual performance tremendously. If on the other hand you unintentionally use ICT in the wrong way, failing to take into account the strengths and weaknesses of the human brain, then instead of increasing the power of your brain, you shackle it in BrainChains. Since you do this unknowingly, I'd like to explain what science knows about how your thinking brain works and how you can unchain your brain.

First of all, let's be clear about the nature of this ICT revolution: it is certainly not one where supercomputers or a network of computers will replace the human brain. People who make this claim often use the example of the IBM Watson computer winning in Jeopardy or the earlier example of the IBM supercomputer "Deep Blue" beating the world chess champion Garry Kasparov. These kinds of declarations are based on a double ignorance: ignorance about computers, and above all ignorance about the workings and abilities of the amazing human brain.

Well-informed IT people do not fall into the trap of the News-week article "The Brain's Last Stand"[2], published shortly before the Deep Blue vs Kasparov match. Quite the contrary, Kasparov himself writes: "The AI [Artificial Intelligence] crowd [imagined] a computer that thought and played chess like a human, with human creativity and intuition, [but] they got one that played like a machine, systematically evaluating 200 million possible moves on the chess board per second and winning with brute number-crunching force[3]."

After playing for a while, a 6-year-old will have better knowledge and better insight into what the game of chess is about than the biggest supercomputer. Why? Because the only tool capable of insight and knowledge is the human brain. In his workshops the influential scientist Gregory Bateson often said that a computer will only get a little closer to the unique abilities of a human brain the day it answers a question with "This reminds me of a story", using original, creative metaphors to provide meaning.

The real heart of the ICT revolution is that, together, the power of modern ICT combined with the unique ability of the human brain to reflect can lead to insights and knowledge that separately they never can or ever will realize. The combination of, on the one hand, the digital processing, storing and networking power of modern computers that make massive amounts of data and information easy to retrieve and process and, on the other hand, the unique reflecting power of the human brain that is the only tool that can reflect in order to generate knowledge and insights, is unbeatable. The revolution is one of close synergy between ICT and the human brain, where ICT amplifies the strengths and complements the weaknesses of the human brain and vice versa.

▶   **For an optimal synergy between your ICT and your brain, you need to know something about your brain.**

By the way, Kasparov himself was very aware of this and experimented with a chess game where the players were allowed to use chess computers. Playchess.com followed up on this idea and in

2005 organized a big tournament, where the company discovered that mid-level chess players who made good use of average chess computers were able to beat the best chess supercomputers as well as teams of grandmasters[4].

Today we have almost as much computing power in our smartphones as the super-computer that beat Kasparov in 1997, and yet we are still only at the beginning of this revolution of collaboration between brains and computers. One of the places where this is particularly evident is the workplace, where during most of their working day professionals do not make the best use of their ICT to increase the performance of their brain; in fact, it's much worse than that, they use ICT in ways that ruin their intellectual productivity and creativity.

This book is therefore written for people who want to understand their brain better, who want to break the BrainChains they unknowingly fabricate and who want to improve their intellectual productivity, creativity and problem solving. It is a book for all brainworkers who want to release the full potential of both their brains and their ICT.

In the first section I explain how your thinking brain works. For most people this is new and surprising information that, by itself, often leads to higher intellectual productivity and new ways of working.

In the second section I explain how you chain your brain when you do not take into account the strengths and weaknesses of your thinking brain, how this makes you much less efficient and effective than you could be and how this also has a negative influence on your behavior. I know from the experiences of those I have coached and trained that these insights by themselves will already inspire you to make better use of your brain.

In the third section I give examples of tips, tricks and experiments to unchain your brain and become more efficient and effective. The solutions range from those that can be implemented by the individual to those for companies as a whole. I'd like to advise you, however, not to jump straight to the third section because a good understanding of the brain and the BrainChains will make you much more creative in finding your own personal solutions.

1.3 THIS IS CERTAINLY A BOOK FOR YOU IF YOU FEEL THAT YOUR ICT USE HAS A NEGATIVE IMPACT ON YOUR PRODUCTIVITY

Before launching into the book, let's first check if you really need it. It takes just 10 simple questions to find out. If it turns out you don't need it, don't waste your time. Instead, give it as a present to somebody who really needs it; the questionnaire will clearly show you who that person is.

Of course you may simply want to know how your brain works either to achieve optimal intellectual productivity or simply because the subject fascinates you.

If your answer is yes, skip the following questions and start reading Section 1.

If your answer is maybe or no, or if you got this book as a present, then first read the statements below and see if they apply to you. In these statements the word "online" means Internet, e-mail, text messages, social media etc...

A THREE-MINUTE TEST TO KNOW IF YOU NEED THIS BOOK

1 At work I usually juggle at least five tasks at the same time, constantly switching back and forth between them, often without completing them (for example interrupting the writing of a memo to answer a call, then answering a few e-mails, being interrupted by my boss or a colleague with a more urgent request, going back to the last e-mail, then to the memo etc...) **YES/NO**

2 I always check my e-mail before doing other things **YES/NO**

3 When I'm online and someone needs me, I usually say "just a few more minutes" before stopping **YES/NO**

4 I am regularly online on the toilet **YES/NO**

5 I usually sleep less than 7 hours **YES/NO**

6 I often experience a continuous (low) level of stress or tension **YES/NO**

7 At work, I am only able to work undisturbed for 45 minutes on a single task (no phone, no e-mail, no messages) twice a week or less **YES/NO**

8 Even if I am not disturbed, I find it difficult to stay concentrated on a book or an important but long report for at least half an hour **YES/NO**

QUESTIONS 1 TO 8:

- You answered yes only once: Reading this book is not urgent, but you may learn a lot of fascinating things about your brain that will help you to be more efficient and effective.
- Your only yes is that you sleep less than 7 hours: Go straight to the chapter entitled "BrainChain #4" about the impact of sleep on intellectual productivity and creativity.
- You answered yes more than once: The more times you answered yes, the more urgent and important it is to read this book. Your efficiency and effectiveness at work will improve by at least 20% and more likely 50%. The more yeses, the greater the gain.

****

9 I regularly make phone calls while driving Yes/No
10 I sometimes text (SMS) while driving Yes/No

QUESTIONS 9-10:
- You answered yes to at least one of these questions: Turn immediately to Section 2, Chapter 8 and read it now. For you, this is urgent and important. You can read the rest of the book later.

TEN QUESTIONS TO KNOW HOW DIFFICULT IT WILL BE FOR YOU TO CHANGE

If you want to have an idea of how easy or difficult it will be for you to break your BrainChains and significantly improve your intellectual productivity, answer the following 10 questions:

1 I sometimes find myself looking forward to, even longing for, the next time I'll be online **YES/NO**
2 I sometimes spend time online rather than going out with others **YES/NO**
3 I sometimes lie about how long I've been online or try to hide it **YES/NO**
4 I regularly go to sleep too late because I stay online too long **YES/NO**
5 I find that the longer I spend online, the lower the satisfaction, and yet despite this feeling I stay online **YES/NO**

6 I often stay online longer than I had originally planned **YES/NO**

7 When I cannot get online or when I try to reduce my time online, I feel anxious, nervous, restless, moody or irritable **YES/NO**

8 Others in my life sometimes complain about the amount of time I spend online **YES/NO**

9 Going online lets me escape when I have problems or feel a little bit depressed, anxious or nervous **YES/NO**

10 I have tried several times to reduce the time I spend online, but I have not succeeded **YES/NO**

- You answered yes three times: It will be difficult for you to become more efficient and more effective because always being connected has become a bad habit. However, if you apply the ideas in this book, your intellectual productivity will improve extremely significantly. Do bear in mind though that in the beginning you will need a lot of willpower, even if you use the best tricks and tools I describe in Section 3.

- You answered yes more than three times: You are probably so addicted to being connected that you won't be able to find the necessary motivation and willpower to change. You also probably have such a strong streak of rationalization that you have convinced yourself that you are the exception to all the research. On the other hand, you bought this book so there is hope. If you received the book as a present from somebody who cares about you, the message is crystal clear and this might motivate you to change. And of course if you do succeed, the return will be so much higher for you than for anybody else.

WARNING

If you answered "yes" several times in these questionnaires, think twice before you read this book. It may seriously harm your peace of mind.

At the moment you can still claim ignorance if you do things that totally ruin the quality and the quantity of your brainwork, that sometimes undermine your relations and that may even be very dangerous. However, once you have read this book, if you still keep doing these things, you will feel stupid or guilty or both.

For the same reason, don't give this book to anybody you think will answer "yes" many times unless you are certain that the person can handle the brutal facts.

YOUR THINKING BRAIN AND ITS TWO FRENEMIES; KNOW THEM BETTER TO USE THEM BETTER

1 WE ARE ALL BRAINWORKERS AND OUR SUCCESS DEPENDS ON OUR INTELLECTUAL PRODUCTIVITY

We are living in a world where our success depends on the quantity and quality of our brainwork, but a majority of brainworkers unknowingly ruin their intellectual productivity because they have no clue about what the human brain can and can't do. Isn't it strange that you don't know how your most important tool works?

▶ **Your success depends on your brainwork, therefore you should know how your brain works.**

As I explained at the start of the foreword, pure "brainless" work has all but disappeared from the workplace, meaning that in today's world we are all brainworkers.

For one of my client companies in the industrial maintenance industry, building scaffolds is a very important part of their business. These scaffolds are dozens of meters high, with extremely high safety standards for the builders and the users.

When they started to operate in Asia, they could not find people trained as scaffolders. Hearing that in Nepal there are villages where people do not suffer from a fear of heights, they went over there, with two containers of scaffolding materials. With the permission of the elders, they invited young men to the village square. There, without much explanation, two experienced scaffolders built a simple cube. The onlookers were then invited to copy the structure. Some young men immediately got it, demonstrating that they had the excellent spatial and dexterity skills needed to copy the structure. They were hired and further trained at a special scaffolding school and became excellent scaffolders... with one interesting characteristic: They were illiterate, they couldn't read or write.

At a keynote speech for the top 300 managers I asked them "Are your illiterate scaffolders brainworkers?" 25% of the managers said no. The further away they were from the shop floor, the less the managers considered the scaffolders to be brainworkers. Then I showed them a picture of one of the huge scaffolds they built and asked my question again. Now the response was almost 100% yes. You not only need skillful hands but also very good brains to build such a scaffold safely.

2 THE ICT TOOLS ARE NOT THE PROBLEM; IT'S THE WAY WE USE THEM

A few years ago, while coaching professionals and managers, both individually and in groups, I became worried that because they knew little or nothing about the human brain, they were using their great information technology in such a way that it undermined their intellectual productivity, both in terms of quality and quantity. I became even more alarmed as I prepared for a keynote presentation and discovered the massive amount of research supporting my first impression. It spurred me on to dedicate five years screening more than 600 research publications, reading more than 400 of them and writing this book. The findings made me so upset that my working title became "How we unknowingly f*** up our intellectual productivity by always being connected and multitasking".

The World Wide Web started as a tool for scientists to exchange information. The www is still a fantastic source of information if you already know enough to differentiate the trustworthy information from the massive amount of trivia, junk, swindle and deceit.

Technological companies spend billions on the design of software and hardware like smartphones and tablets to seduce billions of customers to stick around on their site *to consume, if not guzzle, trivial information* in ways that make you reveal as much valuable personal information as possible about you and your contacts (whom they cleverly call friends) to sell their ads. They invent *gadgets* to keep the consumers glued to their screens,

THERE IS NOTHING WRONG WITH THE TECHNOLOGY

TOOLS

THE PROBLEM IS THE WAY WE USE THESE GREAT TOOLS.

connected all the time and everywhere, busy with software and media designed to be as sticky if not as addictive as possible. In the future smart watches, smart glasses and smart rings will chain and enslave these poor brains even more. Being connected has become the equivalent of hyperactively skipping from one snippet of information to another, just for the fun of it, without properly digesting any of it.

Your job as a professional, however, is *to digest, understand, process, produce and create information, knowledge and insights* both for your company and for your personal development and career. If you use all the great information technology in the same way as the billions of mere consumers and let yourself be seduced into being online all the time and everywhere, then you are caught in an information consumption or even addiction trap. You are enslaved rather than free, following rather than leading and trapped in a place where there is no room to be really focused, intellectually productive and creative.

As a brainworker you have to be in charge of your ICT to lead it where you want to go, to stay with the information and to reflect on it. When you are continuously in reactive consumption mode, you have no time or space to process the information and develop your own creative ideas or to develop them into something of value. You ruin your performance when you use the very sticky and addictive apps and gadgets, developed to consume information, in order to produce professional information.

While some consumer ICT gadgets are interesting for professional work too, brainworkers should use this technology differently, adopting a fundamentally different attitude and being aware of the risk of becoming inefficient and wasting massive amounts of time on them. You should react against their stickiness and frequently disconnect to do the harder work of reflecting, having real conversations, doing some thorough reading and creating knowledge.

I think this was a dilemma for Microsoft when it produced Windows 8. They chose to seduce the billions of swiping page-hopping consumers, while frustrating millions of professionals who don't need distracting apps and sticky social media. To do their knowledge work for many hours a day they need equipment developed not for consuming but for processing information: professional software large screens, good keyboards and mice, a brain-friendly office and good ergonomics to avoid ruining necks, thumbs, wrists, shoulders and backs.

This conflict between consuming trivia and processing-creating information is also the major cause why MOOCs (Massive Open Online Courses) are failing. A MOOC is an online college or university course, sometimes developed by the best of scholars and teachers, and often available for free, that anybody can follow anywhere in the world. They seek to enable people in low-quality colleges in the USA as well as in the poorest of countries to get good-quality teaching, democratizing higher education. As a study by the University of Pennsylvania Graduate School of Education showed[1], however, the results are worse than disappointing despite the big and enthusiastic investments in effort and money. This study looked at millions of people who registered and found that only between 27% and 68% even bothered to look at at least one lecture and only 2% to 14% more or less completed the course. An experiment providing online tutors did only marginally better[2].

One of the most important reasons for this major failure has to do with the enthusiastic initiators totally underestimating, on the one hand the extent to which our behavior is influenced by the way a context is marked, and on the other the extent to which being on the www has become a context heavily marked for the consumption of trivia, which is the opposite of an environment for learning. To process information we need a totally different context, one that enhances reflection and real conversations and discussions. These are hard work and require prolonged periods of being completely disconnected from any distractions (more on this in the following chapters). This is the kind of context, structure and environment that a good college or university provides, even if their professors are not the best scientists in the world, provided that they teach and train their pupils and students to disconnect to reflect. This is the total opposite of the www context.

If my hypothesis is correct, MOOCs have no chance of succeeding, unless they teach and train their students to systematically disconnect to reflect and process information, something that seems to me to be very difficult to do while being online. My hypothesis seems to be supported by the fact that in the PENN study completion rates are somewhat higher, but still extremely poor, for courses with lower workloads for students and fewer homework assignments (about 6% versus 2.5%), clearly demanding less of the hard work of processing information. Some MOOC pioneers think the solution is to put the emphasis on connections and communication among students in social media style rather than on the content delivered by a professor. As we will see further on though, virtual meetings and discussions do not make any sense whatsoever when nobody takes the time to prepare thoroughly beforehand, with the hard work of studying, reflecting on and processing the facts. Without this preparation, communication between students becomes nothing but an idle exchange of baseless opinions.

My own experience as a student and a very successful teacher has taught me that one of the important roles of a professor is to enthuse students about the subject and in this way motivate them to do the hard work of studying and maybe even prompt the student to choose the subject as his profession[3]. Even the best MOOCs can't do this. The live course of a good teacher in the company of other interested students is to a MOOC what a live concert in the company of other fans is to the same concert on TV.

3 AMAZING FACTS ABOUT YOUR BRAIN

Let's first get acquainted with this most important of tools: your brain. If you want to get the best out of your brain, you should know the basics of how it works and how you can best use it for optimal intellectual productivity.

3.1 160 BILLION CELLS AND 8 QUADRILLION CONNECTIONS

The human brain is the most complex object in the known universe. The whole World Wide Web, with all its servers, Network Access Points, backbones, routers, modems, hubs, bridges, switches and all the computers linked to it, is a very simple and primitive network compared to one single brain.

In our brain we have 80 billion neurons (from the Greek word for string), of some 10,000 different types. Each neuron cell functions like a small computer or microprocessor processing electrical signals. At the same time each cell is also acting as a chemical factory, sending chemical signals to other cells. These chemicals are called neuro-transmitters: they transmit messages from one neuron to another. The cells influence each other *and* the connections between other cells. An important neuro-transmitter is dopamine, which among other things gives us a feeling of excitement. Others are similar to opium, which among many other things kills pain and gives us a feeling of satisfaction. We will discuss these later to better understand why it is so difficult to disconnect from the Internet and why many people become really addicted to it.

Our brain also has some 80 billion Glia cells. Until recently scientists thought that the Glia cells only provided structural support, metabolic support, insulation and a matrix for development. Since our neurons are not regularly replaced like most other cells in our body, they have to be kept in shape and nurtured caringly by these Glia cells. Now scholars are beginning to discover that these cells also play a role in the information processing of our brain because they influence the connections between the neurons[4]. As we will see in the chapter about sleep, these Glia cells also control waste management. You can easily imagine how very important this is given that the brain cells produce and release chemicals all the time.

This brings the total number of brain cells that help us to process data to about ± 160 billion, or 160,000 million. This is 48 times more than the number of people on earth connected to the Internet in 2012. It is half the number of all the stars in the Milky Way.

The neurons that play the lead role are linked with 1,000 to 400,000 other neurons. This gives us more than 8 quadrillion ever changing connections. If we consider the vesicles in the connections as transistors, the brain has 400 quadrillion transistors. See next page.

The brain as a whole is a sort of super-super-super-computer or rather billions of microcomputers perfectly coordinated in a gigantic network of networks of networks of networks. Each single cell in itself already functions as a little network. For storing new information and skills we do not necessarily need new cells, just new connections. A lot of this connecting, disconnecting and reconnecting happens while we sleep.

Until rather recently these connections were considered more or less like the copper wires transmitting electrical current quickly (1.2 to 250 miles per hour) but passively from one cell to another. It turns out, however, that these brain wires are not passive at all. They influence the flow of messages, they can send messages back and they are able to do quite a lot of information processing by themselves[5], making the total computing power of the brain unfathomable for people who are not used to dealing with astronomically big numbers. This amazing network is the brain! The brain is the network!

	(short scale=ss)	US-UK (long scale=ls)	EU	SPINNAKER (GOAL)
Neurons ("processors")	80,000,000,000	80 billion	80 milliard	1 million (modeled)
Glia	80,000,000,000	80 billion	80 milliard	
Firing of neurons 0–500/second (for this comparison 100)	8,000,000,000 000	8 trillion/s	8 billion/s	9 billion(ss)/sec
Anatomical connections: synapses 1,000–400,000/neuron (for this comparison 1000)	8,000,000,000,000,000	8 quadrillion	8 billiard	
Functional Connections/second (current passing from one neuron to the other)				9 trillion(ss)/sec
Vesicles ("transistors") (For this comparison 50 active)	400,000,000,000,000,000	400 quadrillion	400 billiard	1 billion(ss) On 50,000 chips
Energy consumption	30 watt *not included: cooling, energy transport, support etc... = total body in the service of brain)*			50,000 watt (Chips only, not cooling etc...)
	1,5 kg			450 kg
Computation	(massive) parallel, distributed			Hierarchical and distributed
Fault tolerant	Very much			A little
Learns (reorganizes itself) with experience	Very much			Potentially

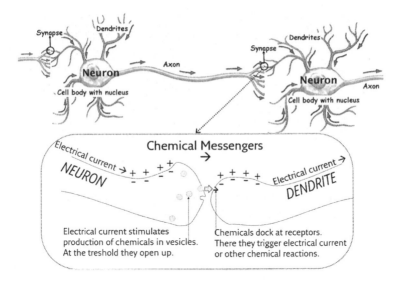

For those interested, here's a quick word on how information is transmitted among brain cells. This also explains how each neuron is not only like a computer, but also like a chemical factory. The neurons receive information, process information and pass it on to other neurons. A signal produced in a neuron travels to the next neuron via the axon (from the Greek axon, "axis"). It travels along this axon as an electrical current. Some axons are only a few micrometers long to reach a neighboring cell, others are about 60 inches long to get information to and from our big toe. The axon branches out to connect with the dendrites (from the Greek dendron, "tree", because they look like branches) of other neurons.

The connections between the neurons are called synapses (from the Greek syn- "together" and haptein "to link"). Where a branch from an axon reaches a dendrite, there is a gap. To cross the gap the current provokes the production of chemicals in little bubbles (vesicles). When the chemicals in the bubble pass a threshold, it opens up into the gap and the chemicals float to the other side, where they are absorbed. In the cell on the other side these chemicals provoke all kinds of chemical reactions that stimulate or inhibit that cell and that may produce an electrical current to pass a message on to other neurons.

Hence, what happens at the synapse is not just a passive transmission of the current, like the link between two copper wires. Each synapse modulates the signal and functions like a set of many sophisticated transistors that actively influence the signal, increasing it or decreasing it, very much influenced by signals coming from many other neurons that connect in the neighborhood. The synapse can also send a feedback-signal back to the cell-body. This whole process takes about a millisecond.

Hence, each synapse is like a chip consisting of many transistors. The thousands of synapses/chips together function like a microprocessor that, along with other fascinating parts of the cell, turn each neuron into a real computer.

The cell on the other side does not just transmit the signal either. Depending on the specialization of that cell, the arriving chemicals can provoke many different bio-chemical reactions, which may end up sending a new electrical current along its axon to a network of other cells.

All 160 billion brain cells are active and work together at the same time. Together they carry out tens of thousands of tasks simultaneously, without any central control and without us being aware of this. This gigantic network of networks of networks has no central decision maker. The most important central organ is a clock, our biological clock that synchronizes these trillions of interactions. It is a most beautiful example of what IT specialists call distributed computing, with a sophistication that is way beyond anything we can achieve with the most modern computers and computer networks, even the world wide ones.

Another superior feature of our brain is that it is amazingly fault tolerant. We can lose many cells through natural ageing or by accident, without impairing the whole system. This is possible because the brain continuously programs and reprograms itself, it wires and rewires itself, and it can change itself and heal itself, especially while we sleep. This is done all the time for individual cells or groups of cells and connections, but even big parts of the brain can take over the function of completely different parts. This is still a faraway dream for computers, where one faulty transistor can wreck a computer chip[6].

If you want to know more about this plasticity of the brain, read the fascinating book "The brain that changes itself" by Norman Dodge[7].

In brief, your most important tool, your human brain is by far the most amazing computer you could possibly imagine. The human brain is so mind-boggling in fact that even for a human brain it is, for the time being, impossible to fully understand it. In the table I compare SpiNNaker, one of the most sophisticated brain simulators, with the real brain. It's unbelievable yet true: The inventors of a computer that primitively mimics 1% of the brain are proud that their custom-built chips use only 1 Watt each, and that the computer, when finished, will consume only 50,000 Watt and weigh only 900 pounds[8] (see table below). Hence a computer that very primitively mimics the working of a human brain would be the size of a big hangar, weigh a massive 40,000 tons and consume roughly all the megawatts of three nuclear power plant. And yet you carry more than that amount of computing power around in your skull as only 3 pounds of wetware consuming a mere 30 Watt! The human brain is utterly amazing and totally unique!

3.2 NOT A MACHINE COMPOSED OF PARTS, BUT A NETWORK OF NETWORKS OF NETWORKS

Before researchers were able to observe the actual activity of the whole brain of a living person with modern neuro-imaging techniques (often called scanners), they thought about the brain as a machine and they looked for which specific hardware parts were responsible for which specific purpose. For example, 175 years ago Pierre Paul Broca discovered that people with aphasia, a disorder where people have difficulties understanding and finding words, had lesions in a very specific area of the outer layers of the brain.

After the invention of MRI (Magnetic Resonance Imaging) and above all the more recent fMRI (functional Magnetic Resonance Imaging), it became possible to see the activity of the brain cells in real time without radiation or injections. These images very clearly showed that the brain is not composed of different parts like a machine, but that it is a very complicated network of networks. This amazing brain network has a fascinating feature in common with the Internet: there is no central decision-making organ, although, as I will explain later, there are several high-level networks connecting to each other and influencing each other. What before looked like parts and areas turn out to be nodes, important relay stations in these networks. These connect with many other networks all over the brain[9]. As we will see further on, one of the domains where these modern techniques are creating a revolution is in the study of emotions.

In a sense this network works like the www, with links in all directions, but (as far as we know) not in a logical way, but more in an associative way that we do not yet understand (more on this in the section below on the archiving brain). Similar to the www, this huge network in our brain also has the advantage that when one connection is broken we can still get to the information via other links.

While the networks and the connections in these networks continuously change and develop, interestingly enough the cells themselves don't. In a creative research project Jonas Frisen measured radioactivity in different cells, radioactivity that had settled in the cells as a result of open-air experiments with atomic bombs. This enabled him to measure the age of different body cells and their turnover. He found that all cells in our body are regularly replaced, except for the egg cells in the ovary and ... the neurons in the brain. An exception to this is the part of our brain that is responsible for long-term memory, where there is a continuous replacement. Production in this area diminishes with age, but never stops[10]. There we make about 700 new cells and several thousand connections every day. This is a lot, but not enough to replace the redundant cells that are discarded. There is therefore a gradual net loss that, at a normal pace, does not cause any trouble thanks to the fault tolerance of the brain.

3.3 OUR BODY-BRAIN: CONNECTED TO EVERY SINGLE CELL OF THE BODY

To make matters even more fascinating, the brain communicates in both directions with every single one of the 50-100 trillion cells in the body. This body-brain is busy with the maintenance of our bodies, adjusting to constant changes in its environment. It does this totally autonomously, on automatic pilot. We don't have to think about things like keeping our heart beating, our blood circulating, our gut digesting or our kidneys filtering. Our body-brain takes care of this without us being at all aware. It performs all these tens of thousands of tasks at the same time with what IT specialists might see as the ultra-sophisticated distributed computing I mentioned above. This means that every cell is like a little computer that influences and is influenced by trillions of other computers. Together they process billions of routines in parallel, they lead each other and they decide together in a complex network that works at astonishing speed. The branches of this brain-system run through the whole body. They direct the working and the multiplication of all the cells; they even influence the genes in our cells. On the other hand, the cells in our body also give feedback to the body-brain so that it can adapt and adjust efficiently and at a high speed. All this activity is synchronized by the biological clock that we will discuss in more detail in the chapter about sleep.

The body-brain influences all cells in our body via three systems:
- the nervous system that reacts super-fast, via electrical currents in the nerve cells and via chemicals where the messages pass from one nerve cell to the other. In a fraction of a second, for example, it prepares your body to fight or flee in a dangerous situation.
- the endocrine system that reacts more slowly, sending hormones as its messengers via the bloodstream.
- the immune system that is a sophisticated defense system that sends out messages that coordinate actions, thereby enabling us to protect ourselves against intruders such as germs and against rebels such as cancer cells.

There is a very close interaction between these three systems. They all link into the central switchboard of the brain, the so-called hypothalamus, where the different streams of information come together, not only the unconscious information which is needed for our autonomous "automatic pilot" to maintain the biological functions of the body, but also our conscious observations, emotions, fantasies and thoughts. It is through this junction of information channels that for example stress sets off the avalanche of chain reactions that enables us to achieve extraordinary feats very quickly (More on this in chapter about the third Brain-Chain: Stress). It is also through this passage between mind and body that our body-brain and our cognitive-brain influence each other. Your brain is just a part of your body. We need a well-functioning brain-organ to be able to think. When your body has the flu, your brain has the flu too, and this will influence your thinking. On the other hand, from research in the field of psychosomatic medicine we know that our thinking can also influence the way our body functions, for example aggressive thoughts and fantasies can increase our heart rate and blood pressure.

To make this story about our brain even more interesting, and even more complicated, the circulating chemicals can play a role in all three systems. Many messenger-molecules play the role of hormonal transmitter as well as that of neuro- or immune transmitter. Particular hormones, which were previously thought to be produced only in the brain, also appear to be made by cells in the defense system and the endocrine system. If your defense system is stimulated, this influences the brain, even our reflecting brain. If our brain is stimulated, that influences the defense system!

The central switchboard where all three systems interconnect also works in close contact with the emotional system, which plays an important role in the development of basic emotions such as hunger, thirst, aggression, anxiety and sexual desire and their impact on our behavior. Here too the brain communicates very intensively with the immune system, creating a direct link between emotions and the reactions of our immune system.

Moreover, many of the messenger-molecules have multiple effects in our body. Oxytocin for example is a hormone that has long been known for its role in increasing the power of the contractions in a pregnant womb, but more recently it was discovered that it also has a positive influence on trust, bonding, caring and discrimination. Endorphins, which we produce in our brain in stress situations and are chemically similar to the synthetically produced morphine, increase our tolerance for pain and at the same time give us a high, factors that were very useful for our ancestors in the savannah when they had to fight for survival.

The main reason for our brain's complexity is evolution. The nervous system was not logically designed for the human being, but evolved over hundreds of millions of years, starting from one specialized cell. More than 500 million years ago there was already a kind of worm with a symmetrical nervous system and a rudimentary brain consisting of one node (ganglion). Again and again random genetic mutations occurred and when one of these increased the chance of survival or procreation, it had a chance of being added to the nervous system and becoming a starting point for further improvements. On the other hand, evolution rarely takes something away that is no longer useful. As a result the nervous system is very complex with lots of redundancies. This makes it simultaneously difficult and extremely interesting to study for so many very different scientific fields.

3.4 UNBELIEVABLE BUT TRUE: OUR BRAIN IS DIRECTLY CONNECTED WITH OTHER PEOPLE'S BRAINS

To top it all, our brain is not only connected with every cell of our body, but there is also a surprisingly direct, unconscious connection with the brains of other people via our senses. I know this sounds like vague new-age superstitious nonsense, but it is a fact. When we see someone move a hand, especially if that hand is doing something we are interested in, like taking a biscuit, the cells that make our own hand move fire up as if we had moved it, even when our hand is motionless. When we observe an emotion in another person, our emotional brain cells fire up, as if we have that emotion ourselves, even before we are aware of our empathic emotion. The cells in our brain that do this are called "mirror cells" or "mirror neurons". (More on this in the chapter about emotional shortcuts and empathy.)

All these research insights about the brain as a network of networks of networks lead to a totally new domain in brain research: "connectomics", where scholars try to map all these connections[11]. The dream of these colleagues is to do for the brain what the Human Genome Project did for the knowledge about genes and heredity, to map the "Connectome" of the whole brain in a Human Connectome Project (HCP).

Given the multiple layers of complexity, you can appreciate the huge and daunting task set by President Obama's BRAIN (Brain Research through Advancing Innovative Neurotechnologies) initiative, also commonly referred to as the Brain Activity Map Project, whose goal is to map the activity of every neuron in the human brain. This task is tens of thousands of times more difficult than putting a man on the moon and thousands of times more difficult than mapping the human genome.

4 OUR UNIQUE REFLECTING BRAIN AND ITS FRENEMIES

4.1 OUR THREE BRAINS IN A NUTSHELL

In the last 20 years, many psychology researchers have found evidence that we have three cognitive, decision-making brain systems[12]. I will call them the reflecting brain, the reflex brain and the archiving brain. Ideally they collaborate for an optimal intellectual performance, although sometimes they compete with each other.

I'd first like to give you a summary of the key features of these brain systems because it is difficult to explain any one of them in detail, without referring to the others.

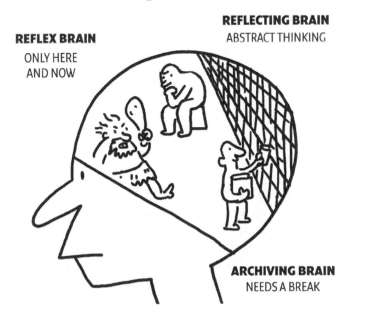

REFLEX BRAIN
ONLY HERE
AND NOW

REFLECTING BRAIN
ABSTRACT THINKING

ARCHIVING BRAIN
NEEDS A BREAK

OUR SLOW SOPHISTICATED REFLECTING BRAIN

We are constantly thinking. This constant self-talk is about what we are doing, the situation, our goals, ourselves. The French philosopher Descartes said: Cogito ergo sum, I think, therefore I am. But the reverse is just as true: I am, therefore I think. Sum ergo cogito! As I described in my book "Stress: Friend and Foe"[13], this inner chatter even has an important influence on our emotions, behavior and body.

This thinking happens in the brain system that I call the reflecting brain.

The most important and uniquely human quality of the reflecting brain is that with it we can think about things that are not actually present, things that do not even exist. Hence it is not only able to think about the present but also about the past and the future. We can think, fantasize and invent stories. This brain system is responsible for conscious reflecting, logical, analytical and synthetic thinking, creative thinking, problem solving, thinking ahead, reflecting on the past and deep thinking.

This reflecting brain is slow, it needs sustained attention and concentration, and because of this it consumes lots of energy and easily becomes tired. For the purposes of this book it is very important to note that the reflecting brain can only handle one thought at a time; as such, it is like a serial processor.

The reflecting brain can think long-term, set long-term goals and be proactive, something that no other animal is capable of. For these reasons, psychologists sometimes call it the "goal-oriented brain", in contrast to the "stimulus-oriented" reflex brain.

One of the things that is uniquely human about the reflecting brain is that it can take precedence over our reflex brain. For this reason, this reflecting brain network is sometimes called the control network or the controlling brain.

OUR FAST PRIMITIVE REFLEX BRAIN

The oldest of the three systems, in evolutionary terms, is very fast, unconscious and autonomous. For the purpose of this book, to make reading and remembering easier, I will refer to it as the reflex brain, because it is as fast as a reflex. In psychological research it is often called "the stimulus-driven system"[14]. It is a kind of "snapshot brain" because its conclusions are in an extreme way based on the here and now and nothing else. In his excellent book about this brain "Thinking fast and slow" Daniel Kahneman calls this "What You See Is All There Is": WYSIATI[15]. I prefer to call it "SNIA": Sensory Now Is All, because what exists for our reflex brain is not only what you see here and now, but also what is immediately present in the sensory world of hearing, smell, taste, touch, balance, temperature, pain, acceleration and body awareness. As a result, our reflex brain is totally reactive, unable to be proactive or reflect on what has happened.

This brain can process many inputs at the same time, it does not consume much energy and it is lightning fast because it works with many genetic and acquired shortcuts. The natural, genetically defined tendency is that our fascinating primitive reflex brain reacts faster than our fantastic reflecting brain. This was a big advantage for the survival of our human ancestors in their life or death struggle in the savannah a few million years ago. Yet it is often a liability in the jungle of the 21st century because the speed of this system comes at a price: if we don't give the reflecting brain the opportunity to check its rapid conclusions, the reflex brain makes a lot of irrational mistakes.

Part of this reflex brain is the affect-network. Emotions too activate super-fast shortcuts that are very useful in many situations, so useful in fact that managers and other professionals should use them better by reflecting on them, rather than ignoring them. On the other hand, as we all experience regularly, emotions can cause major problems if they are not controlled or guided by an emotionally intelligent reflecting brain.

A feature of our reflex brain that was important for our survival in the savannah, but that causes lots of problems for brainworkers today, is that its attention is unconsciously captured by novel or sudden sensory changes, such as smells, sight and above all sounds. This attention to stimuli, even when it's unconscious, interferes not only with the conscious attention that our reflecting brain needs in order to do its thinking, but also with the work of our archiving brain that tries to store the information in our memory. What's more, each time a stimulus captures the attention of our reflex brain we get a little shot of dopamine in our brain, which may stimulate us to seek out these stimuli and even become addicted to them. This explains to some extent why people can become addicted to the continuous stimulation of ict gadgets in their pocket. (Much more on this in the following chapters.)

In the table below I summarize the most important differences between the reflex and the reflecting brain systems.

THE REFLEX BRAIN	THE REFLECTING BRAIN
Sensory Now Is All	No limits. Can think about anything: present, past, future and pure fantasy
Automatic	Deliberate choice
Fast	Slow and inhibiting action
Reactive: stimulus-driven	Proactive: goal-oriented
Unconscious, implicit	Conscious, explicit
Parallel processing	Serial, sequential processing
Generates conclusions, impressions, intuitions lightning fast	Comes to conclusions slowly and deliberately, step by step
Cannot deal with inconsistencies and will automatically change the perception of reality to create consistency	Can deal with lack of consistency
Fundamentally selfish	Can be ethical and wise
Switches tasks rapidly and easily, independent of the working memory	Switching tasks is difficult, error-prone and limited because of the limitations of the working memory
Uncontrolled stimulus triggers attention	Controlled, goal-oriented, chosen attention
Automatic	Controlled
Intuitive	Reasoned
Effortless	Effortful
Follows habits	Can override habits
Black and white	Can manage nuances and trade-offs
Most often involuntary	Voluntary
Heuristic	Analytical / Trial and error

Domain-specific, stimulus-bound, contextualized, pragmatic	Specific or general, abstract, decontexualized, hypothetical
Experiential	Rational
Associative, detects simple relations	Rule-based
Holistic	Analytical
Is magically fast at pattern recognition, stereotyping	Analytical/deductive
Shotgun/buckshot approach	Rifle approach
Very bad with numbers and statistics	Can be good with numbers and statistics
Jumps to conclusions about causality, can't handle probability or statistics	Can handle probability and use statistical reasoning
Chooses the most plausible, which is easier and faster than the most probable	Given the chance, chooses the most probable, but is often overtaken by the reflex brain's faster "most plausible" choice
Jumps to unequivocal beliefs	Can handle doubt, ambivalence, lack of belief
Easily anchored	Often not aware of the anchoring and other biases and heuristics of the reflex brain
Low demands on cognitive capacity	High demands on cognitive capacity
Relatively independent of IQ	Highly dependent on IQ
Nonverbal	Rather verbal
Passes impressions, intuitions and feelings to reflecting brain	Checks the inputs from the reflex brain and can overrule them
Often bypasses the reflecting brain to influence behavior directly	Often unaware of reflex-sources of thoughts and feelings
Automation: incorporates learning from reflecting brain with lots of training and fast feedback in a predictable situation	Feeds new shortcuts, biases, intuitions to reflex brain

Evolved early in evolution	Evolved very recently in evolutionary terms
Shares parts with animals	Uniquely human

OUR ARCHIVING BRAIN WAITING FOR A BREAK

Every day our brain takes in billions of bits and bytes of information. The brain cannot afford to throw all this data into one big pile. It has to be ordered and stored in such a way that it is available for future use. This filing away is done by our archiving brain, which is like a team of millions of tightly connected librarians, archivists and cataloguers, who have only one client: you, or rather your reflecting brain. They take in the billions of bits and bytes coming from the outside world via all our senses, together with the ideas generated by our reflecting brain, and then decide what to discard and what to store in our long-term memory. They stockpile this information in associative ways that are still unknown.

Recent research seems to indicate that the fact that older people need more time to retrieve information from their "archive" is more related to the fact that their database is so much fuller than that of young people. The longer retrieval time is therefore normal and predictable in a mathematical model, rather than the result of a deterioration of the memory system [16].

Modern functional brain scans show that the reflecting brain and the archiving brain are in balance: when one is activated, the other is deactivated and vice versa[17]. As we will see further on, they compete for time and space in our working memory, a part of our brain that can be compared with the central microprocessor in a computer. The archiving brain is always active, always on alert; therefore it is sometimes called the "default-mode". It never rests, unless our reflecting brain occupies all the processing power. While the reflecting brain can and should take regular breaks and sleep, the archiving brain will jump at the slightest opportunity of a tiny little bit of free processing power to do its job. Because it is most active when there is no specific cognitive task to fulfill, researchers sometimes call it "task-negative", contrasting it with the "task-positive" reflecting brain. The archiving brain becomes most active when its only client, the reflecting brain, leaves it alone and sleeps or takes a break, even a micro-break of a few minutes or seconds.

4.2 YOUR REFLECTING BRAIN IS YOUNG, UNIQUE AND FANTASTIC BUT IT CANNOT THINK TWO THOUGHTS AT THE SAME TIME

AN AMAZING AND UNIQUELY HUMAN ABILITY: REFLECTION
The reflecting brain is the one that plays the leading role in this book. It is the most typically human part of our brain. The human being is the only creature who can reflect. It is the thinking brain that we are aware of, identify with and are proud of. Our proficiency in abstract reasoning determines the quality of our reflection and our IQ in general[18]. The quality of this talent is genetically determined.

▶ **The human being is the only creature who can reflect and who eats his food cooked.**

While the reflex brain can learn by experience and is based on the immediate here and now, the reflecting brain can think about things that are not present, things we have never experienced in the past. It can even imagine things that do not exist (yet). It can think about things that may happen in the future, it can think "what if..." and "on the one hand..., but on the other hand". It can imagine a future event and make you act to realize it or avoid it.

This competency of reflection is very much younger in evolutionary terms than the reflex brain. If we link it with the appearance of the first drawings, paintings and a rapid development of tools, it was probably only fully available some 50,000 years ago with Homo Sapiens Sapiens[19]. If we consider the development of tools as a first indication of a reflecting brain, then some primitive reflective thinking was available 2 million years ago. In contrast, the reflex brain is more than 500 million years old.

The reflecting brain is exclusively human. Only a few animals can reflect in an extremely rudimentary way. The limit for the most talented in this, the chimpanzees, is some 250 symbols that they can recognize and manipulate in a very primitive way.

▶ **There is no road to reflection; reflection is the road.**

Reflection is sustained, focused critical thinking with a purpose. The goal is finding a solution to a problem, an answer to a question. It is conscious, persistent, logical, critical thinking at an abstract level: manipulating concepts, mental images, memories, hypotheses and theories in the absence of the objects or the phenomena we are thinking about. It's about defining goals, making plans, conscious decisions and choices.

It is thinking about the different choices in order to come to wise, ethical, sometimes innovative choices, conclusions and decisions, the best we can make with the knowledge we have.

It is thinking based on knowledge. You have to know the subject through undisturbed study, thorough deep reading, hands-on experience and real conversations and discussions with others, while being very aware that your knowledge will always be incomplete.

It is thinking wide, with a systems view, for example taking into account how your decisions will impact other key players.

It is thinking deep: gaining deep knowledge of the issues, problems and challenges. Looking for verification, analysis and synthesis.

It is thinking ahead: thinking about the long-term consequences

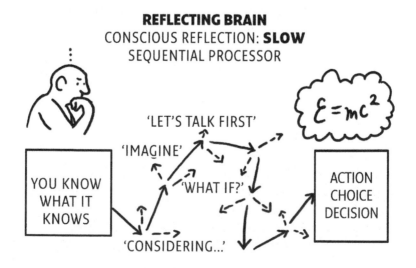

REFLECTING BRAIN
CONSCIOUS REFLECTION: **SLOW**
SEQUENTIAL PROCESSOR

'LET'S TALK FIRST'

'IMAGINE'

$\mathcal{E} = mc^2$

YOU KNOW WHAT IT KNOWS

'WHAT IF?'

ACTION CHOICE DECISION

'CONSIDERING...'

of your decisions, for example considering very different possible scenarios.

It is thinking back to learn from former successes and failures or mistakes.

It is critical thinking, meaning that we have to dare to let go of our certainties and face uncertainty. We should even increase uncertainty, by questioning and challenging our past conclusions, hypotheses, practices, beliefs and values as well as so-called common sense, accepted "truths" and standard methods and models. You have to postpone judgment to give opposing views a fair chance. You need this ability to be imaginative, to think out of the box.

It needs to be particularly critical towards the fast conclusions of the reflex brain.

It requires emotional intelligence in order to be aware of the way your emotions steer your thinking and how your decision will affect others.

The main steps in the "classic" reflecting processes are:
- Analyzing, selecting and ordering facts in a logical way to produce usable information.
- Looking for additional information and other reliable opinions.
- Forming a synthesis and finding patterns, leading to knowledge about how it all fits together.
- The next step is to find basic principles, develop a deep understanding and create a temporary (new) meaning. To do this you need to look at the knowledge from different perspectives.
- The next step is to make a wise choice, the best decision that one can make with the available knowledge.
- The next step is to start all over again as soon as you get new data, information, knowledge or insights.

All these steps need focus, effort, energy and time. The result is a continuous process of learning, development and creation: always confident, never certain.

▶ **The result of reflection:**
always confident, never certain.

This is a theoretical model. It is not always necessary to go through every single stage of every step. To come to good decisions, it is acceptable to jump to conclusions once in a while or to take a decision intuitively if you are an expert, as long as you are aware that intuitions are only correct under very specific conditions (more on the risks of following your gut in the next chapter) and as long as you are always willing to question your opinion and to reflect on it when new data or information is available.

> **"Original concepts don't come out of computers. They come out of the insight you have into the problem... invention is arrived at by intelligent stumbling."** AMAR BOSE 2013. NYT

An important role of the reflecting brain is to be a guard and protect us from the superfast decisions of the reflex brain, to scrutinize, filter, amend, accept or, if necessary, override its fast intuitive decisions.

Some scholars call it lazy, compared to the fast reflex brain, because without a conscious effort from the owner of the reflecting brain, and without the effort needed to develop soft-wired shortcuts, for example ethical ones, it leaves the decisions to the fast reflex brain, which often misleads it and leads to bad decisions and behavior.

Reflecting and conscious thinking consume a lot of energy, literally, as I will further explain in the chapter about willpower and decision fatigue. Therefore, by getting enough good sleep and having moments where we disconnect, you kill two birds with one stone: your reflecting brain recuperates and relaxes and your archiving bran gets a chance to do its work. Hence, breaks are an integral part of the reflection process. Breaks and sleep are crucial because the reflex brain still functions well on a minimum of sleep. That was good for our ancestor in the savannah who tried to survive even when he was exhausted, but for us it means that the reflex brain gets an unfair advantage over a badly treated, tired reflecting brain.

MULTITASKING IS LIKE JUGGLING MANY BALLS WITH ONE HAND; IT CAN'T BE DONE

In our modern world, multitasking has become the rule, not only at work, but also at home. Most professionals see it as an unavoidable way of dealing with the continuous avalanche of information. It is stimulated by a social environment where everybody else seems to have already seen the latest note from the boss, the latest strategic document from the CEO, the latest YouTube hit, the latest digressive Facebook message and the latest totally irrelevant Tweets. It is symbolized by a computer desktop with many programs open at the same time or by the millions of people who are glued to the screen of their smartphone while they are doing all kinds of other things, even driving. We keep our brain running fast to keep up with everybody else and as a result our reflecting brain stalls.

Multitasking is a concept that comes from the computer world. It means that the processor in a computer (a so-called serial processor), which can only do one task at any one time, switches so fast between several tasks that it seems to be doing all these tasks at the same time. In fact it is constantly switching between tasks, while also freeing up space by putting some information into a temporary memory. Temporary memory is like a slate, a blackboard or whiteboard. It has a limited capacity. Once it's full, you have to wipe off the old stuff to make room for new ideas. As we

will see, this metaphor is useful in order to simplify what's happening in our brain when we multitask.

When we talk about human multitasking we can differentiate between two kinds of multitasking. The first is "simultaneous multitasking", trying to do two things at the same time. The second is "serial multitasking", doing parts of many different tasks one after the other.

You will see, however, that your reflecting brain makes no distinction between these two types of multitasking because in both cases your reflecting brain is constantly switching between tasks.

There is another type of work that's sometimes called multitasking: doing many different tasks one after another, such as that done by an operator or an administrative assistant. I do not include this type in the discussion because most of these are brief, well-defined, time-limited tasks that can be finished in one go. This work is more like a rapid, continuous succession of short single tasks. It is single-tasking. Much of it can even become routine and be delegated to the reflex brain. However, when this work requires reflection and the person is switching back and forth between unfinished tasks or trying to do them at the same time, then it will belong to one of the first two categories.

SIMULTANEOUS MULTITASKING

Simultaneous multitasking is something our reflex brain can do. Our "body-brain" also does this all the time, and not with a few but with many thousands of tasks at the same time. Our reflecting brain, however, can simply not do this. Period. The bottleneck is our very restricted conscious attention. Conscious attention is

PARALLEL MULTITASKING

Task 1

Task 2

SERIAL MULTITASKING

Task 1   Task 2   Task 3   Task 2   Task 3   Task 1

the ability to deal with desired, relevant stimuli, while excluding unwanted irrelevant ones. Our reflecting brain cannot give conscious or focused attention to several thoughts at the same time, not even to two tasks, except when the two tasks are extremely simple like recognizing letters that are part of a word, simple enough to be processed by the attention area of just one half of the brain[20]. Normally the attention areas in the two halves of your brain collaborate to give full attention, but for extremely simple tasks, like recognizing a letter, they can split the job.

There are many very sophisticated research methods to demonstrate that the thinking brain cannot multitask, but there are also very simple tests. Take a look at this well-known picture, where you can see both an old lady and a young lady. Once you have discovered both images, try to consciously see both at the same time.

You will discover that you can't. If you try really hard, what happens? You switch very fast between the two images. That is exactly what happens when we "try" to multitask: you may have the impression that your conscious brain is doing several things at the same time, but in reality it is switching all the time between the different tasks. As we will see later on, the switching causes big efficiency problems.

The only kind of multitasking the reflecting brain can do is collaborating on certain tasks with the reflex brain, letting the reflex brain automatically handle routine tasks, while the reflecting brain sticks with conscious attention. Therefore it is possible to knit and watch TV, until you drop a stitch and then you miss the heroine being kissed!

This limitation of our attention results in a worse than zero-sum game. Imagine that you are trying to listen to two conversations at the same time at a dinner table or trying to keep listening to your neighbor while you are answering a phone call. If you think you can pay attention to both, you are absolutely totally wrong. When you pay attention to the phone, you just don't listen to the conversation and vice versa. Hence, you miss parts of each conversation if you switch back and forth. The subjective impression that you can divide your attention is created by your brain, which fills in the blanks. If you drive while you are making a phone call, you cannot pay proper attention to the lane that you're driving in. When your lack of attention makes you cross over into the wrong

SIMULTANEOUS MULTITASKING: INFORMATION LOSS

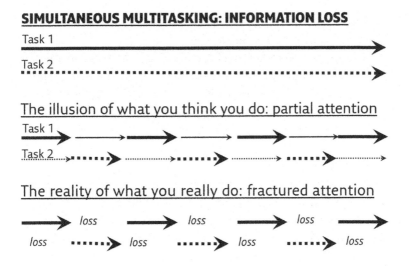

The illusion of what you think you do: partial attention

The reality of what you really do: fractured attention

lane, your reflex brain might fill in the central road markings where they were supposed to be and make you think you're driving OK, but you aren't and you only realize this when you switch your conscious attention from your phone to the road.

I call not paying full attention "worse than a zero-sum game" because it is worse than just not registering one conversation while listening to another one. Each time you switch, you lose even more, because as we will see later, switching attention itself takes time and some information is simply lost between the cracks. What's more, information that we didn't pay conscious attention to doesn't get stored in our memory and all that switching consumes a lot of energy.

Here's an example of how researchers demonstrate this zero-sum game. People lying in a brain scanner were instructed to give a signal when they saw a particular letter on the screen or hear that letter in their headphones. The visuals and the sounds were presented at the same time. To increase the need for concentration, the letters were shown along with four others and the sounds were pronounced by different people. One of the things that became very clear on the scans was that the two senses compete for attention and that this is very much a zero-sum game: when attention switches to the sounds, the attention for the visual input decreases and vice versa[21]. This "un-attentional blindness or deafness" is something to think about next time you are on the phone while driving (see Section 2).

In summary, our reflecting brain functions like a serial microprocessor and not like the fantastic distributed and parallel processing going on in other parts of our brain; it can only process one thought and its context at a time[22]. So when we think we multitask, we are actually constantly switching between tasks.

SERIAL MULTITASKING
This inability to multitask also has severe consequences for the other kind of multitasking: serial multitasking, trying to think about many tasks rapidly one after the other, without finishing them. This is sometimes called task-switching, switch-tasking or task-hopping. Although task-hopping is the most graphic term, I prefer to use task-switching because it is the switch that is the big problem. This is something our reflecting brain can do, but at a very high cost.

Some jugglers juggle with 20 balls, but no juggler can juggle more than three balls with one hand. That is what you are trying to do when you multitask with a brain that can only handle one task at a time. You have only one ball in your hand at any one time while the others are up in the air. Some of the balls are simple plastic ones, but often there are precious crystal ones too. The precious crystal ones can be compared to caring for a child, a very important task or a very dangerous one. When you multitask, don't be surprised that inevitably you will regularly drop balls. Don't be surprised either if you drop one of your most precious ones, like forgetting a baby in the back of the car.

It is quite amazing to see the real-time pictures of modern brain scans that can actually make visible what researchers have until now only guessed[23]. When we do one very simple task, both frontal lobes collaborate. When we do two simple tasks the left and the right more or less split the job. When we start on a third task, one of the first two just disappears from the brain scan. Writing a report, you might be able to take on a second task, like checking one single e-mail, without losing your train of thought. But if that e-mail asks for a decision or something else that requires some thinking, that would amount to a third task and your brain would be overwhelmed and make stupid mistakes[24].

As you can guess from what we have discussed, in the end the two kinds of multitasking boil down to the same fundamental mechanism: task-switching. When you try to do simultaneous multitasking, like doing e-mails while participating in a meeting, you are all the time switching back and forth between the two tasks, losing information from the one while attending to the other because the reflecting brain cannot do two things at the same time. When you are doing serial multitasking, you are all the time switching back and forth between many tasks. As you will learn in the following paragraphs, the switching causes major problems for your intellectual performance.

Hence, the many professionals who think that "just quickly doing this little e-mail or phone call in between doesn't make a difference", as well as those who think that they can do two things at the same time, are absolutely, completely, totally wrong; they utterly underestimate the negative impact of switching between tasks. To be optimally intellectually productive, you need to focus on one task only.

TASK-SWITCHING MAKES DELIVERY TIME LONGER

You may think "So what? In the end it takes exactly the same amount of time to do the tasks, regardless of whether I do them all at once or in pieces. It is purely mathematical." Looking at the figure, where I compare single-tasking and task-switching, at first glance you seem to be right, but in fact you are totally wrong. You are trying to multitask with a brain that can only handle one thought and its context at a time, so every single task will take much longer.

Imagine you have three tasks and each takes 30 minutes to accomplish. If you do one after the other, the total job will take 90

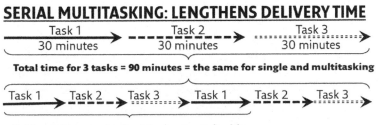

SERIAL MULTITASKING: LENGTHENS DELIVERY TIME

Task 1	Task 2	Task 3
30 minutes	30 minutes	30 minutes

Total time for 3 tasks = 90 minutes = the same for single and multitasking

| Task 1 | Task 2 | Task 3 | Task 1 | Task 2 | Task 3 |

Delivery time per task = 60 minutes = double

minutes. Now imagine you are switching between these tasks. As you can see in the picture, mathematically speaking, the three jobs together still only take 90 minutes but each single task now takes 60 minutes because each one is interrupted by the other two. You may react with a "So what?" because the total time for the three tasks doesn't change. The problem is that the need for more time to finish a single task generates problems when your work is a link in a chain, when your output is the input for other people to do their work.

Hence, you may take on a task in a project that everybody knows takes only 30 hours to deliver. If you multitask they will have to wait 60 hours. Since very often in an organization, your output is the input for other people, these people are waiting for your input to start their work. Since you are delayed, they will start another task, and in the end, when everybody working in a delivery chain is multitasking, lead times run out of control and you will never deliver on time, if your deadline didn't take into account the interruptions caused by your serial multitasking.

Imagine you arrive at the checkout of your supermarket. There are three lines.

In the first line there is a man with 40 items in his trolley.

In the second line there are 4 people with 10 objects.

In the third line 4 people with only 5 objects are screaming that they are in a hurry. Therefore in that line the cashier, using one single cash register, tries to satisfy these four customers at the same time by multitasking! She is registering

- two objects from client 1,
- three from client 2,
- three more from client 1,
- five from client 3,
- one from client 2
- two from client 4,
- another one from client 2 etc... etc...

Which line will you choose? Which counter will take the most processing time, which one the least? But of course the problem is more important than just a longer delivery time. Which cashier will make most mistakes, which one the least? Which cashier will burn out very quickly?

It is evident that cashier number three and her customers are in big trouble. Well, that is exactly the solution you choose when you multitask. Day in, day out, you force your brain to function like cashier number three causing much greater trouble than you think!

Therefore, when people ask you to do something, you should think how much time the execution of the task will take you and then make it a rule that you never put tasks on a to-do list, but go immediately to your diary and find out when you have time, when you are going to do the task. If there is no time to do it at once or in big chunks, you refuse the task or you negotiate putting other tasks on the backburner or delegating them. If you start doing the job in bits and pieces, you will not only be inefficient but you will disappoint everybody, and yourself first and foremost. (More solutions in Section 3.)

TASK-SWITCHING SLOWS YOU DOWN AND RUINS THE QUALITY OF YOUR BRAINWORK: BUSY BUT NOT PRODUCTIVE

Would you want to be operated on by a surgeon who runs back and forth between four patients and in between has a quick look at her e-mails? Would you like your car mechanic to be multitasking while he is doing a brake job on your car?

No, and not just because it would take longer. You know the quality of the work will be lousy and dangerous.

The only exception is where after a prolonged period of training, routine tasks are taken over by your reflex brain so that these no longer require much conscious thinking or continuous attention. This is why surgeons with many years of experience will not make mistakes when, during a routine procedure, they talk about other things; novices on the other hand will make mistakes under these circumstances. You can safely have a discussion while driving your car as long as the driving and the conversation is routine. Similarly, an experienced cook can prepare a complex dinner without making mistakes and without losing track of his conversation with a guest.

Let's continue the comparison with a computer. The more tasks your little laptop or desktop computer has to do at the same time, the more programs are open and the more switching it has to do, the less efficient it becomes. I can recall plenty of occasions where I have opened up several spreadsheets at the same time and my laptop has slowed down to a snail's pace. In this respect, our brain performs exactly like our laptop computer: each time we switch tasks we pay a significant switching cost. Software developers, for example, need 15 (!) minutes to recover from a phone call interruption[25]. To put it simply: instead of your brain spending maximal time and energy working for you, you force it to spend a lot of time and energy getting in and out of tasks.

IT specialists use a very meaningful word for this when they talk about microprocessors: they call it **context-switching**. The word says it all! Every time you switch, for example, from a Word text to a Powerpoint presentation, your computer does not just switch from a text to a slide but has to switch the whole context.

Imagine you are making a PowerPoint presentation and you want to cut and paste data you already have in a Word file. It looks simple: you open the text file, cut, go back to your PowerPoint and paste. What happens in the background, however, is much more complicated. Your computer has to put the whole PowerPoint-context in its temporary memory and then fetch the whole Word-context from its permanent memory in order to put it in its working memory. If in between you look at an e-mail, both Word and PowerPoint are put into the temporary memory etc... In computers this context-switching is very difficult to program, it is where things go wrong and it uses a lot of energy. You might remember that the first iPhones were not able to cut and paste between programs and how hundreds of thousands of (potential) users complained that such a super-simple feature was missing. IT experts explained to me that in fact it was not a simple feature at all, but an example of the difficulty of programming context-switching.

Something similar happens in your brain[26]. The working memory is the brain system that manages information for a comparatively short time. In a sense it is somewhat like the processor in your computer.

Imagine you are trying to write a memo about a very complex subject for the next strategy meeting. This very rich context uses all the working memory in your brain. Then you hear the sound of an e-mail landing in your inbox. You see in the pop-up that it is from the HR director. You think "This is a simple question; it is only going to take a minute..."

But it's not that simple at all for your brain! Your brain has to put the very complex context of that memo in the temporary memory, fetch the HR context from the long-term memory to answer the e-mail, then put the HR context in temporary memory, go and get the important strategic memo-context from the temporary mem-

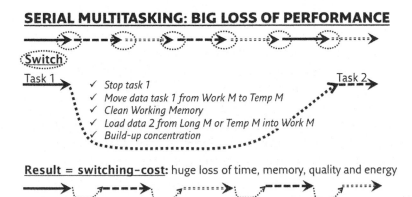

SERIAL MULTITASKING: BIG LOSS OF PERFORMANCE

Switch

Task 1

✓ Stop task 1
✓ Move data task 1 from Work M to Temp M
✓ Clean Working Memory
✓ Load data 2 from Long M or Temp M into Work M
✓ Build-up concentration

Task 2

Result = switching-cost: huge loss of time, memory, quality and energy

ory and from there continue working on the memo.

Hence, the very complex memo-context was pulled out of your long-term memory, put into working memory to work on it, then put into temporary memory to make place for the HR e-mail-context, and then transferred back into working memory etc etc...[27] It's obvious that this can't be very efficient. This switching causes problems. You pay a heavy switching-cost every time you do so. Every single additional switch will further decrease your performance[28].

This juggling of information back and forth takes time, time that you cannot spend on the task. For complex work, multitasking easily takes four times as long. Often it is much more!

Even for just two very simple simple tasks it can take 100% more time.

If you don't believe this, do a simple but very convincing test. It will take only 2 minutes. Take two pieces of paper, a pen and a watch or stopwatch. It is easier and more fun to do this together with another person, letting the other person be the timekeeper, but you can do it by yourself too.

The test consists of two very simple tasks. The first task is writing the word MULTITASKING and the second one is giving each letter its serial number. You will do both of these tasks twice, the first time single-tasking and the second time multitasking or task-switching. In both cases the result looks like:

M U L T I T A S K I N G
1 2 3 4 5 6 7 8 9 10 11 12

First round: single tasking: take a blank piece of paper, start the stopwatch, write MULTITASKING, and then in one go give each letter its corresponding number, stop the stopwatch and write down the score on the paper.

Second round: multitasking: put the first piece of paper out of sight, take another blank sheet of paper, start the stopwatch, write M, give the M its number 1; then write U, give the U its number 2; then write L, give the L its number 3; etc.... It looks like:

```
M  U  L  T  I  ...

1  2  3  4  5  ...
```

Continue until the end, stop the stopwatch and write down the score.

Now, compare the scores.

When I do this in groups, multitasking takes at least 50% more time and for many people it is almost 100% more time. Some people even make mistakes the second time.

This is the most super-simple dual task I can imagine of and yet when you do it while multitasking it takes up to double the time to accomplish and even runs the risk of making mistakes.

It does not need much imagination to understand what the consequences and costs are of multitasking for the difficult, complex tasks of your daily work.

The cost is bigger when the tasks are rather complex or emotional, when you are under stress (see BrainChain #3) or exhausted e.g. from working in an open office (see BrainChain #5), when you switch between thinking about people and about things, when you feel overloaded or when you feel negative about the first task you were working on. When you switch from familiar to unfamiliar tasks, the cost is even bigger than the other way around. To top it all, the negative impact of these factors is additive![29]

The loss is greater when the switch is triggered by an external cue (such as the 'you have mail' notification) rather than being a personal choice to switch, for example to fetch an e-mail you need for the task at hand[30]. In general your brain needs 2 minutes to get back to its former level of concentration after an interruption of half a minute[31].

There is only one exception to this rule that multitasking is so extremely inefficient: if you are doing rather simple, routine, related tasks and quality, especially accuracy, is not required, then a little task-switching can make us more productive than just single-tasking because the multitasking is less boring and increases arousal and alertness. This also explains why the only

people who feel and perform better in open offices are people doing routine work[32], especially when they are extraverts, who need
a higher degree of stimulation to perform well, or people who are
so used to this very inefficient multitasking that this has become
their pathological norm e.g. young people and hypertaskers.
(More on this in the paragraphs about the three myths of multitasking below.)

To put it simply, instead of your brain spending maximal time and
energy working for you, you lose it uselessly in the black hole of
multitasking.
  Just the little "ping" sound of an e-mail landing in your inbox or
the little pop-up announcing an e-mail, causes a 1.5-minute drop
in your concentration, even if you don't read it. If you are working
on a memo for 60 minutes and you have 20 "ping" sounds, you
lose your concentration for 30 minutes. But it is actually worse
than that because of the time needed to get in and out of the task.
As I mentioned earlier, people involved in creative work like software development need 15 minutes to recover from one phone
call. Why?

> **Every change of tasks, every simple
> disturbance, every distraction is a switch
> and the more switches the more time,
> energy and quality you lose in the
> bottomless black hole of multitasking.**

A huge chunk of lost time results from the restart cost, the time it
takes after the interruption to get back to the same level of speed
and concentration. For each switch, you have to mentally disconnect from task A and mentally connect to task B and its specific
thinking frame, its specific context.

The slowing down is further worsened by having to clean your
working memory slate of the remnants of the old task, and if this
is not done perfectly, because you are switching too fast all the
time, the leftovers interfere with the new task[33]. A big switching
cost is caused by "task-set inertia", the carry-over from a previous

task that is not wiped out completely from the working memory when we start a new task. The other big cost results from backward-inhibition. Imagine you switch from task A to task B and then back to task A. To fulfill task B, A needs to be inhibited. The more A is inhibited, the more difficult it is to get back into it when you return to task A[34].

> **"Any man who can drive safely while kissing a pretty girl is simply not giving the kiss the attention it deserves"** ALBERT EINSTEIN (PROBABLY APOCRYPHAL)

The second problem is that our temporary memory is limited in capacity, therefore the more you switch, the more you forget[35]. Depending on the complexity of the tasks, it can only retain between one and seven tasks. It's also "first in, first out": The earlier tasks are continuously overwritten by new tasks[36]. The information is lost unless you take a brain-break to let your archiving brain store the information from the temporary memory in the long-term memory[37]. In that sense, when you take regular breaks your temporary memory functions more like one of those modern whiteboards, where you can write on them and then, before you wipe it clean for the next explanation, you push a button and the board takes a little break to take a digital copy of what was on the board and then sweeps it for you. If you forget to take this short break to copy what's on the whiteboard to memory, it's lost.

When in real life, you switch frequently, without breaks between the switches, a lot of information and thoughts are just never archived. As a result, when you then go back to the original task after a few task-switches, you almost have to start from scratch again. The more you cut up the tasks into little pieces and the more switches, the more information you lose.

The third problem is that this switching back and forth wastes a lot of brain energy. (More on this later in the chapter about decision fatigue.) It is one of the reasons why so many people working in open offices are exhausted at the end of the working day (See BrainChain #5).

The fourth problem, as you can imagine from the paragraph above, is that at each switch many things can and do go wrong. The result is simple: the more you switch, the more stupid mistakes you will make[38]. You will lose even more time because you have to redo more tasks and correct more errors, which often takes more time than doing things right first time.

On the shop floor this will also lead to unsafe behavior. In other situations it causes inefficient meetings due to bad listening and communication.

The conclusion is very simple: multitasking is very bad for your intellectual productivity. Except when your intellectual work is of a routine nature, multitasking has nothing but disadvantages. Every change of task, every simple disturbance, every minute distraction is a switch and every single switch costs you dearly in time, energy and quality[39]. The more switches, the more you lose in the bottomless black hole of multitasking. Until today, you could claim ignorance, but from now on the big question is: why would you want to keep working so inefficiently and continue ruining your intellectual performance? As of today you should ruthlessly and radically reduce the number of switches.

OUR REFLECTING BRAIN NEEDS BREAKS BETWEEN TASKS TO BE REALLY SHARP

As I will describe in more detail in the chapter about 'right-tasking' in Section 3, we need ample switch-breaks, i.e. brain-breaks between tasks, to give our archiving brain a chance to put our memory in order and store important new information before starting a new task. These breaks are also important to refuel, as I will describe in the chapter on willpower. The more complex and different the domains that we are switching between, the more time we should take for a break. There is also some evidence that we need a relaxing break of about 5 minutes to switch between multitasking and single-tasking in order to get out of our multitasking mindset and to be able to perform a task that requires undivided attention[40].

STOP MULTITASKING; START RIGHT-TASKING

<u>Multitasking</u>

➜⟍ˌᴵ➜ˌᴵ➜⟍ˌᴵ➜⟍ˌᴵ➜⟍ˌᴵ➜⟍ˌᴵ➜⟍ˌᴵ➜

<u>Right-tasking: batch-processing</u>

undisturbed *undisturbed* *undisturbed*
➜ ➜ ➜

⌢Finish batch⌢ ⌢Finish batch⌢ ⌢Finish batch⌢
Have a Have a Have a
break break break

Another reason why we absolutely need these breaks is that some tasks are incompatible, if not antagonistic, or mutually exclusive; this is especially the case for tasks dealing with on the one hand the physical, mechanical and mathematical world and, on the other, tasks dealing with the emotional and social context. Psychological research, recently confirmed by research with fMRI brain scans[41], suggests that the two domains even suppress each other.

When we move from struggling with a difficult mathematical problem to having to make a decision about donating to a charitable organization while looking at the picture of a starving child, we will have less empathy. The rational-cognitive mode we started with has a powerful effect on the next task because the brain areas it recruited keep interfering. Hence, we need a break not only to give our reflecting brain time to recover and let our archiving brain store the information in its memory, but also to give our reflecting brain enough time to switch from physical reasoning to social reasoning.

Therefore, if in a management meeting two successive points on the agenda clearly belong to different domains, one dealing with numbers, figures, costs etc. and the other where you have to get inside the mind of customers or employees, you should have a break in between where you do nothing but make small talk. Otherwise, your decisions risk being callous or at least lacking emotional intelligence. You should also organize the agenda of the meeting in such a way that these two kinds of discussions are not mixed up, but rather that similar topics are grouped together. The same is true if you yourself have to switch from concentrating on a physical subject to focusing on a social one: have a break and drastically reduce the number of such switches.

I have read that Dale Carnegie often told a story of two lumberjacks who were out chopping wood. One man worked hard all day and took no breaks. The other took many breaks during the day and a nap at lunchtime. At the end of the day, the woodsman who had taken no breaks was upset when he saw that his mate had cut much more wood. He said, "Hey man, I don't understand. Whenever I looked at you, you were sitting down, you even took a nap, and you cut more wood than me." His mate answered "Well, didn't you see that when I was sitting down, I was sharpening my axe?" Taking a break for a brainworker is not losing time but refueling energy and sharpening your axe (think about the archiving brain) for the next task.

THREE MYTHS ABOUT THE MULTITASKING ABILITIES OF WOMEN, KIDS AND HYPERTASKERS

THE MYTH OF MULTITASKING WOMEN

Everybody seems convinced that women can multitask, or at least that they can do it better than men. In fact, this is basically a myth. If women multitask, their efficiency decreases just as much as it does for men. This is certainly the case for simultaneous multitasking. For serial multitasking, there is some research that suggests women may be slightly better than men, although most of the difference seems due to the fact that women plan the multitasking better. Interestingly, when women have the choice, they multitask less, task-switch less and allow fewer task-irrelevant distractions to interfere[42]. So part of the legend about multitasking women is that they multitask less, and that makes them more efficient.

So what is the origin of the myth of the multitasking woman? In all likelihood, it derives from the fact that women – and cooks for that matter – do manage better than the average man to multitask routine jobs that do not require continuous attention, for example having multiple pots on the stove and managing to get the different dishes on the table at the same time. As I will describe in the next chapter, after spending many hours practicing and perfecting a skill, the whole process passes from the reflecting brain to the reflex brain and thereby becomes automated and intuitive.

THE MYTH OF SUPER-TALENTED HYPERTASKERS

Communication Professor Clifford Nass and his team wanted to find out what the special skills were of people who do a lot of multitasking, the so-called hypertaskers. Since we know that theoretically it is impossible to multitask, they had the bright idea of studying hypertaskers to find out what these people have that average people don't. Some people in their team betted on better memory management, some on superior switching and others on better filtering.

To their great surprise, they found that all people who hypertask think they are brilliant at it, but in reality they are very clearly no better at all, in fact much worse. It will be difficult to change these people's behavior because the more they are convinced about their superior multitasking abilities, the more they do it and the worse they are at it in reality[43]. The people who think that they are not good at multitasking, and who do it the least, turn out to be better at it; they are better at blocking out distractions and focusing on a single task[44]!

▶ **Hypertaskers are suckers for irrelevancy.**
CLIFFORD NASS

Hypertaskers are worse at filtering out irrelevant details, worse at keeping information in their head ordered and available, worse at remembering information and worse at switching between tasks. "We think of them as filing cabinets in the brain where papers are flying everywhere and disorganized, much like my office"[45]. No wonder they also made more mistakes. Moreover, the irrelevant stuff works like a candle for a moth, it attracts them. "They're suckers for irrelevancy," says Nass[46], who by the way is not your typical "soft" psychologist. He started out as a mathematician, became a computer scientist, co-developed the 286 microprocessor at Intel and did most of his research on man-machine interaction.

Other researchers confirmed these findings in a study where people were asked to memorize words in a particular order while driving a car. However, these researchers also found that there are 2.5% of people whose driving performance is not negatively impacted[47]. The problem of course is that 100% of heavy multitaskers erroneously believe they belong to this 2.5%. So probably do you. They also forget that the two tasks were much simpler than anything a professional tries to combine at work. Moreover, it is most likely that the phenomenon has nothing to do with "hypertasking" but that these people reduce the impact of distraction by reducing the variability in speed and steering, thereby freeing mental resources to maintain situation awareness[48].

THE SORRY MYTH OF HYPER-CONNECTED, MULTITASKING YOUNG PEOPLE

DIGITAL NATIVES: TRAINED IN MULTITASKING FROM THE CRIB
For a long time I thought that the inability to multitask was just a problem for older generations like my own. Indeed the older one gets, the more difficult it becomes to multitask[49]. I really thought that the hope for the future in a hyper-connected world lay with the youngest generations, the so-called "digital natives" or "net generation", those who started to hyperconnect and multitask at a very young age, doing their homework with the TV or radio turned on, having three windows open on their computer, with five IM conversations happening simultaneously, tweets popping up, Facebook or a Whatsapp beeping for attention, their mobile phone signaling a text coming in every 5 minutes...

When are you online?
Every day. As soon as I come home.
I open Facebook all the time,
even when I sleep! I put the volume
so loud that I hear it when a messages
drops in and often I wake up to answer.
ALEJANDRA (14 YEARS)[50]

As I studied the research to test this hypothesis of mine, I made many interesting discoveries. Before outlining each of these, it's first worth noting that the only thing I guessed right was that the digital natives multitask much more and spend less time focusing on one thing.

In an analysis of 3,372 computer sessions of students, multitasking was present in more than 70%, was most frequent in over 50% and occurred exclusively in around 35% of all sessions. By comparison, less than 10% of sessions were exclusively work-focused and only 7% were exclusively sequential[51]. For 8-18 year olds in the USA, the total time spent with media went up between 1999 and 2009 from 7.3 to 10.45 hours a day, while the time spent reading print went down from 43 to 38 minutes a day, and the time spent multitasking several media at the same time went up from 16% to 29% of the time[52]. In the UK, 11 to 15 year-olds spend 7.5 hours a day in front of a screen. The average 6 year old has watched a screen for the equivalent of more than one full year of their life[53].

Interestingly 75% of college students in the US think that receiving and sending text messages during class is disruptive to learning, but... 40% feel it is acceptable to text in class[54]. With an almost 100% penetration[55] of phones from the age of 12-13 on, that amounts to a lot of distraction. The minimum schools should do, if they can't or don't want to forbid the technological distractions for longer periods, is to organize regular 10-minute technology breaks and to require the pupils to disconnect in between.

Although research on Internet addiction is all rather recent, it looks increasingly like children and adolescents run a higher risk of becoming addicted if they do not learn to control the pull of always being connected[56], if they are bamboozled by their reflex brain instead of learning the hard work of disconnecting and using the reflecting brain.

Another and most worrying issue of multitasking is that in the USA 70% of young adult drivers text, 81% reply to texts and 92% read texts while driving!!! What's more, they do this despite considering that these behaviors are very risky and riskier than talking on a cell phone[57] and that they should be forbidden[58]. The awareness of risk, however, has no influence on the dangerous behavior. (More on this in the chapter on phones and driving in Section 2.)

Since risk awareness does not help, researchers went looking for other factors determining this risky phone use, not only while driving but also in hospitals, on the plane etc... They found that the heavier mobile phone users are young extroverts, with poor self-esteem. To stay safe these people should have less stimulating mobile phones with less intrusive features[59], which of course is the opposite of what marketers want to sell to heavy users.

HYPER-CONNECTED CHILDREN PERFORM WORSE INTELLECTUALLY, EMOTIONALLY AND SOCIALLY

So, what did I discover in my survey of the research about digital natives?

My first discovery was that young people who use ICT a lot are not ICT-savvy at all. There is only a very small percentage of the digital natives who have anything but a very superficial and narrow grasp of ICT. Many young people, even at university level, only use the online tools at the most simple, shallow and consumptive of levels.

▶ **Digital natives are mostly digital naïve.**

Sue Bennett concludes in her reviews[60]: "The digital natives who have a better than a just superficial knowledge about ICT are a very small minority". Below you will see that this conclusion has important consequences for the way parents and teachers educate and teach these children. It clearly is a myth (see below) that the "old" school system is an obstacle for the development of digital natives. Moreover, given that only a very small minority of digital natives is digital-savvy, that they are the exception rather than the rule, it would be a major mistake to adapt the teaching methods as if it was the case for a majority. ICT-savvy schools should teach their pupils how to use ICT much better instead of adapting their teaching to their pupils' most shallow and distracting use of it. Parents and teachers should think carefully about the real value of what young kids can do with their ICT gadgets *before* they encourage their use rather than later trying to limit and channel their behavior. As we will see, going with the flow and allowing the digital natives to stay hyper-connected, even in learning situations, is certainly not a good idea.

"The fact that children nowadays make use of many electronic devices and are called digital natives does not make them good users of the media that they have at their disposal. First, they are capable of playing with technology, but not really using it efficiently. They can Google®, but lack the information skills to effectively find the information they need, and they also do not have the knowledge to adequately determine the relevance or truth of what they have found," conclude Paul Kirschner and Aryn Karpinski[61].

My second discovery was that young people who multitask a lot are like the adult hypertaskers: they are worse at it, not better. When digital natives have to perform a task, with multiple channels of information open at the same time, they do significantly worse than their peers or the older generations who don't multitask so much. The older generations are actually better at paying attention and concentrating on one task while there are multiple distractions going on at the same time. Even if ICT multitasking while studying were only half as frequent as the research suggests, and the loss in intellectual productivity were only half of what the researchers I mentioned in this chapter found, then the efficiency and effectiveness of students would still suffer significantly enough to warrant a call to arms by teachers and parents to teach kids a more efficient use of ICT.

My third discovery was that hyper-connected children do significantly worse at school. The more kids (of the same class, the same intelligence) multitask, be it in high school, college, university or business school, the less they can concentrate, the less time they study, the worse their homework, the more time homework takes, the lower their grades, the less they read, and the less happy and more lonely they feel[62]. It is a causal relationship because when parents and educators set limits on the multitasking, the grades improve. When half of a class is allowed to text during the lesson and the other is not, the non-multitaskers do significantly better. If you then do it the other way around, the non-multitasking half again does better[63]. A German study showed that even when a student is not multitasking and does not have non-course related stuff on her screen, her comprehension and recall suffer when her neighbor does[64]. It's worth noting that the difference in task and school performance was already obvious in the old days of MySpace: the heavier the use of MySpace, the lower the grades[65].

The sorry fact is that in their hyper-connected, multitasking context, young people do not learn to develop the single-minded concentration needed for thinking, reflection and innovation. A hopeful sign is that when they start university, at least some young people become aware of the negative impact of always being connected and even demand clear rules about not using ICT in the classroom because they know this helps them[66].

My fourth sorry discovery was that the two things hyper-connected adolescents do better are rather low-level ICT skills. The first thing they do better is fast information retrieval. Ask any question and they will find the answer faster than many adults. Too often, however, they paste this information together, often in a nice lay-out, but without reflection and without understanding the fundamentals. What admiring adults forget is that in the 21st century finding information and pasting it together has become a low-skill ability. So low, in fact, that I am convinced that retrieving information and pasting it together is exactly the brainwork that software like Google will be able to do for us very soon! What the software will never be able to do, however, is to reflect on the information. Reflection is a high-level skill, a real value-adding and uniquely human competency. This is what we should be ensuring that our kids are able to do.

The other thing many, or at least the gamers, do better is that they usually outperform people, both young and old people who do not have this experience, in reacting quickly. Journalists often describe this as proof that these children are smarter or even better fit for the 21st century. If they were to take the time to look at the research, they would realize that these game-trained kids only outperform the others on fast, simple, visual, perceptual decision-making tasks that do not require reflection and only use the multitasking reflex brain[67].

My fifth sad discovery was that there is a strong negative link between hyperconnectivity and emotional and social development. A survey of 3,500 girls, for example, showed that the more these tweeners were connected and multitasking the more they felt socially unsuccessful and not normal, the more they had real friends the parents perceived as bad influences and the less they slept[68]. These kids are sometimes described as "Screen Zombies", glued to their screens, disregarding real life around them. But in fact, many adults are not so very different. We do not know for certain yet to what extent hyperconnectedness causes the development problem or vice versa. It most probably works in both directions, feeding a vicious cycle. In any case, this is a very worrying result, an area begging for more research.

Once result that offers hope is that face-to-face contact seems to compensate for this negative effect. Let me quote the head of this research, the Stanford professor Clifford Nass: "Kids in the 8 to 12 year-old range who communicate face-to-face very frequently show much better social and emotional development, even if they're using a great deal of media....Higher levels of face-to-face communication were associated with greater social success, greater feelings of normalcy, more sleep and fewer friends whom parents judged to be bad influences. Children learn the difficult task of interpreting emotions by watching the faces of other people. It's hard work, he added, and is unlikely to be done if everyone at the dinner table is peering at the screens of their smartphones... When we media multitask, we're not really paying attention to the people around us and we get in a habit of not paying attention, and thus when I'm talking with you, I may be hearing the words but I'm missing all the rich, critical, juicy stuff at the heart of emotional and social life[69]."

My last discovery was that the way young people use their ICT creates a new social divide. The social divide is not between the haves and the have-nots, but between the heavy users and the medium users[70]. Children of more well-off families spend 90 minutes a day less time with these reflection-killers and time-wasters than children in low-income families[71].

The sad overall conclusion is that my original hypothesis turns out to be totally and utterly wrong. In my survey of the research to find support for my idea that the digital natives are the hope for the future, I was proven absolutely wrong and I made six very disappointing discoveries.

THE PROBLEM IS NOT WHAT KIDS DO WITH ICT, BUT WHAT THEY DON'T DO

As with TV, the problem with hyperconnectivity is not what you learn, but what you don't learn, not what you do, but what you don't do, such as verbal interaction, having real social contact, learning by doing and by manipulating objects, physical activity,[72] concentrating, paying attention, deep reading, studying and thinking.

Recently I met a young family where a one and a half year-old was playing with a tablet. The parents were delighted that their child was able to play the game of dragging stars, squares, circles and triangles into the proper "holes". Each time he got it right the program played a happy tune. I asked them if the kid also had the real thing, one of those wooden cubes with differently shaped holes in it, where children have to find out how a ball fits in a circular hole, a cube in a square one etc...
He didn't. They answered, "Why should we get one of those, if he can play this game and many more on our tablet?" These parents did not realize that the learning is totally different and much richer and more multisensory when a child struggles and knocks about the real thing.

In the same week I met a couple who were proud about the way their 10 year-old was building complex constructions with Lego... on the computer screen, as if this were the equivalent of building a real structure with real blocks.

Again there is nothing wrong with what these children learnt on a tablet, the problem is what the children are not learning anymore because they are not handling real objects.

Another illustrative example is typing versus handwriting. Some educators no longer put the energy and effort into teaching children handwriting; they take the road of least resistance and teach very young kids how to use a keyboard instead, as if the only goal of learning to write is to get letters and words on a screen or on paper. Don't get me wrong: it is a very good idea to teach kids to touch-type at a very young age, but these teachers forget that what we do when typing is totally different from what we do while writing. It is a very different exercise of visual and motor coordination. To cut a long story short, when we write by hand, the visual attention and the motor input are concentrated together on the tip of the pencil, we even feel the structure of the paper as if we had a sensor located in that tip. When we type, the visual and motor activities are disconnected: the eyes concentrate on the screen (or go back and forth if the person is not touch-typing) and the motor activity is focused on the keyboard.

In principle, different does not mean worse. Nonetheless, the result at the keyboard is immediate. The advantage of writing is that it is a slow, highly coordinated visual and motor process that demands full concentration and sustained attention to what's happening at the tip of the pencil in order to get a result that is legible for others.

In the process, a child also learns about pattern recognition. On a keyboard it's an "A" or a mistake. One of the discoveries while learning to write by hand is that there are many scribbles that can be recognized as an "A" even when they are far from perfect. Compared to typing, handwriting training results in better letter recognition and better long-term recall by children as well as adults. As a result, handwriting lays a much more solid foundation for reading. This pattern recognition and the fact that hand-written characters are more permanently etched in our brain are not only the basis for reading but also for many higher-level language skills[73].

Moreover, I think that slow writing on paper is better preparation for "slow thinking". Slow thinking is the term Daniel Kahneman[74] uses to describe the activity of our reflecting brain. I know from experience that my thinking and recall are better when I take notes with pen and paper, although that might be the result of being from an older generation that did not grow up with ICT. I did not find any research on this subject, but I know from having worked with secretaries, in the pre-personal-computer era, that touch-typing my dictated texts almost completely bypassed their reflecting brain and was taken care of by their highly skilled reflex brain, in such a way that they were able to deliver a perfect error-free text, without remembering the content. When they took hand-written notes for the minutes of meetings, however, they often recalled better than myself what was said and by whom. Therefore, I fear that taking notes on a laptop might lead to more text, but less recall, less understanding and above all, less reflection. The jury is still out on this.

Just before my book went to the publisher I got hold of a not yet printed research paper that supports my musings. Pam Mueller and Daniel Oppenheimer of Princeton discovered in a series of experiments that taking notes with pen and paper results in fewer notes, better factual recall and better conceptual learning, when compared to taking notes on a laptop, even when the laptop users were urged to take less verbatim notes. Their conclusion is that pen and paper forces students to not just record but to process the information[75].

In any case, the conclusion is that there is nothing wrong with kids learning to use the technology of a keyboard, but it's a mistake to think it is the same deep learning as handwriting, and we should think carefully about what else we are throwing away, with regards to important further learning, when we eliminate handwriting.

Last but not least, one of the things many hyper-connected kids don't do enough or for long enough is to interact socially in real life because they immediately and continuously interrupt real-life contacts with virtual ones. Here too it clearly isn't what they do that's the problem, but what they don't do when they no longer give their undivided attention to the other person and all the subtle non-verbal and verbal messages that are exchanged.

Barbara Frederickson summarizes this very well: "It's micromoments like these, in which a wave of good feeling rolls through two brains and bodies at once, that build your capacity to empathize as well as to improve your health." The disconcerting part of her article is where she explains that having this emotional contact is a skill that withers when you don't regularly exercise it[76]. The impact of these social contacts on health might seem farfetched, but as I summarize in the Stress BrainChain, a massive amount of research shows that good social contacts are probably the most important positive influence on our resilience in stress situations.

A CHALLENGE FOR PARENTS AND TEACHERS

Interestingly enough, the very smart and probably rather nerdy, ICT-savvy (top) employees of Silicon Valley giants like Google, Apple, Yahoo and Hewlett-Packard got it right and pay a lot to send their children to private schools that do not use computers at all. These parents limit the use of electronic devices for their children at home too[77]! For many of the real-life games that are so important to learn at a very early age, you only get one chance. If you didn't have the opportunity to play and struggle with a wooden box when you were a young child, then the opportunity is missed. In child development, the postman does not ring twice.

It is probably no coincidence that Google founders Larry Page and Sergey Brin, Amazon founder Jeff Bezos, Microsoft co-founder Bill Gates, Wikipedia founder Jimmy Wales and designer of The Sims games Will Wright all went to Montessori schools. One of the characteristics of these schools is to stimulate independent multisensory exploration in a "well-prepared" environment, characterized by limited but carefully chosen materials that support the child's development and as soon as children are ready for it, they are stimulated to work together in a non-competitive way, even without grades.

These parents probably know from first-hand experience how counterproductive and creativity-killing hyperconnectivity and multitasking are. They are intelligent and ICT-savvy enough to realize that heavy use of the Internet and electronic gadgets has nothing to do with Digital Literacy.

It is probably no coincidence that Randi Zuckerberg, who has been on the front lines of technology and social media since her days as an early executive at Facebook, when her own child became interested in tech gadgets, wrote a little children's book "Dot", which in a lovely way invites children to reboot, recharge and restart by disconnecting from their tech-toys and going into the real world[78].

Parents and teachers really have to educate children to use all these great technologies to their advantage instead of their disadvantage. It is not about fighting great ICT like modern Luddites, but about teaching children to shut off all media (except music for some extraverts) until they have finished their homework. It is about teaching children and adolescents how to use ICT to really learn something and to study behaviors, to set priorities amongst the ever increasing things they can do with their ICT, to manage these and above all to disconnect and batch-process. It might help if parents, teachers and children would have a minimum knowledge about how the human brain works.

▶ **To get the best out of ICT, parents, teachers and children should first of all learn about how our fascinating brain works and only then learn about ICT**

What's most important and urgent is that they have to teach children to pay attention, focus and concentrate on one thing for a long time. Girls have an advantage here, to the extent that they read books much more than boys, which is an excellent training in paying attention. It has the added advantage that this is a good training in reflection too.

Convincing kids that multitasking is very inefficient can be done in a very entertaining way. There are so many inexpensive tests, games and little experiments schools could use to convince pupils and students that multitasking is a very bad idea. One of them is to replicate a set-up used by researchers who put half of a group of students in front of a TV where a teacher was presenting a subject in a multitasking environment that resembled the CNN TV news, filled with its multiple visual and auditory channels. The other half got the same teacher as a talking head without any other distracting information. The students clearly remembered much less when all the distracting channels were on together than when they were presented separately[79].

Too many educators are unaware of the consequences of letting children and students multitask. They let their students use their computers and iPads to take notes and do course-related work, without actually checking what they do. Researchers discovered that in some courses only 10% of students had anything course-related on their screens. When questioned about this, the students, even at top schools like MIT, were convinced that they could do other things like social media without missing important information.

We know from the research about multitasking that this can only be wrong and indeed researchers found that when you let only half of the class, at random, use their computers, the half who is not connected scores significantly better on all measures of understanding and recall[80]. Moreover, students largely underestimate the amount of time their screens are filled with non-subject related material as well as the negative impact of this multitasking on their learning[81].

These educators think you have to go with the flow of modern times and let the students be connected; they think that it's the teachers who have to be interesting enough to lure the students away from digital distractions. It is very naïve to think teachers and lecturers, even very good ones, can win this battle for attention against this very addictive hyperconnectivity[82].

This easy 'going with the flow' really is an immense missed opportunity for schools and colleges. Children should learn the difference between being led or even enslaved by ICT in a distracted and consumptive way, on the one hand, and using ICT in a controlled, focused and productive way, on the other. Too often, parents and teachers fail to distinguish between these two approaches and too easily think that distracted, consumptive use makes children ICT-literate, which it doesn't at all.

Paul Krishner and his team[83] describe three legends in education that are relevant for this discussion. They are variations on one central theme, namely, the erroneous idea that it is the learner who knows best and that he or she should be the controlling force in his or her learning. Let me quote them:

"The first legend is one of learners as digital natives who form a generation of students knowing by nature how to learn from new media, and for whom "old" media and methods used in teaching/learning no longer work.

The second legend is the widespread belief that learners have specific learning styles and that education should be individualized to the extent that the pedagogy of teaching/learning is matched to the preferred style of the learner.

The final legend is that learners ought to be seen as self-educators who should be given maximum control over what they are learning and their learning trajectory. It should be clear by now that students are really not the best managers of their own learning with respect to navigating through and learning in the digital world, choosing the best way in which to study and learn (i.e. learning styles), or gathering useful information from the Internet.

A continuum of available evidence exists for refuting these and other legends. At one extreme are urban legends for which there is a tiny bit of incomplete support – but the legend itself is false or at least a severe overgeneralization (e.g. the claim that giving learners full control over the learning process will have positive effects on learning). At the other extreme of the continuum are urban legends for which there is strong empirical evidence for the opposite, showing that they are totally counterproductive in education (e.g. the claim that children are capable of effective multitasking). Finally, there are urban legends for which researchers claim that there is evidence, and for which there are even empirical studies purporting to support the legend, but the research itself or the body of research is flawed."

Although the modern ICT gadgets are particularly addictive and the smartphone is always within reach, the situation is fundamentally no different than what intelligent parents did a generation ago with that other great technology: TV. They did not forbid it, but taught their kids how to make good limited use of it. If they didn't, they ended up with underperforming, uninspired and uninspiring couch potatoes who developed obesity and diabetes at a scarily young age[84][85]. These kids have more social problems, are less engaged in school, participate less in extracurricular activities, don't sleep enough[86] and are more prone to aggression and delinquency[87]. They run a higher risk of developing attention problems[88] and have inferior cognitive and language development[89]. They have higher material aspirations, are more anxious and, last but not least, are less happy[90]. Of course it might be that passive, bored, moody children may be more prone to becoming addicted to TV, but there are clear indications that the cause-effect relationship is the other way around. The introduction of TV in a community which did not have it before makes people less creative in problem solving, less able to persevere at tasks and less tolerant of unstructured time[91]. This is all the more startling when you know that one-fifth of 0 to 2 year-olds and more than one-third of 3 to 6 year-olds already have their own TV in their bedroom[92].

Children's TV, games, social media or Web surfing do not require sustained, deliberate attention. On the contrary, these media are made to hold the attention by continuously switching and doing so ever faster, trying to glue the young user to the screen, so that they are still there when the commercials come along.

To help children not to become ICT slaves but clever ICT users will demand a considerable, very deliberate and sustained effort from parents and teachers.

A CHALLENGE FOR MANAGERS AND EMPLOYERS

Special attention should be given to Generation Y, those born in the 1980s and also known as the Millennials, and those who come after them. As I described in "The sorry myth of hyper-connected multitasking kids", these young people are always connected, love continuous distractions and incessantly switch back and forth between work and social media, multitasking all the time. Despite all the research to the contrary, they are too often convinced that they are good at multitasking and that it has no negative impact on their performance. Even if it does not bother them, the research shows that it greatly undermines their performance, especially when work needs focused attention to reflect.

The hyper-connected Baby-Boomers and Generation Xers may still vaguely recollect how much more efficient they were before they became hyper-connected. This recollection often frustrates them, but this frustration can be put to good use by motivating them to make the effort to break their BrainChains.

Many young people of Generation Y, who have now joined the workplace, never experienced how amazingly productive one can be with persistent undisturbed, focused attention. For them undisturbed attention feels boring. They prefer the continuous fractioned attention, to the extent that some even really like the fun of the continuous distraction of an open office. However, even though they may complain less about the buzzing, distracting environment of an open office, and may even like it, the negative impact on their intellectual productivity when reflection is needed is the same as for anybody else.

A young director in a broadcasting company was asked to take over the production of a TV series. His team were mostly Millennials who had lots of creative fun in their open office, thoroughly enjoying the continuous flow of the very creative ideas they generated together. His challenge was that they had extreme difficulties turning these sparkling ideas into a program, and the implementation was so bad and slow that often they were unable to complete their best ideas in time because they were so inefficiently distracting each other all the time. Even during meetings where choices and decisions had to be made, they remained glued to their smartphones and continuously distracted each other with the latest Tweet or Whatsapp. The manager urged them to differentiate between free-wheeling creative time and undisturbed focused implementation time and to start batch-processing these in two different blocks. He scheduled the meetings to finalize the storyboards in a separate office. When he asked them, however, to put away their phones for these meetings, most were not happy with this idea, panicked or revolted and missed the deadlines.

The dilemma for employers and managers is similar to the one of parents and teachers: go with the flow and adapt the workplace to these young employees' incessant, hyper-connected and distracted way of functioning, or convince these people of the importance of disconnecting and of separating into different batches the easy consumptive fun of being connected, on the one hand, and the effort of productive thinking without distraction on the other. With this batch-processing (see Section 3), they may even discover the efficiency and fun of undisturbed reflection. This will be difficult, however, given that so many managers have themselves become inefficient, hyper-connected hypertaskers.

5 YOUR REFLEX BRAIN IS LIGHTNING FAST BECAUSE IT RUNS ON SHORTCUTS AND HABITS

5.1 THE PRIMITIVE REFLEX BRAIN: REFLECTION'S FRIEND AND FOE

Although the reflecting brain plays the leading role in this book, you should know the basics about the reflex brain because it is our reflecting brain's most important friend and enemy, simultaneously a great helper and a fierce competitor and misleader.

Although I discovered in my teaching and workshops that most people have never heard of their reflex brain before, I reduced my original chapter about the reflex brain to just a few pages because in the meantime the Nobel Prize winner Daniel Kahneman has written such a fantastic, readable, must-read book about the reflex brain, with dramatic examples and short, convincing tests you can do yourself. You simply lose the right to call yourself a brainworker, knowledge worker or professional if you have not read his book "Thinking Fast and Slow"[93].

The reflex brain is our automatic, fast-action hero. It is very fast and a great help for our slow reflecting brain. Without its ability for example to take over routines that we can do without thinking, our reflecting brain would never have the time, energy or brainspace to do its thinking.

This reflex brain is the oldest in evolutionary terms; other animals have it too. It was very useful for our ancestors to survive in the savannah where acting with lightning speed in life-threatening situations was much more important for survival than reflection. Therefore this reflex brain is very much survival-driven and also fundamentally selfish.

An ancestor with only an intelligent reflecting brain would never have survived. Imagine if, confronted with a saber-toothed tiger, he had started reflecting "Considering that this animal is 10 times bigger than I am, considering that his teeth are as big as my head, considering that my uncle and my father were killed by one of these and considering that there is a tree 10 meters behind me, I therefore come to the conclusion that I should run fast and climb up that tree..." We survived because we had a very fast brain system that in a fraction of a second processed all the information so that our muscles had already started running before we had even consciously taken the decision. The reflex brain also continuously feeds its very fast intuitions, first impressions, conclusions and feelings to the reflecting brain.

While your reflecting brain takes the long and difficult road of thinking (what if... let's postpone judgment...are you certain... do we have alternatives... let's imagine...), your reflex brain jumps to its conclusions very fast for several reasons, such as:
- it can process information in parallel. This means it can process many inputs from different senses at the same time;
- it sees patterns at lightning speed. It is a magical master in recognizing patterns. The downside is that often our reflecting brain cannot undo this;
- it takes lots of unconscious shortcuts. The downside here is that its conclusions are often wrong. Although its errors are very predictable[94], it can be extremely difficult for our reflecting brain to correct them;
- it is based on firm beliefs and these are difficult to correct for our rather slow, questioning, doubting, analyzing, logical, rational reflecting brain;
- it does not need conscious attention or willpower and so consumes little brainpower and can go on forever while the willpower battery of our reflecting brain is empty. The disadvantage is that it will take over the lead from our reflecting brain when we are tired.

Some of the ways it deals with the incoming information are innate reflexes; others are reflexes, habits and intuitions learned by experience. Both help us to speed up the decision-making process. Many of these shortcuts are, or become, involuntary. Once you have learned to read, ride a bike or drive a car, you cannot unlearn this. Once you see a face on the moon, you cannot not see it, even if you know they are mountain ranges. Once you recognize a face, you cannot stop your brain from recognizing it. If you have learned to recognize a painting of Van Gogh, you will always recognize it. With lots of practice you may become an expert and learn to recognize his drawings or intuitively know that a painting is a fake. These shortcuts are very useful when speed is important or in order to take over routine work.

However, famous cases of experts whose intuitions about a fake artwork, financial decisions, business or political decisions proved totally wrong demonstrate that it is important not to trust the "gut" of your reflex brain too much and to use your reflecting brain to question its suggestions. In daily life this is also true for your first impressions of people, your gut feeling about the price of a purchase or the likelihood of a terrorist attack, disease or car accident.

Take this example from Daniel Kahneman. Let your reflex brain answer the following question immediately, intuitively: A toy bat and a ball together cost $1.10. The bat costs one dollar more than the ball. How much does the ball cost?

Don't read on: answer first: the ball costs ....

If your conclusion is $0.10, it's the same as the answer of 50 to 80% of people[95].

Now, with or without pen and paper, let your reflecting brain do the calculation. What do you discover? Your reflex-answer was wrong because the answer is $0.05 (5 cents). The more time pressure I create in my workshops, the more people get it wrong, even when the participants are CEOs, financial directors, bankers or accountants. Imagine this was a real situation where a professional in a company has to very urgently react to a purchase of $110,000 or $1.10 million... Speed is the worst enemy of reflection because your reflex brain will take over.

The conclusion is that sometimes the shortcuts help us, but sometimes they lead to totally wrong judgments when we let the reflex brain decide about things (like dollars) that were totally ir-

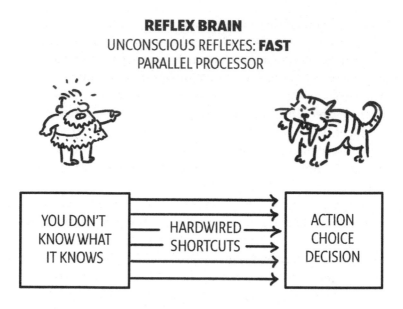

REFLEX BRAIN
UNCONSCIOUS REFLEXES: **FAST**
PARALLEL PROCESSOR

| YOU DON'T KNOW WHAT IT KNOWS | HARDWIRED SHORTCUTS | ACTION CHOICE DECISION |

relevant for our ancestors in the savannah.

The reflex brain uses both hard-wired shortcuts and soft-wired, learned shortcuts, which are intuitions or biases that we unconsciously absorb from our family of origin, education and culture. Other intuitions originate in the reflecting brain but with training, practice and experience gradually move to the reflex brain where they become expert intuitions. We often call them intuitive, common-sense decisions. Some people glorify these intuitive gut feelings, ignorant of the fact that in business in a majority of cases these are just 50/50 bets. More on this later.

In the research literature, the hard-wired shortcuts our reflex brain takes are called cognitive biases and heuristics and were discovered by the creative research of many psychologists (more on these in the paragraphs below). They became widely known outside the field of psychology through a very important publication by Kahneman and Tversky in an economics magazine[96]. Lots of people, especially economists and business people, suddenly discovered what psychologists and sociologists had known for ages: that the homo-economicus who chooses rationally and consistently based on what yields the greatest benefit does not exist, and that forecasts and decisions that people, governments and companies make on this basis are in fact worthless.

What the reflex brain does with information happens unconsciously and only its conclusions are passed to our consciousness. Then the reflecting brain can accept its output at face value or postpone judgment, it can question it, investigate it and reject it. Unfortunately, in many situations, all the reflecting brain can do is rationalize our unconscious reflex-conclusions after the facts.

5.2 THE SECRET OF THE SPEED OF YOUR REFLEX BRAIN: SHORTCUTS

EXAMPLES OF HARD-WIRED SHORTCUTS: HEURISTIC AND COGNITIVE BIASES

It is easy to imagine what the reflecting brain does. It is the brain you are aware of because you use it to think consciously. You are more or less aware of what it does. This is not the case for your reflex brain because it does its work unconsciously.

Strange irrational things happen when the reflex brain is not corrected by the reflecting brain. You will find dozens of examples and experiments in the books of, for example, Kahneman[97] and Ariely[98]. It is important to know the basics because the reflex brain has a major influence on your choices and decisions. These mechanisms are studied with the most modern brain imaging techniques and even exploited by marketers to make us choose what's best for their company and not for us, their clients, while they themselves are most often not aware that the same mechanisms influence their own professional and management decisions[99].

Did you know that when you have to choose between three similar products with three prices, your reflex brain will choose the middle one and that your reflecting brain will usually go along with this? You can imagine how easy it is for sales people to exploit this bias.

Did you know that when a group of people only get a few seconds to guess the result of 9 x 8 x 7 x 6 x 5 x 4 x 3 x 2 x 1 and another group 1 x 2 x 3 x 4 x 5 x 6 x 7 x 8 x 9, the first one guesses on average 4,200 and the second one 500, while the actual result is 362,880? Even scholars, professionals and managers who deal with numbers get this wrong all the time. Try and guess why the results are so different just by reversing the order of the multiplication and why both groups guess so wildly low. (I will share the reason with you very shortly.)

Did you know that managers, for the same reason, will make very different decisions when they first discuss a million dollar purchase and then one costing tens of thousands, compared with when they do it the other way around?

Did you know that most people think it is less likely to win in a lottery when you use the same numbers that drew a big win in the last one?

Did you know that when people have to make quick decisions they make more unethical ones than when they have time to reflect?

There are many different types of bias; in fact researchers have described about a hundred biases and heuristics[100]. That said, this research area is in a bit of a mess because people from very different disciplines have sometimes discovered the same thing but given it a different name[101], therefore scholars are trying to sort out what the root mechanisms are[102]. Let's take a look at some of these different types of bias.

The second example I gave above illustrates the **Anchoring bias**. It is one that has been studied a lot. If you give a group of people just a few seconds to guess 9x8x7x6x5x4x3x2x1 and another group to guess 1x2x3x4x5x6x7x8x9, our reflex brain gets anchored by the first numbers you read. Hence when you start with 9 8 7 you guess higher (average 4,200) than when you start with 1 2 3 (average 500)[103]. Moreover, both groups are anchored by the fact that the numbers are all below 10 and hence they totally underestimate the real result: 362,880. With just a tiny bit of time for reflection, their error would be smaller.

If you then ask both groups to guess the price of a bottle of wine or a box of chocolates, the second group will systematically guess a lower price i.e. people anchored to a number around 500 guess lower than people anchored to around 4,200. The amazing fact is that even very experienced scholars, mathematicians, accountants and managers fall prey to this bias. As a manager you should not forget that when you start a meeting by discussing a

SPEED

THE WORST ENEMY
OF REFLECTION.

multimillion deal, afterwards you will take much less time to decide about a $200,000 expense than if you discuss them in the reverse order. You can use or abuse this knowledge.

Introspection bias or better than average bias: We systematically overestimate the reliability of our self-assessment and underestimate the reliability of others to assess themselves. We think we are above average: 75% of managers, for example, think that they belong to the top 20%. 90% of drivers think they are better than average drivers.

Availability bias: Our reflex intuitions about the likelihood of any event happening are most often totally wrong because our reflex brain overestimates the representativeness of events we can easily remember, and we best remember events that we can easily imagine, usually the ones that can vividly be described in words or images. As a result, the idea that comes to mind first is the easiest one to imagine and remember, not the most likely one. Hence we dramatically overrate the occurrence of events reported by the media because the media report on subjects that are unusual and of special interest and not about what is usual or representative for our lives. They also over-report items for which they have pictures and vivid anecdotes. As for TV news, it only tends to pay attention to events they have footage for and will neglect or ignore more important or more representative events for which they don't have any film. As a result, we massively overrate the occurrence of these events. After a murder, people think that crime increased a lot in the last year even when it actually went down significantly. People overestimate the chances of winning in the lottery because the one winner gets lots of attention, while the many millions who lost money are never mentioned with the same vivid drama. We overestimate the risk of being killed by a terrorist attack in the most extreme way and heavily underestimate the risk of dying because of using a phone while driving. After 9/11 many more people died in car accidents than in terrorist attacks because, out of fear of an attack, they took the car instead of the plane.

Because of this fundamental bias amongst the media and their voters, governments follow the same logic and make laws and spend billions to fight the rarest of life threats while totally neglecting the most common ones.

Halo effect: We overestimate the abilities of successful people while underestimating the role of luck and the environment. When they fail, we underestimate their abilities. This is the trap into which almost every single guru-written management book falls because the writers are led by the quick and simple conclusions of the reflex brain, which in complex situations are often wrong. Look what happened to the companies they called "excellent" or "great" like Data General, Digital Equipment Corporation, Eastman Kodak, Kmart, Wang Labs, Abbott Labs, Walgreens, Pitney Bowes, Circuit City and Enron. Even Fanny Mae was supposed to be great. Although they present their work as research, the authors do not invest in the rules and rigor of real scientific research that lead our reflecting brain to come to truly valid conclusions. Instead they invest in marketing and present vivid illustrations that trigger the availability bias.

Beauty bias: We overestimate the abilities of attractive people (with the exception that women underestimate the abilities of attractive women).

Familiarity bias: We let our choices be influenced by familiar aspects that have nothing to do with the choice. Would you believe that significantly more people whose name starts with a P choose Pepsi and with a C choose Coke? The more letters a brand, made up or real, has in common with our name the greater the likelihood we will choose it. Because of this bias, managers too often hire people like themselves.

Bandwagon bias: Others influence our decisions more than we think, leading to group-think.

Hindsight bias: After the event, we think that we already knew the facts beforehand and that we could have predicted what happened. In experiments about this bias, people are usually very surprised when confronted with the proof that they really didn't have a clue, or a wrong idea about what was going to happen.

Retrospection bias: We see the past as more positive than it really was.

Gamblers' bias: We think that an outcome of a random process that has not occurred for a while is more likely to happen. Therefore we choose a different lottery number each time and we sincerely think that after a win, the chance to win with that same number is much lower. Therefore people are amazed when the same person wins the lottery twice in the same week or in the same year, or as has also happened, in the same lottery. Rationally speaking, the chances of winning a second time with the same number are exactly the same as winning the first time.

Confirmation bias and selective perception: We tend to select information that supports our conclusion and overlook information that goes against it.

Stereotyping: We assume qualities in people based on the group they belong to, without checking. Very sophisticated experiments have shown that the reflex brain stereotypes, even in people who consider non-discrimination as one of their main values and who sincerely and consciously practice their belief.

Loss aversion: Losing what we have feels worse than not getting what we could have gotten. People as well as businesses put a lot more effort into avoiding small losses than maximizing long-term gains.

Outcome bias: We judge the quality of a decision based on its outcome (which could be coincidental) rather than on the quality of the decision-making process.

Post-purchase bias: After we have bought something, we see the advantages more than the disadvantages of our choice.

Self-serving bias: When I am successful, this is due to my superior personal skills and abilities; when I fail it's due to circumstances or others.

When a company is successful, how often do you read or hear about CEOs who explain that the success had a lot to do with luck and that therefore their bonus is exaggerated? How often do CEOs say or suggest that the success of the company is the result of their superior abilities and that therefore their bonuses are well deserved?

When their decisions go wrong, how often do they explain it as bad luck, unfortunate circumstances? How often do they explain it as the result of their wrong decisions?

Actor-observer bias: When I am successful it is because of my abilities. When somebody else is successful this is due to circumstances. When I fail, the reverse is true.

Cheating bias: When we have to act without time to think we tend to cheat and act unethically, significantly more so than when we have or take time to reflect[104]. The faster your decision making, the higher the risk of behaving unethically. Professor Murnighan comments on his research showing that 87% of people don't lie for self-gain if given 3 minutes to think, while only 56% are honest when they have to make an immediate decision. "Immediate, automatic moral intuitions tend to be selfish, given that self-interest is a basic, instinctual response to external stimuli. In contrast, conscious, deliberative thought adds social concerns, setting off a battle within the individual that pits the strength of self-interested intuitive desires against the constraints established by social learning."[105]

By the way, did you know that you cheat less in the morning than in the evening and why? More on this later.

Substitution heuristic is a surprising, interesting and very important one. If the reflex brain cannot easily find the answer to a question, it will answer an easier, related question. If the reflecting brain is not on guard, it will accept the answer without realizing it is the right answer but to a simplified or different question. If in one of those many Employee Satisfaction Surveys you are asked, "How satisfied are you in general with your supervisor", this is a difficult question. To answer correctly you have to use your reflecting brain and compare different situations at different times, different managers you had, your expectations of what a good manager is etc...and then try to average your answer to all these sub-questions. The reflex brain has a quick and simple solution. It instantaneously makes a snapshot of how you feel about your boss in the here and now and gives that as an answer. Especially when you try to answer in a hurry, you don't realize that it substituted the difficult question "what do you think about your manager" with the much simpler one "how do you feel about your manager at this very moment".

It is a tough job for the reflecting brain of a manager to choose between different candidates for a job, taking into account the data of their bios, feedback from former employers, the results of their assessments etc etc... The reflex brain comes with a rapid answer, which the manager calls her gut feeling. When the manager is in a hurry and does not make time for reflection or for a real conversation (see below) with a colleague, she will be particularly prone to following this intuition. She will not realize that the reflex brain unconsciously substituted the original difficult question "who is the best hire" with the easy question "who looks like the best hire" and that its conclusion comes so fast and easily because of its beauty bias, stereotyping, familiarity bias, selective perception and other biases.

If after reading this you think "All these things will never happen to me", "I am too intelligent to fall into such a trap", then you are a victim of the **"blind spot bias"** or **"bias bias"**, special cases of the "introspection bias" that make you think that you have fewer biases than other people. In every single piece of research done on this, people who think they would never fall into such a trap are as biased as anyone else. And there's worse: even after a cognitive bias has been explained before an experiment, many people still score no better in the next test. The problem is that the short-circuits in our brain are unconscious, so if we make mistakes we do not realize it. What's more, helped by the hindsight bias, even our reflecting brain will help to keep our self-image intact and rationalize our decisions after the event. As a result, our biases are often not corrected, especially if you don't take enough time to reflect and have real conversations.

Our reflex brain also uses perceptual shortcuts, which in most situations help us to reach quick conclusions about reality, without having to wait for our slow reflecting brain. Beware though, sometimes these perceptual shortcuts can deceive us or even be dangerous. Some of these shortcuts are related to the fact that the reflex brain cannot deal well with perceptual inconsistencies, with conflicting sensory cues about reality. In such situations the reflex brain will sometimes automatically change our perception of reality in order to create consistency. Just look at the so-called Kanizsa's triangle (see page 60) and try not to see a white triangle pointing down. You can't because your reflex brain follows the cues about a triangle and makes you see lines even where there aren't any.

Based on this feature of our reflex brain, people have developed many other sensory illusions; some of these can be highly amusing, others extremely dangerous. Take this scenario for example: while paying attention to your phone, you veer into the middle of the road and the central road marking disappears (as you're now driving over it). In some circumstances, your reflex brain will change your perception of reality and create an illusion of seeing a line where there is no longer one. (More on this in the chapter about driving while being on the phone.)

POWERFUL SOFT-WIRED SHORTCUTS: HABITS

When you start learning to drive a car, all the information about what you have to do is consciously processed by your reflecting brain, which can only handle one task at a time. Consequently, when you are thinking about braking, you forget the clutch, when you think about the clutch, you forget to look in your mirror etc etc... At first you feel hopeless, overwhelmed that there are too many things to think about at the same time and left with a feeling of "I will never learn this". Indeed, if you only had your reflecting brain, you would never manage.

However, when you keep practicing, after many frustrating hours and many mistakes and particularly thanks to immediate feedback, such as the car stalling, your reflex brain gradually develops "soft-wired shortcuts". The conscious knowledge of your reflecting brain gradually transfers to your reflex brain where it becomes unconscious and little by little driving becomes a habit. The big advantage is that your reflex brain can then process many inputs very quickly at the same time, and you can still drive safely while your reflecting brain is thinking about very different things. Some people even erroneously think they can safely phone while driving, but that is a different question altogether (More on this in Section 2).

In a chain of behaviors, like driving a car, doing routine surgery, waking up and getting ready, one behavior or its consequence can be the trigger for the next, so that we can go through complicated routines without thinking. This is sometimes called chunking. This ability of the reflex brain to combine many bits and pieces of behavior into one efficient "chunk" makes our lives much easier and simpler.

Sixty years ago behavioral psychology researchers discovered, first with rats and later with children and adults, that to learn a new behavior or habit quickly you should get feedback, preferably rewarding, every time and immediately. The reward can be intrinsic, meaning that mastering the skill in itself makes us feel good. For example, the reward can be the effortless scoring of a goal or a fast connection with a potential client. Or the intrinsic reward can be that you immediately "knew" or "felt" that something was wrong when you entered a burning house as a fireman or when you looked at a budget proposal as a financial director or when you saw a patient in the emergency room as a doctor, and that closer examination later proved you right. However, once the new behavior is basically acquired, it becomes most resistant to unlearning when the rewards come only once in a while and are unpredictable. Later it became clear that this was related to the way our reward system in the brain functions. More recently Gregory Berns and his team have found ample support for this idea when he examined people in a brain scanner while they were given rewards. The fruit juice or water activated the pleasure systems in the brain visibly more when it was given in an unpredictable way than in a predictable way[106].

▶ **First we make our habits, then our habits make us.**
CHARLES C NOBLE

This principle is also true for highly skilled professionals like surgeons. For the very experienced ones, through years of training and having been supervised by a superior who gave immediate feedback, part of their work has become soft-wired habits. As a result, as I mentioned before, minor distractions that briefly occupy their reflecting brain do not interfere with their routines, while the same distractions cause mistakes in trainees[107].

In the army soldiers are drilled to execute all basic operations without thinking. As a result their brain is free to make much more important decisions especially when things happen that are un-habitual or unusual. If, under attack, they had to think about their basic behavior and all the basic instructions about how to load a rifle, aim, look for cover, communicate to others etc... they would not survive very long. Thanks to their training, which is a lot about habit development and feedback, their brains can deal with more important decisions.

Not all habits are related to motor skills. There are others, like intellectual habits: once your reflex brain takes over, you don't have to spell the letters or the words anymore to read a book and your reflex brain can do simple mathematics instantly. There are also social habits like "manners" or "etiquette" that make social interaction and collaboration smoother, more efficient and predictable. Rules are helpful too, but a habit is more powerful. Knowing that for most drivers the rules have become habits makes traffic much smoother. In the army, knowing that your mates have developed the same habits makes it possible to function as one without much communication about the basics. This is also true at work, be it in production or in meetings. Developing strongly shared habits makes the collaboration smoother and more predictable.

In a company all the habits together define the company culture. This is what doesn't change, even when you gradually replace all the people. Most of these habits made sense at one time, but sometimes they outlive their utility. Changing company habits or company culture is even more difficult than unlearning a personal habit and learning a new one: it takes time, patience and lots of practice and immediate feedback.

One of the most important features of our brain is that with lots of training, behavior and reasoning can move from the conscious, energy-, willpower- and time-consuming reflecting brain to the unconscious, effortless reflex brain and become automatic, spontaneous[108]. We develop learned reflexes, intuitions and habits. Once a particular behavior or reasoning becomes a habit, we don't have to think about it any more and we can do it with little brain effort. Habit formation helps us to be much faster and more efficient. The reflecting brain is then freed up for other thinking and... for learning new habits. During a normal day we do hundreds of things without thinking, without making conscious decisions. Without these habits our brain would be totally overwhelmed, overloaded and unable to function.

> Ninety-nine hundredths or, possibly, nine hundred and ninety-nine thousandths of our activity is purely automatic and habitual, from our rising in the morning to our lying down each night. Our dressing and undressing, our eating and drinking, our greetings and partings, our hat raisings and giving way for ladies to precede, nay, even most of the forms of our common speech, are things of a type so fixed by repetition as almost to be classed as reflex actions. To each sort of impression we have an automatic, ready-made response.... So far as we are thus mere bundles of habit, we are stereotyped creatures, imitators and copiers of our past selves.
>
> WILLIAM JAMES (1899)[109]

Modern brain scan technology also shows that when behavior becomes a habit, the control of the behavior literally moves to other parts of the brain and that in a subtle way the reflecting brain keeps monitoring the reflex brain[110]. The latter is important because the reflex brain itself does not know if a habit it developed is a good one or a bad one. We need the reflecting brain to decide if the habit is appropriate, good, useful, wise or ethical.

As I have already mentioned, our habits also allow us to multi-task: while our unconscious reflex brain takes care of routine tasks, the reflecting brain can be involved in very different thoughts. The more sophisticated the reflex habits of professionals, athletes, surgeons, soldiers, managers and firemen, the more room this makes for the reflecting brain to be effective. If a soccer player has to think about how to pass the ball, there is less chance that he will pass it to the right person. If after hundreds of hours of training and playing with a ball, giving the most sophisticated passes left and right has become a habit and happens automatically, then the reflecting brain is free to anticipate, to find a solution for out-of-routine situations and to give the pass at the right moment to the right person. After hundreds of hours more of playing and training, even that becomes a habit his reflex brain can take care of and his reflecting brain can move to an even higher level and think quickly about tactics and strategy. But even at that level with many more hours of playing, many tactical decisions become intuitive, taken care of by his reflex brain. At that point his reflecting brain is free to think quickly when something happens that does not belong to the learned routine, unless his reflecting brain is already occupied by worries. Of course he couldn't do this while being on the phone. Even the best tennis, soccer or golf player in the world couldn't play a decent game while being on the phone. Why do you think you can.

As you have certainly experienced yourself, habit formation can cause a lot of trouble when we need to unlearn a habit, when an old habit, like always being connected, becomes inefficient, stupid or dangerous. Luckily, about a hundred years ago a group of psychologists distanced themselves from all kinds of unscientific opinions about why we behave as we do, such as psychoanalysis, and started empirical research on how people learn and unlearn behavior. In the beginning they over-focused on modifying the behavior itself. Later they also studied ways to change the thinking and feelings that accompany behavior. They produced thousands of research publications, resulting in a wealth of scientific knowledge about the most efficient ways to change behavior. Some of the most recent brain research is even sponsored by companies who want to know how they can best influence the habits of their customers.

The simplest model that is still very useful for understanding, learning and changing habits is the A-B-C model. ABC stands for Antecedent, Behavior, Consequence. Sometimes this is described as Trigger, Behavior/Habit, Reward. Originally the B only referred to Behavior, but later it was expanded to thoughts and emotions. (More on unlearning bad habits in Section 3).

5.3 BEWARE OF YOUR INTUITIONS OR GUT FEELINGS

In the paragraphs above I mentioned several times how hardwired and soft-wired shortcuts, presenting themselves as intuitions, can help us to make fast decisions, but that they can also lead to wrong decisions, especially when they are no longer steered by reflection or conversations. The result is that much more often than you think, following your intuitions is just a 50/50 bet. In fact, it is even worse. Because if you were to toss a coin to decide, you would get it right in 50% of the cases, whereas when you follow ill-founded intuitions, you will get it wrong more than 50% of the time. The more you are convinced about your expertise, the more often you will be wrong, except when your intuitions are developed under the rather strict conditions set out below.

This is why choosing which stocks to invest in is done as well by monkeys throwing darts as by experts. Of course you will not believe this because of the availability bias: the media write much more often about the very few, often very temporarily successful experts than about the thousands who lose money all the time. Moreover, several of the soft-wired shortcuts I described will prevent you from learning from your wrong bets so that you can keep your objectively baseless belief in your system or your expertise intact. Following the flow of your reflex brain is easy, going against it and challenging its primitive conclusions and your own beliefs is hard work.

▶ **Gut feelings are often nothing but 50/50 bets.**

It is quite amazing how often the same people who ignore all feelings, both their own and those of others, and who glorify their dispassionate decision making so profoundly believe in their gut feeling. When they are questioned about the wisdom of following their gut feeling, they often refer to management heroes like Steve Jobs who they say followed their gut feeling against all odds.

Steve Jobs himself couldn't have disagreed more. He wrote: "If you read Apple's first brochure, the headline was 'Simplicity is the Ultimate Sophistication.' What we meant by that was that when you first attack a problem it seems really simple because you don't understand it. Then when you start to really understand it, you come up with these very complicated solutions because it's really hairy. Most people stop there. But a few people keep burning the midnight oil and finally understand the underlying principles of the problem and come up with an elegantly simple solution for it. But very few people go the distance to get there"[111].

Intuitions have been the subject of very interesting research, essentially representing two schools of thought. At one point the most important representatives of each school had a conversation to find out what they agreed on and what they didn't. One was the Nobel Prize winner Daniel Kahneman, the other was Gary Klein, a world famous authority on naturalistic decision-making. If you are interested in the subject of intuitions, and as a manager or other professional you have no choice but to be deeply interested in it, you should read their article: "Conditions for Intuitive Expertise"[112]. It is so interesting and important that my only advice to you is: Read it. Period. In the meantime, let me just give you the conclusions with a few personal tweaks.

To make good intuitive decisions there are a few conditions.
- You know that developing and using intuitions only works in a more or less predictable, structured environment, where it is possible to learn the regularities of that environment. Fire fighting and medicine are such environments; the stock market not at all.
- You are an expert in the sense that in the past you learned not just from experience, but especially from continuous fast objective feedback about your decisions, good and bad.
- You do your homework and take the time for hard study, thorough reading, real conversations, deep reflection and you sleep on the information and knowledge acquired.
- You evaluate and challenge your intuition before following your gut and let it continuously be challenged by others.
- You know that gut feelings often blind people to unique new aspects of the situation that other experts, following different intuitions, might see.
- You know how the reflex brain with its many shortcuts, including emotional ones, can completely fool you.
- You know, and you are convinced, that your own subjective experience of the accuracy of your decisions is not at all a reliable indicator of the objective accuracy of your intuitive judgments and decisions.
- You stay within your clearly limited area of your true expertise and don't fall for the temptation, as so many famous managers and experts do, to make judgments that are outside it.

- You know and accept that, in some situations and under some conditions, decisions based on algorithms are better than human judgments.
(list adapted from Kahneman and Klein[113])

If these conditions are not met, your intuitions are nothing but superstitions that you developed to remain confident against all odds in uncertain and unpredictable situations.

Experts, professionals and certainly managers have an above-average desire for control over their lives, and people with a high desire of control show more superstitious behavior to fulfill that desire[114]. It is difficult for them to live with feelings of uncertainty and of not being in control. When they have to choose or decide in a fundamentally unpredictable context, they will develop a "theory", a belief system to retain their basic feeling of being in control. Given the objective unpredictability of the situation, this is an unjustified feeling that they have influence on the situation, while from a purely rational or scientific point of view they have no influence whatsoever. This is by definition a superstition, an illusory sense of control over uncertainty.

What's more, although their decisions are in fact rationalized bets, they will bet right once in a while and that will reinforce their belief, as happened to the world famous pigeons of B.F. Skinner[115].

Skinner put a bunch of hungry pigeons in a cage. He then attached a machine that at regular intervals dropped a few corn grains into the cage. When he returned hours later the pigeons had developed different kinds of "superstitious behavior" or "intuitions". One pigeon turned around at regular intervals, another one made intricate dancing steps, another a pendulum motion, yet another extended his neck as high as possible etc... These pigeons had made a link between the desired event that was totally out of their control, grains dropping into the cage, and what they were doing at that very moment. Since they increased that behavior, once in a while the grains would fall exactly when they were performing that particular behavior, reinforcing that behavior even more.

Some 30 years ago I suggested to a sporty intern of mine to study superstition in athletes[116]. He discovered a few interesting things. First that the less certain the outcome, for example when the outcome was dependent on others like team members, referees etc., the stronger the belief in good-luck charms and rituals. In team sports like soccer, for example, where the result depends on your 10 mates, the 11 competitors, the referees etc., they were more frequent and more developed than in individual sports like tennis where the result depends on you, your competitor and the umpire. Secondly, losing did not change the belief in the superstition; it was protected by the thought "without my amulet, four-leaf clover, strict order of dressing... it would have been much worse". Later research confirmed that the more unpredictable the outcome, think stock market, the greater our belief in our rituals and systems. Our belief systems, predictive tools help us to cope, give us a feeling of control and confidence in situations that are objectively unpredictable. This is true not only for athletes, but also for people choosing letters to play scrabble[117], putting in golf[118], playing baseball[119], studying for exams[120]...and experts trying to predict the outcome of unpredictable processes like the stock market. Their gut feeling, their belief in their system stays intact, even when things go totally wrong. As a result, they do not reflect on the feedback and improve their rational decisions, but instead keep making irrational bets governed by the cognitive and emotional shortcuts of the reflex brain.

"IT WOULD HAVE BEEN MUCH WORSE
WITHOUT MY LUCKY CLOVER!"

5.4 THE GARDEREFLEX BRAIN NEEDS "MADMAN'S GUARDS" AGAINST UNETHICAL BEHAVIOR

You don't need much imagination to picture the role cognitive biases, or hard-wired shortcuts, play in today's hectic, hyper-connected world of business. High up in the banking world in particular, leaders have suffered from many of them, including the halo effect, introspection bias, bandwagon bias, hindsight bias, gamblers' bias, confirmation bias, selective perception, outcome bias, post-purchase bias, self-serving bias, substitution and cheating bias.

It's also very important to know that our primitive reflex brain has no morals, no ethics; it is fundamentally and genetically selfish. As far as ethics and morals are concerned, we cannot trust the spontaneous, fast, primitive reflex brain. Its fast decisions and intuitions are fundamentally selfish, self-interested relicts from the survival and procreation strategies of our ancestors in the savannah. Confronted with the daily struggle for survival, the savannah dweller simply did not have the luxury to reflect and to consider the many interpretations, social concerns and potential ethical consequences of his actions.

The problem is not that it is unethical but that just like animals it is non-ethical. Ethics emanate from our reflecting brain. The only thing we can do is to train the human reflex brain so early on and so continuously, by creating a predictable educational situation with immediate feedback, that it develops some soft-wired shortcuts towards ethical behavior. Without this relentless training, called education, the primitive, selfish, non-ethical reflex brain will take the lead and dominate.

Here again, the solution is to take time to disconnect to reflect and to have real conversations. For example, in a situation where people have to make an ethical right-wrong decision, even if this has negative consequences for themselves, 87% tell the truth when they have time to think about it, while only 56% do so when they have to make an immediate decision[121]. Moreover, when we are tired we make more unethical decisions because the never-tiring reflex brain takes over the decisions, resulting therefore in our decisions being more ethical in the morning than in the evening[122]. (More on this in Section 2 in the chapter BrainChain #1.)

> **"Having time to think things over may not make much difference in big-time financial swindles, but our findings suggest that it would make a considerable difference in innumerable instances of lying and fraud that happen every day in the business world."**
>
> KEITH MURNIGHAN. KELLOGG SCHOOL OF MANAGEMENT.

In French a guard rail is graphically called "un garde-fou", "a madman's guard" to prevent madmen from falling overboard or driving into a ravine. We all need two "madman's guards" to protect us from unethical decisions: one is internal, the other external. The development of our internal "madman's guard" is continuously influenced by the external one, consisting of the values, limit-setting, behavioral rules and consistency of feedback from our social context, starting with our parents and teachers and later our spouses, children, peers, bosses and boards. Ideally these values are so well-trained from early childhood on that they became part of our reflex brain's fast soft-wired shortcuts.

The external ones are very important too because when we do things that do not fit very well with our own values, we all have a tendency to adapt our standards after the facts to our behavior. Due to this gradual adaption we all run the risk of progressively deviating from our initial standards, lowering our internal "madman's guard", without being fully aware of this. The continuous recalibration by our external guard should prevent this from happening. When this recalibration does not happen, the internal guard keeps lowering and the madman goes overboard. This recently happened in a few rather extreme financial and sexual scandals and other unethical behavior of very high-profile people, where the colleagues, family and friends of the perpetrators had also lowered their external "madman's guard" to very low levels.

These guards are even more important for people in positions of power because power makes people more self-centered and as a result they run an even higher risk of making unethical decisions[123], especially in a company culture that on the one hand promotes shooting from the hip, fast decisions and following gut feelings and on the other discourages listening to outsiders and the minority, disagreements, real conversations, reflection and real team decisions.

> "Organizations with a 'fast pulse' or tendency to reward quick decision-making may suffer ethical penalties by discouraging contemplation and conversation... At a minimum, our results suggest that individual, organizational actors facing right-wrong decisions should take the time to think or to consult an ethical colleague."
>
> KEITH MURNIGHAN OF THE KELLOGG SCHOOL OF MANAGEMENT

The paradox, however, is that people who need more external control and pushback get much less. Way too often, especially around people in positions of power, the external "madman's guards" are weakened and lowered instead of strengthened. Top people too often have a tendency to create a clique of "yes-people" around them, where nobody gives sincere feedback anymore, while in fact continuous sincere feedback is the only way to keep the moral soft-wired shortcuts from eroding. They end up in an artificial bubble where nobody takes care of the "madman's guards". Quite the contrary in fact. Within this bubble, many people in the company as well as in private life will, even spontaneously, cover up the vices and failures of the leader. The people who remind the person of the values, or otherwise disagree, are fired or demoted and the leader divorces the person who knows him best when she tries to raise the "madman's guard". This process often leads to toxic narcissism, but that is another story that I have described as "Pain in the ass management"[124].

This is no excuse for people like those who ruined their banks that then had to be bailed out by their countries. It is a call to arms for the boards and leaders of these companies to put in place the regulations needed to rein in the reflex brain of their employees, from the CEO to the operators on the shop floor. As long as making money is the only value that counts and the only way to survive in that environment, their self-interested, survival-driven, non-ethical reflex brain will go for the money no matter what. Their slow, potentially ethical, reflecting brain will have to keep justifying the behavior after the facts, by continuously lowering the norms.

The problem for the people at the top is not necessary that their impulses are stronger, but that the internal and external controls have become weaker and weaker. To prevent abuses of power, sexual harassment being a very good example, organizations need strong "madman's guards": strong boards, truly lived and reinforced values, good checks and balances. Regular anonymous 360-degree feedback, executed well and daring to ask questions about ethics (which they almost never do), may unearth undesirable behavior. A healthy team spirit where team members hold each other accountable, with room for mavericks and jesters to challenge group-think, will help. Therefore, in teams you need real "carefrontational"[125] (a combination of caring and confronting) conversations. The big advantage of having a good team is that we ourselves are not conscious of the maneuvers of our reflex brain, but they are often more obvious to others. Important decisions, especially in unpredictable situations, should therefore be discussed in a good team. The decisions will be better if you are aware of biases like group-think, bandwagon and herd behavior, and know the tricks and tools to avoid them. For important discussions, every team should therefore designate a few arch pessimists, devil's advocates or jesters to counter these biases or make fun of them. Another protection is to ask team members to represent and defend each other's projects[126]. Leaders should be confident, but never certain. When you are certain, you stop thinking and listening to feedback. Of course, this process is slower than going with bets made on gut feelings, without thorough discussion and silencing any difference of opinion. It is the choice between letting the fast, primitive, non-ethical, selfish reflex brain reign or giving the slow, creative, potentially ethical and wise reflecting brain a chance to take the lead.

6 EMOTIONS: VERY INFLUENTIAL, HARD-WIRED AND SOFT-WIRED, ON THE INTERFACE BETWEEN REFLEX AND REFLECTION

Emotions have an important influence on our reflecting brain and also, as we will see, directly on our behavior. We already find this idea in the Latin origin of the word e-movere (to move, act out) via the French émouvoir (to stir up). Not only will emotions color or even force our thinking in a particular direction, but if they run high they can even totally block our reflecting brain. This made sense for our ancestors in the savannah to coordinate action at lightning speed without any interference from the reflecting brain, which is way too slow when very acute, life-threatening, problems need to be solved. But it often doesn't make sense for our 21st century lives.

The research about emotions is going through a real revolution because of the results of the very sophisticated neuro-imaging techniques. These sophisticated "brain scanners" allow researchers to see exactly what happens in the brain in real time. In the many scientific fields that study emotions, the results provoke fundamental discussions about different theories: what emotions really are; the difference between emotions, feelings, moods and affect; how they mix; and about their link with what happens in our brain and the rest of our body[127]. One of the most important findings is that there are reactions in our brain and body that have all the characteristics of emotional reactions, except that we are not aware of them. This is why I discuss them here in the chapter about our reflex brain.

For example, before we had this sophisticated neuro-imaging technology, scientists would show people scary, disgusting or happy pictures and ask how people felt before and after. Sometimes they would measure changes of blood pressure, heart rate and conductivity of the skin to find out something about the arousal, but the cornerstone in this research was basically self-report. Now the situation is very different. Imagine, for example, that I show a person a picture of a very scary situation and her body reacts with typical anxiety reactions, while we can see in the brain scanner that the areas that are active in scary situations are active. Asked about what she felt, she says, "I felt really scared". In this situation it is clear: this was an emotion.

Imagine we do exactly the same experiment, with the only difference that we flash a scary picture so briefly that the person did not have a chance to realize what was on it. Asked how she feels, she says, "OK. Not any different from a minute ago", but her body and her brain reacted exactly the same as in the first experiment where she was conscious of what was on the picture. So her reflex brain reacted exactly the same, independent of her being aware of the emotion or not. If we agree that in both cases there was an emotional reaction, then we must accept that the second emotion was totally unconscious and therefore that there are also emotions that researchers cannot study with questionnaires and interviews.

The importance of these findings for this book is that not only do emotional reactions that we are consciously aware of influence our reflecting brain, but so do the unconscious emotional reactions and shortcuts of our reflex brain. In general, intense emotions tend to shortcut the reflecting brain, diverting us from our goal to the immediately present stimuli, leading among other things to selective attention and automatic, superficial, heuristic reactions[128]. This is an excellent mechanism when lightning fast action is required, but a problem when a little reflection would lead to much better choices, decisions and actions.

Some emotions are an interesting mixture of conscious and unconscious. As we have seen above, our unconscious reflex brain is very fast and our conscious reflecting brain is slow. What happens very often is that a particular situation first triggers a very fast emotional reflex in our brain and then in the rest of our body (for example heart beating, flushing, trembling, tense muscles). Meanwhile, the slower reflecting brain becomes aware of these sensations and then, taking account of the situation and with some delay, labels these reactions as an emotion e.g. anger. Our reflecting brain can often react fast enough to influence the primitive reactions of our reflex brain, especially when through unrelenting education and life experiences we have developed soft-wired shortcuts that help to modulate, control or contain our emotional reactions and behavior. As you read in the chapter above about the "madman's guard", our reflecting brain needs energy and easily tires. Hence, its modulating effect on emotions diminishes in the course of the day. As a result the more crude basic emotions like aggression and anxiety of the untiring reflex brain become more outspoken in the evening, especially if we don't get enough sleep. (Much more on this in the chapter Brain-Chain #4 about sleep.)

Not only the physiological reactions but even the resulting behavior can be faster than the conscious awareness of the emotion. For example, a Vietnam veteran goes for a walk in the city, hears a particular creeping sound behind him and in a fraction of second turns around and knocks out the person coming up behind in one strike. In the therapy session he told me, "That creepy sound scared the hell out of me". But in fact that thought and the feeling of anxiety came after the lightning fast physical arousal and behavioral reaction. The very high and repeated anxiety in the war had flagged the creeping sound as life-threatening and the reflex brain started an action so fast that the reflecting brain couldn't stop it in time.

In this situation the sequence is:

Situation → unconscious emotional reaction in reflex brain → body reacts via body-brain → behavior → appraisal → conscious emotion.

We all have these hard- and soft-wired shortcuts that we only afterwards rationalize or label as a feeling. It is fascinating that researchers scanning the brain in real-time are able to show that in such situations the brain areas responsible for thinking react after the bodily changes have started.

As you can imagine, these emotional shortcuts were very useful, if not life-saving, for our ancestors in the savannah because thinking is so slow compared to reflexes. Without this reflex brain, we would never have survived. Helped by strong emotions caused by horror stories of his family members or by seeing his kin being eaten by a saber-toothed tiger, the reflex brain developed a direct link between a dangerous situation and the bodily changes needed to start running. As a result, his muscles had already started running before he even started feeling scared.

On the other hand, our feelings are often caused by our thoughts about a situation. One person's stress is another person's fun! One person might enjoy dangling from a thin rope over a yawning precipice while another person in the same situation would die of terror. The differences in behavioral, emotional and physical reactions are based on the way you appraise the situation. If you interpret a comment from your boss as an aggressive, unjustified criticism from a pretentious upstart, there is a good chance that you will feel angry and your heart might start beating faster while your blood pressure goes up and you might behave in a hostile manner towards him. To feel angry, you don't even need the presence of your boss. It is possible that you only become angry later when you are thinking about what actually happened or while you are explaining it to your spouse. It is also possible that you feel the anger again when you start thinking about the incident months later.

If you had interpreted his comment more sympathetically, for example as a normal reaction of a very insecure person, you would have felt very different, the stress would have been lower or nonexistent and your behavior very different, for example supportive.

A good actor who really gets into the character can feel the emotions that go with the role. Even for a bad actor like myself, when as an adolescent I was playing a motherless child, to a record of Louis Armstrong singing "Sometimes I feel like a motherless child", even having had no personal experience whatsoever of anything like such a situation, sometimes I started feeling like one, looked like one and the tears would well up in my eyes.

In these situations the sequence is:
   Situation → appraisal → emotion → body reacts via body-brain → behavior

The insight that thoughts cause feelings and, from there, physio-logical reactions and behavior became the basis of an impressive amount of research in the field known as cognitive psychology. It also led to one of the very few psychotherapeutic approaches with a proven track record: cognitive therapy. One of the first psy-chiatric problems it was used for was chronic depression. The idea was that people feel depressed because they have chronically depressive-making thoughts. Hence the therapist helps the pa-tient to uncover those thoughts. He then helps the patient to re-place them with more rational, not depressive-making thoughts, and indeed this improves the depression.

Take a look at the two flowcharts on p.118 and p.119. They are of course extreme simplifications of a much more complex system of interactions. For one, the process is described as linear, whereas in fact most arrows go in both directions and there are feedback loops everywhere. For example, the physiological reactions we feel in our body may feed our interpretation. The same is true for our behavior: Aggressively acting out our feelings of anger tends to increase our feelings, while blocking the physiological reac-tions of our body, by giving medication that lowers the blood pres-sure and pulse for instance, decreases the emotion.

The two kinds of emotions, conscious and unconscious, can also combine. This creates opportunities to change habitual emotional reactions by developing new soft-wired emotional shortcuts or by diverting a spontaneous reaction from being acted out. For example, as a young psychotherapist I managed to con-vince a couple that their continuous, sometimes physical, reflex fighting was their only way to express love because they were too afraid of being otherwise physically close. I therefore told them that before getting into a new fight, they should give each other a symbolic present of one dime, so as not to forget their love. Of course the new interpretation completely changed the situation and their appraisal of it. In the beginning particular actions of their spouse still elicited the same reflex physiological response as before, but it no longer led to a fight because that response was diverted by a different "after the fact" interpretation.

A challenge for organizations is that many managers and other professionals, especially the macho male type, tend to ignore or even ridicule emotions, their own as well as those of others. This has a very negative impact on the intellectual productivity of employees because emotions are the motor, or the brakes, of our intellectual productivity. It will make a huge difference for your career and your projects if you can generate positive feelings like Passion, Desire, Confidence, Pleasure, Commitment, Pride, Courage, Belonging, Autonomy, Affection, Love, Trust, Determination, Loyalty, Feeling Respected, Altruism, Empathy, Entrepreneurship and Readiness for change.

You should also know how to understand and deal with negative feelings like Anger, Fear, Anxiety, Paralysis, Apathy, Hostility, Hate, Grief, Antagonism, Discontent, Resentment, Isolation, Distrust, Risk aversion and Resistance, being able to recognize them, respect them, change them, diminish them and ultimately turn them into positive mobilizing feelings. Only when you are able to do this, will you successfully manage the most important influences on the productivity of your people.

More specifically relevant for this book is that ignoring your own feelings is a bad idea because they have such a big impact on your own reflecting brain. If you just ignore them, you cannot reflect on them, you will not learn from them and you will not manage them. You will act on your intuitions and never realize you were led by powerful emotional shortcuts, which like all the others, allow us to make fast, intuitive decisions when there is no time or no resources to make an in-depth analysis. The emotional shortcuts, both the positive and the negative ones, are also rather primitive and can be totally wrong. The best way to avoid taking the wrong emotional shortcut is first of all to disconnect to reflect and secondly to take time for a real conversation with other people, who by definition have had totally different life experiences and will therefore not be guided by the same unconscious emotions. (More on this further on.)

A very special feeling-shortcut that has got a lot of attention from scientists in the last decade is empathy. The reason empathy got all this attention is the discovery of so called "mirror neurons" in the brain. In 1995 Professor Giacomo Rizzolatti and Leonardo

Fogassi planted microscopically small electrodes in the brains of monkeys to measure the activity in the brain cells that plan the movements of monkeys' limbs. They were registering the electrical activity of a monkey picking up a peanut. By coincidence they discovered that exactly the same cells become active when that monkey, still linked to the apparatus, saw another monkey picking up a peanut, even when the observing monkey was totally motionless. It was as if the brain cells responsible for that movement in the observing monkey mirrored what happened in the brain cells of the active monkey. These movement-cells even fire up in the dark when the monkey only hears another monkey cracking a peanut. The researchers called these cells "mirror cells" or "mirror neurons". This was a revolutionary finding. Before, the regions of the brain responsible for executing movements had been thought to be neatly separated in different areas from those involved in observing. Now, it had become clear that the same area of the brain that plans and controls action is also involved in perception and vice versa!

The same intriguing link between action-perception and action-execution was later found in people too. The authors write: "We conclude that although there are several mechanisms through which one can understand other individuals' behavior, the mirror-mechanism is the only one that allows understanding others' actions from the inside and gives the observing individual a first-person grasp of other individuals' motor goals and intentions"[129].

Next, it was found in people that the same thing happens when we observe facial expressions and speech and that the mirror cells take into account the context, and not just the movement. They fire up differently when a cup is grasped or carefully picked up between thumb and index finger and differentiate between moving an empty cup or one filled with tea.

The human being, from very early in life, is a master in imitating, the basis for fast social learning. Now we start understanding that we are really hard-wired for this because the neurons responsible for a particular behavior are working when we see the behavior of another person. It also helps to understand how very young infants start imitating and why they only imitate beings "like-me". On the other hand, it became evident that the mirror cells are less active when the people observed are not like-me, hence this shortcut helps from infant-life on to distinguish people that are not like-me[130].

The most recent developments now address the possibility that these mirror neurons may play a role in the development of empathy because they also mirror facial expressions[131] and they seem to be able to take the intention of the movement, and from there the intention of the person, into account. They help us to "mind-read"[132]. These findings probably also explain the long-known impact of mimicry, where without being aware of it, people tune in to each other unconsciously, imitating each other's non-verbal behavior.

In any case, it looks like the human being is hard-wired for empathy. Empathy is another shortcut that influences our behavior, even when we are not consciously aware of it. Of course there is nothing wrong with that, but it's good to know.

7 OUR ARCHIVING BRAIN NEEDS BREAKS

As I very briefly explained earlier, the information in our brain is continuously rearranged and manipulated by our archiving brain to store it, refresh it and prepare for knowledge and insight. A most important part of this information processing happens when we are disengaged from the immediately present reality, when our reflecting brain is idling, when we don't demand anything important from it. The less input from the outside world and the fewer demands from the reflecting brain, the busier this network of archivists.

When the reflecting brain idles, unoccupied by any task, then the archiving brain is at its most active sorting and re-sorting its enormous database, looking for information that might be useful for the reflecting brain and putting that information at the front where it is easier to retrieve. The archivists are also continuously searching the archive to see if there is older information that may be of interest, trying to make sense of bits and pieces by linking them together. While they are doing this, the archivists are also being creative and often come up with new, surprising associations of information. Many of these are not useful, or even amusing, but some of the associations that the reflecting brain recognizes lead to creative breakthroughs.

Conversely, when we are always actively and consciously dealing with the outside world, for example by being busy with our screens big and small all the time, the archiving brain doesn't have enough capacity to correctly process all the information coming in and link it with data that has already been stored.

Regular idling in the sense of taking brain-breaks, being disengaged, unoccupied, inactive and not involved in any task, is crucial for your intellectual productivity and creativity. Therefore, what most of us consider "lost time" is actually ideal "working time" for your archiving brain, and filling every single minute being connected to your little screen is a disaster for your intellectual productivity and especially your creativity.

The simplest example of this is when you're holding a conversation and you cannot for the life of you remember the name of a person you want to talk about. The harder you try to remember, the more occupied your working memory becomes and the smaller the chance of you finding it. Once you give up searching and in a relaxed way go on talking about other subjects, your processor is no longer 100% occupied, your archiving brain jumps at the opportunity to use the spare working memory and... the name pops into your mind.

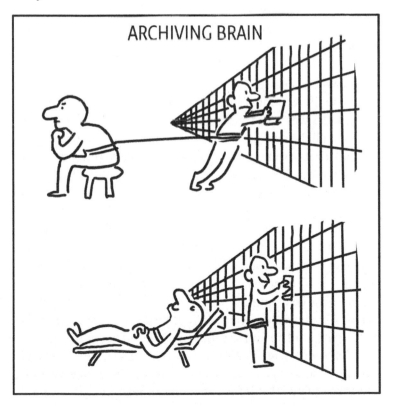

ARCHIVING BRAIN

All of us know the situation where we rack our brains all day long, but cannot find the solution to a problem, and then when we have stopped thinking about it and are standing in the shower, jogging, lying in our bed or enjoying a family meal all of a sudden and totally unexpectedly the solution stares us in the face.

Kazuhiko Nishi, who together with Bill Gates started Microsoft and who developed one of the first laptops when he was 24 years old, got his most creative ideas at moments of lazy relaxation. In a workshop he called it the three Bs of Nishi: break, bath and bed. The film director Woody Allen has his best ideas in bed. Archimedes discovered his law in the bath. Einstein suddenly found the solution to the puzzle of the relativity theory when he was taking a walk on the beach. Professor Kékulé discovered the structure of benzene while he dozed of in front of an open fire. President Clinton said that he had his best ideas when he was playing golf. The real breakthroughs most often happen when we are not thinking about the problem or challenge, when we are not only disconnected but even disengaged, if not totally detached; this gives our archiving brain a chance to delve into the archives of our long-term memory.

Once we know this, we realize that the "Eureka" story of Archimedes is not usually recounted correctly. The essence of the story is that Archimedes was asked by King Midas to find out if the goldsmith had used all the pure gold he was given to make his crown or if he had substituted some gold for silver. Of course Archimedes could not melt that marvelous piece of art with all its golden olive leaves to measure its volume to calculate its density. The wrong version of the story then continues as follows: while sitting in his bath, ruminating about this challenge, Archimedes observed that when he put his arm down in the water he experienced an upward force equal to the weight of the water it displaced. He then cried "Eureka", which means "I found it", did the math and... the king executed the goldsmith.

This story is wrong because if Archimedes had been consciously thinking hard about the problem while sitting in his bath, he would never have made the breakthrough observation. He made it because he was just relaxing in the bath, his mind wandering and absolutely NOT thinking about the problem.

Our archiving brain needs some idle capacity in the "micropro-cessor" of our working memory in order to access and manipulate the internal information, all the billions of bits and bytes that are already stored in our long-term memory. That is why, in a well-prepared brain, we often have our most creative ideas when our conscious thinking uses only 10-20% of our working memory's capacity. The archiving brain then has 80-90% free to manipu-late, combine, store and reorganize the information.

The greatest time of the day for your creative archiving brain is when you sleep. This might sound crazy to you, but getting enough good sleep is an indispensable part of the reflection process! If you are dealing with an extremely important decision, you should al-ways sleep on it. After doing your homework, you need to get enough hours of sound sleep so that the millions of archivists can do their work full time, unhindered by their most demanding cli-ent: your reflecting brain. During sleep they can use your full brain capacity to organize and store all the information, work with the information, your reflections, combining them, linking them to memories that were not immediately consciously avail-able, filling in blanks and creating new associations, coming up with ideas that have never been thought of before.

In my research and workshops, I discovered that in some groups up to 65% of professionals do not sleep enough and almost 100% have no clue how important sleep is for our brain and our intellectual productivity. In Section 2 I have therefore added a special chapter about what happens in our brain when we sleep.

Of course, in order for our archiving brain to do its job well, to turn the information into insights and to come up with creative ideas, it needs to have the necessary and well thought-through information in the long-term memory. Our brain needs to be well-prepared; we need to have done our "homework" i.e. have used our reflecting brain to study a topic deeply without any interruptions or have had undisturbed deep conversations on the subject. This is the hard conscious thinking work I described in the chapter about the reflecting brain. If all you do is continuously scan and skim through information on your (little) screen, without taking the time for deeper reflection, and without sufficient breaks for your archiving brain to store and order this information, it will simply be unavailable for your archiving brain.

Then, both while you are doing this hard homework and afterwards, you have to relax, disconnect and disengage regularly. Why? First of all to give your brain a chance to get lots of information that is still in your temporary memory into your long-term memory. This is not only an important job, but it is also an urgent job because our temporary memory is limited and it works on a "first in, first out" basis. Without regular brain-breaks, more information than you want is just pushed out by new information because it was never stored in the long-term memory.

Secondly because the information in your long-term memory has to be rearranged all the time so that there are enough interconnections to make it retrievable later.

Thirdly to play around with all that information and make new connections that can lead to creative "Eureka" experiences. These creative ideas will not come when you are thinking very hard to find a solution or when you are pecking away on your big or little screen, because when you do that your working memory is totally occupied by conscious thinking and does not leave enough capacity for your archiving brain to process all the information. I hope you are now convinced that taking a break from thinking to deal with your e-mails is no brain-break at all.

> **Being busy with your smartphone all the time is not smart at all; it is brainless.**

Let me build on an idea I learned from Herman Vandenbrouck, who in his research about learning organizations discovered that "Useful Superfluousness" is necessary to be a learning organization. He explains that work has to be organized in such a way that there is some slack. If there is no slack, the organization does not learn.

This is also true for each individual brainworker. People and their brains need slack to function at their best. Therefore I prefer to carry his idea a step further and call it "Indispensable Superfluousness" or "Vital Slack".

Why would you want to let your unrelenting use of ICT asphyxiate your learning and creativity? Being busy with your smartphone all the time, filling all the little gaps of time with little tasks, is not smart at all; it is brainless.

> **Lean organizations are too often mean towards intellectual productivity.**

The lack of slack resulting from consecutive reorganizations, where fewer and fewer people have to do more and more tasks, is one of the ways organizations ruin the brainwork of their people. Lean organizations, for example, are often very mean for intellectual productivity, unless the lean approach is accompanied by a very significant reset of the priorities and in particular the things that the company is not going to do any more.

Conclusion: it is extremely important to disconnect to reflect, but if you want to get the best out of your brain, learn the most, remember the most and be most creative, you should also disconnect to disengage, let your brain freewheel, give it some Vital Slack. In other words, you should first disconnect to focus and reflect and then you should disconnect to relax and disengage.

8 WHY YOU SHOULD COME TO THE RESCUE OF YOUR SLOW REFLECTING BRAIN AND YOUR ARCHIVING BRAIN

The very fast reflex brain with all its shortcuts was excellent for our ancestors and is still very important for us when we need to make very fast, very short-term, simple, snapshot decisions, based on nothing but SNIA (Sensory Now Is All), or when we need to develop new habits. There is nothing wrong with our reflex brain. We still need it, it can be very useful, and its conclusions are often perfectly acceptable. However, we need to know its limitations, so that we don't let it overpower our reflecting brain and its collaboration with the archiving brain.

In general, however, the reflex brain is often far from ideal for surviving in the urban and corporate savannahs of the 21st century, where success and survival depend on our reflecting brain much more than in our ancestors' times. Dan Ariely, one of the creative researchers in this area, writes that the heuristics and cognitive biases of our reflex brain make us "predictably irrational" when we have to make decisions and choices. They are also the reason why so-called gut decisions are more often than not wrong and why common-sense decisions often make no rational sense at all.

▶ **It's worse than you think, and if you don't think, it's worse.**

Life would be impossible without these unconscious shortcuts, but much more often than you think the shortcuts wired in our brain unconsciously induce wrong, stupid, primitive and/or unethical decisions. Therefore, you should rein in your reflex brain

and come to the rescue of your reflecting brain because:
- you are no longer living in the savannah of your ancestors but in a world where your success depends on the quantity and quality of your brainwork;
- your success at work depends on your intellectual productivity;
- undisturbed reflection is paramount for your intellectual productivity;
- undisturbed real conversations and joint reflections are crucial for your intellectual productivity;
- your great technologies easily become an obstacle instead of a support for your intellectual productivity;
- and reflection is hard work that needs a lot of energy, and your reflecting brain can become exhausted, while your reflex brain just keeps on going.

One of the most important things that gives your primitive, reckless reflex brain an unfair advantage over your reflecting brain is the way you unknowingly chain your reflecting brain with the four BrainChains described in Section 2: always being connected, multitasking, chronic stress and lack of sleep.

> **"Give me 6 hours to chop down a tree and I will spend the first four sharpening the axe."**
> ABRAHAM LINCOLN

In my research I found that professionals only have on average (median) two opportunities a week to work totally undisturbed on one single intellectual task for 45 minutes. 14% only had one opportunity a week, and another 14% not one single opportunity! Abraham Lincoln said: "Give me 6 hours to chop down a tree and I will spend the first four sharpening the axe." These brainworkers are chopping wood all the time without first sharpening their intellectual axe by taking time to reflect and by disconnecting to give their archiving brain a chance.

> **Constantly scanning screens of information is like gobbling down your food without digesting it. The result is indigestion, or information overload.**

In the media we often find ignorant articles claiming that with more and more Google-like corporate tools that allow instant retrieval of any piece of information, we no longer need to have the information in our own long-term memory. This is a huge ignorant mistake. Googling information is so easy and so fast that we don't store it in our long-term memory. This is not important if it is about trivia, but to develop real insight and knowledge about important subjects, the most significant information has to be stored in our long-term memory. To achieve this, we need to be focused and concentrated when we study important information and we need to relax and sleep to archive it. Hence, when you are always connected and multitasking, all that guzzling of information is totally useless for developing knowledge.

8.1 WHEN OUR TWO BRAINS COMPETE, THE REFLECTING BRAIN IS THE UNDERDOG

Most often the two brains collaborate well and to our advantage. The reflex brain is at its best in familiar situations. It will come up with a very fast answer and then leave it to the reflecting brain to accept it or not. The way the reflex brain takes care of routines by turning them into habits frees up our reflecting brain for reflection. Together they can multitask.

Think about a pianist. When learning to play the piano it takes hundreds of hours to learn to do different things with both hands. Once this part of the job is taken over by the reflex brain, a pianist can start expressing special effects, creating her very own interpretation. She does not have to think about getting the right fingers on the right notes, but can fully concentrate on the interpretation. Then after another few hundred hours of playing she does not have to think any more how she wants the piece to sound (now it really comes from "the gut") and she can make it blend perfectly with the orchestra she is playing with. She may be so good that even after a disturbing event in her private life, the resulting negative emotions don't disturb her performance too much.

Sometimes the two brains compete. For example for top sportsmen and women, through hundreds of hours of training, the basics of their motor skills have become strong habits: a professional golfer does not have to think about his swing, a tennis player does not think about the technique of her forehand, and a soccer player does not think about how to pass the ball. However, when the champion fails a few times and starts worrying, the negative thoughts of the reflecting brain get in the way of the reflex brain and what before came naturally now goes wrong. This is also the case when a new coach tries to change a particular technique. At first, the performance of the champion becomes worse because the conscious thinking about the new swing or forehand technique gets in the way. It is only after another few hundred hours' training that the new swing is mastered by the reflex brain, which can then do its own thing and not be bothered by the slow, reflecting brain.

On the other hand, and more importantly for your intellectual productivity, the fast reflex brain often gets ahead of the reflecting brain when we do intellectual work. This is very often the case when we are continuously connected, multitasking or when our reflecting brain is tired. Our reflecting brain consumes quite a lot of energy so it can easily become exhausted (see chapter on decision power), while the reflex brain never tires. As a result of this very unfair handicap, our reflex brain is quick to take the lead when we are tired. It's the story of the tortoise and the hare with a new twist: the hare never sleeps while the tortoise does.

Yet when our reflecting brain is not especially tired, it can still easily be outwitted by the speed of the many lightning fast shortcuts your reflex brain takes. The reflex brain, for example, gives you the answer to 2+2= instantly and effortlessly, but it can't handle 19x46=. If the reflex brain does not know the answer, your reflecting brain has to step in, concentrate, take the time and put in the effort to do the calculation. If you don't use your reflecting brain, as we have seen, your reflex brain will guess and often guess wrong because it is very much influenced by the immediately present context, what it experiences in the moment or just before. Think about the anchoring bias we discussed, where the reflex brain makes completely wrong guesses. Another strategy of the reflex brain that will lead you astray is that it will make the unfamiliar familiar and the difficult easy, by answering a much easier question and pass on that answer as the answer to the difficult question (see the substitution heuristic above).

Whenever we fail to take good care of the needs of our reflecting brain, whenever we mistreat it or keep it in shackles with the BrainChains I will describe in the next section, the reflex brain takes the lead. This often makes deciding much faster and simpler in rather straightforward, simple, predictable situations that we know well from experience. However, it will lead to disastrous decisions when the situation is new or very complex, unpredictable or when numbers and statistics are important for the decision. In a fast-paced working environment, where there is no time for reflection and every micro-break is used to gobble up new information from a little screen, the reflex brain will take over and the dozens of biases will beat logic every time.

When the electrical signals of your brain are measured, or you are put in a brain scanner and have to signal simple choices by moving a finger, the muscles of the finger and the brain cells responsible for that finger act milliseconds before you are conscious of your choice. Not only journalists but even scholars have interpreted this as if the human being has no free will. This is a simplistic and wrong conclusion, probably one made by their own reflex brains or by their over-focused reductionist reflecting brain that did not do its homework about the reflecting brain and the interplay between the two brains[133].

The only conclusion we can draw is that for very simple decisions, like moving a finger, especially after some training, the reflex brain is much faster than the reflecting brain. What it does not mean is that this is also true for complex decisions where you have to set a goal, prepare, analyze, synthesize, abstract and imagine the consequences of your decision. It certainly does not mean either that the reflecting brain has no influence on the reflex brain. What this research may mean is that in complex situations where reflection is important, you need to put the brakes on your reflex brain and its intuitions because they may utterly simplify the question in a very primitive way, giving you a fast but totally wrong answer.

I hope that now you have learned more about your three brains and their strengths and weaknesses you are convinced that you have to give your reflecting brain a better chance to play its full rational, creative and ethical role. I hope that you also realize the importance of taking a break and fully disconnecting in order to give your creative archiving brain the best chance of doing its work. And I hope that having learned about the reflex brain and its primitive, fast, non-ethical decisions will help you to recognize your own hard-wired and soft-wired shortcuts as well as those of others, in order to make better decisions in teams at work or at home with your partner, family and friends.

8.2 THE LACK OF UNDISTURBED REFLECTION A PROBLEM FOR YOUR INTELLECTUAL PRODUCTIVITY

In typical company-speak it is no longer fashionable to talk about problems. We are supposed to always talk about challenges. This has some merit because it generates a more positive attitude to tackle them. Often, however, it's just wrong and therefore irritates people rather than motivating them. A challenge is an inciting summons, an invitation to a contest, to heroic deeds, but you have a choice: if you don't like it, you can walk away from it without any risk. You can decide whether or not take up the gauntlet. A problem is an obstacle that gets in the way of your goal. You have to resolve it, whether you want to or not, whether you like it or not. Brainworkers' increasing lack of undisturbed reflection is a huge problem we must resolve; it is not a challenge we can avoid. A major cause of the problem is the wrong way that we use our extremely powerful electronic tools.

> **Brainworkers' increasing lack of reflection is a huge problem we must resolve; it is not a challenge we can avoid.**

With the death of Neil Armstrong we were all reminded how successful NASA was in putting a man on the moon and bringing him back safely within the deadline of a decade, as John Kennedy had envisioned. Did you realize that your smartphone in your pocket has several thousands times more computing capacity than that space capsule? NASA certainly made the best use of the technology available at the time.

You can do the same and use your fantastic modern technology to realize your own dreams and goals. So why would you instead, through ignorance, let these superb technologies become an obstacle instead of a superior resource? Why would you let them "chain the best of your brain" and continuously let them ruin your intellectual productivity, spoiling your bright ideas, energy, time and money? Why would you let them ruin your most typically human, intelligent, conscious, reflecting brain and let it be defeated all the time by the more primitive animal reflex brain?

> **The problem with ICT is not what we do with it, but what we don't do any more because of our way of using it.**

To make the best and most proactive choices and decisions in the complex, unpredictable and rapidly changing environment of our modern times, we cannot and should not give the upper hand to the unconscious, fast, primitive, thoughtless reflex brain. For our ancestors in the savannah who were confronted with a daily struggle for survival, the reflex brain served them well as they did not have the luxury to reflect, to consider many interpretations and possible actions. To be successful in our 21st century jungle, however, we need to regularly disconnect to get out of the reflex mode; this disconnecting allows us to take time to reflect, do some thorough reading, and have real conversations as well as idle and let our archiving brain deal with all the data that has been stored.

Professionals often forget that electronic systems only hold data and sometimes information if the data are ordered in a meaningful accessible way, and that the only place where knowledge, insight and meaning reside is in people's brains. We need the reflection of human brains to turn information into knowledge and wisdom.

YOUR SUCCESS DEPENDS ON YOUR INTELLECTUAL PRODUCTIVITY AND ABOVE ALL ON YOUR ABILITY TO REFLECT

The environment for our prehistoric ancestor was simple: have lunch or be lunch, be fast or be dead. At the age of 15, which was almost halfway through his life, his body was fit to fight or run for survival and for procreation. He went through a coming of age ritual and was considered a grown-up[134]. Simply through learning by imitation, he knew everything his parents knew to survive and procreate.

His pre-frontal cortex, the part of his brain that he needed to reflect and control his impulsivity was not well developed yet. Even today, in boys, this is only fully developed around 25 years of age. For our ancestor this was not too much of a disadvantage. Confronted with a saber-toothed tiger, a tendency to reflect would have been self-destructive. Moreover, his situation was so unsafe and precarious that there was rarely much of an opportunity to reflect long and deep and make plans for the future anyway.

Like any other animal now or hundreds of thousands of years ago, we were bred for lightning fast, impulsive, life-saving brain reactions rather than long and deep reflection. Therefore the primitive fast reflexive reactions come naturally and easy. They do not require sustained effort and energy.

Nowadays you won't survive for long with just these reflexes and the knowledge of a 15-year-old. You need lifelong learning and reflection to acquire ever more knowledge to thrive in the 21st century. Years ago I lived close to a farm that had been in the same family for many generations. The young farmer once explained that if his great-great-great-grandfather had returned to the farm of his father, he would have known enough to be useful from day one. If his grandfather were to return to the modern farm of his grandchild, he would be totally lost and useless because almost none of his knowledge and skills are still used in a modern farm where cows are fed and milked fully automatically. In two generations, the knowledge needed to run a farm exploded.

If you look for the answer to a question on the Internet you get hundreds of thousands of answers from all over the world. Lots of it is utter nonsense. But how do you know what is nonsense and what is not, without knowledge and without reflection? The paradox is that the hyperconnectedness that makes all this information available is, at the same time, for many the most important obstacle to their reflecting brain making good use of it.

INFORMATION
IS ABUNDANT AND CHEAP.

REFLECTION
IS RARE AND PRECIOUS

Reflection and hard thinking require unrelenting effort and energy in the literal sense of the word. Skimming, cutting and pasting information on the World Wide Memory is absolutely no substitute for the reflection needed for optimal intellectual productivity and creativity. As I explained earlier in this section, to be useful, to develop understanding, insight and knowledge, the information has to be reflected on and stored in our long-term memory by our archiving brain. This is simply impossible to do without disconnecting. Period. With continuous fractured attention and without sufficient breaks to relax and archive, we are just scatterbrains or flat brains.

We sometimes forget that thinking ahead, wide and deep is often a lonely business if you want to get to the heart of the matter. You can also do this in a conversation, but how fruitful that conversation will be all depends on how well the participants prepared for it by reflecting and playing around with all the information and knowledge they have in their own long-term memory. I often have the impression that some of my clients can no longer stand this necessary solitude to reflect and therefore welcome all interruptions. Because they are no longer used to being alone to reflect and self-reflect, they feel lonely. The more they feel lonely when alone, the more they connect virtually, because they rather e-mail than talk, like adolescents rather text than talk. The result is that they e-mail rather than think.

Thomas Friedman describes our modern interconnected world as "a flat world"[135]. Due to this interconnection, our 21st century world has become increasingly complex. Abundant information about anything, anywhere is instantly available everywhere. That gives us great opportunities for cultural, scientific and economic exchange and development. At the same time this complexity tests the limits of our reflecting brain, which must make sense of the ever increasing amount of information. Therefore you cannot thrive in this complex "flat world" with a "flat fractured scatterbrain", when you let your one-dimensional (=flat) reflex brain prevail over your chained (=flat) reflecting brain, and when you let incessant distractions continuously fracture your attention.

▶ **With a "flat brain" you cannot thrive in a "flat world".**

To be successful, you need lifelong learning. Learning is the result of study, thorough reading, real conversations, undisturbed reflection and especially of trial and error, of trial and success if... we take the time to do a debrief of our errors and successes, to reflect, looking backward and forward, thinking broadly and deeply. To get there, we need to burn the midnight oil while making room, time and space in our mind for undisturbed questioning and reflection and... idling. To quote Albert Einstein: "It's not that I'm so smart; it's just that I stay with problems longer". Einstein would never have developed his revolutionary theories if he had been as hyper-connected and multitasking as the average modern professional or scientist.

▶ **"It's not that I'm so smart; it's just that
I stay with problems longer."**
ALBERT EINSTEIN

This tenacious reflection may also lead to creative and wise decisions, the best ones you can make with the available knowledge. To quote Steve Jobs again about the revolutionary Macintosh computer: "...Then when you start to really understand it, you come up with these very complicated solutions because it's really hairy. Most people stop there. But a few people keep burning the midnight oil and finally understand the underlying principles of the problem and come up with an elegantly simple solution for it. But very few people go the distance to get there"[136].

THOROUGH READING IS ESSENTIAL FOR REFLECTION

"Thorough" or deep reading is an important part of the reflection process. Thorough reading, the quiet, unhurried and undistracted reading of a book, article or memo, is something totally different from the distracted scanning we do on our computers and smartphones. In a book the authors have studied the subject in depth and then guide and stimulate your own reflection process, your own ideas, associations, metaphors.... When we follow the author, we go deep into the subject. This deep reading often leads to an inner conversation that may go even deeper than the author intended. It doesn't necessarily have to be non-fiction or other knowledge-enhancing reading. Reading fiction too requires skills similar to reflection: varying degrees of abstract, analytical, synthetic, inductive, deductive, associative and creative thinking. That is why it is so important that children should be stimulated by all possible means to keep reading.

This kind of reading is totally different from what we do on the Internet and in e-mails where we deal with a continuous avalanche of quickly written and quickly read, superficial, unordered snippets of information, that do not show connections between different insights and that rarely invite you to think deeper, wider and ahead. The process of quickly and continuously jumping from one bite of information to another even excludes reflection. There is nothing wrong with this kind of scan-reading in and of itself; in many situations at work it is a necessity. It only becomes a problem when it is the only reading we do, with no time left for undisturbed, thorough reading.

If part of your work is reading important texts that are longer than a screenful, you have a special reason to disconnect from your screen and read them on paper. Research shows that reading from paper results in better comprehension and accuracy than reading from a screen, especially if under time pressure, and that it is faster and less tiring.[137] By the way, as we have seen in the chapter on the myth of multitasking kids, taking notes with pen on paper also leads to very significantly better recall and comprehension.

I wonder if there is a link between addiction to all kinds of screens and the sorry fact that in the USA only half of the country's adults and children have in the past year read a book that was not required for work or school and for the worrying fact that US children score the lowest in the developed world on international tests that score their scholastic knowledge and skills. They spend roughly 10 times more time in front of the TV than reading anything[138]. Many young people, especially boys, don't even read anything any more that's longer than a window or a screen. I was recently discussing this subject with a young director of an academy training young people for marketing jobs. He told me that I was not up to date because a great many of his students, especially boys, don't even read as much as a screenful anymore, but only hundreds of Tweets with less than 140 characters, and that they have increasing difficulty integrating, connecting and understanding this daily diarrhea of snippets of information.

It looks like this is another intellectual field where very soon girls will easily outperform boys because girls although they text more, read more books than boys[139] and so still learn to reflect and stick with a subject for longer. What's more, reading fiction is excellent training to learn to understand the mental state of other people[140]. This is a crucial social skill, which in research is often called developing a "Theory of Mind".

There are, of course, many very successful exceptions, for example people with severe dyslexia, who have great difficulties understanding written words. To become successful these people, Richard Branson being one of the best known[141], learned to become masters in learning by doing, in learning by trial and error, trial and failure. They are also masters in developing trusting relations with excellent people, who have the cognitive competences they lack, not only to delegate part of the job to them or let them do the studying, but especially to have real, frank, undisturbed conversations with them.

REAL CONVERSATIONS ARE CRUCIAL FOR YOUR INTELLECTUAL PRODUCTIVITY

In my "Little guide on the big subject of small talk", which you can download from my website www.brainchains.org, I describe that a dialogue can happen at three levels and that mastering each level allows you to have the most intelligent and productive conversations.

1 The first level of dialogue is "Small Talk", which is about neutral facts, clichés. It is not about the content, but about the relationship.
2 The second level of dialogue is the "Discussion", where you bring in your subjective view, your perspective on facts, your opinions, beliefs, value judgments.
3 The "Real conversation" is the third level of dialogue and this is where feelings come in, your own as well as the other person's, and where you create a joint new meaning, resulting in a stronger relationship. One of the most important elements of Emotional and Social Intelligence is being able

to start and develop a real conversation.

These three levels are interrelated and all have their specific value.

Don't think that having real conversations is always preferable. Being socially intelligent means that you understand that in some situations small talk has real value and is much better than a real conversation. Being good at small talk will help you to have better conversations because it is an excellent training ground for listening. If you are not good at conversations, your discussions will often run amiss because you do not have the capacity to separate the objective from the personal feeling. Being good at small talk will build your confidence for discussions and real conversations and provides a shelter to move to if the conversation stalls.

Real conversations, as well as good discussions, are very important for your intellectual performance, for learning and for creating new knowledge, understanding, insight and meaning. Information only becomes meaning, only leads to real understanding, if not wisdom, through reflection. A real conversation is like a joint reflection where we create a joint meaning, and sometimes a creative new meaning.

▶ **The greatest gift in a real conversation, discussion or meeting is undivided attention.**

Let there be no misunderstanding: being connected, exchanging e-mails, tweets or text messages back and forth is just an exchange of information, and a very poor one. It is never a real discussion or a real conversation; it's like eating a bag of chips rather than a proper meal. A rich real conversation is fed by the nonverbal, the tone of voice, the gestures and the facial expressions as well as the verbal. There is much more room for nuance and room to exaggerate, to play devil's advocate and especially to have constructive conflicts. Really knowing and understanding a person and her ideas is only possible via a real conversation. In a real conversation, it is easier to look at the subject from the others person's point of view. This way you often learn something about yourself and your own ideas too.

Two heads know more than one, but in a real committed

conversation, they create something new, something that was not in either head. "From the clash of ideas springs forth the light," said the French philosopher Nicolas Boileau[142] in the 17th century.

Let me quote Mark Strom and Laurent Ledoux[143] on this: "Communication is the sharing of created meaning; conversation is the creation of shared meaning... If we are genuinely to engage in conversation, if we are to take seriously the creation of new meaning, then we will not know in advance what meaning will be created. That can be an uncomfortable place to be. But very often it is exactly the place to which we must go. As leaders, we bear a responsibility to make room and provide contexts for the kinds of conversation where people create new shared meaning."

As for reflection, to create new meaning in a conversation, you need to know what you are talking about, to have done your homework by studying the information. Then you need sufficient undisturbed meeting time, focus, togetherness, commitment and persistence to think ahead, to think wide and to think deep.

In the world of hyperconnectivity we have come to expect fast answers. Fast thinking is reactive and primitive, simplistic and superficial. A fast conversation is impossible; it is an oxymoron, a contradiction in terms. It is often really pathetic to see how many brainworkers, even very senior managers and executives are no longer able to have a focused, undisturbed conversation. They do not know, as I explained earlier, that every single ICT disturbance parks the whole context and content of the conversation into their very limited temporary memory where parts of it get lost very easily.

Some people, not only adolescents who go through a period of being awkward with relationships, but also professionals and managers, hide behind their ICT to avoid conversations and in particular to avoid difficult ones. Look at the terraces on a sunny day. You see more and more couples, families, groups around the table in a restaurant, where everybody spends a large part of the time on their little screen. Thousands of managers, even at an executive level, e-mail while in meetings. They even ignorantly think that they can engage people for their plans with e-mails, corporate social media and fliers, without real conversations.

Could it be that people avoid real conversations because they avoid real relationships, by staying very superficially connected in the virtual world? Being virtually connected is easy; it only asks for a few clicks. Building a good relationship, even if it is only a professional one, is often hard work. Once you are connected, disconnecting from such a professional or personal relationship can be difficult and painful. Electronically connecting is as easy as disconnecting; it only needs one click. It is no coincidence that we have known the word "befriend" since 1559, but "unfriend" and "defriend" have only been used since 2004.

RUSHING THROUGH YOUR NEVER-ENDING TO-DO LIST RUINS YOUR INTELLECTUAL PRODUCTIVITY

Lists of things to do are inexhaustible: to do lists, want lists, need lists, must lists, should lists, wish lists... the opportunities are unlimited. On the other hand, our resources, time resources, life resources and especially brain resources, are limited. This is obviously a truism. But if you look around you, you see so many people frenetically trying to do it all anyway, struggling with to do lists and wish lists, continuously rushing, hopping from one activity to the other, always connected, getting less sleep in order to do more multitasking, and ultimately being unhappy.

Moreover, we know from research with so-called hypertaskers that on top of all the wasted energy used trying to multitask, hypertaskers at the same time spend a lot of brain energy trying not to think about the things they are not doing, that are on their to do list[144].

Since we can't do it all, we have to choose. If you take some time to reflect, you have a five times higher chance that you will do the right things, the most important things, the most ethical things, rewarding things, the most enjoyable things, the most fun things. If you do not take time to reflect, all that stuff that is not really important, rewarding or fun crowds out the best and leaves you unsatisfied and trying to compensate by doing even more.

When you are hurrying all the time, trying to do everything, your reflecting brain does not get a fair chance. Your reflex brain takes over, and since it is only in the here and now, it has also no priorities beyond the 'sensory now' and in the end what you do is more by chance than by choice. Moreover, your archiving brain never gets the breaks it needs to order, store and find all that information.

As I will describe in Section 3, there are tools and methods that can help you to get out of this unwinnable, never-ending race. The number one is to organize undisturbed quiet time to do important brainwork, to disconnect to reflect. That is the "conditio sine qua non", the most necessary precondition. Second is "batch-processing", which will help you to do much more of the things you have chosen and enjoy them more. It will even help you to become more efficient in doing the unavoidable chores you don't like at all. Third, to make the right choices there is the Eisenhower principle that helps you to reflect on the importance of your tasks in light of your priorities. Fourth, to reflect on what work is most efficient and effective to reach your goals, there is the Pareto rule.

The trap is that you need a minimum of time for reflection to make the time for the reflection that you need to become more intellectually productive. The first and most difficult step is to disconnect from ICT distractions, which includes your phone.

WE HAVE LET OUR GREAT ICT TOOLS BECOME WEAPONS OF MASS DISTRACTION
We are living in a world:
- where professional success depends on our brainwork but where professionals don't know how their brain works;
- where fantastic technology makes information cheap and abundant but where the way we use ICT makes focus and reflection very rare and precious;
- where technology makes it easy to connect virtually with anybody anywhere, but where the way we use ICT makes it difficult to have undisturbed real conversations with real people;
- where ICT makes instant answers to our questions possible, but where these continuous streams of immediate answers and questions get in the way not only of reflection and real conversations, but also from planned dependable execution;
- and where modern ICT technology can efficiently provide us with all the information we need for learning, but where

thorough learning is being pushed aside by interruption-driven, immediate reflection-less reactions.

▶ **If Steve Jobs had been glued to his iPhone, he never would have invented the iPhone.**

It is very evident that this great ICT is not a problem for our reflection, learning, conversations and execution. On the contrary, it has tremendous potential to initiate, inspire and support them. The only problem is the way we use the technology, the way we let it lead us astray, instead of managing it to our advantage.

As I mentioned before, I learned from the professionals in my workshops, lectures and research that many never have an opportunity to work 45 minutes undisturbed and that when they have difficult or complex intellectual work to do, for 37% it is very difficult do it in their office, and for 6% simply impossible! These people are brainworkers, but they can't do their most important work at work: thinking, reflecting! Way too many have to escape from their offices to reflect. (More on this in BrainChain #5.)

THE WORRYING BRUTAL FACTS ABOUT THE OBSTACLES OF INTELLECTUAL PERFORMANCE
- 57% switch back and forth all day between five tasks or more, 25% between seven, and 10% between 10 tasks or more.
- 60% try to do two tasks at the same time at least five times a day (e.g. checking e-mails while on the phone or in a meeting) and 13% try to do this 10 times or more.
- 51% have two opportunities or fewer per week when they can work for 45 minutes on one task undisturbed (in the group of managers it is two out of three!).
- 55% experience considerable to high negative stress because they cannot finish intellectual tasks without interruption.
- 50% spend 2-3 hours a day dealing with e-mails (45% spend 5 hours or more).
- 84% check their e-mails whenever they have a free moment and first thing in the morning.

- 25% check their e-mails during meetings.
- And to make matters worse: 75% consider 50% of their e-mail useless. 25% consider more than 70% of their e-mails useless. At Intel one-third of e-mails are irrelevant for the receiver. These unnecessary messages cost Intel $1 billion a year on a total return of $11 billion[145]!
- ... and 72% phone while driving. 0% of them know how dangerous it is and almost all think that hands-free is safer than holding a phone in your hand.

Other researchers have observed brainworkers rather than asking them questions. Their results are significantly worse than what I found in my survey. The average knowledge worker is busy with 10 tasks, or working spheres[146]. They work for 12 minutes on related subjects before they switch to another. They work 3 minutes uninterrupted by incoming e-mails, instant messages, phone calls, tweets, co-workers or other distractions. 41% of the time people do not even resume their original task at all after an interruption, even though they use all kinds of tricks to get back into a working sphere, such as post-its, to do lists, a separate folder or e-mail folder, a stack of paper copies or highlighting key e-mails.

A survey of 1,000 knowledge workers[147] shows that more or less irrelevant interruptions consume 28% of the knowledge worker's day. The cost to business in the USA is $588 billion, assuming an average salary of $21/hour for a knowledge worker. What this research doesn't even take into account is the time lost and mistakes made due to the negative influence of the distraction on the original, more important task.

These interruptions ruin the best of your brain, they make reflection impossible. It is so mind-bogglingly bad that my original working title for this book was: "How we unknowingly f*** up our brainwork". Obviously this loss of intellectual productivity is a huge problem; it is a risk for you, your family, your work, your company and your career.

It is also flabbergasting that organizations invest so much money in hiring the best and the brightest because the quality of their employees' brainwork is their most important competitive advantage, and then organize work in such a way that it makes high-quality brainwork all but impossible. Warehousing them in open offices is one of the worst examples.

> **The hyper-connected, hyper-tasking, hyper-productive brainworker is a total myth. In reality they are hyper-connected, hyper-tasking, hyper-active, hyper-underachievers.**

That the hyper-connected, hyper-tasking employee is hyper-productive is not only a total myth, it is a huge and increasing problem. In reality these people underachieve, and not just a little bit. They massively underachieve.

8.3 COMPANIES SUFFERING FROM CORPORATE BRAIN DISORDER MISTREAT THE REFLECTING BRAIN OF THEIR BRAIN-WORKERS

COMPANIES MANAGE BRAINWORKERS AS IF THEY ARE MANUAL WORKERS

Since we are all brainworkers, the most important competitive advantage of companies is the ability to attract, engage and keep intelligent people with good social skills, to develop good people-managers to lead and coach them and to provide a work environment that enhances brainwork.

Thanks to ICT, the brain of every brainworker is in continuous interaction with other brains that stimulate and feed it. The consolidated brain of all the brainworkers and the connections between them is what I call the "Corporate Brain". Research done by myself and others, however, shows that this Corporate Brain in more than 60% of organizations functions at a less than 60% of its potential! The main cause is that the attitude and methods used to manage brainworkers are basically still the same as those used to manage manual workers in the 19th century. More than 60% of companies are basically people-illiterate. This is what I called "Corporate Brain Disorder".

To get the best out of their brainworkers, managers in the 21st century must fundamentally change their attitudes and behavior to become service professionals. They must provide the services that their employees, their brainworkers, need to perform excellently. To deliver the best possible services, a manager should not only be familiar with the personal instruction booklet for how each team member works but should also know the basics of the brainworker manual in general, and in particular its chapter about the brain.

There are two fundamental premises that too many companies carry over from the management of manual workers 100 years ago to the management of today's brainworkers that are totally wrong:
1 that there is a linear relation between the hours worked and the value delivered.
2 that a company can command brainwork.

The first one is that there is a linear, direct connection between the number of hours worked and the value delivered. If a manual worker, think Charlie Chaplin in "Modern Times", can fix 100 bolts in an hour, he can do 1,000 if you make him work 10 hours. If 1 person can fasten 100 bolts an hour, 100 can fasten 10,000.

Now apply this idea to brainworkers. If a brainworker had two important creative ideas last month while working 8 hours a day, he will have three if you make him work 12 hours a day. If one brainworker has one creative idea a week, 100 will have 100.

This sounds ridiculous and it is, but if you think about it, you see this reasoning happening all the time all around us. Brainworkers and their managers clearly think that if a brainworker is delivering very well on his tasks in an 8-hour day, he will deliver 50% more if you keep him connected 4 hours a day longer, working via a computer at home, smartphone or tablet. As a matter of fact, it's the contrary: always being connected with work will decrease his performance.

As I will explain later on, our brain is much more sensitive to stress than our muscles. With effort and within limits, a tired manual worker can still fix 100 bolts an hour because most of the routine manual work is taken over by his tireless reflex brain. Thanks to his reflex brain, a manual worker can increase his production by training to work harder and longer.

However, working harder and longer will not improve the quantity and quality of your brainwork, but make it worse, with the exception of when your work is very much routine. Working longer increases and protracts the stress, and that handicaps the best, most human reflective abilities of your brain: analytical thinking, synthesis, abstraction, creativity and accuracy. It also decreases willpower, decision power, motivation... The tireless reflex brain that keeps the exhausted manual worker going causes trouble for a tired brainworker.

A second crucial difference between manual workers and brainworkers is that you can demand manual work from manual workers, but you cannot demand the best of brainworkers' brains, you have to deserve it.

You can demand a manual worker to fasten 100 bolts an hour, or to dig 20 tons of coal. For brainworkers, however, you can lay claim on a number of hours they have to spend at work and you can request some basic routine brainwork, but **you cannot demand the best of their brainwork**. You cannot demand one creative idea a day! As a manager, as a company, as a colleague, you can only establish an environment that is most conducive to your brainworkers having creative ideas at all levels, all the time.

You can only earn, merit, deserve the best of their brain! **They volunteer the best of their brains**, not only their creativity but also their motivation, passion, engagement, enthusiasm, loyalty, creativity, entrepreneurship, readiness for change and commitment as well as things like accuracy and safe behavior.

I collaborated for quite a few years with DuPont de Nemours, a company world famous for its safety culture. There I learned that you can to some extent train and request very basic safe behavior, basic instructions that people are obliged to follow. At DuPont though, safety goes way beyond these rules. Most people in the company think and breathe safety all the time, everywhere; they volunteer this behavior. The pride and motivation of the workers and managers is contagious. Working with them really changed my own safety behavior, not only in but also outside their company. The company earns this safety, not only by unrelentingly keeping it in focus, but also by the way they treat their people.

I know companies that have all the same safety demands, rules and regulations, where they even use the same leaflets and posters and where you still see a lot of unsafe behavior. If you go to the website of any one of these companies, you will see unsafe situations and even dangerous behavior everywhere in their own pictures! It is clear that the workers in these companies do not volunteer safe behavior, they don't think or live safety. One of the reasons why they don't is also evident on their website: there are many pictures of directors or the CEO visiting workshops, construction sites and plants, and yet you never see one of these executives wearing helmets, safety glasses, gloves or shoes. These pictures, and more importantly, this behavior of the top managers, send out the message that following the safety rules is just something for the underlings, not for the big shots. Later discussion with the workers confirmed that they weren't at all happy with the way they were treated by their management. One of the most demotivating management behaviors was that when a safety error occurred, it was followed by one big blame game, with the blame constantly being passed onto a person at the level below until it reached the lowest rank possible. As a result, there was no learning, and much worse, people were hiding errors, creating an even more unsafe environment. Modern operators are brainworkers too and they should be treated as such if you want the best of their brains.

COMPANIES MANAGE BRAINWORKERS AS IF THEY ARE ALL THE SAME

A century ago, management did not have to differentiate much in the way they managed individual manual workers. Today, however, if managers want the very best performance from brainworkers, they must adapt their leadership style not only to the personality but also to the basic needs, wishes and values of the individual team members. This is one aspect of the so-called "situational leadership". In other words, it is not sufficient to know the general brainworkers' handbook and the fundamental differences with manual workers; you should also know their personal "Instructions for use". This is not only true for managers, but also for professionals looking for the best possible collaboration with their colleagues.

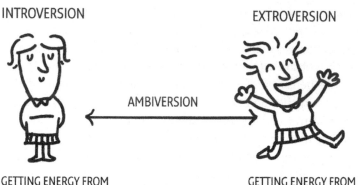

INTROVERSION

EXTROVERSION

AMBIVERSION

GETTING ENERGY FROM
INTERNAL WORLD E.G.
SOLITARY REFLECTION

GETTING ENERGY FROM
INTERACTION WITH OUTSIDE
WORLD E.G. DISCUSSIONS

One of the things you should know is that different people have very different basic attitudes towards deep reflection, thorough reading, real conversations and meetings. The best studied difference is between introverts and extraverts. Some people are clearly at the extremes, but most of us are ambiverts, being introverted and extroverted to some degree.

We know from research that, certainly at the extremes, the cognitive brain of the two types function differently[148] because they deal differently with arousal and that there is a genetic component determining about 40% of this[149].

Let's contrast the differences in black and white. Typical extroverts are usually in a positive mood[150], interested in the outside world, getting energy from time spent with others and losing energy and getting bored when alone. They prefer group meetings more than 1:1 meetings and a 1:1 discussion more than solitary reflection or reading a book or a long memo or a report. Because typical extroverts don't like to study the data by themselves beforehand, they often come to a meeting rather poorly prepared. They think while discussing, creating their meaning in a stimulating meeting. They often forget to listen well. They like to shoot from the hip and generate many ideas[151], get moving as fast as possible and improvise along the way. After a full-day workshop they recharge in good company (with other extroverts) at the bar. They too often forget that they really need the introverts in the team to thoroughly study the facts and to make them stick to the facts.

Typical introverts are interested in their own mental life, getting energy from reflection and reading in isolation, losing energy in meetings except when with a small group of people they know very well. They like to think and listen before they talk. They study the data and reflect longer by themselves before discussing the subject, but then they sometimes lack assertiveness and the social skills to defend their more thoughtful position against the boisterous extraverts. They prefer one-on-one meetings, or meeting with small groups of people they know well. After meetings they need private time to recharge. Interestingly, introverts feel better in meetings when they force themselves to act a little more extraverted, but extraverts don't benefit from acting introverted[152].

The fact that introverts do not react as quickly as extraverts is too often and completely wrongly seen as being shy or lacking intelligence or commitment. Therefore companies tend to hire extraverts, certainly as managers, and these in turn, falling victim to the familiarity bias, then hire more extraverts.

In a good team, however, you need both so that each can balance and enhance the other. You also need a good meeting leader to rein in the extroverts and give space and time to the introverts and invite them to speak up. This is especially necessary in a western (company) culture, which is favorably biased towards extraversion. When the meetings are well facilitated, the two types can make optimal use of the synergy between their verbal styles; the extraverts' higher level of abstract interpretation and the introverts sticking to facts[153].

Moreover, in a well-led team, given enough space and time, the factual knowledge of the introverts and their thoughtfulness often surprises the extraverts, who then learn to appreciate this, rein in their own impatience and give the introverts time to think.

The introverts then learn to appreciate the challenging, on the spot and more abstract creative idea-generating and active style of the extroverts and their greater ability to convince stakeholders, involve the troops, enthuse colleagues and get them going. If this initial appreciation doesn't happen spontaneously, it is the responsibility of the team leader to point this out and make it happen, to get the best out of both brain types.

CORPORATE BRAIN DISORDER IS WORSENED BY THE FIVE BRAINCHAINS

Companies spend millions on top-notch ICT systems to give their brainworkers a whole range of beautiful technologies to get information and to disseminate it to others: smartphones, e-mail, chat, conference calling, VPNS, Twitter, Yammer, Sharepoint, Facebook, LinkedIn, video-conferencing... These resources even make it possible to get a lot of work done at home and spend fewer hours commuting. And yet up to 65% of employees complain that it is very difficult to get the information they really need to do their work well. Amongst other things, the information overload makes it very difficult and time-consuming to screen out the rare, necessary or useful information from the continuous stream of useless messages.

Corporate Brain Disorder is made worse by allowing brainworkers to always be connected, letting them multitask, letting them eliminate their brain-breaks and allowing them to be stressed all the time; these are what I call BrainChains. Often it is worse than that, when companies and managers even dare to demand that their professionals are always connected, that they multitask and eliminate their brain-breaks while at the same time failing to manage stress well and cramming their professionals into open offices. These issues and their solutions are the subject of the next two sections.

SECTION 2

HOW WE UNKNOWINGLY CHAIN THE BEST OF OUR BRAIN

1 WHEN YOU CHAIN YOUR BRAIN, YOU RISK MORE THAN JUST RUINING YOUR INTELLECTUAL PRODUCTIVITY

▶ **Ignorance or neglect of our brain's instruction manual results in clever people underperforming or doing stupid things.**

1.1 A BABY DIES, FORGOTTEN IN A CAR ON A HOT PARKING LOT

A few years ago two mothers, living just a few miles from each other, forgot their babies in their cars in the hot summer sun on the parking lot at their work. Both babies died. Several journalists, especially of women's magazines, came to interview me about the case. Some suggested that you had to be a bad mother if you forgot your baby. One in particular was very tough and not at all convinced by my alternative explanations. I suggested to her that she add a line at the bottom of the interview inviting her readers to send or mail her their own stories where such an accident almost happened to them. The first surprise that made her change her mind was that she received at least 10 times more e-mails than usual for this kind of request. The second surprise was that when she showed some of these emotional e-mails to her colleague sitting next to her, her colleague became very emotional, started crying and said: "I am also one of these bad mothers. The same thing almost happened to me, but at the very moment I was going to shut the door of my car, my baby sneezed. If she hadn't sneezed and if nobody had seen her, I would have lost my baby too."

Discussing that story I explained that there were four typical characteristics that make these kinds of "normal" situations at home and at work dangerous or at least more prone to severe mistakes: always being connected, multitasking, negative stress and lack of sleep. They are a recipe for disaster, especially when all four come into play at the same time.

Imagine one of these young responsible mothers leaving her house with the baby in her arms. She securely fastens the baby into her very safe baby seat, gets in the car as she does every morning to drop the baby off at nursery and then drives on to work. Much of this is a routine that belongs to the reflex brain. Moreover, her reflecting brain is still very much in the home-context, thinking about her lovely baby and how happy she is to have such a good and affordable child-care center.

As soon as she starts driving, however, her phone rings and she gets an angry boss on the line: "We are having a meeting at 10, you promised me all the material about this campaign and I have received nothing". She thinks, "Gosh, I forgot" and says "I didn't know you needed it before the meeting, but I'll send it to you as soon as I arrive in the office". Her body goes into stress mode, with her reflex brain in survival mode and her reflecting brain suddenly 100% in the work-context… and she forgets the precious little piece of home-context that's in the back of the car and forgets to take a turn to go to the child center. All the way to work she is calling all the people she needs to urgently get the information in her mail. She parks her car, gets out while talking on the phone, which is wedged between her shoulder and her ear, rushes to her office and forgets her baby.

It is a tragic example of how always being connected caused multitasking and how our reflecting brain cannot pay attention to two subjects from two different contexts at the same time. As I will explain in this section, the sudden stress makes it worse and of course, as a young mother with a baby, it is very likely that she has been building up a considerable sleep-debt, which further increases the risk of making mistakes.

1.2 A WELL-KNOWN SWISS RECIPE FOR MAKING MISTAKES AND DANGEROUS BEHAVIOR

From the safety managers and plant managers in my audiences, I have learnt about the Reason's "Swiss Cheese" model of risk[1]. It explains a sequence of levels of protection or prevention, each represented as a slice of Swiss Cheese one behind the other. Each

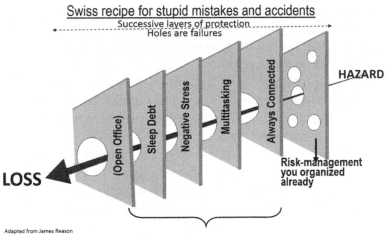

Swiss recipe for stupid mistakes and accidents

Successive layers of protection
Holes are failures

(Open Office)
Sleep Debt
Negative Stress
Multitasking
Always Connected

HAZARD

Risk-management
you organized
already

LOSS

Adapted from James Reason

Risk Management You Did Not Know

level of protection and prevention, even after trying to eliminate all possible risks, has still holes that safety managers continuously try to eradicate or make as small as possible. Failures can arise at any one of the levels; accidents only occur when, for whatever reason, all the holes line up.

I like to use this model to explain that the five BrainChains I will explain in this section do not represent small but very big holes in protecting your intellectual productivity and preventing big, stupid and sometimes dangerous mistakes. The holes are so big and so close that they easily align to cause expensive mistakes.

Ignorance or neglect of our brain's basic user manual and the built-in "holes", makes clever people underperform or do stupid things. It is also a major cause of dangerous decisions and behavior. And yet very often as we go about our daily lives, using our fantastic ICT tools, we fall into that very trap, unknowingly using these electronic tools in totally counterproductive ways that fail to take into account the strengths and weaknesses of the human brain.

Problems with modern ICT manifest themselves in many ways:
- We are continuously guzzling information via our electronic devices to the extent that we can't develop our own ideas. Too often we don't even take time to reflect and digest all the

information. By definition, this is "information overload", meaning that we receive more information than we can process. Most of this overload is not imposed on us by others; we impose it on ourselves.

- We are continuously in our primitive reflex-brain mode, responding without reflection, making brainless mistakes and creating a ridiculously pathetic and counterproductive "adhocracy" in the workplace.
- We are continuously multitasking and task-hopping, making us at least four times less intellectually productive than we could be if we single-tasked or at least right-tasked.
- We generate a continuous (low level of) brain stress, which further lowers our intellectual performance and negatively impacts our body and life.
- We are so addicted to being connected that we skip too many essential brain-breaks and shorten our sleep, handicapping our archiving brain, which further undermines our intellectual productivity.

The result is that we become our reflecting brain's own worst enemy.

▶ **The problem is not the great technology, but the way we use it.**

Some people react to this with a "So what, that's modern life, we'll have to learn to live with it." The answer is NO, NO and NO! Why would you, as an individual brainworker, accept this, knowing that it is bad for the quality and quantity of your brainwork... and even your health? Why would companies accept it knowing that it severely undermines intellectual productivity in general and creativity and safety in particular?

There are many practical tips and tricks to break these Brain-Chains, and I will discuss these in Section 3. Before I do that though, I first of all want to explain exactly how each of these BrainChains ruins your intellectual performance. I hope that this section will not only convince you to take action to become more productive but that this knowledge will inspire you to find your own creative solutions.

2 BRAINCHAIN #1 IS A ROOT CAUSE OF THE PROBLEM: ALWAYS BEING CONNECTED

2.1 THE PROMISES AND PERILS OF ALWAYS BEING CONNECTED (AbC)

As soon as I leave my house and walk out onto the street I see at least four pedestrians busy on their mobile phones, either talking or texting. People also do this in the shop, on their bike, sitting alone or in company on a terrace, while driving their cars, taking care of a baby, hugging or kissing and even on the toilet. I recently read a survey that said 50% of smartphone owners take their phone to bed to make sure they don't miss any calls, text messages or other updates during the night. In a Harris poll, 9% of adults and 20% of people between 18 and 34 admit they've even used their phone during sex[2].

We live in a hyper-connected world that was described very well in "The Global Information Technology Report" of the World Economic Forum in 2012. In their excellent chapter "The Promise and Peril of Hyperconnectivity for Organizations and Societies[3]", four professionals from Alcatel-Lucent describe this phenomenon at a general level.

Always on: Broadband and ubiquitous mobile devices enable people to be connected 24/7 to family, work, friends, interests, obsessions and more.

Readily accessible: A universe of mobile devices and personal computers links people and organizations together; these connections are increasingly available at any time and in any location.

Information-rich: Websites, search engines, social media and 24-hour news and entertainment channels ensure that information

- from the strategic to the banal - is always on hand, in volumes beyond anyone's capacity to consume.

Interactive: Hyperconnectivity ensures that everyone can offer input on just about everything.

Not just about people: Hyperconnectivity includes people-to-machine and machine-to-machine communications, supporting the development of what has been termed the Internet of Things.

Always recording: Service records, virtually unlimited storage capacities, miniaturized video cameras, global positioning systems, sensors and more - combined with people's desire to document their own activities - ensure that a large portion of everyone's daily activities and communications are part of a semi-permanent record. [And since the revelations of Snowden we know that all our information is available for the authorities to scrutinize. TC]

The cumulative effect of hyperconnectivity is that the limitations of time and space have largely been overcome. Experience is virtualized. You no longer need to be in the same room, or even the same country, as your colleague, your teacher or your doctor to accomplish what used to require face-to-face contact (Quoted from page 113).

Through my work advising, training and coaching managers and other professionals, I have come to realize that this hyperconnectivity not only exists at the level of organizations and societies but also at the individual level and that the promises of what it offers get a lot of attention while the very real perils are often neglected.

The trend of "always being connected"(AbC) or hyperconnectivity is still rising, and doing so quickly if young people are any indication. 12% of adolescents send/receive more than 100 texts a day and 18% more than 200. See table. (The data are from PEW4, the figures are medians.)

TEXTS/DAY	2009	2011
Age 12-17	50	60
Age 14-17	60	100
Boys 12-17	30	50

The most important peril for professionals is that hyperconnectivity ruins reflection, real conversations and discussions, and thorough reading; it significantly decreases our intellectual performance. The World Wide Web is dominated by companies that have become masters in keeping their customers online all the time for the consumption of information. If you use ICT in the same way as the billions of mere consumers and let yourself be seduced into being online all the time and everywhere, you are caught in an information consumption trap, where there is little room to be really intellectually productive and creative. As a professional your success does not depend on your ability to consume information but on the way that you intelligently process and produce, if not create, information.

Always being connected forces you to multitask (something your reflecting brain cannot do), causes chronic stress that undermines your intellectual productivity, and has a negative impact on your sleep, which then ruins the work of your archiving brain. These consequences are so important that I have dedicated an individual chapter to each one.

In this chapter I will explain some of the other issues that result from always being connected.

2.2 FROM THE DREAM OF "ANYTIME, ANYWHERE" TO THE NIGHTMARE OF "ALL THE TIME, EVERYWHERE"

Modern technology allows us to always be connected, anytime and anywhere, the implication being that we can choose when and where we want to connect. When these great new technologies are well-used, they can indeed help us to work more effectively and efficiently and to keep in touch with more people. They also make flexible work possible, allowing us to move more easily between our private and professional lives. The use of smartphones in particular provides a lot more flexibility, a faster flow of information, faster decision making and higher productivity. It supports the idea (myth?) of nomadic brainworkers, who are free to choose when and where they do their brainwork.

The reality, however, is that the majority of professionals have switched from 'anytime, anywhere' to 'all the time, everywhere'.

ALWAYS ON - ALWAYS CONNECTED

HOW IT IS SOLD:
YOU CHOOSE. YOU
CAN BE AVAILABLE
ANYTIME, ANYWHERE.

HOW IT REALLY IS:
NO CHOICE. YOU *MUST*
BE AVAILABLE ALL THE TIME,
AND EVERYWHERE.

The freedom to choose has disappeared. People feel they MUST be connected all the time, everywhere. You see people working, sending e-mails and answering business calls all the time, everywhere. They are glued to their little screens and in the future smart watches and smart rings will chain if not enslave them even more.

Between 67% and 80% of cellphone owners check their phone for messages, alerts or calls, even when they don't notice their phone ringing or vibrating. 67% experience "phantom rings", checking their phone even when it is not ringing or vibrating[5]. Some people check up to 30 to 40 times an hour[6].

▶ **The near future: phantom rings from smart rings**

In the Netherlands 99% of professionals and managers feel obliged to use their phone for work outside regular working hours, even during vacations. 89% of them are irritated when others use their phone during meetings and in the company of other people... despite the fact that 40% do so themselves[8]. In my own survey of 1,152 managers and professionals (a split of about half and half), 84% check their e-mails first thing in the morning and then at every free moment during the day.

This sense of obligation sometimes comes from outside pressures. More and more ignorant companies and managers expect people to be connected 24/7, not knowing how badly this affects the quantity and quality of brainwork. In one of my in-house workshops a group of very senior managers told me extremely proudly that in their company they expected e-mails to be answered within 15 minutes, not only e-mails from external clients, but also those from internal clients. This is one of the most counterproductive ideas I have ever heard of. This means that all their highly trained professionals, many of them very expensive engineers, are forced to stay connected all the time and stop whatever important or complex work they are doing every 15 minutes in order to check their e-mail or corporate social media. As we have seen in the chapter about multitasking, every time you stop and restart you lose not just a little bit but a lot of productivity, creativity and accuracy.

Sometimes, when people start doing all this unpaid overtime, on average 6 hours a week, they resent not being paid; some even sue their employer[9], while others become unhappy, demotivated and end up taking more time to do less. Why would a company or a manager want to create an environment that makes it difficult or impossible for employees to use the best of their brains, to be proactive, to really think, to reflect? A few companies go against the trend: having discovered that being 'always-on' decreases productivity, they are now trying to stop or channel the hyperconnectivity (see Section 3).

Very often, however, the "must" is an internal one. Far too many people do not want or do not dare to disconnect, even though all this overtime is unpaid and often not really demanded by the company. Many managers I coach do not get negative reactions when they start disconnecting regularly and batch-processing their e-mails. Quite the contrary in fact.

The brainworkers themselves, especially the addicted ones, think that being connected all the time makes them more efficient. They have clearly never heard about all the research that proves the opposite. They also forget that people with a smartphone work on average six extra hours a week, which makes the supposed advantage less impressive.

For many more than I originally expected, it's even worse: they cannot disconnect anymore. Hyperconnectivity has become a bad habit or, as we will discuss below, an addiction in the psychiatric sense of the word.

Always being connected is not a good idea for a brainworker. Once in a while it is a little more efficient in the very short term, but in the longer term it is less efficient and certainly less effective. In the paragraphs below I will explain how it causes a lot of multitasking and task-switching, generates information overload, causes a continuous low level of unnecessary background stress, leads to bad sleeping patterns, eliminates the time needed for recuperation and is often bad for the quality of your real social contacts. Most important of all, it ruins reflection by giving your reflex brain an unfair advantage, often leading to errors and decisions that are, to put it politely, less than optimal.

2.3 AbC IS A WEAPON OF MASSIVE DISTRACTION IN THE HANDS OF THE HOMO INTERRUPTUS

To be intellectually productive we need to be able to give a topic our undivided attention, but the way we use our ICT means that our planned work and reflection is crowded out by interruption-driven, immediate, and thoughtless or rather reflection-less reactions.

The main distractions are phone calls, e-mails, text messages and people dropping by.

The problem is that interruptions, even entirely irrelevant ones, have a damaging, negative impact on the user's attention and concentration and, from there, on her efficiency and effectiveness as well as on her emotional state[10] and mental energy level (see below). Auditory interruptions are the worst for our concentration and attention, especially when you are reading. This is one of the reasons why doing intellectual work in open offices is so exhausting. (See BrainChain #5.)

Interruptions that demand an immediate response, like a phone call, have a much more negative impact than when the response can be delayed[11] like an e-mail. However, since so many

FROM HOMO SAPIENS TO HOMO INTERRUPTUS
IF YOU THINK YOU CAN CHANGE YOUR BRAIN YOU ARE **WRONG**

600 MILLION YEARS FROM FIRST BRAIN TO SINGLE TASKING HUMAN BRAIN

30 YEARS OF MULTITASKING
*1/20 MILLIONTH OF HISTORY
OF THE BRAIN*

people erroneously think they have to respond to e-mails and other messages immediately, they too totally ruin their attention and concentration. Incoming messages are the most disruptive if they have no relation to the task at hand and less so if they are highly relevant for that task or if they are queued until certain key parts of the task have been completed[12]

Homo sapiens evolved to an inefficient homo interruptus.

A Microsoft researcher, Linda Stone, called this "continuous partial attention"[13]. This term caught on, but is misleading because you might conclude that you can divide your attention between two things that need conscious attention at the same time. You can't. Therefore it should be called "continuous fractured attention" because, as I explained in the chapter about multitasking, every time you switch, you break something and lose some pieces. In reality you switch all the time and your brain guesses the parts that you missed, giving you the impression that you didn't miss anything. When you are having a conversation, this can be annoying, but the effects are more consequential for brainwork where accuracy is important[14] and far more serious in safety-critical situations like driving a car, handling a machine or administering medication[15].

Just dealing with interruptions costs energy, especially when they are unrelated to the task at hand. What's worse, even if they are related and you subjectively consider them to be beneficial for the task, they still come at the same cost. Interestingly, many people who have to deal with a lot of interruptions work faster. They adapt their methods to compensate for the time they expect to lose because of interruptions. They become somewhat more efficient, but they pay a price: they experience a higher workload, more stress and exhaustion, higher frustration, more time pressure and more effort[16].

▶ **Interruption is a hindrance to concentration. That is why distinguished minds have always shown such an extreme dislike to disturbance in any form, as something that breaks in upon and distracts their thoughts. Above all have they been averse to that violent interruption that comes from noise.**
ARTHUR SCHOPENHAUER: ON NOISE. 1851[17]

Even for a simple task like completing a jigsaw puzzle, a single interruption causes a speed reduction of 26%[18]. For a more complex task, it causes a 70% decline in correct answers per minute. It's also worth noting that both these studies were conducted with Millennials (those born in the eighties), who are supposed to be trained for hyperconnectivity from their earliest childhood. Although these young people were clearly not successful in dealing with interruptions, it must be said that it becomes even more difficult with age[19].

As I mentioned in the first section, there is only one exception: when work is very much routine, a few interruptions increase efficiency, probably by increasing the level of arousal[20]. This is probably also the reason why people doing routine brainwork are the only ones whose performance improves in open offices. (See BrainChain #5.)

2.4 AbC TURNS US INTO ADHOCRATS AND OUR ORGANIZATIONS INTO ADHOCRACIES

Reflecting is one of the most important things managers and other professionals do or should do. For their success and for the success of their company, they should regularly think broad, think deep, reflect on the past, think about the future and use their imagination. However, when you are continuously reacting to texts, e-mails and voicemails, constantly receiving information from the outside world, there is no time or space left for your brain to process the information, to store it in your memory, to play around with your own ideas, to be creative, to reflect.

▶ **They don't think, they e-mail.**

It's very important to realize that you are putting your brain in a *continuous impulsive reactive mode*. Your reflex brain gets the upper hand and, since Sensory Now Is All for this part of the brain, the result is intellectually pitiable. Your decisions are very much "ad hoc" snapshots, less discriminative and less accurate than decisions reached when you're using your reflecting brain. This increases the number of big and stupid mistakes as well as the time spent correcting the mistakes and redoing the work.

This reactive mode also ruins meetings and conference calls. Since so many professionals no longer have any undisturbed time to really study the information they have received beforehand and to reflect on it, they come to meetings ill-prepared and with their brains in reactive mode. The only thinking their brains do is reactive thinking triggered by somebody else's statement. As a result, meetings become reactive meetings, a discussion of opinions, triggered by opinions, which are not based on the prior study of facts.

So-called intelligent meeting scheduling makes matters worse for many people because anybody can schedule a meeting for you. As a result, you get back-to-back meetings that leave no time for reflection, no break for your working-memory to pass the information on to your long-term memory, no time for your beautiful archiving brain to store the information and make interesting connections, and no time to prepare for the next meeting.

This way, people become "adhocrats" and their organizations "adhocracies". They no longer behave proactively; they become reactive. This becomes obvious when I force, challenge, tempt and convince my coachees to totally disconnect on a regular basis to make time for undisturbed reflection: thinking proactively,

WE BECOME

ADHOCRATS

IN

ADHOCRAZY

ADHOCRACIES

(REPLACING BUREAUCRATS
IN BUREAUCRACIES)

thinking ahead, thinking wide and thinking deep. At first they feel lost, out of their comfort zone, even anxious. They discover they have real difficulty concentrating, maintaining sustained attention and focus on any chosen subject. They realize that their reactivity has become a habit and that they have to re-learn, re-train the habit of paying sustained attention.

Voluntary attention comes from the inside; it is the ability to concentrate on a task we have chosen. It is under our control and it demands effort and energy to sustain, unless we are in a state of "flow" when it becomes effortless. Without this effort we react to the beep of our inbox and we keep jumping from one e-mail to the next.

Involuntary attention, on the other hand, happens when the reflex brain is caught by something around us. It just happens, it's automatic and it does not demand effort or energy. We cannot easily turn it off because it is deep within our being, having been most important for our ancestral savannah dweller to alert him to anything that could be a source of food or danger. It is the attention we automatically give to the ring or buzz of our phone or the appearance of the "you have mail" icon. Therefore the best strategy is to eliminate these distractions that automatically grab the attention of our reflex brain, to the detriment of our voluntary attention, by disconnecting.

Adhocratizing is one of the reasons why only 27% of change projects and change programs have any success. The leaders or the consultants make a plan and then leave it to the lower levels in the adhocracy to execute. Since the required change activities come on top of their existing frenetic BAHD or MAHD (Brainworker or Manager Attention Hyperactivity Disorder) reactivity, the adhocrats do not have the time or peace of mind to reflect on how to execute the change. Consultants are often hired because the top managers themselves are so busy adhocratizing that they don't have enough time to thoroughly study the facts, to have undisturbed conversations in the team and to reflect themselves. This phenomenon has been made worse by so many ill-conceived "lean" initiatives, where levels of management have been cut out. The result is that, more than before, lots of operational issues that used to be resolved at lower levels of management now land directly on the desktop or phone of top managers, who as a result become top adhocrats without time for strategic reflection or the time to gain a helicopter view of the change initiative. As we will see below, this also has a negative impact on their strategic off-site meetings.

Change never happens in one step. It is a process of continuous learning through trial and error, trial and (small) success, continuous questioning, continuous debriefing and re-briefing, continuous reasoning, real conversations and reflection. Without ample, undisturbed time for reflection and discussions nobody really learns from the mistakes or the successes. As a result, the organization repeats the same mistakes and can't reproduce the successes.

In addition, in their reactive mode the adhocrats more easily fall prey to cognitive biases. The substitution heuristic, for example, will make the unfamiliar familiar and the difficult easy, by answering a much easier question and passing on that answer as the answer to the difficult question. The confirmation bias, selective perception and hindsight bias blind adhocratic executives from any information that goes against their decision. The post-purchase bias will eliminate tough questions about an acquisition and the loss aversion bias will prevent them from being critical about the change project they started and certainly from being critical enough to stop it, even when there are overwhelming signs telling you it was a wrong decision. Having read about these biases in the first section, you will probably already have realized that in change projects, adhocrats should also fear the outcome bias, availability bias, anchoring bias and familiarity bias.

Last but not least, as adhocrats in an adhocracy lead with the reflex brain, without the internal ethical madman's guard of our reflecting brain and without the external madman's guard of strong, ethical company values, adhocrats may do unethical things, things that they would never have done with more time for reflection and real conversations.

2.5 AbC CAUSES INFORMATION OVERLOAD

In 2011, 45% of executives and 61% (!) of Canadian academic/education executives suffered from information overload[21]. When you are always connected you no longer take the time to process all the input and to develop your own ideas. It results in an overload of information that your brain can no longer process and store in the time available, and as a result it becomes impossible to make thoughtful choices and decisions. To add insult to injury, as I will explain in the chapter about e-mail, between 30% and 90% of the information is irrelevant, which further increases the subjective feeling of overload. Moreover, the reflex-brain activity, caused by a continuing stream of new snippets of information, crowds out the duller but usually much more important management brainwork of reflection, thinking ahead, thinking broadly, going deep into a subject and remembering it.

The result is a vicious cycle: when we are always connected, we do not disconnect frequently enough to reflect on the way we deal with all this information, and the more we are connected, the less efficiently we deal with the continuous stream of information. Having all this unprocessed information waiting for you not only pushes you to multitask even more and become even less efficient, it also causes a continuous background of low brain-stress and can be very de-motivating.

The subjective feeling of being overloaded with information is made worse because most of the received information was not requested. Its flood is experienced as out of control, a feeling that easily upsets our stress-balance.

> "In an information-rich world, the wealth of information means a dearth of something else: a scarcity of whatever it is that information consumes. What information consumes is rather obvious: it consumes the attention of its recipients. Hence a wealth of information creates a poverty of attention and a need to allocate that attention efficiently among the overabundance of information sources that might consume it."
>
> HERBERT SIMON. 1916-2001. NOBEL PRIZE ECONOMICS.

There are also indications that being totally reactive during the day has a negative influence on the storing and ordering that our brain does during the night. I will discuss the role of our brain during the night in more detail in the chapter on sleep.

2.6 AbC EXHAUSTS OUR BRAINPOWER, WILLPOWER AND CAUSES DECISION FATIGUE

Reflecting and multitasking consume brain energy, and research shows us that this brain energy is not a wishy-washy new-age metaphor, but should be taken seriously and literally.

Shai Danziger and his colleagues, for example, studied the decision-making process of a parole board that had to decide whether to extend or terminate the imprisonment of criminals. The startling result was that the major influence on the decision of the judge, criminologist and social worker was... their break. It was not just a little statistical difference; as you can see in the graph, where a dotted line indicates a break, it was an important difference[22]. The criminal cases discussed after a break got their jail-term reduced or ended more often.

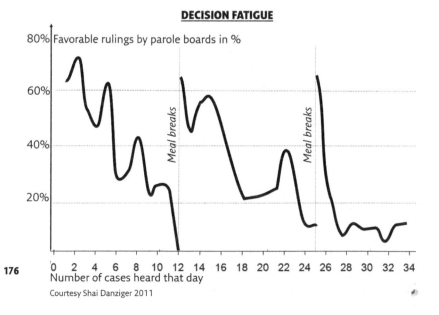

DECISION FATIGUE

80% Favorable rulings by parole boards in %

Meal breaks

Meal breaks

0 2 4 6 8 10 12 14 16 18 20 22 24 26 28 30 32 34
Number of cases heard that day

Courtesy Shai Danziger 2011

This study is one of many demonstrating the phenomenon of "decision fatigue". Research in the lab and in real life shows that after having exerted self-control or having had to make many little choices, there is a decrease of self-control, a decrease of physical stamina, less persistence in the face of failure, more procrastination, less quality and quantity of arithmetic calculations and worse decision making[23]. Just resisting a temptation or distraction depletes your mental energy. You can overcome this low mental energy with high motivation, but this is only possible when the depletion is mild[24].

The problem is that we are not aware of this. We don't have a mental decision gauge and warning light to tell us that the decision-energy tank is low or empty, as is the case with our physical energy. As a result we keep making decisions and we keep thinking they are good rational decisions when they are not! When energy levels are low, our tireless reflex brain takes over from our fatigable reflecting brain and our brain takes all kinds of easy shortcuts that require the least energy, but are not rational.

Reflection, hard thinking, negotiating, making choices and decisions consume mental energy, willpower energy. The more something becomes a routine, the less brain energy it consumes. When you are learning to drive, all the things you have to think about all the time are mentally exhausting, but once driving becomes a habit and your reflex brain takes over, it no longer uses that much mental energy and can even be a relaxing pleasure.

Decision fatigue is a special case of mental fatigue, or willpower fatigue, fatigue of self-control. It is sometimes called "ego depletion", an unfortunate choice of words because it refers to the pre-scientific mythological Freudian ideas about the ego.

It's not only going online that depletes your brain energy; resisting other distractions has the same effect, for example trying to stay focused in a noisy open office, as the following study shows.

Forty female clerical workers were randomly assigned for 3 hours to a quiet office set-up or to a set-up with the typical low-intensity noise of open offices. Subjectively, the ones with the noise did not experience more stress... but the stress hormones in their blood were nonetheless significantly more elevated (!). They also gave up solving a puzzle more quickly after the experience, clearly showing decision fatigue. Interestingly enough, they also made fewer ergonomic, postural adjustments to their computer workstation[25]. As a result the extra concentration needed to compensate for the noise also increased the chronic strain on their body (see BrainChain #3).

As important is the fact that not making a decision, postponing the decision or just sticking to the status quo consumes less energy. That's exactly what happened to the parole board. The criminals being judged just after the break had a much greater chance of being freed, whereas for the ones coming later the judges tended to opt for the status quo. "When in doubt, do nothing" is your brain's guideline, especially when the decision is difficult and your brainpower is running low.

I wonder if this knowledge might be (mis?)used by salespeople and negotiators: let the other party make a lot of little choices and when decision fatigue sets in you come with the questions that require big decisions. The other party will be significantly less rational about them than when you do it the other way around... especially if you ensure that the other party does not consume any drinks or food with glucose because you should not read the word "energy" here as a metaphor, you should take it literally. While exerting self-control, exerting willpower or dealing with disruptions, your brain consumes a surprisingly large amount of glucose. Having a break or just taking sugar gives it a boost[26].

That it really is the sugar that makes the difference is easy to test. After having to make many little choices, half the subjects in a study were given lemonade with sugar and the other half lemonade made with an artificial sweetener. The ones who got the sugar made fewer mistakes in the tests that followed. It turns out that it is the quick energy supplement that makes the difference.

This phenomenon even exists in dogs, making it very clear that these researchers discovered something really fundamental. With dogs, if you put them in a situation where they have to exert self-control and then confront them with the frustrating task of getting food out of a clear plastic container that was open before but is now closed, they persist significantly less in trying to get the food than is the case for dogs who didn't have to exert any self-control beforehand. A glucose drink also made the dogs persist longer[27].

Modern brain scans, where we can follow the activity in the different parts of the brain in real time, have added some startling detail to these studies. In a situation where people have to use willpower, a lack of glucose decreases the activity in the parts of the brain that stimulate self-control and increases the activity in the parts that go for immediate rewards[28]. This response was probably very useful for the savannah dweller to push him to action even when his energy tank was running on empty, thanks to the tireless reflex brain.

By the way, the authors of this study used the results to explain the devilish dilemma that a weight-reducing diet causes for the brain: the energy it costs to stick to your diet reduces the energy your brain needs to maintain the willpower needed to stick to your diet. The more temptations you resist during the day, the more you crave sugar and the more likely you are to succumb in the evening.

At this point you're probably thinking, this is all very fascinating, but what does it have to do with always being connected? Well, the fewer temptations and distractions we have to resist, the fewer choices we have to make and the fewer decisions we have to take, the more energy our brain has to do the difficult, very important brainwork. Continuously resisting the urge to check your e-mails and social media, continuously making small decisions about whether or not to delete an e-mail, respond now or later or decide what kind of answer to give gradually runs down your mental energy. All of these small decisions add up, consuming as much mental energy as one important big decision and... we leave things to our reflex brain, postponing important decisions or making the easiest, most primitive, irrational, impulsive, bad choices.

So if you start your day by checking your e-mails and then spend every free moment during the rest of the day answering them, this is exhausting your mental energy, your decision-making power, your self-control and your willpower. All these mini or micro decisions add up and as a result you literally have no brainpower left to make good rational big decisions. It not only causes a continuous low-level stress, but also a gradual deterioration of the quality of your brainwork. No wonder that the worst decisions, choices, mistakes and misbehaviors happen in the evening. Especially if, as is the case for so many participants in my workshops and lectures, you don't take regular breaks and skip lunch altogether.

Since just resisting all those constant temptations, be they in your pocket or just one click away, is exhausting, you have to organize yourself in a way that limits the temptations as much as possible. Just like if you are a smoker trying to quit the habit, you should not walk around with a packet of cigarettes in your pocket. Or if you are trying to diet, you should not keep your cupboards, pockets and bag full of chocolate. Resisting the easy temptation will exhaust your willpower and you will succumb in the afternoon or evening.

I experienced this myself just after I bought my first smartphone. At first I couldn't resist the urge to look at my e-mails all the time. Then I learned to resist the urge, but I was almost continuously aware of the fact that I was resisting this temptation. Only when I reprogrammed my phone so that I only could get to my e-mails with five clicks, and especially when I was brave enough to regularly totally switch off my phone, knowing that it takes 50 seconds to start it up, input the pin code etc., did the temptation and background tension totally disappear.

Therefore, once you are convinced of its detrimental impact and decide to kick the bad habit of always being connected, you need to do it in a way that not being connected becomes a new spontaneous, autonomous habit, that only connecting at particular hours becomes a routine and so that you no longer have to resist continuous temptations that drain your decision-energy. Interestingly enough, you can download apps that do exactly that: disconnect you from all non-essential connections except at particular times and for particular durations. (See section 3.)

Your tank of brain energy slowly empties during the day. Therefore most people do their best brainwork in the morning after breakfast, unless they totally ruin these golden hours by... doing e-mails first thing in the morning. The same is true for unethical decisions: our decisions are more ethical in the morning than in the evening when the selfish never tiring reflex-brain takes over the decisions [29]. To have the best quality brainwork, real evening people will have to organize a break and a light meal before they start their evening work. I write "real" because there are ever more people who have turned themselves into pseudo-evening people by ruining their morning hours and staying connected way past the time of day when they should disconnect and give their brain a break to prepare for a brain-replenishing sleep. (See BrainChain #4 on sleep.)

If you have an important meeting, a decision to make or reflection to do, schedule a break and a healthy snack before. Scheduling your meetings back to back all day and skipping lunch is the best recipe to make sub-standard or stupid decisions later in the day. Eating lots of sugar will help a little, while also making you fat. It's much better to disconnect regularly, avoid skipping meals and take regular breaks, where you enjoy a piece of fruit.

In brief, for optimal intellectual productivity, you have to organize your work, your life and your decisions in such a way that you keep your brain-energy tank as full as possible. Avoid doing important thinking, important meetings and making important decisions after many little decisions (like doing e-mail), small or big acts of self-control or on an empty stomach.

2.7 AbC ELIMINATES VITAL SLACK AND BLOCKS INFORMATION PROCESSING AND CREATIVITY

Our brain also needs these breaks, periods of disconnection, to detach and disengage from the outside world. When we are actively dealing with the outside world all the time, this uses all the capacity of the information-processing part of our brain and not enough is left for the archiving brain to correctly process all the information that's already stored in our temporary or long-term memory. Moreover, in the chapter about multitasking we saw how continuous switching between different subjects, without a break in-between, results in information being overwritten or pushed out of the temporary memory and never reaching the long-term memory. We described how our brain has an almost infinite database with information that is continuously rearranged and manipulated by our archiving brain during moments of rest to provide knowledge, insight and new creative ideas.

Hence your archiving brain needs idle time to function at its best. Idle in the sense of disengaged, unoccupied, inactive, and not involved in any task.

Don't let your technology prevent you from daydreaming. Your reflecting brain and your archiving brain compete for the same processor, so the less conscious attention your reflecting brain pays, the more room there is for your archiving brain to find stuff in the archives and pass it on to your reflecting brain to leisurely play with. Many of the ideas will be strange, funny or crazy, but often a crazy idea is the first step to a creative one that might lead to an innovation.

Being busy with your smartphone all the time, filling all the little gaps of time with little tasks, is not smart at all; it is brainless. As I mentioned earlier, in a well-prepared brain the most creative ideas will come when you are relaxed and not thinking about the challenge, when you are not only disconnected but also detached. "Well-prepared" also means you disconnected beforehand to reflect, to think, to study and to gain a deep knowledge of the issues. All the things you do not do when you are in reactive mode, glued to your screen full of e-mails.

▶ **Being busy with your smartphone all the time is not smart at all.**

It is extremely important to disconnect to reflect, but if you want to get the best out of your brain, learn the most, remember the most and be at your most creative, you should also disconnect to disengage, to let your brain idle, to give it some Vital Slack. In other words, you should first disconnect to focus and reflect and then you should disconnect to unfocus and disengage.

Conclusion: Disconnect and disengage to be creative! Always being connected blocks the information processing and the creativity.

2.8 AbC OFTEN RUINS REAL CONVERSATIONS, RELATIONS, DISCUSSIONS AND MEETINGS

The relationship between always being connected virtually and real relationships is fascinating. I didn't find much research about the impact of always being connected on the quality of relationships, and sociology is not really part of my expertise, so much of this sub-section is based on my extensive experience with lots of professionals in coaching and workshops rather than on solid research.

On the one hand our fantastic technology allows us to connect with people we love or need, anywhere and anytime we choose. It simplifies staying in touch with family, friends, bosses, direct reports and colleagues. This is great progress for all of us, and especially for the more insecure extraverts, and particularly for adolescents, who can now be stimulated and connected all the time.

In the first section I described how important real conversations are for our intellectual productivity. I called them joint reflections. Once you have got to know someone in person, although a live conversation is still richer, it is then possible to have a good conversation on the phone any time, anywhere if... you are both fully concentrated on that conversation and do not try to do anything else at the same time.

> **"While gadgets like smartphones and tablets certainly do have a huge positive impact upon my working life, it is the people around me who really make the difference."**
> RICHARD BRANSON EXPLAINING THAT NO ICT TOOL IN THE WORLD CAN REPLACE A GOOD ASSISTANT[30]

On the other hand always being connected engenders an interesting paradox when this great communication tool gets in the way of real conversations and relations.

In my own research among managers and professionals I found that 13% regularly prefer to stay connected rather than going out and socializing and that 20% regularly get complaints from family and friends about their virtual over-connectedness.

In the above-mentioned Harris poll, 12% of people in a

relationship said they believe their smartphone gets in the way of that relationship. No wonder when 9% of adults and 20% of people aged between 18 and 34 admit they've even used their phone during sex[31].

This sorry state of affairs and the alienation are beautifully depicted in a two-minute movie by Charlene deGuzman: http://www.youtube.com/watch?v=OINa46HeWg8. This movie would be funny if it weren't so sadly true. This state of affairs is also the source of the new concept of "phubbing"[32]: the act of snubbing someone in a social setting by looking at your phone instead of paying attention, which makes the other person feel less important than your phone.

Always being connected undoubtedly has negative as well as positive consequences for your relationships, depending on how you guard or manage five important boundaries or interfaces:
- the present/absent boundary
- the real/virtual relationship boundary
- the body/mind boundary
- the public/private boundary
- the work/private life boundary

These boundaries are not a problem in and of themselves; it all depends how we cope with them and how we switch between those boundaries all the time, without being aware of the negative consequences.

During a visit to Venice for the Biennale, I was walking along the terraces full of people, friends and families, and was amazed to observe how many people were connected with people other than their table companions, pecking away at their smartphones without talking, preferring virtual friends over real family or friends. It is a fascinating experience to see how so many people continuously switch between being present and being absent.

▶ ### Always connected in company: being alone together

Probably all professionals are sometimes annoyed, if not maddened, when people in a meeting stay connected with their phone or tablet. These people become real zombies for a few seconds or even minutes and when they wake up out of their zombie-state are convinced they did not miss a beat of the conversation. All the people engaged in the conversation know this is a delusion because they typically ask questions that have already been asked or give answers that have been given a few seconds before. At the next meeting it becomes evident that they missed important parts.

Some people really think that they can trick others into believing that they are following the conversation while being busy on their phone. They might even really believe it themselves, as if the other people don't experience their absence while they are faking presence. These micro-zombies think they are the exceptions to the rule that our reflecting brain cannot multitask. While they stay connected with their virtual world, however, they not only ruin their own intellectual productivity, but also that of the other people in the meeting or in the conversation.

▶   **Always connected in company:**
a meeting of micro-zombies

Not only are these people continuously switching between being present and absent, but they are also switching back and forth between the real context and the virtual one,. As we saw in the chapter about parallel multitasking this consumes a lot of brain energy, which is therefore no longer available for making the best decisions. Maybe these people behave this way (as many adolescents do) to escape to the easier, unreal, pimped-up, ever-changing, attractive and addictive virtual world, where it is much easier to control the conversation. Escaping means they don't have to deal with the more difficult real situation that demands more effort, more empathy, social skills and taking into account the nonverbal and all the other aspects of a conversation. This real situation requires more continuous participation and is one where they are co-responsible for animating the conversation when it risks getting off the right track or becoming boring.

It often seems as if the actual real situation, where real people meet real people, has moved into the background and lost its significance, as if it has become merely the backdrop for virtual relations and conversations, which have moved into the foreground and taken center-stage. This is most obvious when people are in intimate relations but are still glued to their little screens. I was stunned the first time I saw a girl sitting on the lap of a boy, embracing him with her left arm and kissing him while at the same time holding her phone in her right hand, behind the boy's head and reading texts. I have since seen several similar situations.

I see young parents busy with their phone, laptop or tablet while holding their baby, as if the baby isn't aware of the difference between undivided attention and absent care. Since this first observation I have realized that this has become rather common. Do they think that a baby does not feel the difference when you are working on your laptop while holding her? Do they not realize how utterly important it is to talk (all the time) to a baby from the very first weeks, even when the baby does not yet talk? Do they not realize that the baby's receptive language development is way ahead of her expressive language? I did not find any research on the language development of babies of Crackberry/iPhone parents, but from what I know about developmental psychology, I am, to say the least, a little worried.

In group coaching sessions and workshops, several managers, already in the old Blackberry days, related how their children took revenge and damaged their Blackberries or threw them away. One of them was sitting on the sofa with his daughter aged 6, watching the television, when all of a sudden his daughter grasped his phone out of his texting hands, threw it on the ground and jumped on it yelling "You did not even listen to me, you never listen to me, you never listen to me, you never listen to me!!!". Recently I saw a 4-year-old playing mama, sitting on a chair with a closed book on her knees typing on it like a pretend laptop, while holding a wooden block between her shoulder and ear. When her mom asked her something, she reacted with a: "Don't you see, I am busy!"

A clever piece of research showed that the impact of mobile phones on conversations is even more subversive than we think. It turns out that the mere presence of a phone already has a negative impact on the quality of the conversation as well as on the quality of the relation of two people talking with each other. The impact was not significant for small talk, but when the two people discussed personally meaningful topics, it had a significant negative impact on the level of trust and empathy[33].

The bodies and minds of hyper-connected people are in different places. Of course this is not new; we all start daydreaming when a conversation or a meeting becomes boring. An important difference, however, is that I start daydreaming when I want to, when I choose to. But hyper-connected people disappear into their virtual world at the sound of a buzz or a ring tone. They don't choose, their virtual world chooses for them. It calls them even when what's happening in the real world is much more important. Some of them are almost never really 100% present, in a continuous state of fractured attention. It is evident that it then becomes quite impossible for them to focus in order to reflect and be intellectually productive.

People who remember the time before the mobile phone should have been prepared for this because even back in those days, it was very frustrating when, after standing in line for quite a while, you arrived at the counter and just as you started your question, the phone went and almost always the clerk dropped you, the real client, for an unknown caller.

A major difference is that those landlines were only at specific locations whereas the mobile phone is omnipresent. As a result there is another interesting continuous switching going on between the private and the public. In private situations, people easily move to the public space of a virtual social network, for example, a picture taken at a dinner is immediately sent to a network of "friends", without asking any of the participants. Meanwhile, in just about any imaginable public place, people start up private conversations, with the result that many strangers are forced to listen to a private conversation. Even if they don't want this at all, even if it ruins their concentration, they can't escape. A ringtone from somebody else's phone can come at any moment and break your concentration, your ecstasy, your relaxation, your joy... when as a speaker you have just captured the full attention of the audience, when you're in a centuries' old church and you're having a moment of contemplation letting the silence sink in, when you're quietly contemplating an amazing work of art, as you arrive at the top of mountain and are taking in the unique view, while concentrating on a difficult document in the "silent compartment" of a train, while enjoying a unique gastronomic meal in the kind of top restaurant you normally cannot afford, while having a very emotional conversation with your doctor...

As I describe in the free booklet about the open office (See Brain-Chain #5), having to overhear half a conversation of a phone call is the most disturbing, unwanted intrusion for brainworkers into their own private territory, ruining their intellectual productivity if they are trying to do some intellectual work[34].

It is an invasion of their private territory, against which there is no way to defend themselves because they cannot shut their ears. This can make people very angry, similar to cases where people have to listen day and night to the music of neighbors who can't keep the volume down. The matter is made worse because many people speak very loudly or shout on their phone, especially when the connection is bad or even when it is good but they don't realize that a low volume of the speaker (or their own poor hearing) does not mean that the other side has the same problem.

Another interesting social boundary that hyper-connected people are continuously crossing is the one between work and private life. Before the mobile phone and the Internet it didn't need much effort to separate work from private life, whereas nowadays this requires a conscious decision of the extent to which one wants the two spheres to overlap and interface. Children, other family members and (virtual or real) friends can now easily contact us at work and we can easily contact them from work. On the other hand, for many professionals the 9-5 boundary no longer exists and they can easily be contacted at home for work-related issues. A majority of people do work-related e-mails at home, often for many (unpaid) hours. As the examples above of the reactions of managers' children show, not everybody is happy with the way this impacts on personal relationships. 83% of iPhone users use their phone in social settings like meals, parties and meetings, at least occasionally. 15% would rather give up sex than go a weekend without their iPhone[35].

As we have seen in the chapter about multitasking, the more different the domains that the tasks belong to, the more detrimental task-switching is for reflection, energy-cost, memory and concentration, accuracy, creativity etc... Hence, when you often switch between work and family, your work will cost more energy, take more time and the result will be of a lower quality.

For all the switching across these five boundaries and interfaces, the question is not: Is it good or bad? It is both an opportunity and a challenge and sometimes a real problem. The question is: Do you manage it, or do you let it happen to you? Do you want this, did you make a conscious decision to let the two spheres interface and to what extent, or were you caught up in it without really wanting it or without realizing the detrimental consequences for your intellectual productivity? The issue is not the overlap between the two domains but the feeling of having freely chosen it, the feeling of being in control, together with the impact on the needs and wishes of people close to us.

For this book, the question is: does it improve my intellectual productivity or does it undermine it? In any case, being half-connected or half-present in a dialogue makes it impossible to have a real conversation, a joint reflection where together you create meaning, if not a creative new meaning, be it at home with your partner or child or be it at work with a peer or a boss.

2.9 A SPECIAL CASE: AbC RUINS OFF-SITE MEETINGS

A special and often important kind of meetings are off-sites. Facilitating these I discovered that executives who are ignorant about the user manual for brains not only ruin the intellectual productivity of their employees, but also ruin their own intellectual productivity. A most typical example is that their off-sites are no longer "off site" because they carry their "site" in their pocket. Always being connected means they are unable to take a strategic helicopter-view of their company or department. This is evident in many of their decisions.

▶ **Hyper-connected executives do not have a helicopter view but a grasshopper view.**

The crucial goal of an "off-site" is to get away from the site, to disconnect from the daily, nitty-gritty, operational, down-to-earth demands at the site and to get in your executive "helicopter" to get an overview, to think, to relax, to idle, to freewheel, to become detached and disengage to be creative.

When executives ask me to help facilitate their off-sites to brainstorm about strategic issues, this has become very difficult if not impossible because the participants check their e-mails all day long. Every stupid little e-mail they check brings them back to their immediate reality and far away from the detachment and disengagement needed to be strategic and creative. Every time they check their e-mail, their brains go back into reactive mode, making it difficult to start thinking proactively and creatively 5 minutes later. Instead of using the breaks to socialize and to let the archiving brain take care of the information learned in the session, they keep guzzling new and often irrelevant information, and lots of information from the session is simply never stored. Their hyperconnectedness gets in the way of defining and reaching their strategic goals.

Asking or demanding that the managers or professionals disconnect doesn't work either because then they can't disengage because they keep thinking about the tasks not being done, the dozens of mails pouring in, how late they will have to work that night to process them and how tired they will be the next morning. As I mentioned above, the problem is made worse in lean companies where the elimination of layers of management means that lots of operational issues that used to be filtered out and fixed at a lower level now arrive on their electronic micro-desk, even when they are at an off-site. This puts their brains in the primitive, "here and now" reflex mode, diminishing reflection and totally eliminating the letting-go, the disengagement needed for creativity.

Each time the managers or professionals try to take an executive helicopter-view to discuss a strategic subject, they are unable to keep hovering over an issue or to get really high in the air because too quickly they are forced or they force themselves to land in the reflex brain's land of SNIA (Sensory Now is All). A few minutes later they take off again, only to stay aloft a few minutes. The famous executive helicopter-view becomes an executive grasshopper-view.

Not being able to disconnect from their immediate reality, their reactive ideas and solutions cannot be anything other than primitive and glued to that immediate reality. The chance of having a good overview or of generating breakthrough ideas is close to zero.

2.10 EXPECTING EMPLOYEES TO ALWAYS BE CONNECTED IS A BIG COUNTERPRODUCTIVE BLUNDER

In "Corporate Brain Disorder", I will explain and support with lots of data how companies spend billions hiring the best and the brightest, and then organize work in such a way that these brainworkers only function at 60% or less of their intellectual potential. One of the most efficient ways to ruin the intellectual productivity of brainworkers is to expect them to always be connected.

If employees are able to have all information with them all the time, everywhere, then a major risk for their intellectual productivity is that at any time of the day, every day of the week, their customers, bosses, colleagues and staff expect them to answer their questions immediately. There are indeed brainless or very ignorant managers and companies that expect their employees to always have their smartphones on. Not only is this plain stalking and should be punished, but most importantly, expecting employees to be always-connected is ignorant (or stupid) because it undermines efficiency and productivity, for many reasons:

It gives an unfair advantage to the reflex brain, resulting in more primitive, snapshot, decisions from the reflex brain.

It prevents them from being proactive.

It makes them *four times less efficient and effective.*

It causes a continuous background stress that undermines the quality and quantity of their brainwork.

It often has a negative impact on their personal relations. Not only do spouses, friends and children complain of the brainworkers' absent-mindedness, but an organization that undermines the social relations of its employees, undermines itself[36].

If the task is safety-related, it makes them unsafe.

With the continuous requests for attention or even the potential call for attention in the background, they are never fully concentrated on the task at hand. This lack of concentration decreases creativity and the quality of work.

It slows down their cognitive brain.

Hyperconnectivity also makes people lazy. Instead of taking time to reflect on the issues mentioned in a mail, to reflect about a solution, they have a tendency to give quick answers off the top of their head or to immediately forward the message to somebody else (this is most often NOT delegating, but dumping) and go on skimming the 100 remaining e-mails.

People also tend to plan less, assuming that there will always be people immediately on hand if an unforeseen problem crops up.

Last but not least, they put themselves in danger when they keep being connected while driving.

For some companies the penny has finally dropped, or maybe they have calculated the cost of always being connected, and they have taken wise decisions to support, stimulate or even put pressure on their employees to disconnect in general and specifically while driving. Some companies give their employees a few email-free hours a week or at the weekend. More often than not this is just silly because it does not address the more fundamental problems of hyperconnectedness. Don't expect your brainworkers to become as productive as they could be if you release their Brain-Chains just a few hours a week and then keep them tightly shackled for the rest of their time, at work as well as at home.

Conclusion: Don't just allow employees to disconnect, but proactively encourage them to do so! Expecting employees to always be connected is an enormous and costly counterproductive blunder.

2.11 WHY IS IT SO DIFFICULT TO DISCONNECT TO REFLECT? ABOUT HABITS, ADDICTS AND SCREEN ZOMBIES

▶

"Perhaps the most ironic aspect of the struggle for survival is how easily organisms can be harmed by that which they desire. The trout is caught by the fisherman's lure, the mouse by cheese. But at least those creatures have the excuse that bait and cheese look like sustenance. Humans seldom have that consolation. The temptations that can disrupt their lives are often pure indulgences."

ROBERT KUBEY AND MIHALY CSIKSZENTMIHALYI

When I got my beautiful new smartphone I became aware how big the impact is of having your e-mail continuously pushed to your phone, how addictive it is. I couldn't resist the lure of looking at my e-mails whenever I had a spare moment. Realizing the significant negative impact it had on my intellectual productivity, I went back to the non-automatic system, which needs five clicks and my username and password before I can get to my e-mail. The result was that I stopped checking my e-mails all the time and became more productive. I was very surprised, however, to discover how difficult it was in the beginning to kick the habit after such a short time of having been always connected. When coaching and training I am very puzzled by the fact that so many people just can't disconnect anymore.

> *I know the hypnosis, as I'm sure you do, too. You start clicking through photos of your friends of friends and the next thing you know an hour has gone by. It's oddly soothing, but unsatisfying. Once the spell is broken, I feel like I've just wasted a bunch of time. But while it's happening, I'm caught inside the machine: I. Just. Cannot. Stop.*
> ALEXIS C. MADRIGALJUL[37]

Did you ever hear or read about a new disorder called Nomophobia? I don't know where it comes from but it means No Mobile Phone Phobia, the fear of being without a phone. I'd like to think it's a joke, but if you look at the statistics, it's a sad reality.

Is this just a very bad habit that is difficult to unlearn? Are these people just trapped? Or is this an addiction?

I'd like to repeat that 29% of cellphone owners in the USA describe their cellphone as "something they can't imagine living without." 67% of cellphone owners find themselves checking their phone for messages, alerts or calls, even when they don't notice their phone ringing or vibrating. 67% had experienced "phantom rings", checking their phone even when it was not ringing or vibrating[38]. Some people check up to 30 to 40 times an hour[39]. This certainly makes one think about an addiction. And indeed many researchers interested in behavioral addictions discovered that there is not much difference between cellphone-addiction and other addictions. Other specialists think it is not wise to label this problematic use as addiction and prefer to speak about problematic or maladaptive behavior[40]. In general I would tend to side with the second approach, but it is undeniable that between 3% and 20% of users are really addicted. The conclusions of the research depend very much on the methodology used, the questions asked, the population studied and above all how stringent cut-off criteria have been used.[41].

Of course you do not have to be addicted to not be able to disconnect. There are rather neurotic, psychological reasons for not disconnecting. For example a need to feel important or to show importance, a need to be included and needed, a lack of self-confidence, being a pleaser, a lack of self-respect, fear of taking responsibility, a lack of willpower etc...

However, when I coached managers, addressing these issues often didn't make very much of a difference. Therefore I very quickly started tackling the problem as the unlearning of a (very) bad habit, and that worked much better. But still the success rate was often lower than I expected and lower than I had experienced as a neuro-psychiatrist or as a psychotherapist in my former career. After a while it dawned on me that often their behavior was very similar, if not the same, as what I had previously observed in drug addicts. When I looked at the research it clearly supported my hypothesis that, for some, always being connected has clearly become a real addiction in the psychological or psychiatric sense of the word.

On the other hand, I think Internet addiction and ICT-addiction are misnomers because people are not addicted to the Internet or ICT but to particular things they do with it. Adolescent girls, for example, are most involved in ICT-mediated communication, while boys are more into games, sex sites and gambling[42].

In my own research I asked the following questions to check for addiction to e-mailing. The questions follow a pattern usually used to check for drug abuse.

1 Do you sleep with your mobile phone next to your bed?
2 Do you always check your e-mail or social media before doing other things?
3 When you're online and someone needs you, do you usually say "just a few more minutes" before stopping?
4 Do you spend time online rather than going out with others?
5 Do you frequently find yourself anticipating, looking forward to the next time you'll be online?
6 Do you lie about or try to hide how long you've been online?
7 Does going online improve a (somewhat) depressed or nervous mood?
8 Do others in your life complain about the amount of time you spend online?

9 Do you feel uncomfortable or stressed when you have no mobile connection?

10 Do you connect (e-mail or Internet or text) as soon as you finish a task or part of it?

What would you call addicted? Based only on the answers of the 1,152 professionals and managers that I surveyed, the conclusions are as follows:

3 or more questions answered positive: then 46% are addicted.

5 or more questions answered positive: then 16.5% are addicted.

7 or more questions answered positive: then 3.2% are addicted.

After going through the research literature I would cautiously say that for 46% their connectivity is a real problem. If you define Internet addiction as "the inability of individuals to control their Internet use, resulting in marked distress and/or functional impairment in daily life"[43], then the conclusion certainly is that 16.5% are addicted, and the family members, friends and colleagues of these people probably agree, unless they are hooked themselves.

No matter the exact percentage, for so many people it is at least a habit that is very difficult to change. What makes it so difficult? What is the trap?

Let me explain why always being connected is so addictive so that it might help you to kick the habit, if not the addiction, or prevent this from happening. If you are not addicted, I still recommend that you read on as you might learn a few interesting things about the brain, behaviors, habits and why it is so difficult for some people to disconnect. If you are responsible for children, it might also inspire you to teach them to use their ICT in a better way.

In any case, do not forget that what I describe in the paragraphs below are genetic tendencies, but these tendencies do not determine you, they are not your destiny and you are not their helpless victim, unless you let your reflex brain ru(i)n your life.

WE ARE WIRED FOR CONDITIONING

You probably know the story of Pavlov's dog. In the 1920s Pavlov[44] was studying the digestive system and, because it was easy to measure, the production of saliva in dogs. He then discovered the dogs started drooling, not only in the presence of food, but also as soon as the lab assistant who usually fed them appeared. He then formulated the hypothesis that anything presented together with the food could elicit this reaction. He checked this with the bell he used to call the dogs for their meals and indeed the bell made them produce saliva. The dogs had developed a so-called "Pavlov reflex" or "Conditioned response". It is important to note that the bell in itself has nothing to do with food. You can replace it with anything you want.

The same thing happens with the sound of your phone, the "ping" sound when an e-mail drops in your inbox and, last but not least, for so many people the slightest feeling of being bored and not filling up every minute of your time. These triggers make you stop whatever you are doing at work or in your private life and reach for your phone. Important work, important conversations, important family activities, real life will not stop the Pavlov reflex of connecting. Very often you disconnect from real human contact in favor of much poorer and less important virtual contact. Just as the dog can't stop his drooling, you can't stop your reflex to connect, unless you break the cycle.

But there is hope, you can help the Pavlov dog inside you from drooling at the sound of the bell. When over a period of time Pavlov fed the dogs without sounding the bell, the conditioned response slowly diminished and in the end was extinguished. For some dogs though, it took quite some time.

By the way, you can also turn this conditioning to an advantage, by creating triggers for productive habits. You can, for example, do the hyper-connected multitasking in a different room, at a different desk or at a different side of your desk, than the one where you do the difficult brainwork. (See Section 3.)

WE ARE WIRED FOR INSTANT GRATIFICATION

In one of the most creative and relevant psychology experiments ever, in 1972 Walter Michel gave 600 kids (4-6 years old) a marsh-

mallow or another preferred treat and promised they would only get a second one if they did not eat the first one for 15 minutes. He then left and observed them from behind the one-way mirror. One-third earned the second marshmallow. You may think "so what…"

Well, they followed up many of these kids several times until 2011, most recently even with brain scans.

The ones who were able to postpone gratification were very significantly more competent and more successful.

- They had higher scores at school and school tests like SAT.
- They were less likely to be obese.
- They were less likely to be addicted to drugs.
- They were less often divorced.
- They had higher emotional intelligence.

This may sound like bad news for the other kids; the good news though is that many learned to postpone gratification later, by the age of 20-25, especially by developing a longer-time horizon.

The brain seems to be wired for instant gratification. This was important for our ancestors living in the savannah hundreds of thousands of years ago. It was very important that they jumped immediately at every opportunity to feed because there might not be a second one.

Being continuously connected can give you continuous instant gratification. Satisfying your need for novelty, for action, for pleasure, for being needed, for feeling important etc…

In 2009, a study by Forrester Research found that online shoppers expected pages to load in 2 seconds or fewer – and at 3 seconds, many abandon the site. Nowadays 2 seconds is even too long for many. How instant can instant be? To me these are suckers for instant gratification, or they are addicted (see below), or both. They are like a kid who continuously eats the marshmallows immediately even when you know that postponing gratification will bring bigger rewards later. Maybe you too should learn to postpone gratification or teach your inner savannah dweller to postpone gratification.

There is hope because our brain is not hard-wired for this. Our genes create a tendency, not a determination. As some of the kids in the experiment learned later in life, we can also learn to postpone gratification.

WE ARE WIRED FOR DEVELOPING HABITS

As I explained in the chapter about our reflex brain, a habit is behavior that has become automatic, involuntary through repetition. The way we (mis)handle our continuous connection has most often become a habit. As a result we do it without thinking and... it is difficult to change the way we do it.

It is not hard to imagine that easy habit formation was an important competitive advantage for the survival of the human race so that the genes governing this have survived until today. The advantage of easily developing habits is that they make our life much simpler. We easily develop routines so that in many situations we can act more economically, without thinking.

Of course, habit formation becomes a problem when it is not managed, when the habits are bad or outdated. Then we have to unlearn these habits, which can be very difficult for really old ones. Fortunately there is a scientific branch of psychology that has been studying this thoroughly for some 100 years. With modern techniques that allow us to study the brain while we are presented with all kinds of stimuli, this research has become very sophisticated. I will explain how you can unlearn habits and learn new ones in the chapter on unlearning habits in the third section.

WE ARE WIRED FOR FAST REACTION

The environment for our prehistoric ancestors was simple: have lunch or be lunch, be fast or be death. Basically, only two things were important: for the individual, survival and for humankind, procreation. The struggle for survival was paramount for 2 million years, until a hundred years ago when in developed countries, little by little, survival and procreation became guaranteed for almost everybody.

When our prehistoric ancestor was confronted with a saber-toothed tiger, a tendency to reflect would have been self-destructive. The ancestors with reflective genes did not have much chance of passing them on to the next generations; the ones with the quick, impulsive reaction genes did. After thousands of generations in this simple environment, the reactive genes were selected over the reflective genes.

Moreover, our pre-frontal cortex, the part that we need to reflect and control our fast impulsive reactions, is only fully developed for boys around 25 years of age. For our ancestors this wasn't too much of a disadvantage because long-term reflection wasn't needed and few lived that long anyway.

These primitive mechanisms still play a role in many ways[45]. Left unchecked and unbridled, our inner savannah dweller prevents us from being reflective especially in an environment that is continuously bombarding us with novel stimuli.

As I described in the first section, controlling your inner savannah dweller needs effort. Letting it ru(i)n your life is easy. Coaching young people to learn to focus and to reflect needs effort and commitment. Letting them follow their impulses to surf the ever-changing Internet is easy.

WE ARE WIRED FOR DANGER

Any development that made the human being more alert to danger enhanced his chances of survival and procreation. We therefore developed, as did all other animals, an acute awareness of potential danger. Signals of potential danger are much more powerful attention-grabbers than signals that everything is OK and humming along peacefully.

Therefore, every time we find an e-mail or message that is frightening, bad news, disturbing or warning us of imminent danger, it strengthens our desire to keep checking our e-mails. The more anxious a person you are, the more often you will check.

It does not matter that most of the e-mails are irrelevant or don't refer to any danger at all. On the contrary, we know from lots of research that when we find the danger-signaling e-mails only rarely, irregularly and unpredictably, it will reinforce this seeking behavior even more than if the signals come on a very regular basis. Then after a while our body goes into alarm-mode as soon as we start looking at our e-mails[46] (remember Pavlov), activating the typical physical stress reactions of our inner savannah ancestor: fight, freeze or flee. This chronic alertness also makes us more vulnerable to disease. (See the chapter on stress below.)

WE ARE WIRED FOR CURIOSITY

There is a link between our being wired for danger and being wired for novelty.

My own experience of finding it difficult to overcome my curiosity when I was always connected made me think of an experiment I learned about when I was a medical student. In this experiment, there were rats in a maze that, while looking in every nook and cranny, got an electric shock in particular places. From a purely behavioral conditioning point of view, this punishment should have stopped their explorative behavior. It didn't. Why? Because finding something new was rewarding even if the discovery was unpleasant. Finding where the safe and where the dangerous places are is vitally important for survival.

For our prehistoric ancestor in the savannah too it was of utmost importance to be quickly aware of small but significant changes in his environment. A shrub moving just a little differently from the grass could be a sign: a threat or prey, get lunch or become lunch. Discovering that one special moving branch even produces brain chemicals that excite us, that give us a kick and prepare us to swiftly attack or run away. Being very curious certainly had risks, but it seems that in the end it was an advantage and the curious ones were more likely to survive and procreate.

One of my coachees called finding a relevant e-mail in a mass of irrelevant ones "finding a rare gold nugget in a pile of shit". He obviously did not like doing his e-mails, but still had major difficulties not looking at his mails all the time and learning to batch-process them. Just finding the rare nuggets, especially when they came irregularly, kept feeding his curiosity.

Curiosity as an explorative reaction to novel objects[47] is old in evolutionary terms, it belongs to the reflex brain, and it does not demand great effort. It is important for survival. Moreover, finding something new gives instant gratification, even if the result of the exploration is irrelevant or negative. As I will explain further on, discovering something new enhances the output of the brain chemical that causes excitement.

Managers and other professionals wade through 100 or more e-mails a day, of which 50% to 95% are irrelevant (the grass in the savannah), but of course they do not want to miss the one relevant e-mail from their boss or a client (the moving branch). The kick of discovering one compels them to keep looking again and again, even if this very much disturbs the work at hand, leaves no room for reflection and undermines productivity.

WE ARE WIRED FOR EXCITEMENT AND... ADDICTION

Amongst the 1,152 managers and professionals of my survey, 84% check their e-mail first thing in the morning and at every free moment. In another survey[48], 1,000 people were subjected to a 24-hour challenge where they were cut off from their digital devices. One participant described the experience as 'my biggest nightmare', 53% of people felt 'upset' when deprived of an Internet connection and 40% felt 'lonely' when not able to go online.

The same survey revealed that younger people, who tend to be heavier users of social media and text messaging, found giving up technology the most difficult while older people (over 40s) generally coped more easily when cut off from digital connections.

Giving up their connection was considered by some to be as hard as quitting smoking or drinking, while one survey participant described it as "like having my hand chopped off".

Only a minority reacted positively to the prospect of being without an Internet connection, with 23% saying they would feel 'free'.

Another survey shows that over a quarter of adults and nearly half of all teens now own a smartphone.

37% of adults and 60% of teens are 'highly addicted' to them.

23% of adults and 34% of teens have used them during mealtimes.

22% of adults and 47% of teens use or answer their handset in the bathroom or toilet[49].

In a sample of 390 phones, 16% of phones had E. coli bacteria on them, which is found in feces. The researchers think it is a question of washing your hands after going to the bathroom[50]. But when I go to the toilets in a company or in a business school, I often hear people using their phones there too. When I ask the question in workshops, up to 70% of participants admit to sometimes using their phones on the toilet.

Looking at these numbers it is clear that many are addicted to always being connected. The reality is probably even worse because it is well known that most addicts tend to underestimate and deny their addiction. Maybe your hyperconnectivity too is not a bad habit but an addiction.

In politically correct lingo people don't use the word "addicted" any more. They call it "dependent" in order to distinguish from the "real" addicts, who of course are "not people like us", although the basic biological and psychological mechanisms are exactly the same.

All addictions are habits, but not all habits are addictions. When it is just a habit, even a bad habit, you do it without much thinking, but you can still choose to do it or not to do it, even if it is not always easy to undo a habit. You are in control of your habit. When you cannot do it, it might feel awkward at first, but you don't feel really bad.

You may have the habit of drinking one or two glasses of wine in the evening. Nothing wrong with that; on the contrary it is even good for your health (unless you are pregnant). If there happens to be no wine in the house, you don't feel bad, you skip it. When you drink six alcohol units every day and you really need them and start driving around to find some when you run out, then you probably are addicted.

When your habit became an addiction, you are no longer free to choose, you are no longer in control, although addicts will usually deny this against all proof to the contrary. Your habit controls you. You need to do it, even if it has a negative impact on more important aspects of your life. Doing it makes you feel better. Stopping makes you feel bad, even physically bad. These withdrawal symptoms confirm the addiction.

The brain chemistry changes, so you crave it. You keep doing it, with lots of excuses, even when you are convinced of the negative consequences.

If we define addiction as the compulsive and chronic seeking of a drug or behavior despite its negative consequences, then there is no doubt that many people are addicted – in the medical, psychiatric meaning of the word – to always being connected, to constantly surfing the web, to staying glued to Facebook or Twitter, to checking their e-mails all the time[51]. Many people are caught in a vicious cycle: the more often they check their e-mails, the more they become anxious about checking their e-mail, an anxiety that can only be alleviated by... checking their e-mail.

As with other addictions, this one too has a negative impact, not only on the addict, but also on his/her relations with others. It interferes with going out in the real world, growth, development, exploration and learning. The withdrawal symptoms users described in the research at the start of this sub-section are a strong indication that this has become a real addiction.

To simplify a complex issue, we can say that there are two general classes of addiction. The first is called the opioid-type addiction, with the opium smoker as its prototype, searching for a feeling of pleasant satisfaction. This is sometimes called the "liking", "hedonic" or "happiness" addiction. This feeling of satisfaction is caused by chemicals we produce in our brain that belong to the opium family. Of course we can get the same heavenly feeling by taking these chemicals directly.

The major difference between this type and the second type of addiction is that, here, once we are in a state of happiness the drug-searching activity stops. There is a pause in which we enjoy the state of well-being, feel satisfied and only start searching for it again when its effect wears off.

The second is called the dopamine-type, with the amphetamine or cocaine user as a prototype, seeking excitement. This is sometimes called the "wanting", "desire" or "motivational" addiction[52]. The addiction to hyperconnectivity is of the dopamine-type. In normal life this is provoked by thoughts or behavior that

increase our arousal, giving a feeling of excitement, a stimulating, activating kick. This does not result in satisfaction and so the search for excitement does not stop by itself, which may result in seeking this state continuously.

Both types are based on normal brain mechanisms that were very important for the survival of our ancestors in the savannah, and to some extent are still important for us today. The dopamine circuits or "I want circuits" stimulate a desire to look, fight or work hard for survival and procreation. They cause a feeling of excitement, eagerness and being focused on a goal. The opioid circuits or "I like circuits" and their feeling of satisfaction slow down or stop the excitement while the feeling of pleasure makes sure our inner savannah dweller relaxes and is motivated to start hunting again later[53].

Normally both systems interact in an interesting balance. "Wanting" and "Liking" are very complementary. The "wanting" system motivates us to search for the fulfillment of our needs and goals. When the need is fulfilled, when we have had a good meal, good sex or read an interesting book, the "liking" system kicks in and we feel satisfied. As a result we stop looking for more for a while, enjoying a passive happiness, but later the memory of the blissful state will start the wanting system again. This is how a runaway is prevented: the satisfaction prevents a never-ending wanting, and the wanting prevents us from staying in a passive satisfied state.

However, the balance is rigged in favor of the seeking, of

discovery, of activity. This was, and still is, an advantage for the survival of the human being.

The disadvantage is that when the system gets out of balance in our hectic jungle of the 21st century where food is everywhere and the source of excitement is beeping in your pocket, it will often be towards insatiable seeking and consumption. Some will even take stimulant medicine or drugs to increase and prolong the activity. For others the excitement becomes overwhelming and anxiety-provoking and they will look for a solution in tranquilizing medication or in the pleasant passive bliss of alcohol or marihuana.

Let me explain this in a little more detail to help you better understand why, once you are addicted to your hyperconnectivity, it can be so very difficult to disconnect. It is not an excuse not to learn to disconnect, but a plea to take it seriously, plan well and use all the tips, tricks and tools you can get to kick the habit.

Hungry rats that are in a cage where they can get a food pellet upon pushing a lever are normally interested in food and not in levers. They push the lever to get some food and once they are satiated they stop until they get hungry again.

But it is possible to set up the experiment in such a way that the rats get conditioned to link the excitement of getting food with pushing the lever. The seeking of the excitement then takes over and the rat is never satiated.

In the fifties, for their studies on learning in rats, researchers[54] put a little electrode in the rats' brain, where they received a tiny current when they pressed a lever. They found by accident that when a particular place in the brain was activated, the rats relentlessly kept pushing the lever while neglecting all other normal behavior, even feeding and sex. The researchers thought they had discovered "the pleasure center" or the "reward center"[55]. Now we know that it is not really a precisely located pleasure center, but a system of millions of cells, connecting to many parts of the brain.

Researchers also found that the chemical dopamine was transmitting the messages, which gave it the nickname "pleasure hormone", which turned out to be a misnomer; it's rather an "excitement hormone". The rats became addicted to pressing the lever because each time they got a little kick. Their desire for this excitement increased, but without satisfaction, and so they just kept on going without taking a break. They sometimes continued until exhaustion set in. By the way, amphetamines and many so-called party drugs belong to the same family as dopamine.

The behavior of many hyper-connected people scarily resembles the rats that push the lever faster and faster, even to the point of exhaustion.

> **What is the machine zone? It's a rhythm. It's a response to a fine-tuned feedback loop. It's a powerful space time distortion. You hit a button. Something happens. You hit it again. Something similar, but not exactly the same happens. Maybe you win, maybe you don't. Repeat. Repeat. Repeat. Repeat. Repeat. It's the pleasure of the repeat, the security of the loop.**
> ROMAN MARS RESPONDING TO THE WORK OF NATASHA SHÜLL[56]

These gamblers on a slot machine are like people losing themselves in frenetically jumping from one mail to the other, from one Facebook link to the other or like the online shoppers in the research I mentioned before who expect pages to load in 2 seconds or fewer.[57]

No wonder that with all these little unpredictable rewards on the phone in our pocket or at arm's length we become addicted to them and are no longer able to disconnect. Just checking your e-mails, messages or social media may become addictive in and of itself, independent of the results. Finding one interesting e-mail among 20 irrelevant ones is a discovery, a hit. The discovery stimulates the production of dopamine, which gives us a little kick, a reward for the seeking behavior, which in turn stimulates us to keep looking for more. Sometimes we find two interesting e-mails in a row, sometimes we have to delete 30 boring ones to get our reward. The result of our reward-seeking is totally unpredictable, and that makes it even more addictive.

Think about her research of Gregory Berns I mentioned before whaer fruit juice or water activated the excitement systems in the brain visibly more when it was given in an unpredictable way than in a predictable way[58]. The impact of the unpredictability of the reward was independent of the conscious preference of the subjects for water or juice. Moreover, his research supports the idea that *"wanting"* is not the same as *"liking"*. Wanting and liking showed up in different parts of the brain: the wanting in the powerful "pleasure systems", the liking in the more neutral ones. Hence you may crave or want a particular behavior, even if you consciously don't like it or like it less than something else.

As in rats, simply the anticipation of the source of pleasure already stimulates the pleasure centers. As a result we are motivated, if not driven, to search for the source of that good feeling[59]. The more unexpected, the more irregular the rewards, the more dopamine is produced, the higher the kick and the higher the risk of addiction. Once a person is caught up in this cycle, the Pavlov mechanisms I described at the start of this chapter kick in to make the addiction even worse because the cues that the reward is on its way (like the bell for the dogs) already cause excitement. This is why many micro-messages like Tweets, texts and Whatsapps are more rewarding than reading longer e-mails. This is one more reason why you should shut off all sounds and icons announcing e-mails or messages.

What makes this story even worse is that your brain gets used to and habituated to the dopamine kick. The brain tries to modulate the peaks to compensate for them. As a result, we need to keep increasing the intensity or duration of the stimulus to get the same level of arousal and pleasure. Once we are used to these high levels of dopamine, normal levels feel like a dip, the more because after a "high", the brain often adjusts, overcompensating to below normal levels. We then need a surplus of stimulus to just feel normal... and we are addicted.

WE ARE WIRED FOR CERTAINTY

If you do not govern your brain, it will seek certainty and try to avoid uncertainty. I know from my own experience how difficult it is not to look at your phone, knowing that messages are pouring in all the time. All those question marks dropping in your pocket two clicks away. Is it important or not? Is it from my boss? Is it from an important client? Is it urgent? What will happen if I do not respond immediately? Rationally we know that e-mail is very rarely really urgent, but you are irrationally drawn to it to resolve the uncertainty of "you never know".

Another aspect of this aversion of uncertainty is that it may keep us away from the hard work of reflecting. Reflection is taking in and processing information in a more or less deliberate way. An important aspect of this processing is deliberately creating uncertainty: looking at the same information from very different angles, asking "what if...?, questioning affirmations, questioning interpretations, challenging your own pet theories, opinions and so-called truths and common sense, considering them for what they really are: nothing but hypotheses. To move ahead, we need to recall an adage from the CIA: "Always confident, never certain". This uncertainty and the stress it causes may push us in two directions. One is to dig deeper and deeper and to increase our knowledge, without ever being certain that our conclusion is the truth. The other one is to reach a quick closure, in the comfort of "the truth", our own truth or the fallacy of a universal truth.

Our inner savannah dweller does not like all these questions and the uncertainty; without the intervention of his reflecting brain he will follow his reflex brain. In the simple, but constantly life-threatening environment of our prehistoric ancestors, "the truths" that they learned from their elders helped them to react very quickly and efficiently. There were not many truths, just a few to procreate and to survive. Doubting these truths risked slowing him down and becoming a death sentence. Two of our strongest cognitive biases (see Section 1) are the confirmation bias and selective perception: to avoid uncertainty we tend to select information that supports our conclusion and overlook information that goes against our idea. The only way to avoid these biases is to stop and think, accept the uncertainty of critical reflection or confront our idea with somebody else in a real conversation or a constructive conflict.

My hypothesis is that we often follow the certainty-seeking savannah dweller inside us and avoid reflection to avoid the stress created by uncertainty.

WE ARE WIRED FOR BELONGING

The human being is a herd animal. For our ancestors in the savannah it was impossible to survive without the mutual loyalty of a tribe, and thousands of years later, when settling, the tribe was the basis for interdependent specializing and sharing of labor.

Thousands of publications, especially in the field of stress research[60], show that belonging to a supportive social system is still very fundamental for health, well-being and life-satisfaction, and that outside interventions to increase belonging increase well-being[61]. It is possible that today with the disappearance or weakening of the classic tribes, people find and create their new virtual tribes in social media and invest lots of time in them not only to belong, but also to gain status. As we will see in the chapter about stress, when the communication is personal and mutually supportive this increases well-being, but when the connectedness is solitary and consumptive, it increase feelings of loneliness and decreases belonging and well-being[62]. In both cases it stimulates the need to always be connected.

WE ARE OFTEN DRIVEN BY RATHER NEUROTIC FEELINGS

One of the reasons why many people stay connected is wanting to help others. There is certainly nothing wrong with that. But when the wanting to help becomes a need to help, it may lead to so many tasks that it becomes impossible to really help.

When wanting becomes needing, a positive stimulant turns into a negative, if not problematic, drive. Other counterproductive drives for not disconnecting that I mentioned before are a need to feel important or to show importance, a need to be included and needed, a lack of self-confidence, being a pleaser, a lack of self-respect, an exaggerated wanting to be loved, a fear of taking responsibility, a lack of willpower etc... This is rather evident with social media users. To quote H. Sashittale and his colleagues who studied peoples' motivations to use social media: "Facebook users are primarily motivated by three desires: (1) to voyeuristically peer into others' lives, (2) to create a distinctive identity for themselves, and (3) to act on their inner narcissistic tendencies" [63].

> **When wanting becomes needing, a positive stimulant turns into a negative, if not problematic, drive.**

The continuous checking of social media is even worse than checking e-mail, because it causes an additional problem: it makes you feel lonely and miserable through a phenomenon called "status anxiety", basically a scientific euphemism for envy[64]. Given that everybody only posts the interesting and positive things about their lives, you get a feeling that your own life is less interesting than average. The satisfaction with your own life decreases. Indeed, the heavier a Facebook user you are, the fewer of your real friends you actually meet and the less time you spend with real people, and the more convinced you are that others are happier than you[65]. When you meet lots of real people in different situations, you get a much more realistic view of their lives.

Originally it was not really clear from the correlational studies what was the cause and what was the effect because it is also possible that people who are depressed and unhappy to begin with tend to use Facebook more heavily. In a prospective research study, however, it became clear that although the user's pre-existing feeling of loneliness had an influence on Facebook use, the Facebook use by itself increases unhappiness[66].

Hence, you feel lonely or unhappy, you look for excitement on Facebook, and once in a while you find something that gives you a little kick, which improves your feelings, but of course not enough to remedy the (mini)depression you are cultivating and so ... you keep looking for more. This causes a vicious cycle: the more you check Facebook, the more unsatisfied, unhappy and lonely you feel, the more you need the little kicks you find among the depressing ones, the more you check Facebook, the unhappier you feel...

2.12 CONCLUSION: DISCONNECT TO BECOME INTELLECTUALLY PRODUCTIVE

Nowadays we live in a much more complex, global, interconnected "flat world"[67] than in the past, a world where the simple and fast reflex brain, with its many shortcuts that helped the savannah dweller so well, no longer provides the best solutions. In the developed world and for many in the developing world, the short-term survival and procreation that needed these fast reactions are basically guaranteed for most people. In the 21st century, the long-term survival of you and/or your tribe (family/company) also depends on your capacity to understand and deal with a very complex environment. Our long-term survival depends very much on our ability to reflect, to think way ahead, to think wide and to think deep. In order to reflect, we need to go against the pull of our inner savannah dweller and resist the call for immediate reaction, disconnect from the bombardment of novel stimuli, focus on what is important and live with the tension created by the uncertainty caused by continuous questioning.

> ▶ **"There is no expedient to which man will not resort to avoid the real labor of thinking."**
> SIR JOSHUA REYNOLDS 1902

Even when we fully realize that always being connected is counterproductive and often even utterly stupid, it will be difficult to disconnect to reflect when we simply follow the impulses and instant gratification of the savannah dweller inside us. Therefore, without a conscious effort, being reactive will always win over from the harder work of thinking and reflecting.

But that is not new: in 1902 Sir Joshua Reynolds wrote: "There

DISCONNECT TO REFLECT
(OR TO HAVE A CONVERSATION!)

is no expedient to which man will not resort to avoid the real labor of thinking." Today, however, the expedient is within reach, in our pocket, 24/7.

Moreover, we should think about the next generation. Research on children and adolescents[68] increasingly shows that they run a higher risk of becoming addicted if they always stay connected and do not learn to control the pulling and pushing of their inner savannah dweller. A very hopeful sign is that many young people, once they get into higher education, realize the counter-productivity of always being connected and limit their connectedness to concentrate on important tasks, even if (or because?) they are privileged digital natives like students at Stanford[69]. If we want our children to become successful as brainworkers in the 21st century, it is the responsibility of parents and teachers to help, coach and structure their kids to tame their inner savannah dweller. Focusing, reflecting and disconnecting requires more effort. Therefore, letting them follow their impulses and giving in is the easiest solution for parents, but this increasingly looks like a very bad idea. Our children have to learn to use these fantastic technologies so that they become their master and not their slave. But that of course... is true for their parents and educators too.

Conclusion:

Disconnect to focus! Always being connected causes continuous interruptions, kills focus, slows you down, increases errors and compromises safety.

Disconnect to reflect: to think far, wide, deep and new! Always being connected makes us adhocrats in adhocracies.

Disconnect to be proactive, instead of being continuously reactive and primitive.

Disconnect to deflect the information diarrhea! Always being connected causes information overload.

Disconnect to be wise! Always being connected exhausts our willpower and self-control, it causes decision fatigue.

Disconnect and disengage to be creative! Always being connected blocks information processing and creativity.

Disconnect to reconnect! Always being connected often ruins real conversations, discussions and meetings.

Disconnect and disengage to think strategically! Always being connected ruins off-sites: disconnect and disengage to think strategically.

Let them disconnect! Expecting employees to always be connected is an enormously costly counterproductive blunder.

Stimulate them to disconnect, don't just let them, make them do it!

Get help to disconnect if your connectivity is a bad habit or an addiction.

3 BRAINCHAIN #2: MULTITASKING AND TASK-SWITCHING; THE SCATTERBRAINED HOMO INTERRUPTUS

In the chapter about the reflecting brain in Section 1, I summarized the most important facts, figures and issues about multitasking. Equipped with this information, you should now be fully aware that when you multitask you are ruining your intellectual performance. For most managers and other professionals the most startling realization is that our fantastic reflecting brain cannot multitask and that multitasking is like juggling many balls with one hand: it can't be done. What it does instead is task-switch, but bear in mind that this makes delivery time longer, slows you down a lot and ruins the quality of your brainwork: you are busy but not productive.

Two of the three myths about multitasking are especially relevant for the workplace. First of all, the super-talented "hypertaskers": don't be jealous of them because the more they multitask, the more they may be convinced that they are good at it but in fact the worse their actual intellectual efficiency.

Secondly, and this is particularly important if you are a manager, the advantage of digital natives in the workplace: this is an urban myth because most of them are not ICT-savvy at all. It's true that some of these young people grow out of it, but for many young adults a distracting hyper-connected world is just normal. It is the world they have known since childhood, and if their parents and teachers didn't teach them how to handle their ICT gadgets well, they perform below their innate competencies, intellectually, emotionally and socially; in other words, they use their ICT as distracting gadgets to gobble up irrelevant information rather than as excellent tools to process and produce information.

3.1 MULTITASKING AND HYPERTASKING, THE NEW INEFFICIENT NORM

The human body is not made for flying. So it is normal, except for a few very disturbed psychiatric patients, that nobody tries. Our reflecting brain is not made for multitasking. So it is normal, except for a few very disturbed psychiatric patients, that nobody tries. Yes? Strangely enough, as we learn by just looking around us, the opposite is true.

Trying to multitask is like denying gravity and yet multitasking has become the norm, with people failing to realize how their intellectual productivity, efficiency, effectiveness, creativity and safety crash as a result. Since the consequences of denying that you can't multitask are not as immediate or painful as denying gravity, then until you started reading this book you could claim ignorance. Ignorance, however, is no longer an excuse. As I warned you at the very beginning, this book may seriously harm your peace of mind!

Research supports these everyday observations that multitasking has become the crazy new norm for most brainworkers. Here are just two examples. Using video analysis and automatic monitoring Victoria Belotti and her team found that the median of open tasks of the professionals she studied was 65! Meanwhile, Gloria Mark at the University of California found that on average employees spent 11 minutes on a project before being interrupted. These 11 minutes are fragmented into three-minute tasks. After

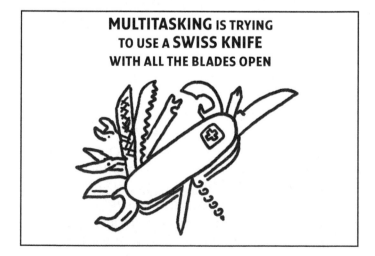

MULTITASKING IS TRYING TO USE A SWISS KNIFE WITH ALL THE BLADES OPEN

distraction, it takes 25 minutes to return to the original task because one distraction has the tendency to lead to another. In 40% of situations the brainworker doesn't even return to the original task[70].

This is no longer multitasking, task-switching or hypertasking, it has become what I call Brainworkers Attention Hyperactivity Disorder (BAHD) and its special case of Managers Attention Hyperactivity Disorder (MAHD). Both are elements of Corporate Brain Disorder[71].

The fact that adolescents experiment with multitasking, as they do with so many other things, is perfectly normal. What is incomprehensible is that professionals too are trying all the time to do two tasks at the same time or switching between many tasks sequentially. To make matters worse, the different tasks are most often not related to different aspects of the same task but to totally different tasks or goals, which further decreases efficiency. This would be fine if they were routine tasks, but most often the tasks require focussed attention. What's more, the tasks are cut up into smaller and smaller pieces, resulting in professionals switching back and forth between tasks ever more frequently and ever faster. This really isn't a good idea because, as we know, the more switches, the greater the loss in productivity. To top it all off, they often even forget to return to an unfinished task.

▶ **Chase two rabbits and catch none.**
RUSSIAN PROVERB

Let me shout again, loud and clear, what I explained in the first section: **THE REFLECTING BRAIN CANNOT MULTITASK!** Period. It is worst when you are forced to multitask, like in open offices, but even when you choose to do it, it is still very bad[72]. Every time you connect with your screen, you disconnect from what you are doing, from the meeting, from a conversation, from more important work, from thorough reading, from thinking, from playing with your kid... Every switch, every hop costs you dearly. The only exception is a situation where your reflecting brain and your reflex brain collaborate, the reflex brain taking over the routine tasks and freeing up your reflecting brain to think.

When you try to multitask it has a tremendous negative impact on your intellectual productivity. Let me summarize the conclusions from Section 1.

- Every single task takes longer as a result of the interruptions caused by the other tasks.
- Every task takes much more time and the process becomes slower because at each switch the slate of your working memory has to be cleaned and prepared for the next task, parking the information of the first task in your temporary memory and inhibiting the first task from interfering with the second.
- It significantly decreases the quality of your work.
- It makes you drop information, and lots of information is never stored because of the continuous context-switching the brain has to do and the juggling between working memory, temporary memory and long-term memory.
- It makes you lose concentration, or if you try to stay concentrated, it costs much more energy.
- It causes many more stupid mistakes that often need more time to correct than doing it right first time. Hence, you lose even more time.
- It kills your creativity.
- It causes unsafe behavior on the shop floor as well as at home.
- It makes the vitally important thorough reading and real conversations impossible.
- In the presence of others, it results in bad listening and communication and is often just plain rude.
- It causes more stress ...

3.2 MULTITASKING AT WORK CAN BE DANGEROUS

When 40% of office workers fail to return to their original task after doing other things in between, this may cause delays and cost money, but it is not dangerous. When this behavior happens on the shop floor in a chemical plant, it can have dramatic consequences. When nurses and doctors are multitasking, it will cost lives.

One of my client companies in industry had major problems at a brand new plant they had built. They were very proud of the plant not only because of the efficient logical layout, which they were certain would result in higher productivity, but also because they tried to make it as pleasant as possible for the operators so that it would be less boring than before. They were therefore surprised when, months later, long after what they considered a normal learning phase, there were still too many errors being made and an unacceptable number of accidents and near-accidents. The operators complained about having more stress instead of less. By visiting this pleasant, even beautiful, plant, it was clear that the work of the operators had been set up to make their routine jobs more interesting. What the designers of the work-process had not paid enough attention to though was that as soon as anything happened that was not routine, the operators were no longer working sequentially but were forced to multitask. Moreover, in the warehouse, for example, the forklift drivers often got their instructions from a computer screen where they also had to input information about the dispatching. Particularly when the drivers were under time pressure, they did this while driving, increasing the risk of an accident by 32 times! (See the chapter later on about being on the phone while driving.)

ANOTHER REAL-LIFE EXAMPLE:
A chemical plant was saved from a major disaster because on one particular day there were fewer traffic jams than usual. As a result a plant operator arrived earlier than normal, smelled something strange, went looking for the cause and found that a heating element next to a high-pressure pipe made from a synthetic material had not been turned off the night before. The pipe containing a highly toxic product was melting. Had he arrived 20 minutes later, a major catastrophe could have happened.

I was supposed to give a workshop about stress for the company's top managers that morning, but instead they used part of the time for an urgent debriefing of the near-accident. It was interesting for me as an outsider to see how quickly and creatively they invented all kinds of technical solutions to prevent this from happening again. What they paid little attention to was the human factor: How come a very experienced operator forgot to shut off this part of the chain while shutting down the whole thing before leaving? With a little probing I *found out that the operator was doing work that in the old plant had been done by two people. The operators clearly preferred the new plant, but what had not been taken into account was that, when a problem occurred that they could not resolve by themselves, they had to ask a colleague on another line for help. When that happened, the colleague had to start task-switching, keeping an eye on his own line, while helping his buddy. Returning to his own line, where he was shutting down in a well-defined order, he skipped one step: it was the price he paid for context-switching.*

No wonder safety managers and plant managers in my audiences are always most impressed with this research and became my most enthusiastic fans. These managers are not only very close to the shop floor, very practical and efficiency-minded but they are in general obsessed about safety. They immediately grasp the practical consequences of multitasking and many start projects to eliminate or decrease multitasking in parts of their organisation. Once they look at work through the lens of multitasking, they always find work situations that can be improved. The best researched dangerous multitasking is undoubtedly using the phone while driving. It is so shocking that I have decided to dedicate a chapter to it. I hope this research will not only make you stop using your phone while driving, but also make you think about the danger of using phones and similar tools on the shop floor.

There is low-hanging fruit for companies who eliminate multitasking for the drivers of their trucks. In naturalistic research where cameras and sensors were installed in commercial vehicles used by 203 drivers over a distance of 3 million miles we learn that there were 4,452 safety critical events. For 80% of them, the driver being distracted was a potential contributing factor. The most dangerous tasks are those that require manual manipulation and visual attention away from the road ahead. Normally a driver glances away from the road ahead for checking mirrors etc. for about 1 second. Looking away for 1.5 seconds turns out to be a high risk and looking away for over 2 seconds the highest risk for an accident. So the use of in-vehicle devices like phones, walkie-talkies, touch screens and dispatching devices should not be used while driving; drivers should not read, write or look at maps while driving. The authors of this study note that these activities are part of the driver's job, but they should not be performed while driving[73]. However, the drivers are too often put under so much time pressure, with their bonuses and lots more linked to their speed, that they do it anyway.

What most people do not realize is that in the developed world, our factories are much safer than our home environment. The most dangerous and literally life-threatening situations happen in our private time when we are hyper-connected, multitasking and under stress. The most tragic example is one I have already referred to, that of very caring, young, hyper-connected, multitasking parents who sometimes forget their baby in the car on a hot parking lot.

The most important in terms of the cost of lives and disabilities is one we create ourselves when we use our phones while driving. From my own workshops and research I learned that 85% of people use their phone while driving. Sales people often use it continuously, from the moment they start driving until they stop. Research by others confirms that about 80% of drivers phone while driving and that 50% are serial, continuous users. These continuous callers use a hands-free phone[74]. They don't know that while on the mobile phone, even if you use a hands-free device, you increase the risk of having an accident up to EIGHT times[75]. When you text while driving, you increase the risk of having an accident ... TWENTY-THREE times. (More on this in the chapter about using the phone while driving.)

3.3 RESEARCH IN REAL LIFE CONFIRMS THE LAB RESULTS

One never knows if real life can be compared with research, which is most often done with students in the laboratory. In the case of multitasking, however, real-life research absolutely confirms the conclusions from the lab research.

In Milan, for example, researchers studied all 58,280 cases from 31 judges filed over a five-year period. To avoid corruption, all the cases were randomly assigned. From a research point of view this was a dream case: a large number of cases, every judge gets the same number of cases, a long duration and random assignment.

The conclusion was very clear: Judges who only open a new case once the previous one is finished, take much less time per case, have a much smaller backlog, have the same number of hearings and perform higher-quality work (fewer cases were appealed) than those who multitask[76].

Elsewhere, researchers found that engineers who have more than two concurrent projects to run are less able to add value. Having two projects instead of one increases the value added, probably because it is good to escape to another task when the first one gets boring or when you are temporarily stuck. From three tasks on though, it goes downhill very fast. If the tasks need to be performed efficiently, e.g. with high accuracy, then quality and added value drop quickly if you have more than two tasks[77]. There is a caveat though: If the tasks are boring and things such as accuracy are not important, having many projects to juggle keeps the interest high and increases productivity.

The risk of having an accident when you are on the phone while driving increases by about four times in simulators in the lab. In real life, however, the risk turns out to be eight times higher (see further on in this section).

3.4 AIM TO BE A RIGHT-TASKER, MOVING CLOSER TO SINGLE TASKING

It really is naive to think we can change the way our brain works. It took us some 600 million years to develop the brain we now have. Do you really think we could change that in 30 years, even taking into account the fact that our brain has much more plasticity than we ever thought? Hence we need to adapt the use of our ICT to the strengths and weaknesses of our brain.

On average, 30 minutes of uninterrupted work on a task is three times more efficient than three times 10 minutes. Uninterrupted work is four times more efficient if the tasks are complex or if the tasks belong to very different domains like work and home. Thirty minutes of uninterrupted work is 10 times more efficient than 10 stints of 3 minutes at it, alternating it with other tasks. The solution is very simple: to become more efficient, to become more intellectually productive, radically and ruthlessly reduce the number of switches.

Even if I have really convinced you that multitasking is just awful for your intellectual performance and productivity, as professionals and certainly managers you cannot totally avoid multitasking. Some multitasking is even a critical part of your job. You are in a very important meeting with a colleague going in-depth into the problem of queues and delays building up in production. One of your direct reports jumps in and needs an immediate decision to resolve an unexpected bottleneck caused by a supplier that has stopped a critical project. What do you do? You have to decide on the spot what has the highest priority. Hence, you interrupt the meeting, you call your boss because you need his approval to deviate from a key agreement, give your instructions... and you go back to the original conversation. The original meeting will have suffered, but that's unavoidable in real life. You need to be flexible. In that same real life, however, it is very obvious that a whole lot of avoidable, counterproductive, even stupid connectivity and multitasking can be avoided with better priorities, better planning and above all more focus and discipline.

> **If right-tasking is like swimming, then multitasking is like treading water; you might stay afloat but it doesn't get you anywhere.**

Your goal is not to become a total single-tasker, but to become a right-tasker, getting as close as realistically possible to single-tasking, and that is always closer than you think. If right-tasking is like swimming, then multitasking is like treading water; you might stay afloat but it doesn't get you anywhere.

Multitask when the tasks are routine and you need more arousal or when it is really necessary, unavoidable and still efficient and if you can afford the price you pay in lost time, lower quality, quantity and safety.

Single-task when the tasks are complex and when you cannot afford lower levels of quality, accuracy, safety, innovation and use of memory.

To be able to right-task there are two necessary conditions: disconnect and batch-process. (You will find more ideas and inspiring examples in Section 3.)

4 BRAINCHAIN #3: A CONTINUOUS LOW LEVEL OF STRESS RUINS THE VERY BEST OF YOUR REFLECTING BRAIN

4.1 NEGATIVE STRESS MAKES SMART PEOPLE BEHAVE STUPID

Stress is one of the most, if not the most, thoroughly researched areas of human functioning. Literally thousands of scientific articles are published every year on stress, an area studied by a great many scientific fields not least because it has to do with biology, psychology and the context in which one is living.

Stress is one of my key areas of expertise; I started doing research on stress in 1976 and later began consulting, during which time I became very interested in the stress caused by always being connected and multitasking. In the Netherlands and Belgium my book "Stress: Friend and Foe" [78] became a bestseller in its category and has remained a long-seller ever since, being reprinted every year and updated every four years. In the book you can find everything you ever wanted to know about stress but never dared to ask.

Negative stress is bad for your intellectual productivity. You do not need lots of research to prove this; you experience it yourself regularly. Just think for a moment: "What kind of intellectual work becomes very difficult or impossible under too much stress, or under stress that has been going on for too long?" When I ask this question in my workshops and lectures, people answer that it ruins their concentration, associative thinking and creativity, analytical thinking and synthesis, abstract thinking, rational thinking, seeing the big picture...

They are right. It is the very best of our reflecting brain that is undermined first and foremost, the very work that computers cannot do, work that requires insight and knowledge. Our reflex brain on the other hand is not easily affected by stress. This was very good for our ancestors in the savannah because this stress-resistant, little power-consuming reflex brain could help them to survive in situations even when they were exhausted.

On the other hand, this also means that in stressful situations, when our reflecting brain is tired, our reflex brain can easily take over. As a result, when we're tired or at the end of the day, we lose sight of our goals and priorities and only react to the here and now. There is also a risk that we will react with very primitive aggression-anxiety or fight-flight reactions in situations where a less stressed reflecting brain would have found better, more intelligent and nuanced strategies to deal with the situation. We also risk making less ethical decisions.

Negative stress can be way too much stress or stress that lasts way too long, even if it is at a rather low level. Under negative stress we make wrong decisions, errors and mistakes. Not the kind of interesting errors we can learn from, not the trial and error kind of mistakes that help us to progress. We make stupid, primitive mistakes we can't learn anything from except that our stress-balance is out of kilter. Negative stress is one of the most important reasons why smart people do stupid and sometimes dangerous things.

▶ **Negative stress makes smart people behave stupid.**

This generates important risks for managers and other brain-workers who have to make decisions under high pressure. Under negative stress their very stress-resistant reflex brain takes over from the stress-sensitive reflecting brain and they make decisions based on primitive heuristics, old learned habits which they euphemistically call "gut feelings", but which are too often just bets. Therefore under high pressure, more than ever and more than anything else, you need to disconnect to have a break and to give your reflecting and archiving brains a chance and to have real conversations with a good team. Of course, under high stress, we tend to do the opposite, taking less time for reflection instead of more, unless we have wise and less stressed friends, family and team members who help us or force us to take time for reflection and relaxation.

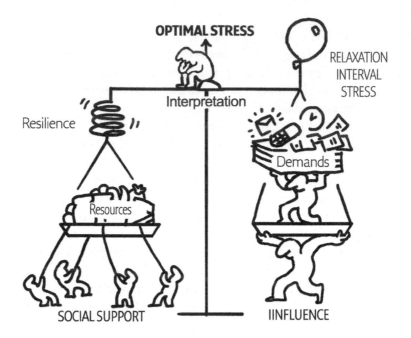

OPTIMAL STRESS

Interpretation

Resilience

RELAXATION
INTERVAL
STRESS

Demands

Resources

SOCIAL SUPPORT

IINFLUENCE

4.2 WHAT IS STRESS AND HOW TO MAINTAIN YOUR STRESS-BALANCE

YOUR STRESS-BALANCE

There are quite a few things you can do to maintain your stress-balance. I explain them in detail in my book "Stress: Friend and Foe" and have included a summary in the figure below. First of all, here's a quick run through the fundamentals in seven questions that you should ask yourself regularly and especially if you become aware of early warning signals.

1 Are the demands on me reasonable? Think about the demands/performance graph below. Where am I situated on this graph most of the time, in the positive stress zone above the dividing line, or below? Am I assertive enough to say "no", "no, unless..." or "yes if..." if the demands exceed my resources and time?

2 Do I have the resources needed to realize these demands? Am I assertive enough to claim the ones I need? Given that I am my own most important resource, do I take good care of myself? Do I invest in the development of my skills? Do I pay

sufficient attention to factors influencing my resilience, like the things I eat, my eating and drinking habits, my sleep, my general fitness etc...?

3 Given that having good social support is one of the most important positive influences on my stress-balance, do I invest sufficiently in my social relations, in my social support system, at home in the first place, but at work too especially in times of high stress? Or do I do the opposite by neglecting them when under pressure, at exactly the time where I need them more?

4 Feeling in control of my life has a big impact on my resilience. Do I feel like I have enough influence on my work and the rest of my life?

5 Since it is not only the level of stress, but even more the duration of the stress that influences my balance, do I make enough time for relaxation and recuperation? Is the quantity and quality of my recuperation (also sleep) good enough to compensate for the weight of the demands?

6 Since my stress-balance is a subjective one, how do my philosophy of life, my basic attitudes and my way of appraising challenges influence my balance?

7 Do I know and pay sufficient attention to my early warning signals and do I take them seriously?

THE RELATIONSHIP BETWEEN DEMANDS, PERFORMANCE AND STRESS

The human being is a fantastic stress machine, not only physically but also intellectually, psychologically and socially. Without this, the human race would have been wiped out hundreds of thousands of years ago. Think about it: can you give one example of something very important you achieved in your life without stress? No, because we need a fair dose of stress to function at our best, intellectually, emotionally, socially and physically. Therefore stress can be positive and negative, healthy and unhealthy, kick-stress and shit-stress, stimulating and paralyzing, exciting and deadly.

The best metaphor to describe what stress really is is a bow. The stress in a bow gives an arrow the energy needed to reach the target! Without any tension in the bow, the arrow won't go anywhere at all. When the bow is drawn too hard, too often, when it's "over-strained", then it loses its resilience. This also happens if the bow is not untied, "relaxed" after every single use! For people too, an important characteristic is that we are built for brief stress not for chronic stress, not for stress without relaxation, without time for recuperation: we too have to untie our metaphorical bow string after every (preferably short) period of stress.

Too many as well as too few demands can result in negative stress. The connections between, on the one hand, the demands, and on the other the results and efficiency of your actions or your well-being and your health is illustrated in the figure below. You perform at maximum efficiency under an optimal level of demands that does not last too long. If too little is required of you, your performance risks being below your capacities and you also usually feel less well. You might then perform worse than somebody who is less able, but for whom the same demands are still challenging. If more is required from you, and the demands are equal to your capacities, your performance improves and you find pleasure in your work. This positive feeling further increases as the demands increase, until the demands become a challenge. But even being stretched is still very healthy under one crucial condition: you make time for sufficiently long and frequent periods of relaxation and recuperation. If there is enough time for recuperation, challenges will even increase your resilience.

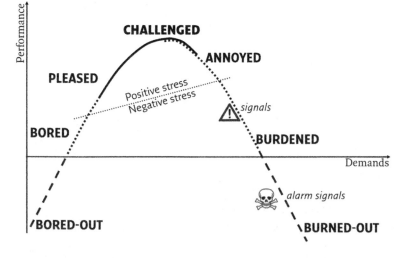

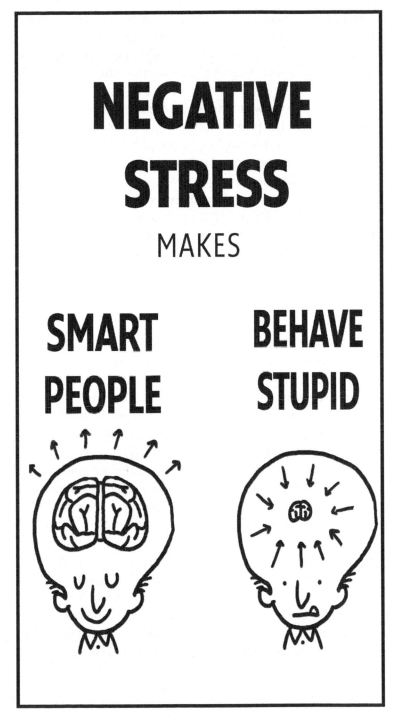

If the demands increase even further or last even longer without time for recuperation, your performance begins to drop and continues to do so as long as the demands last or keep on mounting! Finally the demands may threaten your psychic and physical health.

It is simple to know at what point of the efficiency curve you function. Before the peak you experience an additional assignment as a stimulus, as a challenge or simply as a pleasure. Beyond the peak even a small additional demand can cause a substantial loss of efficiency or pleasure.

If the stress becomes really negative, your body and mind will give you warning signals. These signals are important. You should know your own warning signals very well and take them as a serious call for action. If you neglect them they will turn into alarm signals. If you neglect the alarm signals, you will prematurely end up in the only place on earth where there isn't any more stress for you: a coffin or an urn.

STRESS IS IN THE EYE OF THE BEHOLDER

Research into human stress clearly shows there is usually no direct connection between a stress-provoking situation and a stress response. Between the stress situation and the stress responses there is a filter, a transformer: the way you appraise the situation. Different people can judge one and the same stress situation as irrelevant, a threat, a challenge, a danger, aggression or pleasure. Consequently, their response to it will be different: indifference, fear, anxiety, fleeing, fighting, depression, apathy, joy etc. The way your body reacts and how you behave are very much influenced by the way you appraise the situation.

You misinterpret many of these responses and especially your emotions as spontaneous and difficult to influence. In fact they are not provoked by the objective situation, but by your thoughts about it, and in principle you can influence these. It is not the events themselves but most often your thoughts about them that provoke the stress responses, which if badly managed will lower your intellectual productivity and may increase the likelihood of health problems.

> **"If men define situations as real,**
> **they are real in their consequences."**
> WILLIAM ISAAC THOMAS. SOCIOLOGIST (1863-1947)

The results of my informal surveys in groups show that when asked the question "What is stress?" 80% to 100% of the managers and executives think of (very) annoying, unpleasant experiences. These negative ideas about stress are 50% wrong. Why is this so important? Well, if you think stress is nothing but negative, then difficult situations cause more negative stress more often. Shakespeare wrote: "There is nothing either good or bad, but thinking makes it so". That is true for stress too. Most of what you consider as stressful situations are neither good nor bad in themselves, your thinking makes them so.

Such a one-sided negative vision of stress is not correct. Stress can be very positive, a real motor for success. Stress stimulates and helps you to be creative and to excel in your performance. Regular short exposures to stress at manageable levels, in the right (supportive!) context, make you more stress- and disease-resistant and keep your brain and body in top condition. People who lack a healthy dose of stress not only perform less well but also get sick more often and live shorter lives. The human organism is perfectly made to deal with stress, even with a high dose of stress... as long as the stress does not last too long.

Now that you have this information I can give you a definition of stress: stress is what happens to you as soon as you think that your stress-balance is out of balance. In other words: we experience negative stress when there is no longer a balance between what we *think we must* do and what we *think we can* do about it.

> **Negative stress is a lack of balance between what**
> **you think you must do and what you think you can do,**
> **unless your reflex brain reacts faster than you think.**

What's particularly important to note in the context of this book is that our interpretation of a stress situation can mislead us in two ways. Firstly, we can cheat ourselves by seeing neutral events as potentially harmful. For example, we may experience feedback from a colleague as an insult or as a threat, while the colleague

STRESS IS IN THE MIND OF THE BEHOLDER

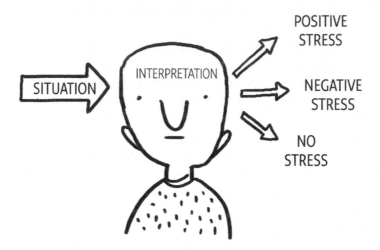

was actually trying to be helpful. Or we react to an unexpected maneuver by another driver as a personal act of aggression, while it might have been a distracted driver who just heard he lost his job. You may also look back at your own behavior, considering it to have been utterly and depressingly stupid, while in fact, objectively speaking, it wasn't your fault at all etc...etc...

Secondly, our interpretation can blindfold us to the negative or even dangerous aspects of a situation or to other people's and our own behavior. For example a smoker who ignores the loud stress-signals of his coughing and struggling for breath with a "my chain-smoking grandfather lived to the age of 86". Or a person who drinks too much and drives his car anyway dismisses the tipsy feeling with a "I've never had an accident". Or a hyper-connected multitasker who never disconnects because she thinks... (fill in your own standard excuse).

As I will explain in the next paragraph, even if you are not consciously aware of it, always being connected creates a continuous state of emergency for your brain and your body. It's most likely that there were stress-signals when you started doing this, just like I experienced during the first few days when I was always connected to my new smartphone. But then you consciously overrode these signals with all kinds of reasons as to why you needed to always be connected. This is like people when they smoke their first cigarettes. The smoking causes clear stress signals all over the body such as in the throat, the lungs, dizziness, palpitations etc.... but they override these because as insecure adolescents they want to conform, and in the end they become addicted and the signals disappear while the cigarettes keep ruining their body. Similarly, even if you feel like you have adapted to always being connected, it is still ruining your intellectual performance.

Of course, as I explained in Section 1, your reflex brain sometimes takes the lead and mobilizes your whole stress system to fight or flee so fast that you can only appraise and rationalize your reaction after the fact. These primitive unconscious reflex stress-reactions were life-saving for our ancestors in the savannah, but in today's environment they lead to behavior that afterwards makes you sometimes despairingly think "Why oh why did I behave like that?".

4.3 HOW THE UNRELENTING LITTLE HASSLES OF BEING CONNECTED ALL THE TIME BECOME HARMFUL

To understand what always being connected does to our health and our intellectual performance, another important aspect of stress to grasp is that chronic hassles, even at a low level, can be as unhealthy as a very stressful big event.

Life events, big and small, have a clear effect on your health. This was very well demonstrated by the researchers Holmes and Rahe a long time ago as well as by many researchers since. Holmes and Rahe gave thousands of healthy recruits a questionnaire where they had to list all kinds of life events they had recently experienced. The events varied from very serious ones like the death of a loved one, divorce and marital problems, via dismissal and reorganizations at work, pregnancy, growth of the family and children leaving home, to relatively minor events like parties, holidays and even receiving a traffic ticket. Months later the researchers checked the medical data of these people and made two important discoveries that have been supported by other research many times. Firstly, that the more events, the higher the risk of becoming ill, and secondly that an accumulation of smaller, relatively unimportant stressors together can have the same negative effect as one very serious stressor[79]. In short, stress is additive.

In most jobs we have to deal all the time with large and small hassles and interruptions. That's just part of the job. When you are hyper-connected, however, glued to your mailbox, you are continuously bombarded with hassles, challenges and problems of all kinds, one on top of the other. Again, they are not much of a stress issue by themselves, but the problem is that, if you are hyper-connected they are additive and it becomes unrelenting chronic stress. It is this chronicity that our brain and the rest of our body cannot deal with.

Let's first take a look at how we react in acute stress situations. Essentially, our reaction is very much like our ancestors' in the savannah who, when confronted with a saber-toothed tiger, had three options: fight and bring the beef home, run away as fast as possible and climb up a tree to save themselves, or freeze.

In the first two situations, in a fraction of a second our whole body is mobilized for an explosion of action and our reflecting brain is put on hold so as not to slow down our reactions. If overwhelmed by the danger, however, if there is no chance to win a fight or to get away faster than the attacker, our inner ancestor freezes, plays death, so that the attacker does not see him or loses interest. This immobility is sometimes called "tonic immobility" because the body is activated and paralyzed at the same time; it actively blocks the strong tendencies to fight or to flee that may be too dangerous for the situation. The blocking of the nervous system causes a degree of anesthesia that makes the ancestor inside us less aware of pain and afterwards he remembers little of what exactly happened in the frozen state. However, when a sudden escape is possible, he can do this with a sudden explosion of energy thanks to the reflex brain that is the last to be knocked out or exhausted.

These reactions were very helpful, even life-saving for our ancestors in the savannah, but can cause problems when we are dealing with the threats of the 21st century with no room to fight or flee, for example when a boss gives totally unjust negative feedback in an insulting way. Internally our savannah ancestor rages, but externally you have to stay politely assertive, but that is not what those hormones are made for. You may also freeze, overwhelmed, unable to react and afterwards not even exactly remember what happened and sometimes explode at an accidental innocent victim like a fellow driver on the road, your partner, your kids or your dog. Moreover, as I explained before, under high stress our reflecting brain is inhibited to the benefit of our reflex brain.

When I got my first smartphone, I realized that I was always more or less consciously paying attention to it and that as a result being connected all the time caused a low but continuous level of stress. Being a stress expert this immediately triggered a warning signal because low levels of stress are as unhealthy as too high levels of stress if they become chronic, with insufficient breaks for recuperation (more about this in my book "Stress: Friend and Foe"[80]).

After an acute high level of stress we recuperate from the acute stress and relax and all the stress chemicals we produced in our brain and body are neutralized to a normal level and a healthy balance is restored. The same chemicals, however, that are so valuable and useful in an acute situation become harmful and toxic when they are elevated chronically, resulting in harmful reactions like chronic high blood pressure and muscle tension, faster heart rate, higher blood clotting level...and a suppressed immune system.

Basically, the fantastic human stress machine is not made for dealing with chronic stress. Healthy stress is interval stress. The intervals should be sufficiently long and frequent to neutralize the stress hormones, to restore the balance and to relax and recuperate. Therefore we need regular breaks, and the higher the stress the more and longer breaks we need. In my whole career I have never coached or treated a professional suffering from burn-out or on the verge of it, who regularly relaxed and recuperated, every day, every week, every month. The challenge is that in times of stress, exactly when we need these breaks more than ever, we tend to have fewer, we sleep shorter, we skip breakfast with a "No darling, I don't have time" and run off to the office, where we also miss lunch and other breaks to keep working, and then we return home where we keep working too late at night.

▶ **Healthy stress is interval stress.**

Being connected all the time causes this kind of chronic low-level stress. When researchers disconnected office workers for five days from their e-mail, their heart rate became normal. Connected to their e-mail it showed signs of being on constant alert, constant stress[81]. Our body goes into stress-mode as soon as we start looking at our e-mails. You may be conscious of this stress or not, but in the background this continuous connection causes a continuous state of emergency, which activates the typical physical stress-reactions of our inner savannah ancestor. These physical reactions become harmful when they are chronically activated, especially with a lack of regular breaks for relaxation and recuperation. People can overcome the negative impact of continuous interruptions with a surplus of effort. Initially they can even maintain the quality of their work, but the price they pay is more stress and frustration[82]. To make matters worse, people who keep doing work-related e-mails all the time have more difficulties mentally disconnecting from work, hence the mental stress never really stops. Always being connected undermines your recovery, especially if you experience a high level of work-home interference[83]. In your stress-balance, regular time for recovery is as important as the stress itself.

▶ **Disconnecting and letting your mind wander during a boring episode of a meeting is much better for your brain and the meeting than connecting and guzzling more data.**

Not only do hyper-connected people eliminate sufficiently long breaks to recuperate, they even do away with the many micro brain-breaks that other people have. They stay glued to their phones in the elevator, while getting a cup of coffee, during lunch, on the toilet, walking to the parking lot, waiting for people to arrive for a meeting, a boring moment in a meeting, unwinding with a little small talk after a meeting, playing with the kids. Don't fill your micro-breaks! Relax! As I explained in the first section, these breaks, mini-breaks and micro-breaks are important for your brain to have a chance to store and manipulate all the information it receives. These breaks are also important to recuperate from the decision-fatigue described in BrainChain #1.

Therefore, taking regular breaks is not only very important for your reflecting brain and your archiving brain, it is as important for the rest of your body. Even if the stress is high it will remain healthy if you take enough time for relaxation and recuperation. With enough time for recuperation your stress-balance will not only stay in balance, but the stress will even improve your resilience.

So now you have yet another reason to disconnect: to recuperate and relax. Disconnecting is not only very important for your reflecting brain and archiving brains to perform at their best, but also to make room for relaxation and recuperation. This knowledge also supports my pleas in the third section for batch-processing e-mails and chores. See the whole batch as one challenge to process in one hour, and take a five-minute break halfway through away from any screen. Stop at the time you decided on beforehand and take a really nice break at the end, of course unconnected.

4.4 THE LOCAL STRESS OF ALWAYS BEING CONNECTED

MOST PROFESSIONALS THINK ABOUT ERGONOMICS WHEN IT'S TOO LATE

Although the local body-stress caused by always being connected is not really a BrainChain by itself, the resulting nuisances can hinder you and sometimes even stop you from doing your brain-work efficiently. The local stress may lead to irritated eyes because of less blinking, tense muscles, neck and back ache, and in the end Repetitive Strain Injuries (RSI). Moreover, the local strain can lead to more general stress.

The inconveniences and disorders I describe in this chapter are not the result of the use of computers, laptops, tablets and phones. They are the result of an uninterrupted, chronic, un-ergonomic, wrong use of them. The prevention and the cure is: regularly disconnect from your screens! Disconnect to take enough breaks to let the poor locally overstressed body parts recuperate. For your joints, tendons and muscles too, the bottom line is: healthy stress is interval stress.

The local stress of always being connected: on my back, a pain in the neck, a headache, no sight for sore eyes and all thumbs

There are other stress factors that can make things worse, like working in a noisy office, which immobilizes office workers even more. This is illustrated well in a study of 40 office workers that I use in my free booklet on open offices, "The Fifth BrainChain". Not only did the noise of the open office exhaust these workers' willpower so that they gave up solving a puzzle more quickly after the experience, but they also made fewer ergonomic, postural adjustments while working, increasing the local chronic strain on their body[84].

There is a very clear relationship between the duration of daily computer use and musculoskeletal symptoms. Pain of any severity is most common in the neck (68%), upper back (62%), shoulders (56%) and right hand (46%). From 3 hours' use a day on, the risk is very high[85]. This is another reason why you should take regular breaks, or at least avoid staying in the same position for a long time.

As I explained in the chapter about reflection, when you need to do some thorough reading, your accuracy, comprehension, recall and speed are better if you read them from paper[86] An additional advantage of printing out texts is that you can read them in a very different body position, with less strain on your eyes and a welcome break from sitting in front of your screen for a long time.

These annoying physical troubles can be improved not only by taking breaks, but also by taking care of the ergonomics of your workstation. This is well-researched and well-known. Ergonomic instructions come with almost every computer you buy (but you probably never read them), and in your company you can easily get this information from any Safety, Health and Environment (SHE) manager or company physician. The problem is that most people only become interested in ergonomics once it's too late. If you didn't think about it beforehand, please do as soon as you start feeling the slightest pain in thumbs, wrists, neck or shoulders. Do take this pain or numbness very seriously, as an alarm signal, because real RSI (Repetitive Strain Injury) can decrease your intellectual productivity a lot and can be extremely difficult to cure. The most intelligent thing to do is not wait for annoying local stress signals but prevent them.

THE USUAL SMARTPHONE AND TABLET POSTURE IS A PAIN IN THE NECK, SHOULDERS AND HEAD

The ergonomics of using smartphones, laptops and tablets are even more neglected by their users than those of desktop computers because these smaller devices stealthily sneaked into our work habits. Have a look around you at people using their phones or do a search in Google Images for "people with smartphone" and you will discover two characteristics. One. When standing: bended and twisted necks. Two. When sitting: slouching and bended and twisted necks. Again, no problem whatsoever if you use your phone relatively briefly and with big intervals, but if you are using your phone all the time you might get trouble due to the tension in your neck and shoulder muscles. This not only happens to adolescents who are Facebooking, texting or Whatsapping up to 3 hours a day, but also to professionals who often spend too much time on the screen of their phone or tablet. Moreover, most professionals also bend their heads when they use their desktop to look at their two fingers pecking on the keyboard. This is a very strange phenomenon indeed: they often spend 2-3 hours typing a day, but do this in the most inefficient way because they never invested a little time to learn to touch-type. By the way, with some initial discipline and time investment this is easy to learn with the open source program TIPP10.

▶ **Don't use your laptop on your lap.**

When you sit straight and you keep your head straight, your head rests on your spine and there is minimal tension in the muscles of your neck. The weight of your head on your cervical spine is 10-11 pounds (4.5-5 kg). If you remember the Laws of Leverage in physics, you will understand that the situation totally changes when you tilt your head forwards. The traction in the muscles of your neck and shoulders increases by about 10 pounds for every inch, adding 30-40 pounds depending on how much you bend forwards[87], which is enough to cause some dislocation of your disc when you do this chronically. To understand what happens to the intervertebral discs, imagine the force exerted in the beak of pliers with handles as long as your neck and a beak of an inch. When you flex your neck often for many consecutive hours, this can cause not only muscle strain and pain in the neck and shoulders, but also disc hernias and pinched nerves and worse troubles after many years. Researchers found that between 53% and 83% of mobile phone users have at least some discomfort in their neck, and often real neck pains[88]. In the media this strain and pain in the neck muscles and spine got the name "Text-Neck"[89] but now I also see more and more "Tablet-necks".

What is less known is that chronic strain on the neck and shoulder muscles can cause headaches because our very strong neck and shoulder muscles are connected to the muscles in our scalp and because the continuous tension may irritate the nerves that pass through them. The most important culprit seems to be chronic tension in the Trapezius muscle, a strong muscle that connects the top of your neck, half your back and both shoulders[90]. When I gave a presentation for the Royal Society of Physiotherapists in the Netherlands, they reported seeing many more people with neck pain, but even among these professionals many of them never made the link with smartphone use.

For the sake of your back, shoulders, neck and head, don't use your laptop on your lap, except for a short period! The same is true for your tablet. Slouching forward on a chair, your neck is bent beyond its comfort zone and the distance to the small screen is still too far to be easy on your eyes, making you squint; the staring diminishes blinking, you get a hunchback, your upper legs and lower back are not supported and your lower back is bent forward beyond its neutral position.

And finally, a word on squinting, which you should avoid at all costs as it is like stress on the eyes. On a regular computer with a good size screen, it is easy in any program to increase the font size to allow comfortable reading. But of course the eyes of smartphone users and smartphone addicts don't have that luxury. Did you know that when working on a screen the rate of blinking goes down by 50%, that our blinks cover less of the eye and that the tears on our staring eyes evaporate faster, causing dry eyes[91]?

If you have a laptop or tablet use them on a table and at work and at home invest in a port replicator or docking station that allows you to connect it with one USB plug to a nice big professional screen and an ergonomic keyboard and mouse[92].

THUMBS DOWN FOR THE USE OF THUMBS

The ergonomics of using smartphones, laptops and tablets are much less known than those of desktop computers and even more neglected by the users[93]. It is evident that your big, clumsy thumbs are the least fit for typing on the tiny buttons of your phone. Although your thumbs can become more agile with training, you are forcing a very unnatural movement on your thumbs, which will cause trouble if you do it a lot. In the past the disorder was sometimes called "Blackberry thumb", though "Smartphone thumb" may be a better term today. It is very frequent too with young people texting and gaming, when it is called "Text-thumb", "Gamers thumb" or "Trigger thumb". In all these situations, you are living under the thumb of your tool.

Your thumb needs to bend all the time much beyond its normal position. This causes a strong stretch and surcharge on the tendons and ligaments on the back of your thumb[94], called hyper-

extension, especially when you type at the bottom of the phone where the keyboard is and when you're texting or e-mailing with one hand. Because the phone is so light, the users underestimate the force that is needed at the base of the thumb. You certainly realize that in normal life we very rarely bend our thumbs so far out of their normal position in that same direction. It is perfectly fine if we do this once in a while, but it is a lot of strain on your thumb if you are glued to your phone and continuously make movements that our poor clumsy thumbs are absolutely not made for. This risks causing RSI around the basis of your thumb. Moreover, the faster you move your thumb, the greater the risk[95].

It is advisable to stop using your thumb as soon as it starts hurting. It is even better to not even get to that point by never typing with your thumbs for a long time. As with most RSI problems, once you've got them, they are often extremely difficult and take a long time to cure[96]. Losing the function of your thumb is awfully debilitating in daily life, especially if it is your dominant hand. Therefore you better prevent this from happening, by interchanging all the time the use of your thumb, with a finger and a stylus, or laying your smartphone flat on a table and pecking on it with two fingers. During the iPhone OS4 event Steve Jobs said: *"It's like we said on the iPad, if you see a stylus, they blew it"*. [97] No-stylus might be stylish, but from the point of view of your poor thumbs, Steve Jobs blew it: please use a stylus, especially if your thumb starts hurting (there are many to choose from[98]). Of course it is even better to recognize the pain in your thumb, wrist or neck as a signal to drastically limit the use of your phone for e-mailing, for all the reasons mentioned in this chapter and the rest of the book in general. Using a stylus or pecking with two fingers on your touchscreen lying down on a table relieves your thumbs, but of course using your phone all day, during every "lost" moment is still by far the least efficient method to do e-mails or any other real work.

5 BRAINCHAIN #4: LACK OF BREAKS AND SLEEP; A WAKE-UP CALL TO SLEEP MORE

You've already learned how important breaks and sleep are for your reflecting brain to recuperate, for your archiving brain to do its work and for your body to handle stress. Below I explain in more detail what happens to our brain and body when we sleep and when we don't sleep enough.

My original intention was to write a rather short chapter on the importance of sleep for our intellectual productivity. However, from my teaching and coaching, from other people's research and from my own, I learned that a lack of sleep has become a problem of epidemic proportions amongst professionals. I therefore decided to go more in-depth into the subject to convince you of the importance of sleep for your brainwork. I hope this chapter will be a wake-up call to start taking your sleep seriously, not just for your intellectual productivity, but also for your general health.

5.1 OUR BRAIN NEEDS ENOUGH SLEEP, MORE THAN ANY OTHER ORGAN

Do you consider sleeping as lost time? Do you try to sleep as little as possible in order to fill your days to the brim with all those important, interesting and fun things you want to do? If so, you don't realize just how crucial getting enough sleep is for your body's general health and, more specifically, for your brain. This is strange because we all know how good we feel and how well we function after a few nights of really high-quality sleep. In spite of this, the majority of people don't get enough sleep.

One of the major habits that destroys brain performance is reducing how much sleep you get or undermining its quality. A lack of sleep has hugely negative psychological and physical consequences, which I will explain later in this chapter. What makes it difficult to break the habit is that we get used to a lack of sleep. We feel as if we adapt to less sleep, even though what is really happening is that we simply become more and more insensitive to the alarm signal of sleepiness. It is as if we have turned off the alarm even though the fire is still burning. Meanwhile, the lack of sleep continues to wield its destructive power and ruins our brainwork. Mind you, way too often when the sleepiness alarm signal goes off anyway, we kill it with caffeine.

Most people shorten their sleep pattern out of ignorance, having never learned how important sleep is. If you think you can use your sleeping time as a reserve of spare time to finish uncompleted business or if you think that your time in bed is simply lost time, think again. By staying awake an hour or so longer, you lose a lot more than you can ever gain. Your efficiency drops significantly so that you need more time to do the same work and its quality will be much lower. You also live shorter, not only due to the much higher risk of having an accident, but also because you will be ill more often and more severely.

Enough sleep is of paramount importance for your intellectual productivity. A lack of sleep undermines your intellectual performance and can be dangerous if you have to perform tasks that are important for your safety or the safety of others, for example driving a car or handling a machine[99].

You need sufficient sleep:
- to recuperate physically
- to restore the energy your reflecting brain needs
- to let your archiving brain reorder and store all the information you took in during the day
- to develop new brain cells (especially for your long-term memory) and new connections between them
- to break down and eliminate the waste products your brain produced during the day
- to process your emotions and maintain your emotional stability

- to activate processes for which there is not enough surplus energy during the day, such as growing, repairing, rejuvenating, restoring your immune system and much more.

Despite this, 52% of adults and 80% of adolescents sleep less than the recommended time for their age[100].

In experiments where people are kept in a situation without clocks, insulated from the outside world, where they get a chance to revert back to their normal sleeping pattern, about 15% of people turn out to be really fine with less than 7 hours of sleep. The percentage of people who can live healthily on 6 hours of sleep is less than 3%.

When I ask people in my audiences, however, 60% of them think they belong to this 12,5% that need less than 7 hours, and in some groups up to 20% think they belong to the 3% who need less than 6 hours. This is of course nonsense. These people are kidding themselves. Therefore if you sleep less than 7 hours, and certainly if you sleep less than 6 hours, you better find out if you are a genuine, genetic "short sleeper", or if you belong to those whose

Healthy sleep:

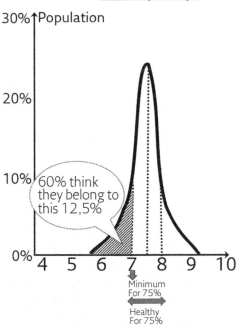

self-deceit is undermining their health and intellectual performance.

For about 40% of the people in my audiences, enough sleep means sleeping one hour longer. If you want to know what it means for you, why not do the three tests later in this chapter to find out if you get enough sleep. Too many professionals who thought sleep was not an issue for them greatly increased their intellectual productivity and especially their creativity, as well as their health, after they looked in the mirror of these tests and changed their sleeping habits.

By the way, both significantly shorter and longer amounts of sleep are less healthy and lead to increased mortality[101]. The problem for researchers, however, is that it is easy to wake up a person to study the impact of less sleep, but it is very difficult to make people sleep longer. The research with children that I will describe at the end of this chapter is a nice exception. For these reasons and because in my work I have not yet met anyone who sleeps too much, I will not discuss the problems of too much sleep.

Our brain recuperates quickly after a short acute lack of sleep, but not after a chronic lack of sleep. When the lack of sleep is chronic the brain adapts, but at a significantly lower level of functioning and does not recuperate quickly with enough sleep. Without enough sleep your brain loses a lot of its potential for concentration, creativity and judgment and as a result the brain of a tired highly skilled professional functions at the level of an unskilled worker[102].

The problem is that for most short sleepers the unhealthy abnormal becomes normal. People can adapt to a chronic lack of sleep, but the research shows that even though these people adapt to higher levels of sleepiness, objective measures of cognitive performance, attention, and concentration remain low, although they are not aware of it (think of the consequences for driving!!). The subjective feeling of sleepiness therefore has no bearing on the lower cognitive performance[103].

You may feel fine with 6 hours or less of sleep, while still undermining your brainpower and building up a sleep debt. Moreover, the cost of a lack of sleep is cumulative: a small lack of sleep every day may result in a big sleep debt over time. Additional wakefulness has a neurobiological "cost" which accumulates over time. As a result, even a moderate lack of sleep can cause serious neurobehavioral impairment, especially in the area of alertness and attention. There is also a significant cognitive loss, comparable with an alcohol intoxication of 0.1% (the legal blood alcohol limit for driving in the USA is 0.08%, in much of the EU 0.05%)[104]; think of the consequences of this for driving a car, controlling machines and... reflection and real converstions.

> **"We now know that 24 hours without sleep or a week of sleeping 4-5 hours a night induces an impairment equivalent to a blood alcohol level of 0.1%. We would never say 'This person is a great worker! He's drunk all the time!' yet we continue to celebrate people who sacrifice sleep."**
> CHARLES CZEISLER, PROFESSOR OF SLEEP MEDICINE
> AT HARVARD BUSINESS SCHOOL [105]

A lack of sleep was fine for our ancestors in the savannah for whom physical survival, based on primitive reactions of the untiring reflex brain, was paramount. However, it is certainly far from ideal if you want to perform intellectually at your best in the complex context in which we live today.

Many people make things worse by making sufficient and good sleep less likely because they drink caffeine all day and stay in front of their screens too late, making falling asleep more difficult and then drinking alcohol or taking a sleeping pill when they go to bed. The latter does help them to fall asleep but it undermines the quality of sleep. Too little sleep or too low a quality of sleep results in a lack of alertness, which then prompts them to drink more caffeine later in the day to stay alert, which makes falling asleep more difficult. The result is that they are stuck in this performance-ruining vicious cycle.

5.2 THREE TESTS TO FIND OUT HOW MUCH SLEEP YOU REALLY NEED

Since there are people who can live a healthy life with less than 7 hours of sleep, but that 60% think they belong to that rare group, why not find out how much sleep you really need.

TEST NO. 1: THE NO-CAFFEINE TEST

The simplest way to find out the minimum number of hours sleep you need to function perfectly well is to eliminate all caffeine or other stimulants during the day. If, after a one-week detoxing from caffeine, you can do your work after less than 7 hours of sleep, perfectly alert and concentrated, without needing to sleep-in in the weekend, without feeling sleepy, without nodding off, without needing a nap, without any of the symptoms of tests 2 and 3, then you are a genuine short sleeper.

Beware, there is also caffeine in black and green tea, in decaffeinated coffee, and of course cola drinks. The amount in so-called "energy drinks" is huge. The name of these drinks is totally misleading because caffeine does not provide any energy whatsoever. It does NOT improve your intellectual productivity, it is NO antidote against a lack of sleep and it does NOT improve your mood (rather the contrary, except to the extent that your negative mood is a withdrawal symptom of your caffeine addiction[106]). Instead, it simply reduces the feeling of sleepiness while in fact your intellectual performance does NOT improve! The only thing it improves is your reaction time, alertness, vigilance and the ability to pay attention (but only to a limited number of objects). (See "Driver on phone meets drowsy driver" later in Section 2.)

Drinking caffeinated drinks is simply disconnecting the alarm signal without taking care of the disaster going on in your brain. The companies producing these caffeinated drinks would be much less successful if their consumers stopped cutting their sleep below healthy levels.

Once you know how much sleep you really need to function well without caffeine, you can return to a healthy consumption which is a cup in the morning and a cup after lunch and not much more than that.

> **Drinking caffeinated drinks is simply disconnecting the alarm signal without taking care of the disaster going on in your brain.**

Bear in mind that when you stop using caffeine it will take you a few days of washout to get over your addiction. Even if you sleep enough you will have the typical withdrawal symptoms, meaning unpleasant feelings and a craving for caffeine that is caused by stopping taking it. Your body had biologically adapted to the caffeine and now needs some time to reorganize and re-adapt to its normal functioning[107]. The most frequent withdrawal symptoms are: headaches in 52% of people, depressed feeling/feeling miserable 11%, feeling no energy 11%, feeling tired/lack of concentration 8% and a feeling like having a small bout of flu 8%. These symptoms start 12-24 hours after the last dose and peak after 20-48 hours.

This is another explanation of the success of the absurdly named "energy drinks": like with any other drug addictions, if you stop taking them this provokes exactly the feelings that make you think "I need another dose". Therefore start the no-caffeine test the day before a long weekend or even better a vacation. Otherwise you will never have the courage to continue the test.

TEST NO. 2: THE SLEEPINESS QUESTIONNAIRE

As I explained above, when we reduce sleep chronically, we adapt rather well to the increased feeling of sleepiness, even though we function under par intellectually. Therefore just following your general feeling of sleepiness by itself is not a sufficient indicator. Feeling sleepy certainly is an indicator, but not feeling sleepy is not by itself a good indicator that you are getting enough sleep. The importance of the subject can be seen by the fact that academics have developed more than 100 sleep questionnaires[108]. Here I have chosen for you the alertness questionnaire developed by James Maas, who studied sleep for some 35 years.

YES/NO 1 I often need an alarm clock in order to wake up at the appropriate time.

YES/NO 2 It's often a struggle for me to get out of bed in the morning.

YES/NO 3 On weekday mornings I often hit the snooze button several times.

YES/NO 4 I often feel tired and stressed out during the week.

YES/NO 5 I often feel moody and irritable, little things upset me.

YES/NO 6 I often have trouble concentrating and remembering.

YES/NO 7 I often feel slow with critical thinking, problem solving and being creative.

YES/NO 8 I need caffeine to get going in the morning or make it through the afternoon.

YES/NO 9 I often wake up craving junk food, sugars and carbohydrates.

YES/NO 10 I often fall asleep watching TV.

YES/NO 11 I often fall asleep in boring meetings or lectures or in warm rooms.

YES/NO 12 I often fall asleep after meals or after a low dose of alcohol.

YES/NO 13 I often fall asleep while relaxing after dinner.

YES/NO 14 I often fall asleep within 5 minutes of getting into bed.

YES/NO 15 I often feel drowsy while driving.

YES/NO 16 I often sleep extra hours at the weekend.

YES/NO 17 I often need a nap to get through the day.

YES/NO 18 I have dark circles around my eyes.

YES/NO 19 I fall asleep easily when watching a movie.

YES/NO 20 I often rely on caffeinated drinks or over-the-counter medications to keep me awake.

If you answered "Yes" to four or more of these statements, consider yourself sleep-deprived, read this chapter thoroughly and then decide what to do about it.

TEST NO. 3: THE "IT'S MORE THAN SLEEPINESS" QUESTIONS
Since a lack of sleep has far more negative effects than just sleepiness, you can double check if you need more sleep by checking if you have any of the following signals.

YES/NO 1 Feeling (a little) depressed, less happy or less enthusiastic without a reason

YES/NO 2 Craving for food, snacks, sugar during the day, even if you eat enough

YES/NO 3 Crying without good reason

YES/NO 4 Having little patience

YES/NO 5 Having trouble retrieving things from memory or having the feeling that your memory is full

YES/NO 6 Having difficulty making decisions, even small ones

YES/NO 7 Being clumsy: dropping stuff, spilling drinks, having more (near) accidents while driving...

YES/NO 8 Having difficulty focusing

YES/NO 9 Not being alert, clear-headed

YES/NO 10 Getting colds easily

YES/NO 11 Getting feedback from other people that you don't look good or that you look tired

YES/NO 12 Having little interest in sex

There is nothing alarming about having a few of these symptoms once in a while, but if you have many or if you have them all the time: think about your sleep first. They might also be a sign that you are (a little) depressed. But from research we know that the first and often the only step you need to cure your depression is getting enough good sleep[109]. As I described extensively in my book "Stress: Friend and Foe"[110], many of these symptoms can also signal that you are under too much stress or that your stress has been going on for too long. Have a look at your stress balance. This too can turn into a vicious cycle: stressed people have a strong tendency to sleep less or to sleep worse, and people who lack sleep experience more stress.

5.3 SCARY STATISTICS ABOUT OUR LACK OF SLEEP

"Insufficient sleep is a public health epidemic". That was the conclusion of the Centers for Disease Control and Prevention after their 2012 nationwide survey[111]. Lots of people, however, seem rather to agree with what Napoleon, who managed on 4 hours sleep a night, is supposed to have said: "Six hours for a man, seven hours for a woman, eight hours for a fool". What this quote does not tell you is that he took a very long siesta every day... or that he lost at Waterloo, just around the corner from where I am writing this.

In the last 30 years, in the Western world, we have reduced our sleep by 1.5 hours on average, creating an intellectual productivity undermining "Social Jetlag" (more on this below) for up to 70% of the population[112]. It is ridiculous to think that in 30 years we can change a biological mechanism that took millions of years to develop. It is not because, thanks to electrical light, we can now stay up as long as we want, that we should do so. Nor is it because we can stay connected with what happens in the world that we should be glued to our screens until we go to bed and are even in bed.

Adults who reported sleeping less than the recommended 7–9 hours per night were more likely to have difficulty performing many daily tasks[113] and felt the need to sleep longer at the weekend[114]. In the USA, 70% of high school students do not get the sleep they need, and in some countries like Korea, where it has been linked with increased suicide, the situation is even worse.

In a nutshell: The very troubling results of several surveys[115]
60% report a sleep problem every night or almost every night and that their sleep needs are not being met during the week.
52% of adults and 80% of adolescents sleep less than recommended for their age.
49% of adults wake up feeling unrefreshed.
43% of Americans between the ages of 13 and 64 rarely or never get a good night's sleep on weeknights.
42% are awake a lot during the night at least a few nights each week.

36% nod off or fall asleep while driving.

32% drive feeling drowsy at least once or twice per month.

30% of adults sleep 6 hours or less per night after a workday. For shift workers it is even worse: between 35 and 44%.

30 to 50% regularly wake up due to the sounds of their phones.

29% fall asleep or become very sleepy at work.

20% have sex less often or have lost interest in sex because they are too sleepy.

14% missed family events, work functions and leisure activities in the past month due to sleepiness.

12% arrived late at work in the previous month because of sleepiness.

84% of bad sleepers say that they just accept it and keep going.

58% say they consume caffeinated beverages to stay alert.

38% choose foods high in sugar and carbohydrates.

5% take stimulant medications or drugs to fight the lack of sound sleep.

In a survey of 2,500 managers in five countries, the average manager sleeps 19% less than the recommended number of hours. 87% have at times had their work, friendships, family life or sexual relations negatively impacted by lack of sleep. After inadequate sleep, 58% are less able to concentrate, 51% have less patience, 49% have less enthusiasm and 25% have impaired judgment. 15-40% said they don't sleep well because of the economic situation[116].

5.4 ALWAYS WIRED, TIRED AND UNINSPIRED

There are several ways in which always being connected may ruin your sleep.

First, especially if you are more or less addicted to your ICT, because you postpone the moment of disconnecting and go to bed later and later.

Second, because you prolong a low level of stress or excitement until the very last moment of your day. As a result your activating stress hormones and arousal hormones are at too high a level to sleep well when you go to bed.

Third, and little known, by the direct effect on your sleep hormones of the light of your screen directed straight into your eyes.

Fourth, because if you keep your phone next to your bed it makes you sleep more superficially because your brain stays "on alert" for its sounds while you sleep, like a mother who sleeps is still on alert for the noises and cries of her baby.

Fifth, because, depending on your age and degree of addiction to being connected, 30-50% regularly wake up due to the sounds of their phones[117].

And last but not least, your hyperconnectivity makes you multitask all the time, and as a result you are so inefficient that you spend much more time on your tasks, trying to complete them and correcting errors; you then try to make up for this by stealing time from your sleep. This of course then makes you even less efficient the next day...

The conclusion is crystal clear: for the quality of your sleep, disconnect and organize a screen-free period before you go to bed. If not, your hyperconnectivity will ruin your sleep and your brainwork. If your brain is always wired, it will always be tired and uninspired if not also dumbed-down.

5.5 LACK OF SLEEP RUINS YOUR INTELLECTUAL PRODUCTIVITY, MAKES YOU LESS HAPPY, LESS HEALTHY AND LESS SEXY

Sleeping enough is very important for your whole body, but for the reader of this book the positive impact on your intellectual productivity is most important. The results of the research about the impact of a lack of sleep are alarming to put it mildly. One night of insufficient sleep already has a negative effect on our cognitive and emotional functioning[118]!

It's very clear and simple: you need enough sleep if you want to get the best out of your brain. Period. Enough sleep is a necessity for the rest of your body as well. Without enough sleep you get fatter, are more prone to diabetes, develop heart problems at a younger age etc, etc...[119].

Without enough sleep your brain loses a lot of its potential, for example concentration, creativity and judgment.

We know that the effect on cognitive performance of 14 days of lack of sleep (6 hours or less a night) is the same as two nights without any sleep[120], hence it seems reasonable to cautiously apply the findings of sleep deprivation to sleep debt in general. In any case, taking all the research together we can clearly and unambiguously conclude that for most people shortening your sleep pattern is not a good idea at all.

There are only two excuses for sleeping less than 7-8 hours for an extended period: having a baby who wakes you up and working shifts. But even then you can do a few things to minimize the negative impact of a lack of sleep on your brain and the rest of your body.

DON'T MESS AROUND WITH YOUR BIOLOGICAL CLOCK

The brain mechanisms that control waking and sleeping, and above all the restoration of the brain, are so essential that you should be familiar with the basics about them so that you know what you are really doing to your brain, body and life when you mess around with your sleep.

We need to sleep at very specific regular hours because that is how our biological clocks are set. These clocks took millions of years to develop so that we can get the best out of the eternal cycle of night and day. We find these clocks not only in all animals, but also in plants and in bacteria. This means that these clocks are extremely old in evolutionary terms and very essential for the functioning of living beings.

The central clock is called the "circadian clock" because it follows a 24-hour cycle, the so-called circadian rhythm. The word circadian comes from the Latin circa=around and dies=day. The clock is set rather precisely at 24 hours and 11 minutes. The main function of this biological clock is to coordinate the activity of the trillions of cells in our body and brain, amongst othet things, to be active during the day and to clean up, recover and restore during the night.

It is a good thing that this clock is very persistent and not easily disturbed by external factors because otherwise things like waking up at night or taking a nap during the day would disturb lots of important processes in our body. This steadiness is absolutely necessary for our body and brain to function normally and is disturbed when we reduce our sleep to less than the biological setting of our clock. In today's world, this steady clock is also in trouble when it has to adapt way too fast to very sudden changes, for example when we travel across several time zones, do shift work, have different sleeping patterns during the week compared to the weekend or have to adapt to the yearly changes to and from Daylight Saving Time. The steadier your clock, the more difficult it is to cope with these disturbances.

There is one thing that has a particularly strong influence on your clock: light. This is necessary because to synchronize the 24 hours and 11 minutes of the central clock with the 24-hour spin of the earth we need the regular light and dark cycle of a day to reset it. This sensitivity to light is a good thing because otherwise, in the long run, the 11 minutes' difference would cause problems. The invention of artificial light, however, is a bad thing because we can disturb this clock with light, especially with the light of modern flat screens directed from a close distance straight into the eye. The biggest disruption can be provoked by light at the wrong moment during the transition between waking and sleeping and vice versa[121].

Even much simpler organisms like plants and even bacteria consisting of only one cell have such clocks. In medical school we were told the story of Jean-Jacques d'Ortous de Mairan who, in the beginning of the 18th century, put mimosa flowers in a dark cupboard with a little peeking hole. He saw that the leaves kept opening and closing in the dark and that all the leaves did this in perfect synchrony. This proved that the opening and closing was not only triggered by sunrise and sunset; inside the plant there is also a mechanism that regulates this 24-hour rhythm for a short time, independent of light.

This clock is not just a metaphor. Researchers have been able to exactly locate the human "central biological clock" in a group of cells, the so-called SCN or Supra Chiasmatic Nucleus, which gets its information from special cells in our eyes that we can't see with but that are sensitive to light. There are only 20,000 neurons in the SCN but they are extremely important because they are the metronome, the pacemaker, the master clock that synchronizes the activities of all the billions of cells in our body.

This clock is very powerful. Researchers put some of these cells in a nutritious solution in little glass containers and discovered that even outside the body, and even if they are put in continuous dark or light, they keep their rhythm, although disconnected from their network they do become irregular after a while. From there, it was only a small step to see if the other cells in our body also have a little clock, and indeed they have, but they need the central clock to synchronize. Hence you have 20,000 neurons, which together are the "master clock" synchronizing trillions of body cells, the "slave clocks", by influencing how the genes in these cells give their instructions to the cell, telling them when to multiply, when to offload their products in the bloodstream etc... It is easy to imagine the total chaos that would ensue without this central timing and tuning, if the trillions of body cells each did their own thing at their own time.

We have known for decades that sleep disturbances such as lack of sleep and shift work increase the chances of diabetes, certain kinds of cancer and especially gastro-intestinal problems. Now we understand that the deregulation of our biological clock influences these disorders: certain cells lose contact with the central clock and keep multiplying (cancer), others lose contact and start or stop secreting their products very irregularly in the bloodstream (diabetes) or in the gut[122].

Here are a few examples of important hormones whose production must follow a steady 24-hour pattern coordinated by our central clock:

Melatonin: This is an important hormone for sleep itself [123]. This hormone plays a major role in synchronizing the internal clock with the day-night or rather the light-dark cycle outside. It induces sleepiness, improves our mood, probably improves our anti-inflammatory system and has many other effects, not all of which are very well documented yet. It is a biological product that is very old in evolutionary terms. It is not only produced in

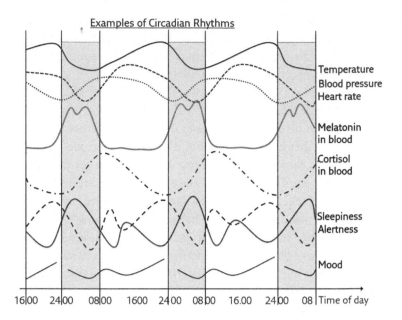

Examples of Circadian Rhythms

Temperature
Blood pressure
Heart rate

Melatonin
in blood

Cortisol
in blood

Sleepiness
Alertness

Mood

16.00 24.00 08.00 16.00 24.00 08.00 16.00 24.00 08 | Time of day

mammals, but also in most other organisms, even in plants where it also follows a circadian rhythm.

Leptin: this inhibits appetite and gives us a feeling of being satiated.

Ghrelin: this increases appetite and makes us feel hungry.

Cortisol: a stress hormone that suppresses the immune system, regulates the body's intake and use of fat, sugar and proteins, for example for building muscles and bones.

Growth hormone does exactly what its name suggests, and this is one of the reasons why academics worry about the long-term consequences of a lack of sleep for children and adolescents. But growth hormone is important for adults too for the uptake of sugars, for our immune system, to make proteins, to keep the calcium in our bones and much more.

Testosteroids: these are co-responsible for vigor, development and functioning of sexual organs, sexual behavior, desire, thoughts and feelings, male looks, bone and muscle building and general health. Recent research, however, shows that Testosterone production is much more dependent on the duration of sleep than on the circadian clock by itself[124].

Thyroid hormones: these regulate energy balance, bone growth, core body temperature and the metabolism of sugar, fat, proteins and vitamins.

Parathyroid hormones: these regulate many things that are important for bone growth such as the calcium, phosphate and vitamin D levels in our blood.

And much more: the clock influences the effects and side-effects of many medications, and also has an impact on when the two halves of our brain are most active and efficient.

Because this clock regulates so many cells, a lot of processes in our body follow a fixed pattern over a 24- or 12-hour period: energy production and restoration, core body temperature, blood pressure, oxygen consumption, the production of digestive chemicals and juices etc... These changes, via their impact on our brain, also have an influence on our behavior, our thinking[125], our management of memory, our emotions etc. This clock is very steady and when it is out of synchrony with the environment, for example due to jet lag, social jetlag or shift work, it needs a few days of exposure to the alternation of day and night (especially exposure to full daylight) to get back in sync.

By looking at this list you can easily figure out that it is not a good idea to disturb this clock by messing around with your wake-sleep rhythm or by shortening your sleep pattern, which causes a continuous misalignment with your internal clock.

As I have already mentioned, the clock has its own internal driver, which is continuously nudged to 24 hours by the light-dark cycle. With the omnipresence of electric light we keep being exposed to light after dusk and until late in the evening. As a result the release of our sleepiness hormone Melatonin is delayed, we become more alert, it becomes more difficult to fall asleep and we go to bed later and later. This can be done by a short exposure to bright light or a long exposure to rather dim light[126].

A recent discovery is that the major influence on our circadian clock is not via the eye cells we use to see, but via specialized sensor cells in our eyes that contain the pigment "Melanopsin". When triggered, these cells send a signal to other cells, most importantly to our central biological clock, where it inhibits the production of Melatonin. Melanopsin is most sensitive at 480 nanometers, the wavelength of blue light. Hence in the morning and noon light, with a lot of blue light, it will stop the production of Melatonin, whereas in the evening, when there is more red and much less blue light, Melatonin production will be stimulated, resulting in a gradual increase in sleepiness... unless you expose yourself to artificial light with lots of blue in it which will increase your alertness at the very moment it should be decreasing to get ready to sleep. The issue is that the maximum sensitivity of the Melatonin-controlling Melanopsin in our eyes is at almost the exact wavelength as where white computer screens (RGB, LCD, LED) peak![127] (See picture.) They emit even more blue light than direct sunlight at noon. As a result, looking at a flat screen, tablet or smartphone at a close distance will decrease Melatonin production and influence your biological clock[128].

Light with lots of blue increases our alertness and attention, by reducing our sleepiness and by halting the production of our sleepiness hormone Melatonin[129]. The production of Melatonin is inhibited on average after 2 hours of exposure, but for some people this already happens after half on hour and at very low degrees of lumen. This is a very significant discovery because

Sensitivity of the eye cells that stop Melatonin production

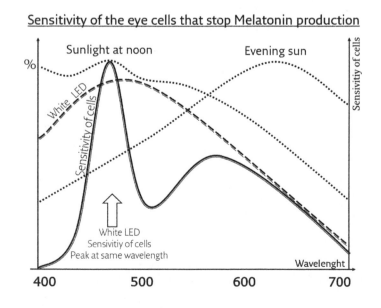

95% of Americans use some type of electronics with a screen like a television, computer, video game or cell phone during a prolonged period at least a few nights a week within the hour before bed[130] and more and more people stay glued to these screens until they turn out their gadget to go to sleep.

The white light of the e-ink screens or e-paper screens of eBook readers that do not have a backlight, the kind where you need a lamp to read them in the dark, is not a problem. These just reflect the ambient light and for your sleep this is no different than reading a printed book. The problem is that to compete with the brightness, contrast and loads of features on the tablets, these readers are being replaced with eBook readers with the same screens as tablets. The light of a modern TV screen has less impact because we usually look at TV from a greater distance.

All this is not much to worry about if you sleep long enough and well enough, but it is something to bear in mind if you have sleeping problems or if you have shortened your sleep pattern beyond what's healthy. The problem is that so many people are fooling themselves about the need to stay behind their screen until they go to bed, and about the hours of sleep they need to function at their best.

OUR BIOLOGICAL CLOCK HATES LACK OF SLEEP

It is not difficult to understand the negative impact on our intellectual performance when we create a chronic conflict with our biological clocks by sleeping too little. But our biological clock can also become totally out of sync with our environment due to sudden changes caused by jetlag, social jetlag (due to short nights in the week and long ones at the weekend) shift work and changes due to Daylight Saving Time. Since our biological clock regulates our cells and a lot of other clocks in our body and brain, these too fall out of sync. Our organs are activated when they should be resting and are slowed down when they should be active. For example we feel shivery because the clock wants to lower the internal body temperature as it always does during the night or we might have intestinal problems, as many shift workers do, because the production of digestive chemicals in the gut is still in its night phase while they are up working and vice versa. Since the clock also makes us alert when we should be sleeping and feel sleepy when we should be awake we sleep even less or worse. These sudden changes also have a direct and indirect negative impact on our brain and from there on our thinking, decision-making, driving, machine-handling etc...The steadier your clock, which is normally a good thing for your body, the longer it takes to adapt. For a very informative explanation about normal and not so normal sleep-wake patterns, take a look at http://healthysleep. med.harvard.edu/interactive/circadian.

The problem caused by jetlag is explained by the word itself. Our clock can adapt to gradual small changes, but struggles with sudden big changes. Before planes had jet motors, people travelled slowly enough for their biological clocks to adapt gradually. With jet planes, the change is so big and sudden that our biological clocks, and from there our whole body and brain, can no longer follow.

For several clock-related reasons jetlag caused by westward travel is less taxing than eastward travel. The more time zones crossed, the longer it takes the circadian pacemaker to reset, the worse the symptoms and the longer it takes to recover. A rule of thumb is that it takes a number of days equal to about two-thirds of the number of time zones that have been crossed. The gastro-intestinal disturbances are well-known, but for the reader of this book it is more important to know that on arrival we do poorly on mental tasks, and for much longer and more severely than people are often aware of, not only because of a drop in attention and concentration but because our reflecting brain doesn't function well.

The general fatigue from travel has the same effect, but that's usually resolved with one good night of sleep, while the impact of jetlag lasts much longer and is made worse by its typical sleeping problems. It not only lasts longer because the clocks influencing our reflecting brain need time to adjust, but also because when we travel eastward we have difficulties falling asleep and sleep poorly during the night because our clock is still set on day-time and when travelling west we wake up too early because our internal clock acts as if it is morning while we are still in the middle of the night. What's more, our sleep is more fractured in both directions.

Other consequences that will undermine our intellectual performance are general fatigue, headaches, mood instability, irritability and digestive problems[131].

When the de-synchronization becomes chronic, because you do shift work or most commonly for non-shift workers when you create "social jetlag", you ruin your brainwork.

Social jetlag is a problem we unnecessarily create ourselves when we artificially lengthen our days and shorten our sleep time so that there is a chronic difference between our biological clock and our social or environmental clock that is too big to routinely adjust. This social jetlag is made worse when we try to make up for the lack of sleep during the week by sleeping later at the weekend because this further disturbs our clock that has to reset again and again on Monday. It is less disturbing for your clock if you go to bed earlier at the weekend instead of sleeping later in the morning. This social jetlag is not only disturbing for office workers, but also truck drivers because they sleep short nights, catch up on sleep at the weekend and then want to participate with family life on Sunday and have their shortest night on Sunday[132]. By the way, social jetlag peaks in adolescence with considerable cognitive and health consequences[133].

Given that between 15% and 25% of people in developed countries do shift work and that between 30% and 50% of them suffer from shift work disorder[134], this is an individually, economically and socially very relevant topic. Shift work has a (very) negative impact not only on health and social functioning, but also on the productivity and safety of employees[135]. Given what we have already discussed, you can imagine how shift work can wreck the sensitive system of our biological clocks.

A lot of research on shift work has been done on hospital interns and residents: young, healthy, bright physicians, who have to do an intellectually difficult job. In many countries they are exploited by making them work weeks of 90 hours or more, with shifts of 24 hours and longer, without enough time to recover afterwards. In some countries like the USA, this has, in theory, been restricted to 80 hours, which is much more than in any industry in developed countries or than for any other profession with life-critical responsibilities like policemen, traffic controllers, pilots, truck drivers and bus drivers.

This makes these interns ideal guinea pigs for real-life research on lack of sleep. For six years I was one of them myself, and I know I made mistakes that I never would have made if I had had enough sleep, to say nothing of the mistakes that I made and am not even aware of because... I hadn't had enough sleep.

For these young doctors, the risk of making serious professional errors and having a traffic accident increases very significantly. Hospital interns scheduled to work for 24 hours increase their chances of stabbing themselves with a needle or scalpel by 61%, their risk of crashing a car by 168% and their risk of a near miss by 460%[136]. Eliminating interns' extended work shifts in an intensive care unit significantly increased sleep and reduced attention failures during night work hours by half![137]

Every shift of more than 24 hours increases the monthly risk of car accidents by almost 16%[138] or 36% when compared with 16-hour shifts.

On the other hand, given the chance to work an average of only 65 hours and sleeping an extra 6 hours a week on average, they made 50% fewer unintentional failures. An impressive result, especially given the fact that most of them were carrying a considerable sleep debt from the "normal" working period before the experiment[139].

Although workers in industry are better protected than medical interns, the research on shift work not only shows an increase in physical problems, but also an increase in mental problems and problems with attention, concentration and reasoning. Shift work in general increases the risks of fatal accidents at work and on the road[140], especially night shifts[141]. The risk of having an accident rises with the number of consecutive shifts (particularly night shifts), the duration of the shift, the absence of breaks and the lack of undisturbed sleep in-between shifts[142]. Famous (or infamous) accidents that are probably due to lack of sleep are the Three Miles Island and Chernobyl nuclear accidents, Union Carbide chemical accident in Bhopal, the Exxon Valdez oil spill and the Space shuttle explosion[143]. In the only two accidents I have had in 48 years of driving, lack of sleep (in one case combined with jetlag) undeniably played a role.

By the way, the reason women suffer more from shift work disorder is not primarily because they are less resistant to it, but because at home, they put sleeping lower on their list of priorities than their responsibilities to the family, such as children, shopping and cooking, typically tasks that many men avoid, giving their sleep during the daytime the highest priority. As a result women more often become really sleep deprived because they sleep (much) less than 7-8 hours.

Finally, an example of a conflict between our biological clock that is millions of years old and our modern lifestyle is the yearly Daylight Saving Time (DST). For whatever (good?) reasons this has been implemented, it certainly did not take our biological clock into account. It is very easy to set our electronic clocks one hour earlier, but it is a challenge for our biological clock to follow due to a net loss of sleep in the following week. Subjectively we seem to adapt in a day or so, but in fact it takes our biological clock about a week. It is worse and takes longer for short sleepers and people who go to bed late and as a result has a marked effect on adolescents, , who should avoid taking important tests in the week following the change to DST, or pay double attention to healthy sleep in that period. The performance of many adults, however, suffers too. This is evident in the increase of car accidents (especially with pedestrians), where the sudden increase in darkness is an important part of the problem, and a rise in severe accidents at work in the week following the change. Changing to DST also has a negative impact on mood and life satisfaction. All these consequences are most evident with the change to DST rather than the change back to Standard Time[144].

TWO VERY DIFFERENT KINDS OF SLEEP ARE IMPORTANT FOR INTELLECTUAL PRODUCTIVITY

What too many people don't know is that when we sleep, we are not just resting in a kind of unconscious comatose state, regaining our energy after a busy day. On the contrary, sleep is a very active dynamic process that has an impact on every single part of your body, and above all on your brain. During the night all kinds of new connections are built and cells duplicate to store the learning of the past day[145]. Sleep is also most important to process emotions and to keep our emotional balance[146].

The activity of the brain during sleep follows a strict pattern. Our biological sleep-clock leads us six to seven times from superficial sleep to deep sleep in four steps. Every step has its own typical electrical brainwaves. Superficial sleep and deep sleep are fundamentally different. This is reflected not only in very different electrical brainwaves (EEG), but also on brain scans and the different chemicals that are produced[147].

During the superficial stages the brain cells are very active, sometimes more active than while awake. Therefore this kind of sleep is often called "Paradoxical sleep". One of the characteristics is that our eyes move rapidly underneath the eyelids, which is the reason why it is called Rapid Eye Movement (REM) sleep. In this phase we very actively process our memories and especially our memories about emotions. The most intriguing aspect of REM sleep, and one that is not really understood, is dreaming. Most of our dreaming happens during REM sleep, whereas sleepwalking and night terrors happen in the deepest non-REM sleep. It's a good thing we are paralyzed in REM sleep; otherwise we would act out our dreams, as sometimes happen in non-REM sleep when people sleepwalk. Everybody dreams, including the people who think they don't. The reason some people think they don't dream is that we only remember a dream when we wake up during a dream or immediately after it.

We need REM sleep and dreams to digest our experiences of the day, especially to develop our memory, to stay emotionally balanced[148] and to stay psychologically healthy. It is during REM sleep that our archiving brain is very active. All the information of the day is not just being stored, it is also being linked with all the information that is already stored[149].

REM sleep softens the memories of heavy emotions. Without enough sleep, people tend to remember negative experiences better than positive ones. During one or more nights of good sleep

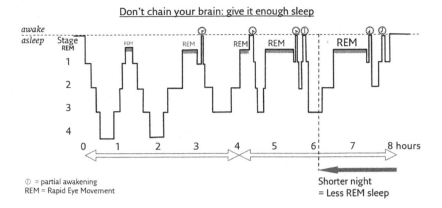

Don't chain your brain: give it enough sleep

① = partial awakening
REM = Rapid Eye Movement

Shorter night
= Less REM sleep

very emotional memories gradually lose their emotional and visceral qualities. Sleep does not make us forget, the memory remains, but it is disconnected from the original strong emotional and physical reactions[150].

A lack of sleep, especially a lack of REM sleep, results in decreased positive emotions like happiness and increased negative emotions, especially anger, anxiety and depression[151]. Sufficient sleep improves our mood; it is literally "therapeutic"[152].

Why we dream what we dream is still very much an enigma. There is no evidence for the unscientific theories of the Freudians about the meaning of dreams, but there is also not much scientific evidence for other theories about the content of our dreams. What we know is that dreams are part of the brain's unique way of selecting, recombining and ordering the billions of bits and bytes of information taken in during the day.

Given that in this phase the sleeping brain is as active as when we are awake, that we have most of this kind of sleep in the last part of the night and that we can easily be awakened, some scholars think that its function is more related to preparing for being awake (no longer being disturbed by strong emotions) than it is for digesting the past per se, while the deep non-REM sleep, where we don't respond to external stimuli, is more important for restoration and recovery[153].

From that superficial level of REM sleep, we move several times per night in stages to deep sleep, the "non-REM" sleep, when the brainwaves become very slow. This stage, most of which happens in the first half of the night, is very important for physical recuperation.

This slow-wave, deep sleep is also very important for storing memories in the long-term memory. Some scholars think for example, that the decreasing memory function of older people is more directly related to a reduction in deep sleep quality rather than to a decrease in memory capacity per se[154]. In an experiment comparing memory in young people and people at retirement age, for example, it was no surprise that immediately after memorizing lists of words the young people remembered 25% better than the older people. The two surprises were that after a night's sleep, the young outperformed the older people by 50%, and that this was mainly due to the seniors' poorer quality of deep sleep[155].

Non-REM sleep is very important to recuperate physically too. Our muscles are relaxed, our temperature is lower, probably to conserve energy, our heart rate and blood pressure go down, the circulation of blood in our brain decreases and our breathing becomes very efficient, slow and regular. Many body functions are reduced, but interestingly enough, other functions that are related to repair, rejuvenating and growth are increased.

It has become very evident that we need both kinds of sleep, REM and non-REM, to retain what we learned during the day[156]. In rats it was demonstrated that poor memory is due to the fact that a lack of sleep suppresses the development of new cells in parts of the brain responsible for long-term memory. As a result the sleepy rats did not learn from experience and repeated the task as if they had never done it before[157].

SUFFICIENT SLEEP HELPS YOUR REFLECTING BRAIN AND IMPROVES YOUR IQ, EQ AND SQ

I explained in Section 1 how with insufficient sleep your brain archive becomes like a library with lots of books lying chaotically around on the floor, never stacked in their proper place, never indexed, never able to be retrieved. But the consequences of a lack of sleep are not just limited to our reflecting brain suffering from a memory problem.

Whatever scientists look at, people with a lack of sleep do worse. The first victims are attention and concentration. Then come patience, a feeling for nuance, the appreciation of complex situations, the assessment of risk, anticipation, logical planning, lateral thinking, creativity, innovation, insight, judgment, rational decision capability, maintaining interest, rational assessment of situations, self-assessment, openness to feedback from others, mood, happiness, communication, enthusiasm, sexual desire, abstraction, synthesis, judgment and especially moral judgment etc...[158]. Name any aspect of intellectual (IQ), emotional (EQ) or social (SQ) intelligence and you will find it is undermined by lack of sleep.

Sleep is especially important for the complex brainwork of highly specialized professionals, managers and commanders in the army because such people have to appreciate difficult and rapidly changing situations, assess risk, anticipate the range of consequences, keep track of events/update the big picture, be innovative, develop, maintain, and revise plans, remember when events occurred, control mood and uninhibited behavior, show insight into one's own performance, communicate effectively and avoid irrelevant distractions[159].

This negative impact is most evident in research about sleep deprivation, where people are kept awake for one or more nights, but even 40-60 minutes a night less significantly reduces your intellectual performance. Caffeine or amphetamines do not improve this high-level brainwork although they will reduce the feeling of sleepiness[160] and increase alertness. With modern technologies, researchers have not only been able to demonstrate this deterioration, but they have also been able to show which phases of sleep are most important for our intellectual functioning[161].

After reviewing the research about the impact of a lack of sleep on decision making, Yvonne Harrison and James Horne concluded: "...[If you need] innovation, flexibility of thinking, avoidance of distraction, risk assessment, awareness for what is feasible, appreciation of one's own strengths and weaknesses at that current time and ability to communicate effectively, then these are the very behaviors that are most likely to be affected by [a lack of sleep]... The impact on these behaviors is likely to be particularly significant in a situation that changes rapidly and personnel have to adapt to a wide range of continuous and unpredictable

developments. Tasks that demand other than well-learned automatic responses will be most vulnerable[162]."

Many people let these crucial higher cognitive functions deterio-
rate the most precisely when they most need them, when they
have to make decisions in times of stress and in crisis situations...
in situations where they often cut back on their sleep[163]. Therefore
the habit of having 24-hour negotiations between politicians and
between politicians and labor organizations is utterly stupid. It is
asking for trouble because it is impossible to make good rational
decisions when you are lacking sleep, especially because overre-
acting to negative information is certainly the opposite of what
one needs for successful negotiations. President Bill Clinton
probably didn't know the extent to which he was right and supported by science when he said: *"You have no idea how many Re-
publican and Democratic members of the House and Senate are
chronically sleep-deprived ... I do believe sleep deprivation has a lot to
do with some of the edginess of Washington today."*[164]

> **"You have no idea how many Republican and
> Democratic members of the House and Senate
> are chronically sleep-deprived ... I do believe
> sleep deprivation has a lot to do with some
> of the edginess of Washington today."**
> **PRESIDENT BILL CLINTON**

Ever since the beginning of the 20th century, the relationship between sleep and emotions has been intensively researched. When
we are well rested, our reflecting brain keeps an eye on our reflex
brain and modulates its fast, primitive, often exaggerated emotional reactions. When we do not sleep enough or when we are
tired or exhausted, for example after a day of work in an open office, it is our reflecting brain that is tired and it is our cognitive
resources that are depleted. This is even visible in brain scans
where we can see that the part of the brain that moderates the
emotional brain is too sleepy to do its job[165]. This not only has a
negative impact on the quality of our thinking, but since our reflecting brain then has difficulties regulating our emotional reflex
brain our emotions become more primitive and exaggerated, we

become over-reactive, over-emotional towards negative stimuli and are much less able to see negative things in their proper context. It also leads to a decrease in emotional intelligence in general and less socially intelligent behavior, due to a lessening of our intrapersonal awareness, interpersonal skills, emotion management, empathy and moral judgment[166]. A well-researched aspect is that with a lack of sleep we have greater difficulties appraising emotional facial expressions[167], which of course reduces our ability to react in an emotionally and socially intelligent way.

WHILE YOU SLEEP YOUR ARCHIVING BRAIN TOILS TO STORE A DAY'S WORTH OF INFORMATION

During the day too many people abuse their archiving brain by filling every single break, mini-break and micro-break with frenetic activity on their ICT tools. As a result the brain can't properly archive lots of information. Although some of it is lost forever, during our sleep our archiving brain finally gets a chance to do its work and order, store and reorganize the information that is still there.

Sleep is a bit like the disk defragmentation and disk cleanup for your hard disk. But our archiving brain is much more interesting than this passive hard disk. It is active! Your archiving brain decides what to discard and what to keep. It continuously rearranges the information in your archive. During sleep the billions of archivists are no longer distracted by continuously incoming information and are undisturbed by our reflecting brain. They can start doing the most important job of selecting, storing, indexing and reordering the billions of bits of information that were registered during a single day. It makes connections with the massive amount of data that have already been stored in the long-term memory. It prepares your brain for the day to come. As a result it enhances learning, conceptual thinking and creativity. It does this by connecting and disconnecting billions of connections between nerve cells[168]. A good full night of sleep – before and after learning – very significantly improves memory[169].

Do you remember your first or second grade teacher? 90% chance you do even 40, 60 or 100 years later. Have you ever needed this information? 90% chance not. Isn't it amazing that this information is still available in your archive: the teacher's name, looks...and this information is still there despite the fact that probably none of the original connections that stored the information so long ago still exist. What a difference between our brain archive and digital archives, which 20 years later nobody can read anymore because the software or hardware no longer exists.

If you don't get enough sleep, there is too much junk information that's not cleaned up, snippets of information that are not linked to each other and valuable stuff that is not put in its proper place. The situation is then like an archive with lots of folders and files lying around everywhere. When the next day you need the information you don't find it and when you are exposed to lots of important new information your memory retains much less. Eight hours of sleep significantly improves problem-solving skills, memory, the learning and retention of motor skills and... creativity. This was even made visible in brain scans where greater activity showed up in several regions of the brain[170]. This is the reason why so often you wake up with a solution you could not puzzle out while you were actively thinking about it during the day.

It is important to know that your archiving brain is especially active during the longer periods of REM sleep in the last part of your sleep. So when you shorten your sleep time you cut off exactly the part that your archiving brain needs most. Especially after a day chock full of information or before a day where you need to make important decisions, you really need that last part of the night. In an ever- and faster-changing environment where we are bombarded with ever more information, more than ever we need enough sleep in order to sort out this continuing avalanche of information.

Having the deep sleep that makes us recuperate physically at the beginning of the night made sense for our ancestors in the savannah for whom physical survival was the one and only priority, and reflection was a luxury. For modern professionals it is the other way around.

LARKS, OWLS AND THE MOST VULNERABLE OF ALL, FAKE-OWLS

In my workshops and coaching sessions I often get questions from people who consider themselves "Owls", i.e. "Evening Types" who function better in the evening. They contrast themselves with "Larks", the "Morning Types" who function best in the morning. Researchers have found that these types are real, that it is partially genetic and that 60% of people are Lark-Owls, functioning somewhere in-between. Typical creative types are often Owls and business types like managers and engineers are often Larks. Interestingly, there might be a link with the way our brain functions. The two halves of our brain do not function in sync. In the morning our left, more analytical brain is faster and in the evening it is the right associative brain. This might also explain why the results of tests and assessment can be very different in the evening or the morning, depending on the extent to which they are typical right-brain or left-brain assignments[171].

Whatever type you are, you always need enough sleep, which is more than the Fake-Owls get. Fake-Owls are a distinction I made myself because in most situations when I am dealing with professionals, "I am a typical Evening Type" is clearly their empty excuse for messing up their sleep habits by going to bed much too late for all the wrong reasons and sleeping way too little because

they have to get to work on time. Real Owls go to bed late and wake up late, so they get enough sleep. The Fake-Owls go to bed late, get up early and live with a chronic sleep debt. This becomes very clear when they do the three tests at the start of this chapter.

In general Larks function better than Owls[172]. Being a Lark is a protecting factor. Being an Owl is a risk factor. They have less healthy life habits, function cognitively below their potential, behave more unethically and asocial and have more psychological and physical problems. Among other things, because they function out of sync with their circadian clock, they build up a sleep debt during the week when their work or family life forces them to wake up early and create a social jetlag by waking (much) later at the weekend. The problem is that in this category researchers do not differentiate between real Owls and Fake-Owls. My hypothesis is that the Fake-Owls more than the genuine Owls run a higher risk of dysfunction and that the core problem is their lack of sleep rather than their bedtime.

LACK OF SLEEP CAUSES ACCIDENTS AND OTHER MISTAKES

As I mentioned earlier in this chapter, a lack of sleep may have played a major role in disasters like the Exxon Valdez oil spill when the helmsman fell asleep, nuclear accidents like the ones in Chernobyl and Three Miles Island and the explosion of the Challenger[173], but you probably didn't make a conscious link with the way you deprive yourself of sleep. Of course you know that a lack of sleep and sleep debt increase the risk of accidents on the road, for adolescents even more than for adults, and that in 40% of cases these are deadly, but do you stop for a rest every time you feel tired?

From national surveys done by American and Canadian authorities we learn that, depending on the generation they belong to, between 25% and 60% of drivers report having nodded off for a moment and 30% having fallen asleep while driving! Drowsy driving is responsible for 20% of all motor vehicle crashes. That would mean that drowsy driving causes approximately 1 million crashes, 500,000 injuries, and 8,000 deaths each year in the U.S.[174]. In Germany too 24% of heavy traffic accidents are the result of a lack of sleep[175]. The risk is especially high for young drivers, and especially teenage drivers, because they sleep less than adults while they should sleep more[176].

How often have *you* had to fight sleep or even nodded off a little while driving? Would you dare say it had never happened to you? Too many professionals and especially managers think they are super(wo)men, getting on a plane on a red-eye flight while already tired, crossing a few time zones and then jumping in a (rental) car. Maybe people keep driving when they are tired because while 85% think that driving under the influence of alcohol is a serious or extremely serious offence, only 50% think the same about driving when tired.

Full disclosure: many years ago I almost drowned myself and my wife in my car in a frozen canal after I returned to Europe after a long stay in Indonesia. Although it happened in winter, on a treacherous slippery road, this accident never would have happened without jetlag. If I had known then what I know now, after all the research for this book, I would have taken a taxi or asked somebody else to drive.

A lack of sleep causes risky behavior, lapses in attention, slower reaction time, impairments to our judgment, difficulties regulating emotions including aggression and a drop in focus. It also undermines our motor skills, decreases coordination, hinders memory recall etc...[177]. One of the trickiest problems is that when we lack sleep, acutely or chronically, the brain tries to steal microsleeps of 1 or 2 seconds. These micro-nods are what you experience when you drive a car tired and that you try to fight by rubbing your eyes, moving about, putting on loud music or stopping for a cup of strong coffee, instead of just stopping and having a 15-minute nap.

To put it simply, a lack of sleep makes us very, if not dangerously, clumsy. You can easily imagine that this not only has consequences for driving a car but also on the shop floor when people drive a forklift, work with heavy equipment and machines, or do fine motor or potentially dangerous manual work[178]. And as I mentioned earlier, hospital interns and nurses make more mistakes and have more traffic accidents when they lack sleep[179]. These are specific examples, but don't underestimate how dire the influence of a lack of sleep or sleep debt is on the quality and quantity of your own brainwork[180]. Read on but be aware that after reading this you can no longer claim ignorance if you keep ruining your brainwork by a lack of sleep.

LACK OF SLEEP ALSO CAUSES DISORDERS AND DISEASES

Although this book focuses on the ways we ruin our intellectual productivity, I'd like to mention briefly that a lack of sleep is not only bad for our brain, but also for the rest of our body. As you certainly understood from reading the paragraphs about your biological clock, every single system of your body is negatively affected by a lack of sleep. As a result, with a lack of sleep, you live shorter not only due to the higher risk of having an accident, but also because you will be ill more often and more severely. Therefore, why would you try to do more by sleeping less, knowing that at the end of our lives short sleepers and normal sleepers have had the same number of waking hours. Indeed, people sleeping between 7 and 9 hours live longer[181].

Moreover, during sleep a unique waste removal system is activated. Remember I called our brain a combination of a computer and a chemical factory? And indeed, as all factories do, these billions of micro-factories produce a lot of waste. Luckily enough, the brain has an amazing drainage system, different from the one in the rest of our body. During sleep and anesthesia this system of drains is open 60% wider and is fully active with the arteries as its pumps to literally flush away the waste produced by the brain cells[182]. One of these "trash" chemicals that build up during the day is adenosine, which interestingly enough inhibits hormones that are responsible for alertness. That way it increases the feeling of sleepiness so that we are motivated to get the sleep needed to get rid of this waste and start the next morning fully alert. Isn't that nice? Brain trash that triggers its own destruction ... if we sleep enough.

One of the best-researched consequences of a lack of sleep is obesity[183]. On average, the people who sleep 8 hours have the healthiest weight. Sleeping less, especially when you sleep 6 hours or less, disturbs your sugar and fat metabolism, makes you crave high-calorie food and you run double the risk of becoming obese, especially if you are a child, young adult or female. An analysis of the research done between 1980 and 2007 convincingly showed that there is a clear association between short sleep duration and increased risk of childhood obesity[184]. Lack of sleep makes you obese for several reasons:

- It messes up the balance between the hunger hormone "Ghrelin" and the saturating hormone "Leptin". One of the consequences is that you crave junk food.
- It lowers the burning of calories because on the one hand with a lack of sleep you move less and on the other hand your thermoregulation is disturbed (think about the shivers you can experience after a night with little sleep).
- During longer days you eat more.
- It suppresses the part of your brain (especially in women) that plays an important role in the inhibition of your behavior, in giving food its affective value, in postponing satisfaction: suppressing short-term gains in favor of long-term ones[185].
- On a calorie-restricting diet, women who sleep enough lose fat, the ones who don't sleep enough tend to lose muscle. If you go on a diet to lose weight, having enough sleep is as important as the diet[186].

Dr. Wright, a sleep researcher, summarizes the issue as follows[187]: "There's something that changes in our brain when we're sleepy that's irrespective of how much energy we need. The brain wants more even when the energy need has been fulfilled."

A lack of sleep may also disturb the way Insulin works in your body, increasing the risk of getting diabetes (also in adolescents!). Together with other factors such as a lack of physical activity this double whammy increases the risk of developing the so-called "Metabolic Syndrome"[188], a disease caused by people's lifestyle and one that is becoming a major public health problem. This is especially the case in sedentary children who are fed on junk food and are glued to their screens, with an increased long-term risk for developing heart diseases, diabetes, strokes and other problems with blood circulation.

A lack of sleep has a negative influence on the production of growth hormone, which is mostly produced during deep sleep. As its name suggests, it stimulates growth in children. But it also stimulates processes that are just as important for adults: regenerating cells, strengthening bones and muscles, burning fat, maintaining the sugar balance and more.

A lack of sleep also undermines your immune system very significantly, not only decreasing the effect of vaccinations[189] but more importantly making bacterial infections, arthritis and allergic reactions more likely[190]. If you sleep less than 7 hours, you have a three times higher risk of catching a cold. Surprisingly, even relatively small decreases in the quality or duration of sleep increase the risk[191].

Chronic sleep disturbance, like that of shift workers, increases the occurrence of certain cancers or makes them worse, especially in organs that are dependent on hormones, like the breast, ovaries or prostate. Shift workers for example run a higher risk of intestinal and prostate cancer, breast cancer and cancer of the lining inside the womb[192].

Cutting back sleep also increases the risk of high blood pressure[193], heart disease[194] and headaches[195]. It undermines your thyroid, which is responsible for your energy levels. It speeds up aging. It makes you look less attractive[196]. It increases the risk of depression[197], suicidal ideas in children[198] and makes you hyperreactive to psychological stress[199].

Finally, a chronic lack of sleep not only diminishes the opportunities and the desire to have sex, it decreases Testosterone and increases Cortisol, both decreasing libido[200]. Why would you want that?

A SPECIAL WAKE-UP CALL FOR PARENTS, TEACHERS AND EDUCATORS

Most researchers agree that healthy adolescents need between 8.5 and 9.5 hours of sleep. An alarming piece of research showed that only 20% get their 8 hours. The problem is that over the years children are gradually going to bed later and later, but still wake up at the same time to go to school.

There is no biological reason why they should sleep less. Quite the contrary: they need more sleep than adults for their brains to mature optimally! In fact, most adolescents are, to use my terminology, Fake-Owls continuously living with a sleep debt, with quite significant negative consequences[201].

The impact of chronic sleep reduction on intellectual performance has been studied very extensively in children and adolescents because many scholars worry about the long-term impact not only on intellectual, emotional and behavioral development, but also on brain development.

Over time, chronic sleep reduction can result in biological consequences such as poor health, especially excess weight, obesity and poor growth (see further on). The psychological consequences found were more emotional problems, lower self-esteem, more depression, suidical thoughts and behavior, behavioral problems, risk-taking behavior, less receptivity to the influence of teachers, impaired cognitive and school performance, daytime sleepiness, depressed mood, alcohol use, caffeine intake, cigarette smoking and even detrimental neurobiological changes[202]. With modern scanners we can see which parts of children's brains develop less when they do not get enough sleep and, sadly, it's the part that is most important for memory formation[203]. Many of these problems have a bi-directional relationship with lack of sleep. The bi-directional relation between lack of sleep and depression has been well studied: lack of sleep causes depression (and more suicide attempts) and depression causes sleep problems[204].

Moreover, the big difference between week and weekend sleeping patterns makes things worse and results in the social jetlag I described above, thus further disturbing sleeping pattrns[205].

▶ **"Almost all teenagers, as they reach puberty, become walking zombies because they are getting far too little sleep."**
PROFESSOR JAMES MAAS (A FAMOUS SLEEP RESEARCHER)

Some very convincing research was carried out by Avi Sadeh, who made perfectly normal, healthy children aged 9-12 sleep one hour more or one hour less than normal for three days. The findings were clear: a little more sleep, even if it is only for a few days, significantly improves the scores on a variety of cognitive tests, even if sleep was more agitated[206]. Another finding was that it is not difficult at all to get children to sleep longer (or shorter). Hence, there is no way for parents to evade their responsibility: preschoolers (3-6) need 11-13 hours, schoolchildren (6-10) need

10-11 hours and adolescents 8.5-9.5 hours.

Another worrying fact is that the problem is worse in lower socio-economic classes where children sleep the least, giving them a supplementary handicap at school[207].

If you have teenagers of your own, they have probably convinced you that they don't need so much sleep, but don't let them fool you. If they made you have doubts, you should know better now. Of course it is more difficult to influence the sleeping habits of adolescents, but from the data about the influence on their brainwork and their bodies, it is very clear: it is worth the (big) effort, if not the fight, and the additional engagement from the parents to achieve these normal sleeping patterns. You too should therefore establish good sleeping habits, setting a good example from very early on.

6 BRAINCHAIN #5 IS OUTSIDE YOUR CONTROL: BRAIN-HOSTILE OPEN OFFICES

Every single time I ask participants in workshops or lectures what undermines their brainwork, with the exception of groups of executives, a majority always complain that one of the major factors is the open offices they have to work in.

There is one other exception though: If you belong to Generation Y, born in the early eighties, you may love the lively, animated, entertaining atmosphere of an open office. You may be convinced it does not hinder your intellectual productivity and creativity. However, think twice because, as I described in the four Brain-Chains above and especially in the chapter "The sorry myth of multitasking kids" and in the separate booklet "The Fifth Brain-Chain", all the research proves you wrong.

Such a high number of negative comments by participants about their open offices spurred me to delve into the research on open offices too. The conclusion from my workshops and from the research is loud and clear: Most open offices are totally unfit for brainwork because they make attention, concentration and reflection very stressful and often nearly impossible.

The goal of this book, however, is to address issues that you can change by yourself or in collaboration with others. For most people doing something about a badly designed office is not within their control. There is almost nothing they can do about it unless they get together and revolt.

The complaints as well as the research, however, were so convincing that I felt I could not just throw it out. Therefore I compiled it into a free separate booklet "The Fifth BrainChain" that gives

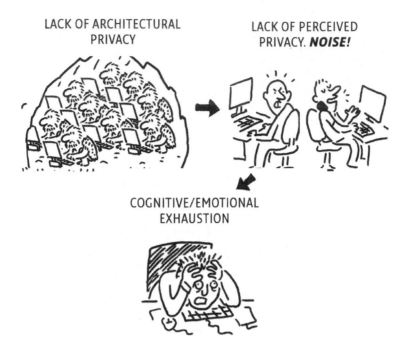

LACK OF ARCHITECTURAL PRIVACY

LACK OF PERCEIVED PRIVACY. ***NOISE!***

COGNITIVE/EMOTIONAL EXHAUSTION

some practical advice and that you can use to prevent bad open offices from being built or to remediate existing ones as much as possible. You can find it at Amazon.com or download free of cost from www.brainchains.org .

In principle the case against all these bad offices is simple and evident. The quality of the office has a major impact on the performance of brainworkers. You do not need the hundreds of studies about the impact of the office on the performance of people to be convinced of this. In case you nonetheless doubt this, I am sorry to say that recent review articles confirm my conclusion from 1999: "Many modern buildings, especially office blocks, make their inhabitants psychologically and physically ill because they fail to take account of the primitive (wo)man in all of us and his/her very fundamental, deeply ingrained in more needs." [208]

▶ **If you work requires concentration do the telephone test. If you can hear any phone conversation you're in the wrong office.**

"Such designs are argued to provide a flexible working environment, to offer space and cost savings and to promote communication between office occupants. However, research suggests that open-plan office occupants may experience a lack of both visual and acoustical privacy and an increase in the amount of unwanted distractions and interruptions. In addition, the proposed benefits regarding improved communication are often not realized. Furthermore, open-plan occupants sometimes experience unfavorable ambient conditions, partly because of the lack of control resulting from a shared office space."

KATE CHARLES AND JENNIFER VEITCH IN AN IN-DEPTH GOVERNMENTAL STUDY IN 2002[209]

"Office type clearly correlates to health, well-being, and job satisfaction among employees. The cell office and flex office both scored high with respect to good health and job satisfaction, whereas open-plan office types generally scored low."

CHRISTINA AND LENNART BODIN 2008[210]

"Research evidence shows that employees face a multitude of problems such as the loss of privacy, loss of identity, low work productivity, various health issues, overstimulation and low job satisfaction when working in an open plan work environment."

VINESH G. OOMMEN, MIKE KNOWLES, ISABELLA ZHAO 2008[211]

"The findings from an extensive body of research, suggest that open plan offices do not generally support advocates' blanket claims of improved communication, satisfaction and productivity. In fact, most findings suggest the exact opposite."

GEORGE MYLONAS AND JANE CARSTAIRS 2010[212]

"There is a need for awareness of the unpredictability of spatial design, and simplistic views of openness as unequivocally leading to flexibility, innovation, and other favorable or desirable organizational outcomes need to be challenged. Furthermore, the findings also show how strategic attempts to plan for flexibility can backfire and that flexibility along one

dimension within the organization can imply a reduction along another dimension."
SARA VÄRLANDER 2012[213]

"Distraction by noise and loss of privacy were identified as the major causes of workspace dissatisfaction in open-plan office layouts. Open-plan office layout is commonly assumed to facilitate communication and interaction between co-workers, promoting workplace satisfaction and team-work effectiveness... [but] benefits of enhanced 'ease of interaction' were smaller than the penalties of increased noise level and decreased privacy resulting from open-plan office configuration...
Our results categorically contradict the industryaccepted wisdom that open-plan layout enhances communication between colleagues and improves occupants' overall work environmental satisfaction. This study showed that occupants' satisfaction on the interaction issue was actually higher for occupants of private offices ... the increment of overall workspace satisfaction due to the positive impact of ease of interaction in open-plan office layouts failed to offset the decrements by negative impacts of noise and privacy..."
JUNGSOO KIM AND RICHARD DEDEAR 2013

"IT'S THE ONLY PLACE LEFT
THAT'S NOT OPEN PLAN!"

7 FOUR BRAINCHAINS COMBINED: E-MAIL AND CO, WEAPONS OF MASS DISTRACTION FOR THE HOMO INTERRUPTUS.

In this chapter I will treat e-mail, social media, texting etc. as one because the negative effects of how we use them are the same. And I will use 'e-mail' to refer to them because in the workplace e-mail is still the most frequent counterproductive distracter of the lot.

7.1 A GREAT TOOL HAS BECOME COUNTERPRODUCTIVE AND CORPORATE SOCIAL MEDIA ARE NO SOLUTION

People send 182 billion e-mails every day or 66 trillion a year[214]. E mail is a fantastic tool that has become the dominant "communication" tool in the business environment. The way we use this tool, however, turns it into a combination of all four BrainChains at the same time: it is the major cause of always being connected, multitasking, continuous low stress and even lack of sleep. An incessant input of email, text and phone makes your brain reactive and reactive equals primitive.

E-mail is not only a huge time-waster but it also ruins our focus, concentration and reflection. I explained in the chapter about multitasking in Section 1 how unexpectedly huge the loss of time and energy. The Homo Interruptus forces his reflecting brain to switch all the time, every single e-mail pushes all the information about the task he was working on a little further to the exit of your temporary memory, it takes on average 25 minutes to get back to the task he was working on and in 40% of cases he doesn't get back to the original task at all[215].

INCESSANT INPUT

OF EMAIL, TEXT AND PHONE
MAKES YOUR BRAIN

REACTIVE

Most people totally underestimate how disruptive and costly the effect is of receiving an e-mail and how utterly counterproductive it is to look at your e-mails all the time. As a result they also have little mercy on the receivers of all the e-mails they send. When a research spy program monitors their e-mail use, they are always surprised that they spend much more time on it than they thought[216].

For too many the amount of e-mail has reached crisis and panic levels. Half of people have the feeling that they have lost control over their e-mail[217] and from the research on stress we know that this feeling has a very negative impact on our stress-balance.

A survey by Harris Interactive found that 94% of employees reach their daily e-mail tipping point at 50 e-mails. Any more than 50 e-mails causes information overload[218]. In my groups, however, anywhere between 75 and 200 e-mails a day is not exceptional. My survey of 1,152 managers and professionals shows that on average they spend 3 hours a day (median) doing e-mails. Doing e-mails has become a big part of their job. I almost wrote an "important" part of their job, but up to 80% of their e-mail is not important at all.

For managers, the consequences of all these hours spent peering at their screens and pecking at their (micro) keyboards are even worse because it prevents them from interacting, communicating, leading and coaching their people. It is their employees who therefore suffer as a result. And although they're not aware of it, e-mailing managers are one of the most significant factors in lowering productivity because most people feel they must respond to a manager's e-mail within minutes. Hence they become even less efficient, firstly because they constantly check their e-mails just in case a superior has sent one and so are continuously distracted by all the e-mails and secondly because they stop whatever work they are doing to respond to one of these e-mails.

For the majority of professionals always being connected leads to more not less work and surprisingly many experience less instead of more flexibility[219]. For younger employees the continuous stream of messages from social media makes the situation even worse.

Little by little, more and more people are becoming convinced that the daily e-mail avalanche decreases productivity in alarming ways instead of increasing it, and they're right. Larry Page, Google's chief executive, does not like e-mail, even his own Gmail, saying the tedious back and forth takes too long to solve problems. He discourages excessive use of e-mail and stimulates quick, unilateral decision-making by others and himelf[220].

▶ **If you use e-mail for anything other than informing people and transmitting simple, unequivocal requests for tasks with little ambiguity, you are creating problems for the receivers, the company and yourself.**

The major problem is that e-mail was not made for communication (two-way) but for sharing information (one-way) and to keep records. Trying to make it bi-directional, a kind of a conversation, creates a lot of back and forth, as anyone who has tried to set up a meeting by e-mail knows all too well. So you can imagine how totally inefficient it is when you try to use it to reach a mutual agreement or a common understanding on more complex or ambiguous subjects. Too many people try to use e-mail for instant communication, answering (and expecting an answer) immediately. In one large company 70% of e-mails were even answered within 6 (!) seconds. This means that all the time, often every few minutes, people were interrupting what they were doing. This totally ruins their intellectual performance. Therefore you will never be as intellectually productive as you could be if e-mail has become your default communication tool. The question "Why did you not respond to my e-mail yet" is the clearest expression of people's confusion about the use of e-mail as a (non)communication tool and their total ignorance of the huge cost of task-switching.

You should not (NOT) use e-mail for the instantaneous exchange of ideas and opinions. If something is urgent, very important or needs discussion: talk. Using the phone and best of all face-to-face conversations is much more efficient and effective. You should certainly never use e-mail in the case of conflict because conflicts escalate more quickly and last longer via e-mail[221].

E-mail is simply too poor to be a good communication tool. Up to 90% of the most important information in a face-to-face meeting is non-verbal. People realize this and try to compensate in their e-mails by using :-), :-(, :-D, (-.-)zzz, (^.~) and other emoticons, which probably should be called idioticons ;-).

For communication, you should only use e-mail when a conversation or a phone call is really impossible, and that is much rarer than most people think. E-mail gets in the way of necessary and important conversations in real life and real time. We have all experienced colleagues, bosses and other important people who disappear and hide behind their computers doing e-mails instead of inspiring, coaching, leading, helping…Using e-mails to avoid real communication, real conversations and difficult confrontations is always a mistake. The most heinous one is firing people by e-mail. The only exception is when you are somewhat autistic because then you need e-mail to avoid the conversations you cannot handle, but you should warn people that you have this disorder ;-).

An additional productivity-killing aspect is that too many brainworkers let their e-mails determine their agenda. They remain in reactive mode and continuously let their reflex brain react to incoming messages instead of deciding what's important and setting their own agenda.

No wonder many people talk about the "e-mail monster" and how to tame it[222]. But in fact it is not a monster at all; it is an "e-mail Frankenstein" continuously producing Frankenmails, because we have created it ourselves. The problem is not the tool but how people and companies use it. As a result it becomes a major source of hyperconnectivity, multitasking, information overload and stress. For some it has even become a major reason why they don't sleep enough.

▶ **Corporate abuse of e-mail is often a symptom of bad corporate communication.**

ICT and consulting companies are now touting and pushing organizations to use social media type communication platforms rather than e-mail. These are software products and services that are supposed to help employees communicate more efficiently than via e-mail. They are supposed to create Facebook-like social communities. They use messages similar to the tweets of Twitter, posting information, video, audio and written material to a feed, "liking" and "sharing" these.

The main advantage of these corporate media tools, if they deliver on their promises, is that people may stop using e-mail for tasks it was never made for like to-do lists, archiving, scheduling meetings, sharing knowledge or even project management. Most corporate ICT tools lack a common and easily searchable archive of knowledge and a high-performing search engine. Therefore, if the corporate social media provide this, these tools are likely to outperform e-mail in making it much easier to find the right information and the right people for a particular task. It is very likely that employees, and certainly those who use social media in their private lives, will use them a lot.

But I would not bet much on these tools significantly increasing real intellectual productivity and creativity. One reason is that searching for information only takes up 19% of the workday[223]. More importantly though, even if 30% of e-mail could move to these platforms, it wouldn't change the fundamental brainwork-killers: hyperconnectedness and multitasking. If corporate social media are anywhere as addictive as Facebook, employees might check them even more often than they check their e-mails now. If they check their Chatter, Yammer and Jive 50 times or more a day as they do with their e-mails or Facebook, if managers and colleagues still expect people to react within minutes to new postings, then the gain in intellectual productivity will be marginal or negative because the brainworkers will still be inefficient, hyperconnected, hyper-distracted multitaskers and task-hoppers.

Moreover, like Facebook "friends" they will often avoid the much-needed real conversations by going online and favoring a connection where a conversation is what is really needed. Hence these corporate social-media tools will only deliver their potential if the workers learn to, and are strongly encouraged to, limit their time online and to totally disconnect on a regular basis to do real value-adding intellectual work and, above all, if the company communication and collaboration cultures are already efficient and sane to begin with, which primarily depends on the management culture.

7.2 E-MAIL HAS BECOME A MAJOR TIME-WASTER. THE COST IS SECONDS FOR THE SENDER, HOURS FOR THE RECEIVER

As we have seen, most users think that most e-mails are unimportant and do not add value. The immense and growing opportunity cost of e-mails impedes real value-adding tasks and so they are becoming more and more counterproductive. The major problem is that low-priority or even irrelevant e-mails are crowding out the high-priority, important ones. Many e-mails, up to 73% of e-mails in fact, are not even job-related[224].

From my research and that of others I learned that in some groups up to 70% and in some cases even 90% of e-mail is "internal spam" or "**iSpam**": it is neither important nor urgent[225] and sometimes totally irrelevant for the receiver! These professionals then spend between 1 and 1.5 hours per day, 1 to 1.5 working days per week, and 1 to 1.5 months a year processing irrelevant e-mail!!!! It is easy to imagine the huge cost of handling all this iSpam! Imagine the even bigger opportunity cost of more important work not being done or being done badly. Moreover, each interruption also has an impact on the emotional state of the receiver. The degree of disruption depends on the user's mental load at the point of the interruption[226].

But even these frustrated people keep checking their e-mail all the time because they not only overestimate the risk of missing an important one, but also because finding that rare nugget in a pile of shit reinforces the seeking behavior, as it does with addicts as I described in BrainChain #1. The automatic monitoring and analysis of video registrations of e-mail users shows that people do not wait to answer e-mails at a more convenient time, as they should, but that 70% of e-mails are opened within 6 seconds of arriving and 85% within 2 minutes[227]. This certainly makes the resemblance between these people and the addicted rats in BrainChain #1 most striking.

Besides, nobody ever looks at only one selected e-mail. Even if you search for a particular e-mail, 90% of the time you get distracted by others. You stop the important task you are doing, go into your e-mail program, get into your e-mail mind, do a few e-mails, switching contexts every time and losing lots of information about the more important task in the process, and then finally exit the e-mail context. When you return to that important original task you have to start over the thinking almost from scratch... how inefficient can you be? The price you pay in lost time and mistakes for doing these e-mails is very high.

In experiments where all e-mail use is automatically registered, it turns out that for some people who check their e-mails all the time as they come in, they spend only 15 seconds on 50% of their e-mail and more than 5 minutes on only 4%. This means that their brain spends more time on switching than on actually looking at the e-mail, time that disappears without any trace in the black switching-hole: Homo Interruptus at its worst.

The total cost of sending an e-mail to (many) more people than is useful or necessary is negligible for the sender; the burden of the continuous flood of iSpam in terms of time, energy and inefficiency for the receiver, on the other hand, is huge. It's the senders who keep the productivity-ruining avalanche going.

Let's do the math: adding just one unnecessary receiver on an e-mail costs the sender 2 seconds. If during a day he does this 30 times, it costs the sender only 2 minutes (even less if he makes thoughtless use of "groups"). The cost in terms of productivity at the receiver's end when he receives 30 irrelevant e-mails a day is over an hour! 30 x 15 seconds to have a quick look at it to find out it is irrelevant and delete it and a 2-minute loss of concentration (not counting all the other important switching costs described in BrainChain #2).

For the receiver the cost is much less of course if he batch-processes his e-mails (see Section 3 for details). If you are not convinced, just try a few days of limiting your e-mail checking to two to three times a day and do it in batches of 30-45 minutes, your gain of time will be at least 25-50%, certainly enough to convince you, unless you are addicted. In the latter case, you will worry about all those e-mails that are urgent, from people who really need you immediately, that are important for your career etc... and all the other usually neurotic excuses.

In any case, the cost for the receiver is still significantly higher than for the sender. If everybody stopped and reflected for just 2 seconds before adding a recipient to an e-mail, if everybody picked up the phone when there's a need for two-way communication, if everybody stopped using "Reply to all", if everybody stopped sending to groups, and if everybody stopped sending cover-my-back e-mails, then everybody would free up massive amounts of time and energy at the receiver's end.

What might prevent people from changing their attitude is an interesting contradiction. 50% of people think they receive much more e-mail than they send and only 12% think they send more than they receive. 26% prefer to send e-mail while only 3% prefer to receive e-mail[228]. Since it seems very unlikely that these 12% cause the problem for 50%, I think people just have the impression that they receive more because they hate it.

Anthony Burgess summarized the main reasons why e-mail has become such a never-ending flow of irrelevant or poor information as four e-mail-deficiencies[229]:

Information deficiency: The recipient is left in limbo about what to do with the e-mail.

E-mails that fail to give the recipients enough information to act upon.

Ambiguous poorly written e-mails lead to misunderstandings.

Poor use of the subject line: it does not say when action is required, which is important for prioritizing.

Poorly targeted: Irrelevant or untargeted e-mails increase the time employees spend reading.

Inappropriate use of the carbon copy (cc) function.

"Cover my back" e-mails.

Overuse of the 'Reply to-all' function.

Information-only e-mails without letting the recipient know this.

Selection of the wrong medium: The communication medium must be appropriate for the message that is to be transmitted.

E-mail is too often used when face-to-face communication or the phone should be used instead.

E-mail used to avoid unwanted social interaction.

E-mail used for tasks with ambiguity: when used by groups,

e-mail is only more effective than face-to-face communication for a task of low ambiguity.

Interruption: E-mails interrupt from more important work.
Recovery from an e-mail interruption takes 1 minute.
Processing and filing of e-mail.
Poor use of subject line makes filing more difficult.
E-mail stays in the user's inbox.

This all sounds very negative. But there is a positive conclusion from his research: training sessions targeted on the sending side of e-mailing can significantly improve e-mail overload.

7.3 CHECKING YOUR E-MAIL ALL THE TIME, ESPECIALLY ON A PHONE, IS RIDICULOUSLY INEFFICIENT

I hope I convinced you in the chapters on BrainChain #1 and #2 that checking your e-mail all the time is very inefficient, but it becomes ridiculously so when you do it on your smartphone!

> Unbalanced brainworkers never have time to watch their daughter playing soccer on Sunday.
> Poorly balanced brainworkers are constantly pecking away on their smartphone while trying to watch their daughter playing soccer.
> Blandly balanced brainworkers keep an eye on their smartphone while they are watching their daughter playing and immediately peck an answer when one of the e-mails comes from their boss.
> Well-balanced brainworkers have their phone in their pocket, get totally involved in the game of their daughter and send their boss a thoughtful answer the next day.
> Inspired by an idea by Jennifer Chatman[230]

You don't need a degree in ergonomics or even a college degree to understand that doing e-mails all the time on the tiny keys of a smartphone with the biggest and the least dexterous fingers of your hand, while the autocorrect tries to make fun of your input, cannot be very efficient to say the least. As I described in the chapter about local stress it is also as bad as you can get it in terms of ergonomics, ergonomic efficiency and risks of getting RSI, neck and shoulder pains and headaches.

To make things even worse, on a phone you tend to handle your e-mails one at a time, which is the least efficient way. If you start with the most recent ones and answer them, you miss information from earlier ones. On the other hand, if you do them in chronological order, you are often answering questions and issues that have already been answered.

Even with the smartest of smartphones or tablets and the best of connections it is much more difficult to access your calendar, a memo or a spreadsheet than on a big screen, and it is impossible to have them open together next to each other. Smartphones have no desktop and on a tablet you lose half of your screen for a clumsy error-prone keyboard. Moreover, in the office most professionals have information at hand that is not easily available on the Internet or that is very difficult to read on a phone. So, after having already read the mail on their phone or tablet, they decide to do it again in the office!

Your concentration and attention on the go is only a fraction of what it is in your office, especially once you have learned to disconnect yourself there from all interruptions. By working on the go you will make more stupid mistakes more often, typically reply to all with a message only one person should have gotten and react in ways you would never do when you are writing in a better suited environment.

As I mentioned earlier, reading off a big computer screen results in slower reading and a decrease in comprehension and recall (and drier tired eyes) compared to reading off paper. So just imagine what you are doing to your poor eyes by reading all the time from a Lilliputian screen. Besides, that small screen showing you only one sentence or paragraph at a time does not allow you to read diagonally, slowing you down even more when the text is longer than a sentence or a paragraph and further ruining your comprehension and recall.

> **Doing professional e-mails on a smartphone has the quality of Linus, from the Peanuts cartoons, playing Beethoven on a toy piano.**

The only way to make reading e-mails even more ridiculously inefficient and ineffective would be do it while you are in a meeting, having a conversation, eating, watching TV ... or of course while driving, which as we will see is rather criminal even if you do it hands-free.

In a creative, thought-provoking piece of research that I hope will be repeated in larger groups and in other contexts, Gloria Marks and her colleagues [231] asked office workers to take five-day "e-mail vacations" where they did not check their mail and then compared the results with how they functioned during three "normal" days. She interviewed not only them but also their closest colleagues. She made them fill in all kinds of questionnaires before and after. She also observed them and recorded their heart rates, and software sensors observed when they switched from one browser window to another. She found that:

- checking e-mails all the time is bad for your health;
- during non-e-mail days employees multitasked much less, reported more focus and their work was less fragmented;
- when catching up afterwards they learned that batch-processing e-mail is much more efficient;
- the colleagues in the participants' work groups did not report detrimental effects when their colleagues were off e-mail;
- face-to-face interactions in the workplace increased and this was considered by all to be a benefit;
- they realized that e-mail hindered their work relationships;
- the most frequently mentioned negative effect of the experiment was a feeling of being cut off from information being exchanged in the organization;
- and the burden of e-mail was caused by:
  1 social norms expecting an immediate response
  2 the sheer volume of e-mails
  3 the lack of self control to not check e-mails all the time.

Of course, it is not realistic for all of us to take regular one-week e-mail vacations. However, what we can all do is to plan short "e-mail vacations" every working day and week. Of course there are professions where always being connected is important, but they are much rarer than you think. There's a 95% chance that your job is NOT one of them. You will be more productive the day you regularly disconnect from all iSpam and iDistractions and batch-process your e-mails. If you think you can never disconnect from your clients, like modern salespeople who are always on the phone even while driving, you are wrong. Once you are convinced how counterproductive it is to always be connected, you will discover that there are in fact many more productive solutions available... even for salespeople. (Much more on this in Section 3.)

▶ **It does not disturb them in thinking, simply because they do not think; they e-mail, which is their substitute for thought.**
PARAPHRASING ARTHUR SCHOPENHAUER: ON NOISE. 1851

8 DANGEROUS BRAINCHAINS: USING YOUR PHONE WHILE DRIVING, EVEN HANDS-FREE

8.1 DRIVING WHILE USING A PHONE: "SUPERMAN DISORDER"

Everybody seems to know that it is very dangerous to use your phone while driving, especially texting, and yet most people keep doing it.

60% of motorists think talking on a cell phone while driving is very dangerous.

45% have even been hit or nearly hit by a driver on the phone.

88% rate drivers who text and e-mail as a very serious threat to their safety and consider such behavior unacceptable.

52% feel less safe on the roads today than they did five years ago, mainly because of the use of phones while driving and especially texting and mailing.

75% indicated that they would lose respect for a friend doing this.

80% support a law banning texting while driving.

50% would support a law banning all phone use while driving.

And yet...

25% of people (60% of young people) text while driving.

80% use their phone and think that making a call does not negatively impact their own driving performance.

98% consider themselves safe drivers.

The result:

660,000 drivers are on the phone at any moment of the day across the USA.

24% of all car crashes involve cell phone use.

The phone death toll = ± 3,300 to 8,000 lives/year = many more than the number of people killed on 9/11 [232].

> **"Safe" drivers on the phone kill more people every year than the terrorists on 9/11.**

This is rather absurd. We cannot consider all these drivers to be so depressive that they want to kill themselves or so cruel that they want to kill or maim others. Hence, it looks like they suffer from a very bad and epidemic case of "Superman Disorder": a pathological delusion in which patients think that using a phone while driving is dangerous only for other drivers, not for themselves, because they psychotically think that they are invulnerable and have unique super-human reflexes and attention powers. As with many other psychotic disorders, no rational arguments can change these irrational thoughts.

Or is it because these drivers genuinely don't know that it is much more dangerous than they think and because they don't understand why it is so extremely dangerous?

Maybe you thought the same until you had read the chapter on multitasking and you realized that nobody can multitask and that doing it in the car might be dangerous for you too. In that case please read on because the research about the use of a phone while driving impressively supports the research about multitasking and lays bare the incapacity of our reflecting brain to multitask.

For more or less rational human beings who are not suffering from "Superman Disorder" and who want to give their reflecting brain a chance to decide about potential life-threatening behavior, I have summarized some of the most interesting research about using ICT while driving. If this chapter convinces only 10% of readers to radically stop this dangerous habit, it might save a few lives, maybe your own.

8.2 THE RISK IS 4 TO 23 TIMES HIGHER; HANDS-FREE AND EYES-FREE ARE NOT SAFE

Back in the early 1960s Martin Cooper, the man who developed the first portable cell phone, testified before a Michigan state commission about the risks of talking on a phone while driving. "There should be a lock on the dial," he said he had testified, "so that you couldn't dial while driving."[233]

David Strayer, one of the major researchers on distracted driving, concluded in 2009: "We've spent billions on air bags, antilock brakes, better steering, safer cars and roads, but the number of fatalities has remained constant. Our return on investment for those billions is zero, and that's because we're using [our mobile phone] devices in our cars"[234].

In October 2011 there was a three-day total blackout of Blackberry services in the United Arab Emirates. The directors of the police departments reported that during these three days in Abu Dhabi there were 40% fewer traffic accidents (normally one every 3 minutes) and no fatal ones. In Dubai there were 20% fewer traffic accidents[235].

In 2013 the media reported crashes not only of cars, but also of planes, helicopters, trucks and trains where the driver or pilot was busy with a phone.

If you think these are only anecdotes, look at the hundreds of research articles that have been published on the subject. The research has been done in surveys, on simulators, on special test tracks, in real driving situations (with or without continuous video monitoring), in 100 cars equipped with multiple sensors and cameras, in brain scanners... you name it[236]. The result is that since reviewing the research for this chapter I never ever phone any more while driving. NEVER!

TEXTING WHILE DRIVING
RISK X 23 !!
TEXTING WHILE DRIVING IS
CRIMINAL

FROM TODAY ON, YOU CAN NO LONGER CLAIM IGNORANCE!

Although there is some variation in the results depending on the method used and the driving circumstances[237], the risk of an accident is four to eight times greater when you phone while driving. And I can't repeat this often enough: CALLING FROM HANDS-FREE AND VOICE-COMMANDED (EYES-FREE) KITS IS JUST AS DANGEROUS[238]. Even people ignoring a call while their phone is ringing run a higher risk of a collision or a speed violation[239].

Researcher David Strayer concludes: "When driving conditions and time on task were controlled for, the impairments associated with using a cell phone while driving is more dangerous than driving while drunk, and doing it hands-free does not make any difference"[240]. The impairment is higher for older people[241], although they try to compensate by driving more slowly and by keeping a steady speed. Moreover, the cardiovascular and respiratory changes show an increase of stress[242].

The conclusion is loud and crystal clear: don't use your phone while driving, not even hands-free. The only advantage of using your phone while driving, if you are only thinking about yourself and not about your potential victims, is that it provides a lot of fresh young organs for transplants. So if you keep phoning while driving, at least have your donor card ready.

▶   **Hands-free and eyes-free kits do not make any difference: The bottleneck is your brain.**

Texting while driving is a recipe for disaster: not only is your conscious brain busy but on top of that your eyes don't look at the road for an average of 5 seconds and your hands are more or less off the wheel. Studies show that there is a logarithmic relation between the risk of an accident and the time you don't look at the road. When you send a text or a brief e-mail, you take your eyes off the road repeatedly for an average of 5 seconds. Five seconds at about 40 miles/hour (70 km/h) means that you didn't look at the road for about 100 yards (110 meters)! That's the same as driving with your eyes closed for the length of an entire football or soccer field and doing so several times in a row!

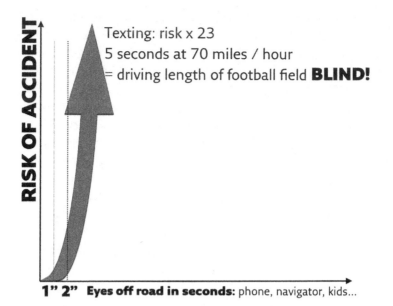

RISK OF ACCIDENT

Texting: risk x 23
5 seconds at 70 miles / hour
= driving length of football field **BLIND!**

1" 2" Eyes off road in seconds: phone, navigator, kids...

Don't think you can keep the road in your peripheral vision. You can't, even if you have the impression that you can. The part of our eye we focus with is a tiny spot in the middle of our eye that covers only 10 degrees. At arm's length this is about the size of a fist. All the rest is fuzzy peripheral vision. A little further on I will explain why we don't experience it as fuzzy. In our peripheral vision, only very colorful objects or things that move will catch our attention if they move against a rather still background. When as a driver you look at the screen of your phone, even if you keep it in front of you, or at the navigator on your console, in your peripheral vision you will not only not see a person or car standing still, but since everything is moving in the background, you might not even see a car moving in your direction.

No wonder the risk of getting involved in a crash is 23 (!!!) times higher[243]. Instead of pussyfooting around the problem, we should call this behavior suicidal or criminal, depending which side you take, the perpetrator's or the victim's. In any case it's very stupid.

A few months ago I took a taxi. When I got in, the driver was watching a TV show on his dashboard computer. I thought the TV would stop automatically once we started. It didn't. I asked the driver how this was possible and he explained that the TV only worked with the hand brake on, but that it was very simple to hack this with a simple short-

circuit. He was rather angry when I told him to stop the TV or take me back to the station to get another taxi.

Most of you will agree that the driver's behavior was stupid, unprofessional and dangerous. Do you think the same about somebody who is texting while driving? You should.

> **"You have to be certifiable to think that you can stare at a small screen and thumb-type on a tiny keyboard for 5 or 6 seconds while going at 65 miles an hour and not be a potential threat to everyone in your path. In the opinion of many safety experts, self-deluding multitaskers have had their way long enough."**
>
> CLYDE HABERMAN QUOTED IN
> THE NEW YORK TIMES 31 AUGUST 2009

Young adults know that texting while driving is very risky and riskier than talking on a cell phone[244] and that it should be forbidden[245]. About 50% of teens and adults have been passengers in a car when the driver used the cell phone in a way that put themselves or others in danger[246]. And yet 70% of young adult drivers text, 81% reply to texts and 92% read texts while driving, notwithstanding their awareness of the risks!!!!! They keep their subjective perception of risk low by driving a little more slowly, which of course doesn't make much of a difference in terms of risk.[247]

The 2010 American Automobile Association (AAA) report concludes: "Young drivers are well informed about distracted driving, but their "heroic" assessment of their own driving and the impact distraction has on their abilities undermines their willingness to change their behavior." Clearly, 92% of young drivers suffer from Superman Disorder.

Since the risk of causing an accident while texting is 23 times higher, I don't think I am exaggerating when I say that texting while driving is criminal, because taking your own life is one thing, but killing or maiming somebody else is quite another.

8.3 WHY USING A PHONE WHILE DRIVING IS SO VERY DANGEROUS

USING YOUR PHONE WHILE DRIVING IS MINDLESS MULTITASKING

Students posted at a residential crossroad with four-way stop signs observed 1,700 drivers approaching. 78% of drivers not using a phone stopped as is required by law, while 74.5% of the drivers on the phone just ignored the stop sign[248].

When drivers got the instruction to take a left turn at an intersection clearly marked with a "no left turn" sign, 80% of drivers on the phone took the turn and had not seen the sign[249].

Using your phone while driving is a recipe for disaster and hands-free kits do not make any difference whatsoever. In a study that compared tuning the radio, entering an address in a navigation system, 10-digit dialing, dialing via contact selection and text messaging, text messaging was associated with the highest drop in driving performance by far. Entering a destination was number two, followed by the two phone-dialing tasks. Tuning the radio had the lowest level of degradation[250]. The research about using the phone while driving perfectly confirms the research about multitasking.

The most important is not only where your hands are and where your eyes are looking but above all whether your brain can handle the two tasks. From what I explained in the first section on the brain, you may have guessed that the answer to that is no. The actual research in simulators and in real life is very clear: the human brain cannot safely handle a phone and a car at the same time. Period.

Unfortunately, the situation is getting worse. Car and ICT companies are selling speech-commanded and even voice-to-text technology that lets drivers not only phone but also text, e-mail, Facebook, find shops and restaurants etc... while driving! As if these companies do not know as well as any researcher in this field, or as well as you after reading this book, that it is not just a question of where our hands and eyes are, but that the major danger is that our brain just can't handle this. Therefore, whatever the sales pitch of your car or phone company may promise, while you are driving, speech-based interaction with your phone or on-board computer is not at all safe and speech-to-text interaction is the worst[251].

> **Hands-free and eyes-free kits are not an improvement because our brain is the major limiting factor. Pending brain-free, driving the only safe way of driving is with no ICT whatsoever.**

Driving a car is an excellent example of simultaneous multitasking. If we had to do this with our reflecting brain only, it would be impossible because that brain system can't multitask and when you are driving you have to think about so many things at the same time. If we only used the thinking brain we would never evolve beyond the stage we all went through the first time we learned to drive: always forgetting something while we were concentrating on something else, always making mistakes while we were concentrating on avoiding other mistakes.

Luckily, through continuous repetition, more and more of these complex procedures gradually become routine habits, stored in the implicit knowledge that your reflex brain uses without much need for reflective thinking. It acts as an automatic pilot for all the routine driving behavior. Contrary to what people think, this takes a few years of driving to become "natural". Therefore, if there is one area where the use of a phone should be completely banned, it is in the hands of the drivers who use them most: young novice drivers.

But driving while on the phone is almost as brainless for experienced drivers because even with the help of our reflex brain we can't drive safely while on the phone because our "automatic pilot" cannot drive the car all by itself, because not all driving is routine. It needs the attention of the reflecting brain, the consciously thinking brain too. Freed from the routine acts of driving, the reflecting brain is available to keep an eye on all the non-routine events that happen on the road. But, as we have seen, the reflecting brain only has a very limited attention capacity.

Remember the experiment I described in Section 1 that showed that visual attention and auditory attention compete in a zero-sum game? When our attention switches to sounds, the attention for the visual input decreases immediately and vice versa[252]. It does not require any further explanation to understand that this so-called "inattentional blindness" is a big risk when you are on the phone or are having an intense, concentrated or emotional conversation while driving. Every activity that competes for the attention of your visual attention or for your reflecting brain in general increases the risk of an accident. Recent research seems to indicate that the reason our attention is so badly messed up is specifically linked to a competition with speech and language. Even preparing to talk is already a distraction, causing a delay in the detection of a hazard by ¼ to 1 second, which at 60 mph (100 km/hr) equates to a delay of 36.8 ft (10.2 m) to 82.8 ft (12.6 m), just the distance you need to avoid a sudden hazard[253]. This is just one more reason why voice-commanded systems and especially voice-to-text or voice-to-email will NOT make the use of ICT in the car much safer.

The other side of the coin is that paying full attention to the road lowers your attention for a conversation, which is not good for the discussion or for your conclusions.

Hence, attention is the core limiting factor, and hands-free or eyes-free kits do not change that at all. As a result, when you drive while on the phone you react more slowly, make riskier choices, brake later or not at all, and/or change lanes without knowing because listening intently competes with seeing. This is also true when you phone on your bike or while walking, but given the slower speed, the consequences are smaller, until a cyclist on the phone... meets a driver on the phone.

As I explained in Section 1, the reflecting brain also has major difficulties switching between totally different domains. Switching from talking about the traffic with your passenger to reacting to what actually happens on the road is easier and quicker to do than switching from a business call or having a difficult and important conversation with your passenger.

USING YOUR PHONE IS THE WORST CAUSE OF DISTRACTED DRIVING

The number of people wounded, maimed and killed by drivers on the phone is staggering. In the USA alone, every year more people are killed by people on the phone than by the terrorists on 9/11. Yet these numbers underestimate the problem because phone use is not routinely or uniformly checked after an accident. Anything that takes your eyes off the road, your hands off the wheel or strongly engages our reflecting brain is a serious risk. Of course there are other causes of distraction that make driving unnecessarily dangerous. For example fiddling around with the car's sound system, looking at beautiful scenery or a fascinating billboard, opening the candy bar you just bought in the gas station, having a difficult or emotional conversation with a passenger, putting on make-up or shaving, looking at and helping a vomiting baby, resetting your navigator, wiping the chocolate crumbs off the candy bar from your lap... One of the riskiest is rowdy situations that can occur when young people are in the car together with a young driver[254]. If your radio is blasting out, you might not hear cars honking to warn you or ambulances asking for room to pass[255].

Taking into consideration all the possible causes of an accident, the phone is by far the most dangerous distraction because it's omnipresent, anywhere and anytime. On a two-hour trip you probably won't eat more than one hamburger while driving, but you may have one phone conversation after another. Of course it's impossible to eliminate all distractions, so we should focus on the worst ones and the most frequent ones and the phone is by far the number one. 80% of drivers use their phone while driving, 40% do it routinely and at any time 7-10% of drivers are on the phone. And we ain't seen nothing yet; wait till drivers start wearing Google glasses.

You can decide not to put on make-up because the driving situation does not allow it, but other people call you all the time without having a clue about the driving conditions. Because of habits, peer pressure, company pressure or addiction, most people cannot resist taking a call, unless the driving situation is really extremely difficult, and even then many still do.

Driving has also become so much of a routine, taken care of by

BRAIN ON PHONE IS WORSE THAN **BRAIN ON 8‰ ALCOHOL** OR **BRAIN ON MARIJUANA**

our reflex brain, that it has become boring. Our unconscious brain has taken over so much of the routine tasks that our conscious brain is bored. We also become overconfident and forget that the unconscious brain can only handle routine and that our conscious brain can only deal with one thought and its context at a time.

The statistics are difficult to keep updated because every year the use of the phone in the car increases. In the USA the National Highway Traffic Safety Administration[256] found that basically 80% of drivers phone while driving and drivers under 25 are the heaviest callers and texters. In the under-25 age group, 60% text while driving. They don't even slow down when they are on the phone and really nothing will keep these drivers from using their phone while driving. Even very bad weather will only stop half of them from using their phone. A driver's decision to call or text while driving depends on how important they feel the other person or the message is; they do not think about traffic situations, personal safety or state laws. Paradoxically, they are well aware of the danger when they are a passenger in the car of a driver who is texting, and they will say something about it, even the young ones.

THE (SCARY) DETAILS
- The most commonly performed potentially distracting behaviors while driving are (in order of frequency not of risk) talking on the phone or with other passengers in the vehicle (80%), adjusting the car radio (65%) eating/drinking (45%), interacting with children in the back of the car (27%) and using a portable music player (30%).
- Men are more likely than women to use navigation systems (55% of men, 46% of women), use smartphones for driving directions (30% men, 21% women) and use portable music players with headphones (4% men, 1% women).
- Women are more likely than men to interact with children in the back of the car (23% men, 31% women) and do personal grooming (3% men, 8% women).
- About twice as many respondents (77%) report answering incoming calls than making calls (41%). More reported reading (10%) than sending (6%) texts or e-mails.
- Men and women are equally likely to make or accept phone calls (42% men, 39% women), incoming e-mail or text messages (10% men, 9% women) and send messages (both 6%).
- More drivers under 25 send text messages while driving compared with older drivers.

- Younger drivers, aged 18 to 20 years old, are more likely than older age groups to make phone calls while driving due to boredom.
- There were very few situations when drivers would never talk on the phone or never send texts or e-mails while driving. Bad weather was the primary driving situation cited by half the respondents (54%) as a reason for not doing so. About 25% said that bumper-to-bumper or fast-moving traffic would influence their decision not to place calls or send messages. However, seeing a police officer, driving at night, driving in a marked school zone or having a baby or child on board were not often mentioned (range from 1% to 6%).
- When asked how they think their driving is different when talking on the phone or sending messages, about half (54%) said that talking on a handheld device and one quarter (25%) that even texting or sending messages makes no difference to their driving performance. Some said they drive more slowly when talking on the phone (20%) or sending messages (31%).
- More younger drivers than older ones (61% versus 50%) report that talking on the phone makes no difference to their driving performance!!!!!
- Some report that they drive more slowly when talking on the phone and this also varies with age, from 14% for the youngest age group to 21% for those aged 45 to 64.
- Paradoxically, as passengers, almost all respondents considered a driver who was sending a text message or e-mail (86% men, 90% women) and reading e-mails or text messages (84% men, 88% women) as very unsafe, and this perception increased with age from 62% in the youngest age group to 96% for adults aged 65 and above.

In an amazing piece of research, 100 cars[257] were equipped with a computer, Doppler radar, GPS, a network of sensors and five cameras. They collected data on 43,000 hours of driving, covering 2,000,000 miles in an 18-month period. They documented 10,000 crash, near-crash and crash-relevant events. Almost 80% of all crashes and 65% of all near-crashes involved the driver looking away from the road in front just prior to the incident.

The rate of inattention-related crash and near-crash events decreased dramatically with age, with the rate being as much as four times higher for the 18- to 20-year-old age group relative to the older driver groups (i.e. 35 and up).

The use of phones was associated with the highest frequency of risky events. This was true for all levels of severity. Less frequent but just as risky is looking at or reaching for an object or having a deep conversation with passengers. By the way, these researchers also discovered that crashes happen about five times more often than reported to the police[258]. Hence statistics based on police reports heavily underestimate the real problem.

Being on the phone ruins your reaction time

When something unexpected happens, something your reflex brain is not programmed for, in a fraction of a second your reflecting brain will come to your help or, much better, it will have foreseen the risk and urged you to slow down, for example when a ball rolls over the road that might be followed by a child... unless it is distracted by a conversation[259], in which case, you then react with a delay of 20% to 90% of a second, depending on your ability, age, tiredness etc.... At only 40 miles/hour (70 km/h) this makes a difference of 5 to 20 yards (4.5 to 18 m), a distance that makes the difference between a near-collision and a fatal accident.

YOUR SPEED		DISTANCE DRIVEN IN 1 SECOND	
MILES/HOUR	KM/H	YARDS	METERS
20	30	9	8
30	50	15	14
40	70	22	20
60	100	31	28
75	120	36	33
90	140	43	39

Even at 20 miles/hour (30km) you would cover 9 yards (8m), which can make the difference between a collision and no accident. The slowing down of our reaction time is the most often observed problem when people are on the phone while driving[260]. Other results are more traffic violations (e.g. speeding, running stop signs), wandering out of your lane and attention lapses (e.g. stopping at a green light, failure to visually scan for intersection traffic)[261].

Our reaction time is greatly improved by driving proactive. However, our reflex-brain that is doing the routine driving is exclusively occupied by the here and now (remember SNIA from section 1). To drive proactively, to foresee risky situations, to think ahead, we need our reflecting brain… that is not available while we are on the phone.

BEING ON THE PHONE RUINS YOUR VISION: BLINDED AND HALLUCINATING

With slower reaction times, people brake late and there are late skid-marks. However, with crashes involving people on the phone there are often no skid marks at all. This means that the cause of the accident is not just slower reaction time, it is NO reaction whatsoever. How is this possible that these drivers did not react at all? How come that after an accident these drivers say "I did not see her…". The awful thing is that they are absolutely right: they really did not see the pedestrian, the other car, or the child running after a ball, for several reasons.

One reason is that when you are on the phone while driving, you suffer from inattentional blindness, like the drivers mentioned above who did not see stop signs or "no left turn". As I explained in the chapter about multitasking, when different senses compete for the same limited attention-resource and you are concentrating on one, you will miss input from the other and vice versa. The more you concentrate on a conversation, the more visual inputs you will miss[262].

Another reason is that you scan less. You may remember from biology classes in school that we only have high-resolution vision in the fovea, a limited spot in the middle of our field of vision. Here the vision cells, named cones, are the most tightly packed with the least layers of cells above. About half of the eye nerve cells serve this one small area. It's only 0.1 inch (2-3 mm) in size and sees only about 10-15 degrees of our 200-degree visual field. Outside

HANDSFREE MAKES *NO* DIFFERENCE. IT'S ABOUT ATTENTION!

ATTENTION

NOT DISTRACTED

ON THE PHONE

VISUAL SCANNING

NOT DISTRACTED

ON THE PHONE

this narrow sector, the so-called peripheral vision is low resolution and becomes fuzzier and fuzzier the farther you get from the center, but is very aware of movement especially against a still background and sees better when it is dark. This was important for our hunting ancestors in the savannah so as not to be surprised by an attack coming from the side.

At a distance of 100 yards, only an area of 52 feet is in sharp focus (100 meters and 17.4 meters, respectively). At arm's length, where a driver keeps her phone while texting, the area that is in focus is 3.4 inches (8.7cm)[263].

Usually people don't believe that their peripheral vision is that

"I TOLD YOU NOT TO TEXT AND DRIVE!"

bad, because they have the impression that their whole visual field is sharp. The reason is that this extreme limitation of our high-resolution vision is compensated in three ways so that even when we are distracted or tired while driving, and our conscious attention diminishes, our peripheral vision does not become unsharp, blurred or gray, which would put us on alarm.

Firstly, because wherever something in our peripheral vision catches our attention, we look at it and at that same moment catch it with our very high-resolution fovea. Hence, everything you look at is in focus.

Secondly, because outside of our awareness our eyes make very small so-called saccadic movements of 1/100th of a second. Our brain then stitches all these sharp pictures together, giving the impression that the high-resolution area is bigger.

Thirdly, especially in situations like driving, our eyes scan our visual field all the time, several times a second jumping from one object in our visual field to another and then again our brain stitches the low- and the high-resolution images together in such a way that we have the impression of having a total field of vision that is sharp and focused. But, if your scanning diminishes, because you are on the phone or tired, large parts of your peripheral vision don't get a focused look at all anymore and you are driving in a visual tunnel with a fuzzy periphery you are not even aware of.

Fourthly, and most fascinating and dangerous, is that it is great that our reflex brain stitches our partial focused views together into a coherent sharp overview but a very dangerous downside to this is that it sometimes fills in the gaps. The amazing thing is that our reflex brain will even fill in things we do not see where they are supposed to be. An innocent example is the illusion in the picture below where your brain sees a white triangle and even its sides, where there is none. A dangerous example is when, while on the phone you drive on or over the demarcation stripes on the road, so that you really cannot see them any more, but your reflex brain fills them in where they are supposed to be, and your reflecting brain is so involved in the phone call that it doesn't get a chance to correct this illusion. This is why one of the most frequent indications that the driver in front of you is on the phone is that he is constantly weaving in and out of his lane. In psychology this phenomenon where our reflex brain fills in reality with the illusionary is called "Subjective Constancy", the basis of many interesting and very funny sensory illusions[264].

YOUR ATTENTION IS SO SCREWED UP THAT YOU DON'T REALIZE HOW SCREWED UP IT IS

Why do drivers think they can get away with this? One reason is that 90% of drivers suffer from "Superman Disorder", thinking that their driving is way above average, they think that they are the exception to the rule that nobody can safely phone while driving. Do you?

Another reason is that when you are on the phone, your attention is so screwed up that you don't even realize how bad your driving is. Since your conscious brain can only deal with one thought and its context at a time, you are totally unaware of all the many driving errors you are making, that you have been crossing the line several times, that you were driving too close, braking late. You just don't hear or see the signals other people try to give you. You are totally unaware of the risks you are taking. Drivers on the phone lack "metacognitive awareness". They are so distracted that they can no longer monitor their own behavior[265].

▶ **There is only one safe place for your phone while driving: in the glove box, switched off and out of reach.**

If you want to see many funny and not so funny examples, just go on YouTube and search for "distracted driving crash", "driving phone crash", "bus driver phone crash", "truck driver phone crash", "metro driver phone" etc...[266]. There are many examples of crashes as they happen, especially from Russia where many people install dashboard cameras because they do not trust the police.

DRIVING RUINS YOUR PHONE CONVERSATION

The other side of the coin, as you can imagine, is that being on the phone results in a significantly lower quality of your reflective thinking and conversations[267]. As I explained in Section 1, listening and looking compete for a limited amount of attention in a zero-sum game. The most dangerous aspect of this is that you are literally blind to what's on the road when you concentrate on listening. But it also works the other way around.

When you concentrate on looking at the road, your conscious brain cannot pay attention to the conversation and you will make major mistakes, and not just in difficult discussions. When drivers were asked simple multiple-choice questions or simple math on the phone while driving, they made 70% more mistakes and they were amazingly stupid mistakes. At the same time they made major driving errors like not staying in lane, not seeing a red light and missing an exit. They just could not do the simplest math correctly, unless they stopped the car. So if you are making a deal with somebody, do it while he is driving, but never do business yourself while you are driving. Business done on the phone risks being very bad business indeed. Moreover, your attention is so messed up that you have no clue how bad the decisions are that you make on the phone while driving.

TALKING WITH A PASSENGER IS DIFFERENT

People usually react with "but what's the difference between talking on the phone and talking with a passenger...". Well, the research clearly shows the difference is big, unless the conversation with the passenger is difficult or emotional and the driving is hard[268]. In the latter cases, the increased risk may be 60%[269].

The more complex the conversation, the more realistic the test situation and the heavier the traffic, then the bigger the difference between a phone conversation and a real conversation. In any case, a 60% increase in risk is very significant, although much less than the 600% increase while on the phone.

The main reason why a real conversation is less risky is that the passenger is in the same context as the driver and adapts the content and the pace of the conversation, sometimes proactively, to the traffic situation. The traffic situation itself becomes part of the conversation, helping the driver to stay focused[270]. The driver knows this and when she has to take swift action, does it without thinking about the passenger. On the phone it takes more time to disconnect mentally. Drivers do not stop mid-sentence and they often add a "Excuse me I have to..." or "Hold on a minute ...". This may only take half a second, but at 60 miles/hour this is a difference of 15 yards (100km/h and 14 meters, respectively). This is the difference between a close call and an accident.

Finally, when you have a passenger with you, you are less likely to text or mail, which makes you a lot safer.

DRIVER ON THE PHONE MEETS DROWSY DRIVER

Do you remember from the chapter about sleep that 32% of drivers drive drowsy at least once or twice a month, that 26% drive drowsy during the workday and that 36% had even experienced nodding off or falling asleep while driving? Lack of sleep impairs reaction time, decreases sustained focused attention, increases distractibility (car leaving driving lane), and reduces the ability to divide one's attention (selective attention as well as sustained attention). Multitasking becomes even more difficult than it already is when wide awake[271]. The conclusion is very clear: tiredness and driving are a lethal cocktail.

▶ **Tiredness and driving are a lethal cocktail.**

For shift workers, for example, the risk of having an accident or making a dangerous mistake is eight times higher[272]. Often without knowing it, tired drivers close their eyes for between a quarter of a second and several seconds (even 30 seconds has been registered) and while they drive the registration of electric currents in the brain clearly shows micro-sleeps where the driver exerts no control at all over his driving.

Before getting to that stage these drivers experience clear symptoms of sleepiness like eye tiredness, feeling of heavy eyelids and yawning. Later they experience alarm signals like nodding off to sleep, struggling to keep their eyes open, difficulty maintaining the correct speed, slow reactions and even their head dropping down but ... a great majority ignore them, especially men, and amongst these young men in particular. The result is more accidents and especially head-on collisions[273]. But as you probably remember from the chapter about sleep, you adapt to the feeling of sleepiness even though your sleep debt still ruins your conscious thinking in general and your ability to focus in particular. Therefore, when you are driving with a sleep debt, you are more hazardous even before you feel the alarm signls.

▶ **Tiredness and driving are a lethal cocktail.**
Throw a phone into the mix and it's catastrophic.

I explained earlier in this chapter that at any moment in time 10% of drivers are on the phone, up to 80% of drivers use their phone while driving, up to 60% even sometimes text while driving, 24% of all car crashes involve cell phone use and 50% of drivers say that talking on the phone makes no difference to their driving performance.

You do not have to be professor in statistics therefore to understand that:

- it is very likely that a driver (you?) might be sleepy and on the phone at the same time. Some people even think that being on the phone while they are driving keeps them awake and thus safer while in fact it makes driving even more dangerous;
- that while you are on your phone, you run the risk that when you make a mistake, the other driver might be sleepy and therefore unable to avoid an accident.

By the way, caffeine clearly helps when you feel sleepy while driving. It improves your reaction time and it counteracts to some extent the sleepiness by increasing alertness, vigilance and the ability to pay attention (but only to a limited number of objects). The improvement is limited, but enough to make a positive difference in terms of the occurrence of (near) accidents with sleepy drivers.

Caffeine, however, does not improve distractibility. It does not improve your reaction when sudden unexpected objects appear in your visual field. The ability to divide attention is even worse when you are sleepy and using caffeine, and multitasking becomes even more difficult[274].

In other words, using caffeine is a good immediate countermeasure when you feel sleepy and there is really no possibility to take a nap. Be aware though that the caffeine only starts working after some 20 minutes. The best solution therefore, if nobody else can take over the wheel, is to drink a caffeinated drink and then have a 15-20 minute nap (to know why not longer, see Section 3). By the time you wake up, the caffeine has kicked in to further help you to be alert. Of course, the safest thing to do is not to drive at all when you are sleepy.

DRIVER ON THE PHONE MEETS PEDESTRIAN ON THE PHONE

The research about pedestrians and cyclists using the phone is as clear as that about drivers on the phone: you run a greater risk of having an accident. Texting is much more dangerous than having a phone call, which is more dangerous than listening to music. And personality factors don't make any difference: it is true for everybody[275]. Due to this inattentional blindness, only 8% of pedestrians on the phone saw a unicycling clown crossing their path, while 60% of people walking with a friend saw him[276].

Inattentional accidents of pedestrians requiring a hospital visit, like walking into a telephone pole while texting, have quadrupled since 2006. The younger the pedestrian, the more they got injured while on the phone. Half were people under 30 and a quarter between the ages of 40 and 60[277].

Of course the consequences are much lighter: "Pedestrian tripped over garbage can and broke his wrist" is very different from "Driver on the phone killed two pedestrians". The pedestrian, however, is the most vulnerable in a traffic environment dominated by cars. The risk of "Distracted driver hitting distracted pedestrian" has become very real. There is absolutely no way a pedestrian on the phone will ever be able to anticipate and proactively avoid being hit by a distracted driver on the phone because the pedestrian on the phone also loses awareness of the environment.

WHEN A SUPERMAN ENGROSSED WITH HIS ICT CRASHES INTO A SUPERWOMAN INVOLVED IN HER ICT

The conclusion is loud and clear: whatever the law says, don't use ICT while driving. NEVER. This could easily save a life or a body, your own or the one of your potential victim. If you kill somebody else while you're on the phone your own life will be ruined too.

From whatever perspective you look at the issue, the conclusion from massive amounts of research is unambiguous: don't use ICT while driving and certainly not for texting or e-mailing. Just don't, not with your phone in your hand, not with a hands-free kit, not voice-commanded, not eyes-free, never. Don't let the ICT and car companies mislead you. They are selling the stuff for their profit and clearly your safety is the least of their concerns. They sell the technology as enhancements, but there is one thing it does not enhance: your safety.

Don't wait for the lawmakers. Why would you if the evidence is so overwhelming? The lawmakers will only move after many more dramatic accidents or better yet accidents with very famous people and even that is not at all certain for the moment.

▶ **When two Super(wo)men driving a car while on the phone crash into each other, both discover they have no supernatural powers.**

Today at any moment of the day 10% of drivers are busy with their phone and 45% of drivers experience a dangerous situation caused by another driver being on the phone. The groundless deceiving dangerous claims of companies selling sophisticated ICT for cars, together with the lawmakers only forbidding hand-held devices, will without doubt increase the false feeling of safety of drivers using these perilous devices with unjustified overconfidence. As a result it is very likely that more and more people will use ICT while driving, further misled by their own addiction to always being connected and their "Superman Disorder".

This in turn further increases the risk that you personally are suddenly confronted with an unexpected, hazardous move of another driver whose brain is occupied by one kind of ICT or another. I hope that after reading this chapter and the one about multitasking, you are convinced that there is a huge risk your brain will not react well enough or fast enough to avoid a collision. Just the fact that 1/10 of the other drivers is distracted for a relatively long time is a sufficient reason not to be involved with any ICT yourself, so that your brain can proactively try to foresee distracted driving. If you are on the phone, there will be no skid-marks on either side and both of you will discover that you do not have the supernatural powers of a Super(wo)men.

8.4 WHY THE AUTHORITIES WILL NOT STOP THIS VERY DANGEROUS USE OF ICT

Given all this research, no wonder the American National Transportation Safety Board, which ordered the above-mentioned study

DON'T USE YOUR PHONE WHILE DRIVING!

JUST DON'T.

of 100 cars, is urging states to make the use of hands-free devices by drivers illegal. This is the only safe and sensible thing to do to save several thousands of lives, tens of thousands of injuries and handicaps, and billions in medical and insurance expenses. In fact they and the AAA go beyond this and advise the authorities to ban all ICT use by drivers, hands-free or not. The problem is that

that the authorities and safety laws have totally fallen behind the research in this field.

Even worse, the fact that countries and states only ban the use of a "hands-on" phone gives the public the very strong, very wrong and very dangerous message that hands-free is safer, which it isn't at all.

> ## The ban on hands-on calling gives the very strong, very wrong and very dangerous message that hands-free is safer, which it isn't at all.

There is little chance, however that a total ban is going to happen because of a collusion between people's dependence if not addiction to their phones, their ignorance about the danger, the populism of lawmakers who do not dare to take away the beloved ICT tools, toys and gadgets of their voters and the lobbying of the automotive and ICT companies.

There is still a lot of work for governments to do to convince people that using a phone while driving is as unacceptable as driving drunk. In an experiment, different groups of young drivers all received the same real case story about a car crash, with just one difference: for one group, it said the driver "was not distracted", while for the others it said "was on the phone while driving" or "was texting while driving" or "had 8 Promille of alcohol in his blood". Then the participants were asked to judge and fine the driver. Who got the harshest sentence? Although driving while texting is many times more dangerous than driving with 0.008 alcohol in your blood, the slightly drunk driver got the worst punishment and... the driver on the phone got fines and jail time similar to the undistracted drivers who had had an accident[278]. It is evident that parents, schools and governments still have a big job to do to make people more aware of the danger of driving while on the phone. On the other hand, the fact that drunken drivers get a harsh punishment is a hopeful sign because a generation ago driving after drinking was considered pretty normal too.

The National Transportation Safety Board (NTSB) compares the wholesale cultural shift necessary to change distracted driving with the one needed for drunken driving, wearing a seat belt and smoking[279]. These shifts also took quite some time and only changed drastically with strict legal obligations and high-visibility enforcement and education campaigns.

As with the use of seatbelts, convincing people of the danger is not sufficient. Campaigns help to make people aware, but do not work without the law getting involved. In Britain, with strict laws on distracted driving, the use of phones while driving is 21% while in the USA it's 70%[280]. In the UK the first drivers who caused an accident using a hands-free set have already been sentenced for careless driving.

Although in the USA 41 states ban texting while driving[281], only 12 states have a ban on making hand-held calls[282]. It is great that more and more states and countries are passing laws that forbid texting while driving and phone in hand driving but not so great that lawmakers aren't also forbidding the use of any phones while driving. California and Delaware and on a smaller scale Hartford, CT, and Syracuse, NY did "Phone in One Hand. Ticket in the Other" campaigns. These reduced the observed hand-held calling by 32% to 72% and the results had not tapered off three months later[283]. In Utah a texting driver can get as much as a $750 fine and three months in jail; if injury or death is involved, the penalties can go as high as a $10,000 fine and 15 years in prison[284]. In other states the fines are $30-60. This will not help much until... lawyers start suing the telecom companies and car companies for willfully building instruments in a car that are life-threatening when used while driving and for misleading their customers about their danger.

In a conversation with civil servants I learned that politicians are aware of the danger of using any phone while driving but that they do not want to introduce a total ban because there is no public support for it. Since their horizon is only as far as the next elections, they do not want to take away the drivers' favorite toy, even if using it is as dangerous as drunken driving. On the other hand, 43% of Americans think that a legal ban is the only solution, while 42% think the solution should be a technical one[285]preventing all these devices from working as soon as the car starts driving or to signal distracted driving.

The second reason why lawmakers do not plan a legal ban on

hands-free and eyes-free use of the phone is because it is impossible to enforce because it is invisible. If you have too much alcohol in your blood you have too much of it all the time, even a long time after you caused an accident. If you phone while driving you are as dangerous as a drunken driver, but only while you are connected. In-between there are no traces of your dangerous behavior, unless the law enforcers and insurance companies would be allowed to check the log of your calls and texts as they are already allowed to do in some states and countries after a heavy accident.

The third reason is that automotive and ICT companies lobby against any such laws.

▶ **ICT in a car: a killer application**

Aside from the drivers and the authorities, the third partner in this collusion are the companies that make a profit through the sale and use of these dangerous devices. The Alliance for Automobile Manufacturers defends the integrated systems in the console of a car, saying they allow drivers to keep their hands on the wheel and eyes on the road while they remain connected[286].

Listen to Ford CEO Alan Mulally: "Ford, The App of Choice for Car Buyers." In perfect collusion with Eddy Cue, chief of Internet Software and Services of Apple, who said: "But we want to take this integration to a whole new level. What if you could get iOS on the screen that is built into your car... so that you could make phone calls, play music, go to maps or get your iMessages right on the screen of your car eyes-free using Siri?" He bragged that in 2014 Honda, Mercedes, Nissan, Ford, Chevy, Lexus, Kia, Mitsubishi, Volvo, Acura and Jaguar would introduce iOS features in their cars[287].

Ford's system that costs several hundreds of dollars allows drivers to use phones, music players and even to surf the Internet... hands-free[288]. These voice-commanded computer systems are as powerful as any PC or tablet, allowing the driver to get instant information about shops, museums and other points of interest in the area, the person who is calling, the tune that is playing... These systems with phone, Wi-Fi, connections for USB and even a keyboard are a billion dollar industry ($ 150 billion in 2009[289]).

> **Smart phones are used by ignorant or stupid drivers, very smart phones by ignorant or very stupid drivers.**

As if the bright engineers and lawyers of these companies don't know the massive amount of research showing that the use of hands-free and eyes-free in a car is brainless, and that voice-commanded e-mails and texting is the most dangerous. They willfully deceive their clients, creating a smoke screen so that you ignore the fact that the issue is the limitations of your brain and your attention and not only hands on the wheel and eyes on the road.

Talking about a smoke screen, being a medical doctor I have been here before, having seen the tobacco industry fighting the scientific evidence tooth and nail and openly and stealthily attacking and discrediting the research that demonstrated perfectly that smoking prematurely kills not only the smoker, but also the bystanders who have to inhale the smoke of others. In the end the industry very reluctantly accepted the inefficient warning "Smoking is bad for your health", while at the same time doing all they could, unethically if not illegally, to make cigarettes as addictive as possible and prevent tougher laws especially in poor countries[290].

Anyway, keep in mind that the primary goal of companies selling this in-car ICT is clearly not your safety, but making a profit selling you these systems. If you look at car magazines or newspaper reports about car shows, it is clear that this is just the beginning. They call them enhancements, but these applications are distractions. They call them "killer applications" and that is what they are, literally.

AT&T looks a little like it could be an exception. They invested a considerable amount of money and time in the "Txtng & Drivng... It Can Wait" awareness program and Werner Herzog made an attention-grabbing movie for it[291]. I applaud the initiative, but I will only be really convinced about their good intentions the day they do the same to convince drivers to stop using their phone and any other device altogether, hands-free or not, and sell cellphones and other in-car ICT that are disabled as soon as it senses that the car starts driving. The apps for your smartphone already exist and some of them are very sophisticated. (See Section 3.)

If carmakers and ICT companies really cared about your safety more than their profit, they would automatically block all use of a phone or a dashboard computer by the driver as soon as the car starts, with the exception of emergency calls and the navigator with a screen as close as possible to the field of vision and impossible to reset while driving. Of course they don't. They prefer to make their distracting products more attractive with too many options left as a free choice for the driver with a token warning like "Use the online services only when traffic conditions allow you to do so safely."

We should not underestimate their power. On 20 July 2009 the New York Times reported: US Withheld Data on Risks of Distracted Driving. The research was only made public when two consumer advocacy groups filed a Freedom of Information Act lawsuit for the documents.

"Joe Simitian, a state senator in California, managed to get his hands-free legislation, an effort he began in 2001, passed in 2006... In each previous year, the bill was killed — after lobbying by cellphone carriers... He said they fought him even though their brochures said that distracted driving was dangerous... In the first six months the California law was in effect, a preliminary California Highway Patrol estimate showed that fatalities dropped 12.5%– saving 200 lives." Matt Richtel.

When lawmakers do not act in the best interests of the citizens and bend over backwards for these lobbyists as they did for decades for the tobacco lobby, our only hope is that insurance companies very significantly lower their rates for drivers using phone-blocking software and start treating DOP (Driving On the Phone) like DUI (Driving Under Influence), demanding a check of the phone record of drivers causing an accident with injuries, treating it as an intentional conduct, refusing further coverage, spiking the rates after an accident or not paying coverage for the damage.

To me, the best solution seems to be a total ban ICT while driving, reasons on the use of all ICT devices while driving.

First of all because this will give a crystal-clear message to everybody that hands-free and hands-on use are equally dangerous, instead of giving the impression that only hand-held phones are dangerous.

Secondly because it will save the lives and prevent injuries of law-abiding citizens and their potential victims.

Thirdly because countrywide information campaigns about the reasons of the total ban will make it clear for all the people who were ignorant about this that hands-free and hands-on are equally dangerous. This will save more lives.

Fourthly because it will allow the police and insurance companies to check the phone record of every driver after every crash and certainly every crash with injuries, without of course revealing either the content of the communication or the interlocutor. In terms of breaching privacy, this is much less than the National Security Agency (NSA) is allowed to know about all of us at any time and everywhere, even about the presidents of allied countries. In developed countries thousands of times more people are killed and injured every year by people using their phone while driving than by terrorists. For the dead and their next of kin, it does not make any difference who did the killing.

Fifthly because as with the development of the technology to enforce speed limits, which in many countries sends people their speeding-tickets automatically without any person being involved, it is not difficult to imagine that once there is a total ban technology companies will grasp the opportunity and develop the necessary technology to find out if a driver is interacting with any ICT gadgets.

If lawmakers do not assume their responsibility, the only hope to save all these lives is that the judges, especially in countries where they are not elected, will use existing laws to stop this deadly distraction. On 6 June 2012 in Massachusetts an 18-year-old veered over the line to the wrong side of the road and caused a fatal accident, killing a father of three. He told the police after the accident that he had not looked at his phone since he left the parking lot, but his telephone records showed that that day (the accident happened at about 2 pm) he had by that point sent and received 193 texts, that he looked at 11 messages in the 10 minutes before the crash and that he was texting just before the crash.

He was convicted of motor vehicle homicide by texting, sentenced to two years in prison and lost his driving license for 15 years[292].

8.5 IF YOUR COMPANY IS SERIOUS ABOUT SAFETY IT SHOULD HAVE CONNECTIVITY POLICIES

DOES YOUR COMPANY HAVE A CELL PHONE POLICY FOR WHITE-COLLAR WORKERS?

A while ago I called a friend to find out a name and phone number. He was driving and while talking to me on the carphone took his smartphone to look up the number. When I said I'd prefer to call later, he said, "Don't worry, I can do that, I do it all the time. Oh and by the way I am also eating a hamburger and drinking a coke".

Today managers and salespeople turn their cars into an extension of their office. Not only do they make phone calls, but they also check and send e-mails... while driving. They take notes while holding the wheel with their knees. They have their tablet or laptop computer open on the other seat. White-collar workers, like my friend, usually have a choice. Their distracted driving is self-imposed. From my workshops I learn that most professionals are unaware of the increased risk of an accident. They think it is some 25-50% increase, and they are willing to take that risk to continue working while driving.

Moreover, almost none of them are aware that the quality of the conversations suffers a lot while driving and leads to bad decisions and bad deals. People on the phone while driving make very stupid mistakes with simple mental arithmetic and multiple-choice questions. Imagine the impact on difficult business conversations. While driving you are much more easily manipulated by the other person when she is single-tasking and you are multitasking.

Many connection addicts and irresponsible companies will never believe this. What researchers predict, reality proves to be right: banning the use of the phone while driving does not diminish productivity. Convinced by the hard data about the risks of phoning while driving, companies who really care about the safety of their employees (and the potential victims) have totally banned the use of phones while driving. They not only report a decrease in accidents, but also no negative impact on productivity! Some report an increase of productivity (see Section 3).

Therefore conscientious and certainly safety-conscious employers should develop programs to create awareness about the danger of distracted driving and ban the use of phones (examples in Section 3), ideally before insurance companies and lawyers hold you responsible and make you pay huge fines for not doing so.

DOES YOUR COMPANY HAVE A CONNECTIVITY POLICY FOR BLUE-COLLAR WORKERS?

RISKS ON THE ROAD

Of course everything I have written about using your phone while driving a car also applies to the work situation and the use of (heavy) company vehicles like a lorry while on the phone. Driving a lorry or a fork-lift truck while being connected similarly increases the risk of an accident between four and 23 times!

Sometimes irresponsible or ignorant companies even expect or force their employees to always be connected, even while driving. They install gadgets in their trucks so that they are always connected and that the drivers can do some work while driving. These drivers then fill in forms, timesheets, client requests, handle dispatches etc... while driving.

Researchers put video cameras in trucks and taped 200 truckers driving about 3 million miles. They looked at crashes, near accidents and dangerous behavior. They too found that texting was the most dangerous thing to do (23 times riskier than undistracted), twice as dangerous as looking at a dispatching device with five to six lines of text. However, since the drivers look at these devices much more often than they text, in the end the dispatching devices turn out to be the riskiest ones. The second most dangerous behavior was dialing a cell phone. Sometimes workers are expected to do so while driving, sometimes they are not obliged to, but given the time pressure and the fact that (part of) their pay may be linked to performance, they can't afford the 15 minutes to stop the truck to respond to messages.

Two years ago Coca-Cola was sued and paid a huge sum because an employee caused an accident while having a business conversation on the phone... hands-free. A quote from the Risk Management Monitor: "Last week, a jury in Corpus Christi, Texas awarded $21 million in damages to a woman who was struck by a Coca-Cola driver who had been talking on her cell phone at the time of the accident. The plaintiff's attorneys were able to successfully argue that Coca-Cola's cell phone policy for its drivers was "vague and ambiguous". They also suggested that Coca-Cola was aware of the dangers but "withheld this information from its employee driver," which led directly to the circumstances that caused the accident. Thomas J. Henry, one of the plaintiff's attorneys, said: "From the time I took the Coca Cola driver's testimony and obtained the company's inadequate cell phone driving policy, I knew we had a corporate giant with a huge safety problem on our hands".[293]

"Typical American"? Of course, but in Europe, just wait a few years. It's coming to a courtroom near you.

We should also think about train, tram and bus operators. A tugboat captain caused a deadly accident while being online. A train conductor went through a red light and caused an accident killing 25 people...while texting. A high-speed train derailed near Barcelona, killing 79 people. The New York Times wrote: "[The conductor] received a phone call from an official of Renfe, the Spanish national railway company, and was "reading a map or some kind of paper document" ...according to the statement by the court." If you have a look at YouTube, search for "bus driver texting" and you will find a hundred examples, including actual crashes.

RISKS ON THE PREMISES

Now that you have read about all this research about the risks of multitasking and the risk of using a phone while doing other things like driving, think about other situations at work where operators are forced to multitask.

In my workshops for plant and safety managers, the discussion about unsafe driving opened many people's eyes to the danger of numerous off-road, in-company driving situations. In many warehouses, for example, the fork-lift drivers get their instructions via a mobile phone. Even worse, in others touch screens and keyboards are installed where the driver receives instructions and has to input a response (= texting = risk x 23!). The distraction is built into the system! Hence, these badly informed companies compel their drivers to do something very dangerous. These are accidents waiting to happen! I am glad that in these workshops many managers who had not already done so decided to add a system that freezes the screen as soon as the truck starts moving.

In these workshops many other examples cropped up, such as a maintenance operator forgetting to fasten one bolt out of seven with major consequences, when he was interrupted by his walkie-talkie directing him to his next job, an office worker who made a three-step fall because he had not seen the stairs...

If you are responsible for safety or if you are an operator yourself, think about other situations on the shop floor where multitasking is a risk factor built into the system.

A "pedestrian" on the phone on the shop floor is a risk factor too
As you can conclude from the risk of being a pedestrian on the phone on the street, being on the phone as a distracted pedestrian on the shop floor is also a hazard, especially in a zone with moving equipment. This should make you think twice before you use a mobile phone in any work situation where a brief lack of attention could cause an accident. As a manager you should consider banning the use of phones on the shop floor altogether, as more and more companies are doing.

HOW TO UNCHAIN YOUR BRAIN. BRAINGAINS AT THREE LEVELS

The goal of this book is to improve your intellectual performance and productivity, enabling you to unleash the amazing potential that can be achieved when man and machine, you and your ICT, are well-balanced. I hope that the first two sections have convinced you that being lured by the addictive, consumptive use of ICT will not make you more productive, but in fact ruin your intellectual performance. Once you understand this, an improvement in intellectual performance and productivity is both realistic and achievable.

The strategies and tactics I mention in this section are the result of discussions I have had with participants in my presentations and workshops about stress management or change management or about the BrainChains. Many ideas were tested out with those participating in my coaching sessions and who came for many different reasons ranging from burnout to leadership development.

Therefore, you should see this section as a toolbox from which you can choose as many tools and tricks as you want to become more efficient. They are inspirational suggestions and recommendations rather than instructions, except for a very few that are so important that they are almost commandments.

1 SIMPLICITY IS COMPLEXITY RESOLVED, BUT SIMPLE DOES NOT MEAN EASY

When I started tackling the issues obstructing the great potential of the brain and ICT working together, at first it all seemed very complicated. After burning the midnight oil and immersing myself in the research, however, I discovered what's essential. As the great artist Constantin Brancusi (1876-1957) wrote, "Simplicity is complexity resolved" ("La simplicité est la complexité résolue"). Brancusi's own art is the most perfect example of this and his words are ones with which I fully agree.

Our scientific and complex subject can also be expressed simply and that is what I have sought to do in the first two sections of the book.

Initially I thought that with this knowledge about our brain the reader would be able to find his or her own solutions. However, I learned from my own experience and the experience of hundreds of professionals in my coaching sessions, workshops and lectures that simple does not mean easy. For most people it is really difficult to change their inefficient habits. This was certainly true for the sculptor Brancusi since he only made about 200 sculptures in his 81-year life, many of which are continuous refinements, if not simplifications, of earlier work.

Therefore, to make it easier for you to apply these simple but often very difficult solutions I have added this third section. Here you will find suggestions about how to be most productive with your ICT. I do not intend to write the ultimate "How to guide" but rather be a source of inspiration. I would much prefer that, based on what you have learned from the first two sections, you develop your own creative solutions for your personal situation.

Solutions to improve your intellectual productivity can always be placed at one of the following levels:

1 **BrainGains at the ME level** is the most important one to start with. You should ask yourself: "What can I do to improve the quality and quantity of my brainwork?" There are many things you can start doing today and for which you need nobody but yourself.

2 **BrainGains at the WE level.** These are things you can change together, not only with colleagues and peers, but also with your family members. For managers there are two more WEs: things you can do with your team for the part of the business you are responsible for and initiatives you can take in your boss's team.

3 **BrainGains at the THEY level** is about initiatives people higher up in the hierarchy can and should take to improve intellectual productivity, either in the organization as a whole or in the part they are responsible for.

I am not presenting these solutions as THE right way of doing things. Nor do I expect you to use all these tools and tricks. Consider them more as a toolbox where you will find tools that have helped my clients or that my clients invented once they had understood the basics.

In this section as in the previous two, I will treat social media, IM, texting and messages as one and use the term "e-mail" to refer to them all because their negative effects on our intellectual productivity are very similar.

2 BRAINGAINS AT THE "ME" LEVEL

Always being connected, multitasking, chronic stress and lack of sleep are the result of bad habits and sometimes addiction. Sometimes these are difficult to change. In case you don't succeed through willpower alone, at the end of this chapter I will also explain in detail *how* to change your strong habits.

2.1 CHAINBREAKER 1: DARE TO DISCONNECT SEVERAL TIMES A DAY

The single most important solution to get the most out of your brain and your ICT is to plan regular slots for uninterrupted, focused work or conversations: Disconnect.

The minimum for every single manager or other professional is to have one hour a day totally disconnected from any interruptions. If you have to fight for it, fight tooth and nail. You may forget every single piece of advice in this book, but if you implement just this one, it will significantly improve your intellectual productivity.

Just before this book went to press I discovered a unique experimental field study that supports my point: "People report a higher performance on days when they have implemented a quiet hour than on days without a quiet hour. They also report more progress on tasks worked on during the quiet hour than on comparable tasks during a day without a quiet hour. These effects were not due to an increase in hours worked during the day, and they could not be attributed to differences in daily stressors. Furthermore, participants evaluated the quiet hour positively, both directly at the end of the study and three months later." König 2013[1]

▶ **A most important rule for intellectual productivity: Totally disconnect one hour a day**

This disconnected time is not only very important to work efficiently, but also to be creative. Dan Russell, a senior manager at IBM's Almaden Research Center says, "If you don't have that sort of free time to dream and muse and mull, then you are not being creative, by definition." After realizing that he had become a slave to e-mail, he now only checks them twice a day, leaves his cellphone in his car, does not use instant messaging and regularly schedules uninterrupted time in a nearby office[2].

You too should become totally single-minded about disconnecting. All means are allowed to reach this goal. You will have to be creative, relentless and even ruthless about this, towards your environment and towards yourself, in order to protect yourself from all non-critical interruptions. Dare to disconnect! Lay claim to this quiet hour!

Some people are convinced that frenetic multitasking is at the core of their responsibility and that people need their immediate answer or action all the time. Task-hopping is only acceptable when the tasks are routine and you need more arousal or when it is really necessary or unavoidable and you can afford the price you pay in lower quality and quantity of work. Most of the time, however, task-hoppers are dead wrong about this, which shows when they become ill and things keep running smoothly or when they start right-tasking, not being available anytime and anywhere, and everything runs even better. If you think you are the real exception, then tackle it the other way around: keep multitasking all the time, but organize one hour every day to single-task undisturbed.

More professionals than you expect say they have no time to reflect on a plan while at the same time "having more time to plan" is at the top of their wish list. Quite amazing because what it boils down to is: I have no time to plan, and as a result I lose so much time on my tasks that I have no time to plan.

None of the many suggestions in "how to" books and courses about organizing your work, getting things done, time management etc... have any chance of being effective if you don't manage to disconnect, if you are the slave rather than the master of your fantastic ICT tools.

When the tasks are complex and when you cannot afford lower levels of quality, accuracy, safety, innovation, use of memory or engagement from your interlocutors, earmark time to disconnect and single-task.

First find out at what time of the day your reflecting brain works best. When I ask this question to people or teams I coach, many don't even know, because they let themselves be disturbed at every hour, if not minute, of the day. If you don't know, start experimenting with timeslots of protected brain-time at different times of the day to find out.

For most people the best hours are the morning after a good night's sleep (see BrainChain #3). Owl types work better in the evening, but most so-called Owls are Fake-Owls, working late not because it is the best time for their brain, but just because they are running around like crazy all day and even their evenings are lost in connection. In this case, one hour of being disconnected before you go to bed is acceptable as a start.

Whatever your best brain-time is, declare it sacrosanct, use it to do your most important brainwork and let NOTHING disturb you. Safeguard this time like a treasure. Don't let anybody steal it from you.

Before you claim your quiet time, be certain that you can manage it, that you can kick the habit yourself. All your electronic devices have a special BrainGain button: push it for 4 seconds and they go into brain-protection mode, which means "dead". Turn off your e-mail program completely when you're doing really important work. Give your mobile phone to your assistant or to a colleague and ask him or her to only interrupt you for very urgent matters. If you don't dare to disconnect your phone, get a second one whose number you give to a limited number of people only to be used in emergencies (more on this later in this chapter).

If your task is reading difficult texts: print it and read it on old-fashioned paper in a place where you are totally disconnected. This has another important advantage. You have probably already experienced being able to immediately spot important details or mistakes on paper that you missed on the screen. Not only was your observation correct, but the advantage of paper goes beyond this. Research shows that reading from paper results in better comprehension than reading from a screen, especially if under time pressure and that it is faster and less tiring.[3]

An interesting experience is that disconnecting to reflect may ripple from the Me to the We level.

In one of the Dutch ministries I often work with, a highly qualified and respected professional realized that the quality of the difficult and thorough analyses he had to make suffered from continuous interruptions. He decided to apply what he had learned in my workshop and put a poster on his door: "At 11 o'clock I am totally available for you". He closed his e-mail program and disconnected his phones. This very much improved his effectiveness and creativity. His colleagues, however, at first reacted negatively to the fact that he was no longer always immediately available for their questions. In the discussion that followed he explained why he had changed and they decided to follow his example. This then automatically escalated to the next level because they were no longer available all the time to immediately react to questions from higher up in the hierarchy. By then they were so convinced of the advantages of the new system for their intellectual productivity that they made a convincing case. It was decided that one particular phone number would always be picked up immediately for very urgent or very important things. Team members would take turns to man that phone number.

A second time for disconnecting that works well for many people is taking 20 minutes of disconnecting on Sunday evening to plan the week, to decide what the most important tasks are, what you should delegate and to make sure there is enough quiet time every single day.

Then, every day, no later than one hour before you go to bed you take 10 minutes to look at the next day and what the most important things are that you need to do and write this down so that your archiving brain can take it into account while you sleep. Then you totally disconnect at least one hour before you go to sleep.

If you are really unable to disconnect and while trying to do so you discover that you are addicted or at least have a very strong bad habit, then please read the final paragraphs of this "ME" chapter very carefully. Another possibility may be to look for a coach or therapist trained in behavioral and cognitive therapy. I have also discovered that there are digital detox camps[4], although personally I don't think this is the most efficient way of dealing with the problem.

2.2 CHAINBREAKER 2: BECOME A RIGHT-TASKER: RUTHLESSLY AND RADICALLY REDUCE THE SWITCHES

As a modern professional, you cannot totally avoid multitasking. Some multitasking is critical as it is part of your job. However, if you analyze your interruptions, you will discover, just like so many other people, that a lot of them are irrelevant. Continuously checking your e-mail and texts is the worst, unless you are hooked to their even worse cousins, social media and news feeds.

Rule Number 1: Ruthlessly and radically reduce switches

Rule Number 2: Disconnect to reflect

Rule Number 3: Disconnect to relax

As you can imagine after reading the chapter about multitasking, the principle of right-tasking is very simple: reduce the number of switches by all possible means. Basically this means that you make room for both single-tasking and multitasking and you manage both well so that the multitasking does not crowd out or kill the single-tasking.

Your goal should be to reach an optimal level of connectivity and of multitasking. For 80% of people, this means reducing both considerably. To tame multitasking you have to put it in a cage, otherwise it will kill the important tasks. As I explain below, the cage for this dangerous, productivity-devouring animal is batch-processing. Batch-processing means first of all that you put a sturdy do-not-disturb cage around your important work, so that the e-mail monster and other distractions cannot disturb or kill

STOP MULTITASKING; START RIGHT-TASKING

Multitasking

→ ⌐→ ⌐⋯→ ⌐→ ⌐⋯→ ⌐→ ⌐⋯→ ⌐→

Right-tasking: batch-processing

undisturbed ———→   *undisturbed* ═ ═ ═ ═ ═→   *undisturbed* ⋯⋯⋯⋯⋯→

⌒Finish batch⌒   ⌒Finish batch⌒   ⌒Finish batch⌒
Have a   Have a   Have a
break   break   break

your reflecting. Secondly, you put a cage around your multitasking and the many other little distracting chores and you eliminate them for a limited time.

This of course does not mean that your whole life and everything you do has to be planned. On the contrary. Once you manage the important things better, there will be more room for serendipity, unexpected encounters, learning, discoveries and fun.

If you think the message "reduce the switches to the bare necessities" is enough for you as a call for action, you can skip the paragraphs about the Eisenhower principle and Pareto rule and jump straight to the section about batch-processing.

In my experience, however, people have great difficulties implementing this simple idea because their priorities are not explicit enough. It is much easier to choose what to do or not do and to drop the unimportant distractors if you know what's really important for you.

BEING CLEAR ABOUT YOUR PRIORITIES IS THE FIRST IMPERATIVE CONDITION TO RIGHT-TASK

THE EISENHOWER RULE

In the chapter about multitasking I explained that for many tasks the best thing you can do is NOT to put them on a to-do-list, but to look in your calendar WHEN you are going to do them and refuse the task or set conditions if there is no time for it. But even before you look at your calendar, you need to ask yourself "should I do

Eisenhower principle

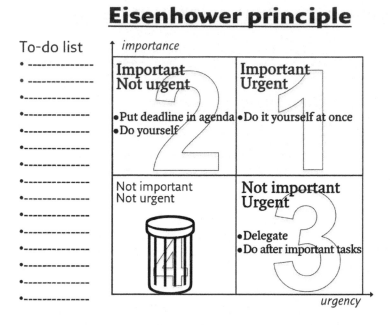

To-do list

- --------------
- --------------
- --------------
- --------------
- --------------
- --------------
- --------------
- --------------
- --------------
- --------------
- --------------
- --------------
- --------------
- --------------
- --------------

↑ *importance*

Important
Not urgent

- Put deadline in agenda
- Do yourself

Important
Urgent

- Do it yourself at once

Not important
Not urgent

Not important
Urgent

- Delegate
- Do after important tasks

urgency →

this yes or no, even if I have time for it". To quickly decide it will help you to start thinking in terms of the Eisenhower principle and even to develop an Eisenhower reflex. The Eisenhower principle is: "What is important is seldom urgent and what is urgent is seldom important." To be successful, focus on the important things and manage the urgent ones wisely.

Most people deal with e-mails as if they are all important and urgent. A majority even responds to e-mail within two minutes[5]. How can you fight this primitive and totally counterproductive bad habit, Pavlov reflex or addiction?

This principle gives you a simple matrix:

#1 Important and urgent: For high performance they take ± 20% of time

For example: Crises, deadline-driven projects, a complaint from an important client...

#2 Important not urgent: For high performance they take ± 70% of your time

For example: Preparation for important meetings or projects, planning, building important relationships, strategy development, formulation and implementation etc...

#3 Urgent but not important: For high performance they take no more than ± 10% of your time
For example: Lunch with team, many meetings, interruptions, phone calls...

#4 Not important and not urgent: For high performance they should take no more than ± 1% of your time
For example: Timewasters like social media and web surfing, 50-80% of e-mail, desk cleaning...

Take 5 seconds to score each task on your to-do list (if you have one) and every meeting on your agenda. You can use the same matrix to quickly delete lots of e-mail. In the beginning this will take a little longer than five seconds, but after a while it becomes natural and very fast.

Next, decide what to do and when. When consciously filtering all incoming distractions based on their importance, you end up doing much less of the not important ones and thus become more productive in your work.

1 Do the important/urgent tasks immediately.
2 The most important quadrant for your intellectual performance is: important/not urgent. For these you should immediately block time in your diary for ample undisturbed brainwork. If you don't plan these tasks, they will become important and urgent, and the quality of your work will be much lower.
3 If a task is not important but urgent, refuse, delegate it to somebody for whom this is an important challenge or do it after the important ones.
4 Never accept non-important and non-urgent tasks. Just dump the non-important non-urgent ones, don't bother or do them as a break, to relax after working hard on the other ones... There is the risk that basically irrelevant timewasters like social media and e-mail end up taking much more time than you planned because they are so addictive. So if you can't limit these activities to 10 minutes, just stay away from them until all your work is done.

Bear in mind that the less real pleasure you get from your work (pleasure belongs to the important category!), the more you will yearn for fun (fun is not important). Therefore first do your Pareto-pleasure exercise in the next section so that you know what activities have the most positive impact on your intellectual performance as well as on your pleasure.

By the way, you should consider meetings with yourself, which I will describe in the section about batch-processing, as important. If you don't mark them immediately as an important appointment in your calendar, the unimportant ones will take over. These meetings with yourself are an example of important tasks that should never be on a to-do list, but always in your calendar.

THE FOUNDATION OF THE EISENHOWER RULE: BE CLEAR
ABOUT YOUR AMBITIONS, PRIORITIES AND GOALS
To be able to apply the Eisenhower rule at its best, you must be clear about the following:
- What are your priorities, not only at work but also for your life as a whole?
- What activities add most value and pleasure?

Too many managers and executives I teach and coach do not know what the cornerstones of their happiness are, what their priorities in life are. You might wonder what this has to do with right-tasking. Well, right-tasking is about making the right choices. These choices, not only the big life-defining ones but also small everyday ones, should on average be in line with what is fundamentally important for yourself. There's no way that you will become really efficient if you don't have a clue about what you really want from your life. This is so important that ALL the executives I coach have to start with a reflection on their priorities in life.

Being more conscious about the cornerstones of your happiness helps you to:
- Realize a better balance between the needs of your work, your family and yourself.
- Feel less lost and stressed when you have to make important choices and reduce the risk of making the wrong choice.
- Prevent yourself from jumping at an opportunity, without giving the consequences much thought.
- Reduce your workload by making it easier to say "no" to demands that do not fit in with your priorities.

Your priorities set the direction you want to go in. What gives you pleasure keeps your engine running. When the two work together and feed each other, you get the best results. There is nothing wrong if sometimes there's no synergy. If for example, you have fun for fun's sake. Or if you are working hard to achieve your priorities, but you don't really enjoy what you are doing, that too can work for a while, although it will be very difficult to sustain.

Further discussion of this very important subject would lead us too far away from the goal of this book. However, I would like to point out that since lots of people find it too difficult to start thinking about these cornerstones, I developed a tool that will help you to reflect on what your priorities are and what gives you most pleasure. You can download this "homework": "The cornerstones of happiness" at www.brainchains.org. The best way to get the most out of these exercises and reflections is to do them together with your partner/spouse. Make a copy of these pages, fill them in separately without consulting with the other, and afterwards spend a weekend away together in a nice hotel without children, e-mail or telephone to compare and discuss the results and to develop your *joint* priorities as a couple or as a family.

To do this exercise well takes some time. Organize some undisturbed time out. The time spent on this exercise is an investment that will save you from lots of unhappy days.

Once I coached a very successful manager from the aviation industry who said: "My philosophy is: if you don't have goals, you never get lost". He had developed a very hedonistic, ad hoc approach to life and was happy grabbing any opportunity that popped up. I think we all need a dose of that approach, to be flexible and to keep life interesting and exciting. However, during the coaching it became very clear that for important work-related choices, renovating his house and his relationships with his wife, children, family and friends, he had very specific priorities, ambitions and plans, but he did not let these interfere with his enjoyment of the here and now and... decided not to take the very nice promotion he was offered to become an executive because it would ruin his pleasure. Doing "The cornerstones of happiness" with his wife when the big promotion was offered, made it very clear what their joint priorities and their joint pleasures were, to the extent that it became almost self-evident that not accepting a promotion that almost everybody would jump at, was the right thing to do.

BEING CLEAR ABOUT WHAT ACTIVITIES ADD MOST VALUE IS THE SECOND IMPERATIVE CONDITION TO RIGHT-TASK

THE PARETO RULE

Once you know what your priorities are at work and in your private life, the Pareto rule will help you to find out what activities add most value. The Pareto Rule states that 20% of your activities generate 80% of your results. Or the other way around: 80% of your activities generate only 20% of your results. Don't take this famous 20/80 rule too literally. The essence is that to be effective you need to identify the high performance or high value-adding activities.

Hence during your week, reflect once in a while, or even more efficient, every evening for 5 minutes while you are travelling home, on which activities that day added the most value to realize your long-term or short-term goals and priorities. If you regularly do this it will help you to say no to non value-adding tasks and to stop yourself from spending a lot of time on these.

If you are overwhelmed with tasks you need to filter, you need to invest a few seconds to decide if the task belongs to the 20% of high value-adding activities or not. If they do, then concentrate on these first and make time for them. If not, forget about them, unless they give you a lot of pleasure (see below).

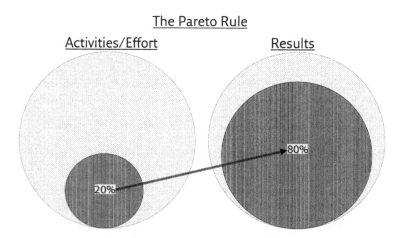

The Pareto Rule

Following your social media, for example, is a huge counterproductive and addictive timewaster that never belongs to this 20%. If it is really fun for you, read on and do a Pareto-reflection exercise for your fun activities. As for your e-mail, 80% is low value adding. For a lot of people, 80% of their e-mail does not add any value whatsoever! So find ways to eliminate these as much as possible (for tips, see the chapter about e-mail below).

ONLY FOR THE DARING: THE POWER OF PARETO^2
(PARETO SQUARED)

If you want to become a really top performer, once you've got the knack of "thinking Pareto", do a daring Pareto^2 (Pareto-squared) or even a ruthless Pareto^3 (Pareto to the power of three) reflection exercise, at least to get a better insight into what your job is really about.

You start with the Pareto rule that 20% of activities generate 80% of results. Then for these 20% of activities you do another Pareto to discover which 4% of your activities (20% of 20%) generate 64% of your results (80% of 80%). This will require some hard out-of-the-box thinking. From my coaching experience with managers I know that coachees, even very senior executives, are often flabbergasted by what they learn from this exercise.

Extreme^2 Pareto

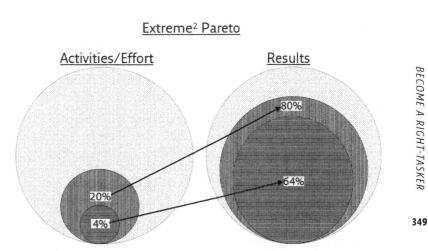

Activities/Effort   Results

Then for the really daring amongst you, or just for the fun of it, there is the Pareto[3] reflection. If 4% of your activities generate 64% of your results, then 1% of your effort generates 50% of your results. It sounds absurd, but bringing this reflection to its conclusion will give you an inspiring new view on your work. This does not mean that from then on you will only do this 1%, but when you have to make choices, you always apply your limited resources, brain-time and brain-power first of all to the 1%, 4% or 20% of activities that generate the most results.

This Pareto exercise is especially important for perfectionists. Perfectionists spend 80% of their time to reach the last 20% of perfection. For most of us and for most tasks 100% perfection is not necessary. For people like a programmer to get the last bug out of a software program or for a brain surgeon it is, but these are the exceptions and there is a 90% chance that you are not one of them.

PARETO FOR PLEASURE

Once you have the picture of Pareto at work, I suggest you do a Pareto pleasure reflection. Life is not just about being efficient at work, having a successful career etc...To realize your goals, your priorities have to be clear, but you should also enjoy what you are doing. What sense does it make to strive for goals and priorities while not enjoying the journey? With enjoy I don't mean fun, but real joy, real pleasure, real fulfilling happiness.

Pleasure is often related to succeeding in activities that are at the limit of your abilities, about developing your skills as a professional, as a parent, as a friend... It is often about doing something significant and meaningful for others or even for a cause bigger than yourself. Therefore, what are the 20% of your activities at work that give you 80% of pleasure, the 4%-->60%, the 1%-->50%? Once you are aware of these, don't compromise on them.

Finally, what about the fun in your work and your life? There is nothing wrong with this more hedonistic superficial, short-lived fun, notwithstanding that it is not fulfilling in the long term. Therefore, why not reflect for a few minutes on the 20% of activities at work and beyond that are most fun, that are the spice of your work and life? Once you have clearly defined them, why not make time for fun as well.

Beware though, you have to bear in mind when making room for fun that there can be a risk, especially if you don't experience much real pleasure and joy. The effect of fun activities is short. They are not fulfilling like real pleasure or real happiness, which can make you feel happy for a long time. So you may rather quickly long for another "dose" of fun. Moreover, many fun activities habituate. This means you will gradually need more of them to get the same kick. This is particularly true if being online is fun for you. You will have to be very strict with yourself to limit the time you spend online. If you don't, it will become a major brain-waster if not an addiction, crowding out the pleasurable as well as the important.

PARETO FOR LIFE

Interestingly enough, once they get the idea, most people can do this extreme Pareto rather easily for their work, but when as a coach I then ask them to go beyond this and to reflect in the same way about the rest of their life, they are lost. I coached more than a hundred professionals, managers and executives individually and more than about two hundred in groups at INSEAD. When I asked them the "simple" question: what do you want to achieve in your life? Many did not have an answer. To help them I developed the tool I described above. Once you know what your life priorities are and what gives you most pleasure, you can also start Pareto-thinking about non-work subjects like your family life and your own development, health and well-being.

THE ULTIMATE GOAL: BECOMING AN EISENHOWER-THINKER
AND PARETO-THINKER WITHOUT DOING ANY EXERCISES

Once you know your priorities and goals, you can formulate sub-goals for the next period, for the next month, week and day. As I described before, the ideal is to decide each evening what's really important the next day and earmark time for it. You can do this on Sunday evening for the following week.

Of course you should not be doing explicit Eisenhower and Pareto exercises all the time for the rest of your life! The goal is to do it as a learning exercise, in the beginning as a very conscious exercise. After this exercise, however, while you are becoming a right-tasker, more and more it will become spontaneous Eisenhower-thinking and Pareto-thinking in the back of your head. Then you only do explicit Eisenhower and Pareto exercises when the circumstances change or when you feel you have lost your right-tasking and are becoming inefficient again by being hyper-connected, multitasking, stress or lack of sleep.

BATCH-PROCESSING IS THE MOST CRITICAL SOLUTION

Do you remember the simple but very convincing experiment of Section 1, where you had to write M U L T I T A S K I N G in capital letters and then give every character its serial number and that the second exercise where you had to switch tasks took 50-100% more time than the batch-processing method in the first step?

If doing this super-simple simplistic easy task in multitask mode results in an intellectual productivity loss of 50%, you don't need a super-brain to imagine what the gain in intellectual productivity can be when you stop switching between intellectually much more challenging, difficult or complex tasks.

TO RUTHLESSLY AND RADICALLY REDUCE SWITCHES: BATCH-PROCESS

For real maximal intellectual productivity the dream would be to eliminate multitasking altogether and to work in one batch from start to finish, but this has become impossible in most jobs. A certain degree of multitasking might even be part of your job responsibility. However, once you are convinced about how counterproductive always being connected and task-switching are, the most important thing to do is to start batch-processing.

Before you start doing this, you first need to eliminate most of your to-do list by immediately planning tasks directly into your calendar; this will help to eliminate delays in the delivery time. As I explained in the chapter about multitasking, multitasking not only prolongs the execution of a single task, but when this task is a link in a chain of events, it totally ruins delivery times at the end of the chain. Therefore when people ask you to do something, you should think how much time the execution of the task will take you and then you should make it a rule that you never put tasks on a to-do list, but go immediately to your agenda and look when you have time to do it. If there is no time for it, refuse the task. If the request comes from a superior, you negotiate to find out what other task you can drop, postpone or pass on to somebody else.

While you are looking for space in your diary, you also avoid doing the task in bits and pieces by planning it preferably in one undisturbed batch or at least in big consecutive chunks. This way you will be able to make significant progress on several tasks in a day, much more than when multitasking.

This is a necessary step to start systematic batch-processing, which is THE most imperative method to become much more intellectually productive, especially when your work is not routine work. Bulk-processing or batch-processing is many times more efficient than doing your work in bits and pieces all day long for the many reasons you now know having read the first part of this book. The most important one is how your brain works and especially the concept of context-switching and the huge loss this causes in terms of time, efficiency, memory, concentration, creativity etc...

Uninterrupted work is up to four times more efficient if the tasks are complex or if the tasks belong to very different domains like work and home. Thirty minutes of uninterrupted work is 10 times more efficient than 10 three-minute stints alternating it with other tasks. Don't forget: every single switch, every distraction, even a minor one causes a loss of productivity.

▶ **Batch-processing: to turn the scatterbrained Homo Interruptus back into a productive Homo Sapiens**

As we will see later in this chapter, you should first of all handle your e-mails in batches, not only for the reasons discussed in the chapter about multitasking in sections 1 and 2, but also because it is purely mathematical: each time you go to your e-mail there are a lot of little time-consuming actions you take to get to an e-mail and answer it that you only have to do once if you bulk-process your e-mail. This of course is the worst when you do e-mails on your phone. Taking your phone, logging in, scrolling to the e-mail, reading e-mails that you have already partially read and then stopped reading to go to an important meeting etc... Doing e-mails all the time on your phone is even more inefficient than doing it all the time on your desktop computer, which is already very inefficient.

The objection I hear most often is: But there might be a very urgent e-mail. This is a typical reaction of a connection-addict. It is not at all rational. It is a cop-out. This becomes clear when I ask these professionals: How many e-mails did you receive this week that would have caused a real problem if you read them with a two- to three-hour delay? The answer is always "zero". Then I ask about the last month and the answer is ... zero.

When people are still reluctant or worrying, I advise them to keep their "out of office" reply on all the time with a nice friendly explanation about their e-mail management method and including an emergency telephone number for real emergencies. Some people used a small cheap second phone for this with a different number, a very small investment for their peace of mind. The most frequent and important disadvantage of having such an emergency phone is that nobody ever uses it, which can be an important blow to your feeling of being so important and indispensable.

Last but not least, since making progress is what motivates people most[6], batch-processing will make you feel much better, happier and more enthusiastic about your work every time you finish a batch, rather than after finishing just a little piece. If you want to further increase that great feeling, set a goal and why not set a reward. Write down in one sentence what you want to achieve in that particular batch and why not promise yourself a reward like getting a cup of coffee or reading an article in the newspaper or a magazine at the end. Do not link your reward to any screen, like surfing the Internet, doing social media or a game. Get away from your screen for all the reasons explained in Section 2. In your break you should move, walk, or even run at full speed, even if it is only a few flights of stairs. Remember the "tonic immobility" of the Stress BrainChain. Break out of your frozen position. Moreover, if the reward is Internet-related, you will always spend more time on it than you planned.

- *Work on one single task or logical parts of it, undisturbed*
The first kind of batch-processing is for important brainwork where you need your reflecting brain to be at its best, like writing an important memo, making a plan, thinking about a solution or an important choice to make, preparing for an important meeting, studying a file, reading a book, making a presentation, having an important conversation etc... In all these cases the most efficient approach is to do this work all at once without being disturbed (with the strongest possible emphasis on "undisturbed").

▶ **Reflection takes time: reconquer your time**

If the task is really too long to handle all at once, divide it into more or less logical chunks of at least 45 undisturbed minutes, like subchapters, parts you can finish in one go if you work on them undisturbed. This way you don't have to store much in your temporary memory. After you finish an important part, don't waste the accumulated knowledge in your temporary memory by immediately doing e-mails, but take a break (see the next BrainGain) to give your brain time to order and store the important information in your long-term memory. Your reflecting brain needs these breaks to digest and store the work it did. Then you start with the next chunk etc...

- *Bundle related tasks into one batch*
The second is to bundle together tasks that are related to the same subject and do them in dedicated blocks of time.
The less the tasks are related, the higher the switching cost, the more brain-energy they cost, the more stress they cause, the more you forget and the more mistakes you will make... Doing your e-mails is an extreme example of doing tasks that most often have no relationship to one another.
Separate work tasks from home tasks because these too are totally different domains. You will forget more and make more mistakes when you mix them and switch between them.
- *Assemble unrelated tasks, e-mails and chores in one batch*
The third is where you assemble all kinds of small unrelated

355

tasks, most often doing e-mails, in one big batch of at least 30 to max 45 minutes, and you do nothing but that with your brain, your computer and your desktop in e-mail-mode. After you have processed e-mail for half an hour or 45 minutes, please take a break and have a (healthy) snack or do the bundle with the most unrelated tasks (like e-mails) just before your lunch break! As I explained in the chapter about decision-power, several researchers demonstrated that making decisions and choices is a summative process: making all these small decisions and choices required by e-mails, even if it is just about deleting or not, consumes more brain energy than making one big decision. Moreover, after half an hour your brain is all over the place and in reactive mode, so you need a short break to refocus your brain on the task, meeting, conversation or whatever is next.

You should also batch-process your chores. We all need to do chores we really don't like, little ones and big ones. First think if there is really nobody else you can delegate these to, ideally somebody who likes these tasks or for whom they are new and still a challenge. You might be able to swap chores with a colleague who dislikes tasks that you like. If we cannot delegate or swap them, we tend to postpone them or procrastinate because usually they are not urgent. Just knowing you have that long list of chores is unpleasant, but what's worse is that we tend to postpone them until they become urgent and then they get in the way of more important work. Therefore you should batch your "shit work" into "shit batches", as one of my executives called it, for example scheduling in your diary one hour a week for it. Just call it SB meeting so that nobody else can schedule a meeting at that time of the week.

This has several advantages. When you get the chore and you cannot delegate it, you don't have to swear, stress or worry, you immediately file it in the "shit box". That in itself will make you feel much better. Secondly you don't have to worry about it because you know you will deal with it. Thirdly, when you start your SB, you most often will adopt a kind of cleaning-up attitude that will help you to do it much more efficiently. Cleaning a lot of shit in one batch is much more efficient than doing it in little bit and pieces. As a result these postponed annoying little chores no longer get in the way of more important work. Last but not the least, cleaning up a lot of garbage in one go gives you a feeling of having accomplished something, a feeling you never get if you get rid of it bit by bit. Of course this is true for your e-mail batches too.

- *Make a home batch*
  When you still have to work from home after a full day of work, even after you managed to gain lots of time by breaking your four BrainChains, make a home batch, a dedicated timeslot for dealing with work at home. Being connected all the time at home ruins your family life and sets a very bad example to your children. If your children are adolescents, you should reread the chapter on them in the Hyperconnectivity BrainChain and reflect on how you can help them avoid being totally inefficient. Set an example by making one home batch instead of being partially present all the time. Agree on the time with the family, be totally disconnected while you are working on it and then disconnect and be really present, engage, enjoy and recuperate.
  If you are always connected at home, not only are you an example of a badly balanced brainworker, as described in the chapter about e-mail in Section 2, but you are declaring your family less important than whatever is on your phone all the time, and that is an awful feeling, the worst kind of phubbing (snubbing someone by looking at your mobile phone instead of paying attention). Before you know it the whole family will be more engaged with the virtual world than with their real family, including you. And remember, when the subject is the development of children and your relationship with them: the postman never rings twice.

PUT THE BATCH-TIME IN YOUR CALENDAR
It is absolutely critical to earmark time for these batches, so put them in your calendar. Given that in most companies calendars are public and anybody can ruin your batching intentions at any time, give your batch-processing times a name of a meeting and plan them for the rest of the year as weekly recurring meetings.

Many of my coachees have called them MWM meeting (meeting with myself). One quality manager called them QTM meetings (Quality Time with Myself). Another used TT meetings (Thinking Time), and the manager I mentioned above called them SB meetings.

Many professionals, even executives I coach always complain that the circumstances and culture in their companies don't allow them to reduce their hypertasking. This is usually a load of baloney, to put it politely. Some multitasking is unavoidable and part of your job. Without exception, however, a lot of multitasking is unnecessary, counterproductive and can be eliminated with batch-processing, creativity, guts, ruthlessness, discipline and focus.

The secretary general of a global company tried to follow the advice of doing real brainwork first thing in the morning, before reading his e-mails, to keep his brain uncluttered and focused on the important things. Because he had to make an exception for e-mail from the CEO and CFO, he had those e-mails colored red. Then he discovered that while looking for the red e-mails, he couldn't stop himself from reading other e-mails... The solution was to create a rule in his e-mail program that automatically put all incoming e-mails except those from the CEO and CFO in a folder "Inbox2". Opening his inbox first thing in the morning, the only e-mails were those from the CEO or the CFO. A quick Eisenhower-check helped to decide whether to deal with them at once or postpone them until his e-mail batch. From then on he was able to keep to his scheduled times for e-mail.

TAKING A GOOD BREAK AFTER EVERY BATCH IS NOT A LUXURY BUT A NECESSITY

I sincerely hope that what I wrote about the necessity of regular breaks for your intellectual productivity was convincing enough to motivate you to systematically plan regular breaks in your working days.

Ample brain-breaks between tasks are crucial for our archiving brain to put our memory in order before starting a new task. These breaks are also imperative to refuel our brain energy. On top of that, they are absolutely indispensable to switch between very complex or very different tasks and especially between thinking about people and about things. You should at all costs avoid going straight from one meeting to the next without a brain-break or filling these breaks with e-mails. Therefore don't organize back-to-back meetings, and encourage the same behavior from your manager, the president of the meeting and the other participants or your team members.

Similarly, regular breaks are very good for your health too, especially if you move about in these breaks. Hence, it is more than evident that breaks are not lost time, but an investment to produce more, better and healthier brainwork.

If you are not used to taking breaks, you may need a few tricks. One is to include them in your planning and calendar and set an alarm or timer. When you have meetings scheduled back to back, set a timer and leave the meeting in time to have a break before the next one.

A very efficient help is to find a buddy, somebody who is going to join your plan. You can then put each other under pressure to take these breaks.

There is another strange but helpful tool I discovered: smokers. The addiction of smokers forces them to take regular breaks. This is the only advantage of a nicotine addiction. As a non-smoker (and I hope you are too), you can turn this to your advantage by asking a smoker to come and get you to join her break (but not the smoke) every time she feels the urge.

Of course your buddies' timing does not always fit the timing of your meetings, tasks and batches, but a non-ideally timed break is better than no break.

A MOST IMPORTANT CHAINBREAKER: TAME THE E-MAIL MONSTER

Please bear in mind that I am not an email-management or time-management specialist. The strategies and tactics I mention in this chapter are the result of discussions I have had with participants in my presentations and workshops about stress management or change management or about the BrainChains. Many ideas were tested out with coachees who came for many different reasons ranging from burnout to leadership development. It is significant that very often when discussing issues of self-management and managing other people, e-mail turns out to be an important obstacle to becoming more efficient, even for very successful and very senior people.

E-MAIL IS NOT A MONSTER BUT AN E-FRANKENSTEIN

By now you certainly realize that much of the stuff you do when you are always connected is not efficient, important, urgent or value-adding. The next step is to kick these brain-wasting habits. Although the long-term awards are big, this is not going to be easy. In the short term, it might make your work not less but more difficult. Moreover, if you are addicted, it will be very hard to forego the short-term rewards. First of all, you need to be convinced of the fact that e-mail is only useful for the exchange of facts and information and that it is an awfully inefficient tool for sharing opinions and communication.

Before you start taming your own Frankenstein, check if you are addicted. Do the test in Section 2 in the chapter about e-mail. If you are addicted it will be very difficult to become very intellectually productive again. You will invent many excuses and rationalizations as to why you shouldn't do things differently. The first step to change, as Alcoholics Anonymous realized, is to admit you are addicted. The second step is to read the chapter below about changing habits.

For the reasons I explained in the second section of this book, switching back and forth between e-mails and other work is the least efficient way of dealing with both. The most important victims are your other tasks and activities. You are less present, concentrated and attentive, and less focused on the tasks and especially the people you are interacting with. This is not just the case if you do e-mails during meetings or interrupt other tasks "to quickly do a few e-mails", but also if you do e-mails just before important thinking tasks, meetings and conversations.

The following may surprise you, but the second most important victim is the e-mailing itself. Doing it in bits and pieces, especially on a smartphone is the least efficient, most time-consuming way of doing it.

360 YOUR BEST WEAPON: BATCH-PROCESSING

As I described in Section 2, one of the major disadvantages of e-mail is that it was made for information (one-way) and not for communication (two-way). The problem is that it is still useless for communication, but too many people try to use it for communicating anyway, by answering (and expecting an answer) within 2 minutes. In one large company 70% of e-mails were even answered within 6! seconds. This is not just utterly counterproductive, as I explained in Section 2, it is totally crazy. It means that for 70% of e-mails people interrupted whatever (important) work they were doing, totally ruining their intellectual productivity.

In the not so good old days when Internet connections were not as ubiquitous as today or when family members still revolted against staying connected all the time, many professionals would return from a trip or a vacation to find hundreds of e-mails in their inbox. They would then sit down behind their computer and process all of them in two or three hours or even less if they used mini-batches (see below).

If you try to do that many e-mails in your normal hyper-connected, task-hopping workdays it will take you at least four times longer, especially if you do it on your phone. Or do you have so much idle time to waste?

This is an example of the huge advantage of bulk-processing e-mails.

Ideally you not only bulk your e-mail management, but you also limit the time. So how do you do all this in practice? The first and most important step is to ring-fence your e-mail time. Limit it to four times a day. Put these times in your agenda so that nobody can schedule a meeting at that time. Even five times a day is acceptable if you keep to those times and to the time limit. There is no strict rule. Experiment to find your own solution and then keep to your e-mail time and its duration. Interestingly enough, many people who went from checking their mail all the time to doing it four times a day discovered that three times or even twice a day works even more efficiently.

As for limiting the time, set an alarm and when it sounds just close your e-mail program. "Even if I didn't finish?" Even if you did not finish. For one thing, you will discover that nothing horrible happens and, more importantly, it will force you to become more efficient by using the tips and tricks from this chapter.

When the issue is the batch-processing of e-mail or any other intellectual work, ruthlessness is the only real solution. Don't worry about going to extremes. If the subject is important, there's still a 90% chance that it is not really urgent and if it is urgent, people should call you. If you are worried anyway or if this goes against a totally destructive e-mail culture in your company, you may need to camouflage your dedicated e-mail time by giving it a fake meeting name. It might also be helpful to use a very friendly out-of-office message saying that you are unable to read your e-mail but that if it is very important or very urgent people can always reach you on your mobile phone or even better on the cheap emergency phone that you bought for your own peace of mind.

Going "cold turkey" is the word drug addicts use when they try to kick the habit straight away. It is the fastest and probably the best method, if you can get through the initial stage where the anxiety runs high. If you really can't get yourself to ruthlessly ring-fence your connection time, do it in small steps and see how far you can get. Start going to the bathroom, the water cooler or the coffee machine without your phone. Then take a lunch break with only your emergency phone. If you can't manage these experiments, you are a real addict. Get professional help if you want to ever reconquer not only your intellectual performance but your life too.

Once you are able to disconnect for five minutes to half an hour without anxiety, gradually increase your disconnected time. If necessary, take very small steps. Even if you stubbornly add only two minutes a week, you will get to the minimum goal of being half an hour connected, half an hour disconnected. Once you get there the significant increase in intellectual productivity will most likely sufficiently motivate you to limit your connection time to a few times a day.

When it's e-mail time, you get your brain and yourself organized to do nothing but e-mails. When you do it on a professional computer and the biggest professional screen you can get, you have your e-mails and the things you need to do them really efficiently (your calendar, your contacts, your folders, the timeline of your most important project or whatever takes most of your time on your desktop), you get your brain in email-mode and off you go for 30 minutes. You will fly. If you batch-process e-mails, the overall gain in time will be 25-50% with a much better quality of response, less stress and much fewer stupid mistakes and, most importantly of all, your other more important work will gain the most in quality and quantity. If you can't get a nice big screen from your company, buy one yourself. It's worth the investment.

Telecom companies and smartphone producers try to convince you that you can do this on a phone. This is pure baloney (and I am being very polite now). Even on a tablet whose screen is halved by the keyboard, it is much less efficient and far more difficult and tiring than on a nice big screen with a real keyboard. You should make it a rule to use your phone and tablet as an exception, not as a rule.

SUB-BATCH OR MINI-BATCH YOUR E-MAIL
If you have lots of mails in an inbox you want to clean up, avoid at all costs doing them one by one in bits and pieces of "lost" time. Moreover, the default order in which your mails are usually ordered is by date. If you start looking at the most recent ones you may miss information from previous ones and if you start with the oldest, you might answer questions that have already been answered in the meantime. You will be surprised how fast and how many mails you can process if you "sub-batch" your e-mails by sorting or arranging them. In MS Outlook click on "arranged by" at the top of the list and order them by subject, by sender or whatever is most logical or efficient for you to manage many different mails at once.

Usually you only need to do two well-chosen sub-batches to process e-mail very quickly. For example, you start by arranging them by sender, scan them fast to see if you got any from really important people and do these first without looking at the others. Then you sort them by subject. Scan them quickly and react only to the really important subjects (remember Eisenhower).

Then you process all the others, but still in sub-batches. With the preview on, you know at a glance what the mini-batch is about and you can often answer, file or delete 10 e-mails at once.

This is most efficient of course on a big screen in your office, where you have a much better overview and all information you need in sight, rather than on the micro-screen of your phone where it is ridiculous to try to be efficient.

Some people like to archive their e-mails in separate folders or to give them labels. That's what I used to do myself. I realized that this is a waste of time if you have an excellent desktop search tool. Since even in the latest MS Office the search tool is less than mediocre, I keep using my x1 desktop search tool (Copernic is an alternative) and I put all the mails I want to keep in one archive batch. I flag a few e-mails before filing if I cannot respond or delete immediately. My e-mail program opens on these flagged ones (see below).

Warning: when you are doing an e-mail batch, do not follow any links to the Internet in your e-mails, especially in your digital detox or iDetox period because the temptation will be too great to start surfing and task-hopping.

WHY YOU SHOULD NOT DO E-MAILS INSTEAD OF
"LOSING TIME"

If at this stage you are asking yourself "why not do e-mails instead of wasting all these precious little empty timeslots in the course of a day", you have probably been task-hopping or multitasking while reading this book, or you have jumped directly to the solutions without reading the first two sections. The answer to this question is explained in the chapter about e-mail in Section 2.

Let me summarize the most important reasons why you should batch your e-mails.

The "lost" time is often the "micro-breaks" that your brain (and the rest of your body) needs to recuperate and relax (see section 2 about "interval stress"). These are precious moments to relax and free yourself from the continuous low level of stress that e-mail causes.

The "lost" time is the perfect time to let your reflecting brain idle between two important meetings so that your archiving brain gets a chance to digest the information from the last one and prepare for the next one.

The "lost" time is the time when your archiving brain will play around with your long-term memory to prepare for the most creative solutions.

The "lost" time standing in the elevator in your office or your client's office is perfect not only to reflect or let your brain idle, but also to say hello. Why not have a micro-conversation? Why not meet a real person who might be going to the same meeting and who will have a very different impression of you after such a brief friendly interaction?

The "lost" time waiting for a meeting to start is the perfect time for some small talk. "What? Doing stupid small talk rather than important e-mails?" Yes, yes and yes! Relaxed small-talk leaves enough idle spare brain-capacity to allow your archiving brain to prepare for the meeting and, if you came running straight out of another meeting, to store some of that information too.

Especially just before an important meeting, while you are waiting for everybody to arrive, "small talk" is also the perfect oil to grease the relational machine of the meeting and to put the introverts at ease. These are also the moments when you might learn things "off the record" that you will never find in e-mails. Moreover, I recently discovered that small talk has been the subject of serious research and it turns out that small talk also has an influence on the efficiency of the meeting, to the extent that the authors advise managers to start every meeting with a few minutes of small talk, especially when there are introverts in the group[7]. Can you imagine just before an important football match a coach allowing his players to sit there not talking to each other but doing e-mails? By the way, if you want to learn more about the importance of the much underestimated small talk, go to my website www.compernolle.com and click on "Free texts to download".

Filling the "lost" time before an important meeting or any important task with e-mails also ruins much of the beautiful preparation work that your archiving brain has unconsciously been doing, it ruins your concentration and it even squanders precious brain chemicals that you need so dearly to get the best out of the meeting. It literally lowers your decision power, willpower, self-control... and even your IQ. Why the heck would you want to do this? Or do you really think you have such a huge surplus of brain-power to waste?

DON'T START THE DAY WITH E-MAIL IF YOU HAVE IMPORTANT, DIFFICULT OR CREATIVE BRAINWORK TO DO
Doing e-mails first thing in the morning is like shackling your brain immediately. Make it a rule never to start your day with e-mails, certainly not when you have important intellectual work,

reflecting or meetings that day.

Don't even think about opening your e-mail first thing in the morning. Doing that is enough to kill your concentration for many hours and to get your brain in its primitive reactive mode. Moreover, all the little and often unrelated decisions you have to take when doing your e-mails also diminish or exhaust your willpower and decision power, as I explained in Section 2, handing over decisions to your primitive reflex brain. Only do your e-mails after you have done the most important and most difficult brainwork.

The ideal approach for your reflecting brain is to decide the evening before what really important work you will do the next day. Write this down. This way you will focus your fantastic archiving brain while it is doing all its beautiful archiving, memorizing and reconnecting during the night. If you really want to get the best out of your brain, do the most creative and difficult intellectual work first thing in the morning without looking at your e-mails. Starting with your e-mails is enough to undo a lot of the beautiful work your brain has done for you during the night.

ELIMINATE ALL SIRENS THAT LURE YOU TO YOUR INBOX

The songs of the mermaids were so beautiful and hypnotic that no sailor could ever resist them and as a result all their boats crashed on the cliffs. Therefore the Greek hero Odysseus stuffed the ears of his men with wax and asked them to tie him to the mast and thus became the only man ever to hear the Sirens and survive. You have to be as creative and ruthless as Odysseus if you don't want to be lured to the cliffs of your e-mails where your productivity will be stranded.

▶ **Eliminate all Sirens that lure you to your inbox where your intellectual productivity will be stranded on the e-mail cliffs.**

- *Turn off all visual and auditory inbox alerts*
  This first piece of advice only takes a couple of minutes to implement and will save you tons of time and concentration. As we described in Section 2, visual and auditory alerts by themselves cause a drop in concentration. So turn them off on all your phones, desktops and tablets, except for your sep-

arate emergency phone if you have one. If they are not off yet, stop reading and do it NOW. If you don't, no matter what your rationalization is, it is a clear sign you are addicted. You will be unable to execute any of the other advice. You probably need professional help.

These alerts are one of the hypnotic Sirens luring you to the cliffs of your inbox where your intellectual performance will crash.

- *Don't use your inbox as a to-do list*

  If your e-mail inbox is full of to-do items you have created an inbox full of Sirens that will lure you to the cliffs of all your other e-mails and leave your intellectual performance stranded.

  First of all, as I described in the chapter on multitasking, to avoid promising things you can never do in time because you're serial multitasking, never put important tasks on a to-do list or leave the mail as a reminder in your inbox. Instead, immediately note in your calendar when you will do them. If a task is not important enough to put in your calendar, why would you do it anyway? If the task is answering an e-mail, then it will become part of the next batch of e-mails you process.

  If you really need a to-do list, put it anywhere you want, as long as looking at your to-do list does not bring you anywhere close to your e-mail. By extension, never put your to-do items in the task manager that is part of your e-mail program (unless you really never switch to your e-mails when you look at your to-do list), because if you do you are simply creating another Siren that's going to crash your intellectual productivity on the cliffs of your e-mail.

- *Don't allow ANY timewasters in your inbox*

  Every time you get an e-mail from a source that regularly sends irrelevant e-mails make a rule at once to automatically delete them in the future, or if you don't dare to do that for a particular sender, put it in a dedicated "iSpam" folder or in your Archive folder, where you can always find it with your search program if you need it (99% of the time, this is never). In MS Office, you just have to right-click on the mail and in two clicks your rule is made.

Disable all automatic feeds from social media, news sites, blogs etc... If you think you cannot survive without looking at them, you are an addict or you have too much time to waste. If you think it is just a bad habit of doing this at the wrong place and the wrong time, make a rule that automatically puts all of them in a separate "timewasters" folder, and only look at them to relax at the end of your workday. Well ... if you really do not have anything better to relax your brain like going to the gym or having fun with your spouse, kids and (real!) friends.

If you still look at that folder at times you decided not to do it, nest that folder in a cascade of folders that will force you to open at least five folders to get to it and give these folders names that warn and scold you.

By the way, you probably won't believe this, but people who thrive on intellectual productivity and creativity discover, sometimes after a very difficult iDetox period, not only that they become more productive but even that they can live better without most of these timewasters.

- *Don't let your office program and your e-mail program open on your inbox*

  First of all, reset your e-mail program so that it opens by default on your calendar or to do list (if you have one), not your mail program, and leave that on your screen. Although it gets you closer to the cliffs, you can also set the "For Follow Up" folder as the default. When you systematically flag e-mails that you weren't able to finish, at the next batch-time your e-mail program opens with the most urgent or important e-mails.

  How to set this up in MS Outlook? Start with the Tools (2003, 2007) or File (2010) tab. Select Options/(Other)/Advanced Options. Click the Browse button of "Start in this folder". From the "Select folder" choose what you want Outlook Office to open at startup. If you want to open with the "For Follow Up" folder, expand the Search Folders. Click OK/OK/OK.

  You can even configure your e-mail program to open with an empty inbox so that you avoid temptation when you need to search for a particular e-mail or you need to write an urgent e-mail that really can't wait until the next batch-processing slot.

To do that, make a rule that immediately redirects ALL your incoming e-mail to your custom-made "Inbox batch". That way your inbox is always empty. An advantage of this approach is that, if you still go to your inbox outside your set 'Batch time" you can nest this "Inbox batch" in a "danger" folder and that one in a "Are you certain?" folder and that one in a "only for batch time" folder. You can make it as difficult as you need to and the names of the folders as scolding as you want to avoid going to your inbox outside batch time.

- *Put wax in your ears and tie yourself to the mast.*
Good luck.

DON'T ANSWER YOUR E-MAILS IMMEDIATELY, NOT EVEN WITHIN THE HOUR; 24 HOURS IS THE HEALTHY AND PRODUCTIVE STANDARD

Until now you could claim ignorance about how counterproductive it is to always be connected. But as of today, it is not because everybody else is totally f***ing up (excuse my French) their intellectual productivity by trying to answer e-mails immediately that you should too! This is totally irrational, unnecessary and utterly stupid, if not crazy, and you should refuse to enter this productivity-ruining madhouse.

Revolt, or at least be wiser yourself. There are in fact no e-mails that need a response in less than 24 hours. If somebody sends you one of these, the sender is the idiot. The sender should know that if something is really urgent and important they should contact you by phone. Period.

If you do not have the courage to just stop checking your e-mails all the time, make a nice out-of-office message that you leave on all the time and tell people that to be more productive you only check your e-mails three times a day and that people should call you if they have an urgent request. If you feel too uncomfortable doing this, buy the emergency phone I described above. If you feel like you need to explain the reasons why you do this, refer to this book!

If you are a manager, and certainly if you are an executive, you will increase the productivity of the brainworkers in your company enormously if you establish a 24-hour answering rule for the whole company. If you set a rule that e-mails have to be answered within 24 hours, this means that people only need two batches a day to answer them all. With such a simple rule the gains in productivity will be massive. No strategic intervention you can imagine will ever have such a return on investment.

DON'T TRY TO COMMUNICATE BY E-MAIL: APPLY THE RULE OF THREE

Apply the rule of three: as soon as three mails are exchanged on a subject and it's still not settled or whenever there is the slightest suspicion that it will take more than three e-mails to get an agreement, pick up the phone, go and meet, or have a conference call.

DON'T ANSWER ALL MAILS

Way too many people still think they have to answer all mails. Some older professionals might have kept this habit from the days they got letters, and you always answered letters. Younger people have got into the same habit from texting, Tweeting and Facebooking totally irrelevant information back and forth. You don't have to answer, really. Sometimes it helps to think, "If this were the pre-email era, would I take my pen and paper and write a letter?". If the answer is no, more often than not it is not worth an e-mail either. As I mentioned before, I learned from my research that 50% to 90% of e-mail is internal spam, iSpam, anyway.

Many professionals are doing this already with cc-mail. They make a rule that automatically redirects ALL cc-mail to a dedicated cc folder, to look at when they have time, which is usually never. If you are afraid of being so drastic about this, you can make automatic exceptions for e-mail coming from particular sources. A less drastic, less daring, step-by-step approach is to make an ad hoc rule every time you receive irrelevant cc-mail, so that at least e-mails from that source or about that subject won't arrive in your inbox in the future. The best solution however is to make your automatic reply very polite and not make any exceptions. This depends on how high you are in the hierarchy, the company culture and your assertiveness.

If you feel uncomfortable doing this, you can make your rule in such a way that it redirects all cc-mail before it reaches your inbox and automatically sends all cc-mail senders a reply that you have real work to do, that you have no time to read the hundreds of cc-mails you receive and that they should resend the mail with your name in TO if they think it is really important for you personally to read it. An example: "Dear correspondent, the hundreds of cc mails I receive are becoming a real obstacle to doing more important work than looking for the very few relevant or important ones. Therefore, if the mail you just sent me is urgent or important, please mail it directly TO me or give me a call at my private emergency phone 123 45 67".

This healthy basic attitude, however, of not reading all your e-mails is impossible if you think that your opinion is always indispensable or that awful things will happen if you do not answer all e-mails. In that case look for a psychotherapist.

IN CASE OF ANY DOUBT: DELETE

An important trick when you do your e-mails is: if you have the slightest doubt about the usefulness of an e-mail, delete. If you don't dare, archive. Do not waste your time putting them in neatly ordered folders. 99% of these e-mails are not worth the time you spend on archiving. Put them in one huge archive folder with one click or sweep. In the extremely rare case you might need one of these e-mails later, you will find it in a second with one of the high-performing desktop search programs like x1 or Copernic.

Every time you delete an e-mail take a second to think if you should not take five more seconds to make a rule that automatically redirects e-mails about this subject or from this person to the archive folder or deleted folder so that they never again appear in your inbox.

Don't forget that with regards to e-mails, the postman always rings twice: if by accident you deleted/archived an important e-mail, the sender will react. If she doesn't, the mail was not worth your time in the first place.

STICK TO YOUR OWN RULES AND FORCE OR INVITE YOUR CONTACTS TO HELP YOU

As you learned from the earlier examples I gave, several of my clients bought a small, dedicated emergency phone for urgent calls. The number was only known by their spouse, children, boss and team members, with the clear instruction only to use it for emergencies. This opens up a whole range of new possibilities for eliminating disturbances, distractions, task-hopping and information overload while showing that you are really very committed to your job by giving your private phone for emergencies. You feel much more comfortable and you become more assertive about eliminating irrelevant e-mail at the receiver's side.

Tell everybody they should not e-mail but call you if they have an urgent question. Put this in your e-mail signature. The message in your signature could be: "I need to give my full attention to project x. I am therefore limiting how often I check my e-mails." Another person made it: "I want to give my internal and external clients my undivided attention, therefore I will limit my email-checking." If you have an emergency phone, you can make your life even easier, by adding: "If you have an urgent question, please call or text my private emergency phone at 123 4567". Somebody made it very simple: "To be more efficient I only check my e-mail three times a day. If you have an urgent or important question, call me on my emergency phone 123 4567".

You can put the same message on your voicemail and shut off your regular phone too if you have important or difficult work to do.

Recently I mailed somebody who had attended one of my presentations and I received an interesting out-of-office reply:

Dear (future) friend or client,

Thank you for your mail.

I have chosen to spend radically less time with my computer and smartphone.

This does not mean that I am saying 'no' to you.

Rather, it means I am saying 'yes' to what I value most: focus (also for my work with clients), connection (with real people) and beauty.

For an optimal You<>Oscar communication:

1. Urgent? Call me. I will answer immediately or as soon as I stop meeting or driving (I value life too).

2. Important? Text me.

Thanks for your collaboration! :)

Oscar

The ideal solution is to collude with as many people as possible to do the same thing. If you receive e-mail TO you that is irrelevant for your job, send a return e-mail, asking to be kept out of the loop unless it is absolutely necessary that you get involved. If you are good with macros, you can send a standard reply with three clicks, saying "Thank you for your mail. I think, however, that it is not necessary to keep me informed. Please take me off your mailing list or group on this subject". Since the MS Outlook macro-function is very customer-unfriendly, unless you know how to program in visual-basic, I use the "Macro-Express" program to make these kind of macros. I used to do this with two macros, but with the "reply and delete" quickstep in the latest versions of MS Outlook I can do it with one: I click "reply and delete" and then I can choose between three self-made macros that insert a boilerplate reply, going from a very friendly suggestion to a very assertive demand to delete me from the group or mailing list.

Depending on your position in the hierarchy, you can kindly invite or forcefully invite others to sort out your e-mails for you. The only thing you have to do is to make a nice out-of-office message and put the same text in your signature.

"Given the crazy number of e-mails I get, the risk of missing your most important or most urgent e-mails is increasing by the day. Therefore, please always add a Priority code in the subject line of all your e-mails to me: P1 is high priority and P5 is very low priority. E-mail without a P-code will be considered low priority. If it is really very urgent or important it is always better to call me on my private emergency cell xxx.xxxx." You then also do this yourself with all the e-mails you send.

If you are not high enough in the hierarchy to be so assertive, just make your message friendlier, or present it as an experiment, a pilot and invite as many colleagues as possible to join your experiment. Once many people join your endeavor, you can make rules that automatically file the e-mails into two or three folders. It then also becomes very easy to let the "Awayfind®" program send you a message on your "private" mobile phone whenever a top-priority mail drops in your box[8].. Moreover, but keep this a secret, as you will see in the real-life examples below, you will discover that nothing bad will happen to you if you simply never look at e-mails in the P4 and P5 categories. In the rare case that you need the information in one of them, a good desktop search program will find it for you in seconds.

You might not dare to do these kinds of experiments, fearing negative reactions, but I hope you realize that these are just examples of the many ways you can creatively deal with the daily e-mail avalanche. You only need some creativity and (a lot of) assertiveness. If you do, you will discover that the negative reactions are very seldom, if at all. It is much more likely that others will follow your example and you can start dreaming about the whole company falling in line behind you.

HELP TO STOP THE E-MAIL AVALANCHE FOR OTHERS

If you are serious about taming your email-Frankenstein, you should also help others with theirs. When you send an e-mail, ask yourself: If the e-mail system were down, would I print this and fax or send paper copies to all these people or call them? If the answer is "No", why the heck do you create yet another Frankenmail? As we saw in Section 2, a major source of the continuous e-mail diarrhea is the asymmetric relationship between the sender and the receiver. In a way the sender has the power and the receiver is the victim. The million-dollar (literally) question is how can we discipline the senders and empower the receivers. I don't know the ultimate answer, and therefore a lot of my suggestions are more guerilla and subversive techniques than real solutions.

The really structural solutions can only be realized at a company level, but what everybody can start doing is simple things that make a big difference if lots of people do them. I have therefore included these in the section about BrainGains at the WE level.

ONLY FOR THE DARING: DO A CLEAN SWEEP

From the real-life examples below, I learned that more often than not, simply moving all the e-mails in an inbox into oblivion did not cause many problems. So if you're overwhelmed, if not depressed, by a huge inbox because you haven't yet used the strategies and tactics mentioned above, why not select all the e-mails in your inbox and put them altogether in a "WIHT" ("When I Have Time"?) folder. You will then discover that WIHT really means "never" and that the WIHT folder is only really useful for finding a few mails with your search-tool. If you are worried about possible negative reactions, invent a nice excuse.

A FEW MORE REAL-LIFE EXAMPLES

Just a few examples that might seem extreme at first glance in order to show that you can be much more daring, if not ruthless, than you think you can to eliminate Frankenmail.

Many years ago, in the days when there were still a few faxes around, a senior executive was exasperated by his ever-overflowing inbox. He calculated that at his salary level, just processing useless e-mails cost the salary of four full-time high-level management assistants[9]. Of course, this did not even calculate the huge opportunity cost of the really important things he could have done in that time.

We did an experiment: he made an MS Outlook rule, replying to all internal e-mails with the out-of-office message: "I cannot answer your e mail now. If you just sent me an e-mail about something very important or very urgent, please fax it to me at number 1234 (the number of his secretary)". The reasoning was: if what anybody e-mails you, at your level, is not important enough to print it and find a fax, it is not important enough for you to read it. He went from 80-100 e-mails to 3-10 faxes per day! With one simple Out of Office message, he freed up 1 to 1.5 days a week for really important work. Following up two months later, he reported that not reading his e-mails hadn't caused a single problem.

For his vacation, an account manager in one of my groups asked the IT department for a second e-mail address. He then gave this address just to his clients and made a rule that all other e-mails got an automatic reply about his dedicated e-mail hours and about his private emergency phone. All these mails were also automatically moved to a separate WIHT folder, leaving only e-mail from his clients in his inbox. Not looking at the WIHT folder caused only minor problems.

Another manager found 900 e-mails in his inbox after his holiday. This caused a conflict with his wife when on the next vacation he wanted to do his mails every day to avoid a repeat of such a huge backlog. My advice was to use his Out of Office message: "Since after my vacation I will have between 600 and 1,000 e-mails in my inbox, there is a risk that your e-mail will be answered late or not at all. If your message is very important or very urgent, please mail me at my private e-mail address me@myprovider.com." This e-mail address was an alias he specially made at his private provider. He sent a similar e-mail to his customers, with another alias. E-mails to both aliases were automatically forwarded to his company address. He only received five e-mails to the aliases he made for in-company mail. After his vacation, people commented on his commitment to the firm by giving his private e-mail address while on vacation. What they did not know, is that upon returning, he did a search of his inbox and moved over 800 internal mails from his inbox to a separate "vacation" folder. He only kept the messages from his clients. He then did a quick and dirty 45-minute check of his vacation folder using two mini-batches. The original plan was to process the "vacation" folder as soon as he had time for it. Of course he didn't have the time and three months later he realized that out of all those mails in the "Vacation" box he only used information from... about 10. In the meantime he had been able to give much more attention to the mail from his customers.

I was able to convince another manager, who found 300 e-mails after his sick leave, to do another experiment: to only read the e-mails from customers and to send all the people on his internal mailing list a message that something had gone wrong with his inbox, politely asking them to resend all the important e-mails sent to him between July 8 and 25. He received... 15 e-mails! This means that only 5% of the e-mails sent to him were important enough for the sender to mail a copy! Why don't you do this experiment just once to find out what percentage of your e-mail is really relevant?

As you can see from these examples, you need creativity and guts to tame your Frankenstein.

2.3 CHAINBREAKER 3: LET YOUR BRAIN IDLE BETWEEN TASKS AND GET ENOUGH SLEEP

GIVE YOUR BRAIN A BREAK

As I described in the chapter about the reflecting brain, taking a break between tasks is very important to give our archiving brain a chance to put our memory in order, to refuel and to be able to switch between the incompatible physical/mechanical and social contexts. Therefore in the right-tasking figure (p.343) the word 'break' is not a detail, it is crucially important.

If you are a Screen Zombie, constantly glued to your big or small screen, you are screwing up the best of your cognitive brain because your archiving brain and your reflecting brain need a lot of regular loafing about!

As I described in the chapter about the reflecting brain, our long-term memory is like an almost infinite database packed with information from our whole life. We need the idling so that our archiving brain can handle and store the information and to present it to our reflecting brain. Even rats, with which we share most of our genome, only remember new experiences if they are allowed a break after the events. During these periods of stillness, the part of the brain called the hippocampus, which plays a crucial role in memory, repeatedly replays memories of experiences they had previously during the day[10].

▶ **"All truly great thoughts are conceived while walking."**
FRIEDRICH NIETZSCHE, TWILIGHT OF THE IDOLS

In 'Twilight of the Idols', Friedrich Nietzsche writes: "All truly great thoughts are conceived while walking." It is not always necessary to go for a walk, although this would be ideal if you are doing difficult, important or creative brainwork. A break could also be to run up and down a few flights of stairs, to speak with somebody, clean up your office or your desk, do some easy reading, get a coffee and have a chat with other people there, preferably a few floors up or down from yours etc... it just needs to be an activity that does not require much thinking or reflection.

BRAIN AND BODY SAVER: SLEEP SUFFICIENTLY

CHECK HOW MUCH SLEEP YOU REALLY NEED
There is a 75% chance that you need about eight hours of sleep if you want to get the best out of your brain. The advice is therefore simple: go back to your normal sleep pattern. Period. For most professionals in my audiences this is on average one hour more than they get.

There are of course about 15% people who are genetically short sleepers and who live healthy lives with seven hours of sleep or less. Up to 60 % of the many managers and professionals in my workshops or coaching sessions behave as if they belong to this 15%, which of course is nonsense and with some probing questions it almost always turns out that they do not really belong to the "natural" short sleepers, but are fooling themselves because they have got used to the sleepiness of unhealthily low levels of sleep. If you think you belong to the 15% nonetheless, read on.

If you really think you need less sleep than 7-8 hours, do the tests in Section 2 in the chapter about sleep, bearing in mind that you might have switched off the alarm signal of sleepiness. Pay special attention to how you feel after a few nights of good sleep, maybe on a good relaxing (disconnected) vacation.

If, after doing the three tests, you find out that you sleep enough and well enough, just skip this chapter unless you want to improve the way you cope with jetlag or shiftwork.

If you know you have a sleep problem or you discovered you might have a chronic sleep debt, make re-establishing healthy sleep a priority. If you regularly use sleeping pills or tranquilizers to sleep or have a lot of caffeine or other stimulants to stay alert, then please read on. You will find plenty of tips and tricks below.

If necessary, get help from a sleep clinic because changing bad sleeping habits after many years can be difficult, especially if you take sleeping pills because these are very addictive. Therefore, don't use sleeping pills; this solution is worse than the problem.

CHECK IF YOU DON'T HAVE A REAL SLEEP PATHOLOGY
Do you regularly wake up with a choking or gasping sensation? Did your partner observe that you snore very loudly or sometimes stop breathing? Do you wake up several times during the night and have the feeling of having slept very badly night after night, even if you spend enough hours in bed? If the answer is yes, then you should have a health check-up to assess whether you have a sleeping pathology.

The most frequent one is sleep apnea. This is the name given to a disorder where people stop breathing for 10 seconds or longer while they sleep. This results in a drop of oxygen in the blood. As a result you may lie a sufficient number of hours in bed, but with such a low quality of sleep that you experience all the symptoms of an important sleep debt. Very often this is the result of an obstruction in the throat. Therefore it is called Obstructive Sleep Apnea (OSA).

You are more at risk of OSA if you're a man over 40, especially if you are obese, have a large neck and a small jaw bone, a large tongue or tonsils, an obstruction of your nose or chronic sinus problems, have gastro-esophageal reflux (acid from the stomach coming into the esophagus and sometimes mouth and which may cause chest pain and regurgitation) and if others in the family have OSA. Of course you don't need to have all of these characteristics.

People with OSA of course have symptoms caused by a lack of sleep such as sleepiness, for example while driving, or a lack of energy during the day, forgetfulness, mood changes and a decreased interest in sex. Rather typical are restless legs (leg cramps or tingling) while you sleep, loud snoring and waking up with a sore or dry throat. People with OSA also often complain of headaches when they get up.

If you have an Android smartphone and are ready to tinker a bit with a phone-mike, you might give SleepAp (in the beta-stage of development at http://www.sleepapnet.com) a try for a quick checkup of your sleep. If you have several of these symptoms, however, you should see your physician. The main reason is that you run a much higher risk of developing not only a severe sleep-debt but also of high blood pressure, stroke, heart failure or mood disorders like depression.

USE TWO BEDTIME ALARMS
Bedtime alarms are as important as your wake-up alarm if the sleep tests show you should sleep more. You set one bedtime alarm to disconnect from screens at least one hour (ideally 1.5-2 hours) before you should be in bed and the other to start your going to bed routine half an hour before you should be in bed. Once you have set the alarms and made an agreement with your partner about your bedtime, going to bed becomes a healthy routine and you don't have to wait for each other.

Once your bedtime is regularized, disable the snooze button of your wake-up alarm and get out of bed at once. You will feel much better. The only exception to this rule is when you set the alarm 15 minutes early to spend a little cuddle time with your partner before you get out of bed because that is also good for your alertness and concentration during the day and much more, but that's another story.

If you use and stick to these bedtime alarms, your intellectual productivity will go up. And there is a bonus: 9 times out of 10 your sex life will also improve.

IF YOU TAKE SLEEPING PILLS, STOP USING THEM

If you use sleeping pills or tranquilizers to sleep, it will be very hard to stop, but it must be your top priority because these pills do not restore healthy sleep. You can start applying the advice below, but even if you do, stopping the pills can be very difficult because they are very addictive. One of the reasons they are so addictive is that the most important withdrawal symptom is horrible sleep.

Withdrawal symptoms are the phenomena that happen to your body and mind when you stop using a drug and that are caused by nothing else but stopping the drug. Hence, in this case stopping the drug by itself causes sleep problems. This of course makes you think "I really can't live without them" and you take them again. Imagine a person with no sleeping problems whatsoever starts taking sleeping pills. If he does this for a few weeks and then stops taking the pill, he will have sleeping problems (caused by nothing but stopping the pill) and have difficulties stopping them.

So if you are on sleeping pills, try to apply as many as possible of the good sleeping habits listed in the next section and once you have developed these healthy routines, stop the pills. You can stop them in two ways. One is going "cold turkey" as some smokers and other addicts do. This will be awful for quite a few days, especially at night when you will often have many nightmares and wake up often until your body finds it new healthy balance. Therefore you should do this at the beginning of a vacation or when you can afford to feel awful during the day.

The second is to do it very gradually. Through your physician you can ask the pharmacist to make capsules with your sleeping drug that contain three-quarters, one-half and one-quarter of your regular dose and then take the time to taper them out. If necessary you can also do this in smaller steps over a longer period. In some cases, to avoid withdrawal symptoms I had to ask the pharmacist to make capsules with 1/10th of the regular dose and let the patient withdraw from the pills over a period of 10 weeks.

DEVELOP HEALTHY SLEEPING HABITS

If you have a sleeping problem, there are many measures you can take to restore a healthy sleep pattern. I explained them in detail in my bestseller "Stress: Friend and Foe"[11] and have summarized them below. If you do not have a sleeping problem, try out some of these tips and you might be very surprised how they can still improve the quality of your sleep, especially if your sleep is disturbed by a young baby or by shiftwork (more on shiftwork in the following paragraph).

- To restore your biological rhythm, be consistent: go to bed and wake up every day at the same time, including at the weekend.
- If you need to catch up on sleep at the weekend, go to bed earlier as it will disturb your sleeping pattern and your biological clock less than waking up later... and don't take naps of more than 20 minutes. As I explained in the chapter about sleep, the need to sleep in during weekends is not only an important signal that you don't sleep enough during the week but it also creates jetlag every week. Moreover, sleeping longer at the weekend will diminish your subjective feeling of sleepiness and fatigue, but it does not correct your performance deficits[12]!
- If you are not rested after a night's sleep, there are two reasons why you need to disconnect from all your screens, including the smaller ones, at least one hour before you go to bed. As I described in Section 2, the first one is that most interactions with a TV, computer, tablet or phone are exciting. The second one is that the light of modern screens of monitors, tablets or phones (and LCD light bulbs) beaming straight in your eyes from a close distance tend to suppress the production of the sleepiness hormone Melatonin. Therefore the first thing to do for the screen-addicts amongst us (yes, me too, I still work too late too often, including to finish this book) is to disconnect from ANY screen at least an hour,

but much better two hours, before going to bed. During that time do something you enjoy that relaxes you. If you don't know what to do anymore, or if you are bored, without a screen, you'll have to admit you are really addicted and need to make a plan to cure your addiction and get a real life.

- If you really cannot avoid working at your computer until you go to bed, consider wearing amber "blue blocking" glasses. Another possibility is to install the free little f.lux program that adapts the wavelength of your screen to the time of the day (e.g. less blue and more red in evening)[13]. But this is only a bandage not a cure.

- Never look at a screen, tablet or phone IN bed. Avoid doing activities in bed like surfing the Internet, getting involved with social media, doing e-mails, gaming and texting. Very passively watching a relaxing TV program like a comedy, on a screen at a distance, can help you to relax. This is perfectly acceptable as long as it doesn't finish later than the healthy bedtime you have set for yourself, you are able to switch off the TV after that one program, you avoid programs with suspense, fear and aggression that make you alert, and you don't do it in bed. Most often the TV in the bedroom is an enemy of sleep. Don't sleep with the enemy, especially when you have a sleeping problem. Ban the TV from your bedroom and stop watching TV at the second bedtime alarm you set so that you start your bedtime routine on time.

- To restore healthy sleep, you should only use your bed for sleeping and sex. Good, pleasurable sex is OK because the excitement is followed by (deep) relaxation.

- If you use your smartphone as an alarm clock, make a special sleep-profile and turn all sounds and vibrations off (30% of people and 50% of the younger generations regularly wake up during the night because of the sound of their phone). I learned from my clients that way too often, just setting the alarm clock is enough to make them think "Just one quick look at my e-mails...or one message", and there they go again. Having the phone as an alarm next to their bed also seduces them to start doing e-mails first thing in the morning. Therefore it is a much better idea not to use your smartphone as an alarm and not to put your smartphone next to your bed or even in your bedroom; this should certainly be the case if your phone sometimes wakes you up. After a few nights to adjust to the idea that the world will not fall apart if you miss that very late or very early phone call, you will sleep better. Moreover, this turns out to be a very strong symbolic statement for the hyperconnectivity addicts that they really mean business. It is like a smoker who no longer has any cigarettes in the house.

- There is a general misunderstanding about the impact of alcohol on sleep. Alcohol makes you feel sleepy, but it decreases the REM sleep and in the first half of the night it will make your sleep less deep, while in the second half when the alcohol is metabolized, the rebound effect will make you wake up more often, leading to a more fragmented night's sleep. Hence, one (=1!) little nightcap (=one old fashioned measure of liquor or one old-fashioned glass of beer or wine) may help you to fall asleep. Anything more will undermine the quality of your sleep. If you have a sleeping problem, stop drinking alcohol 2-3 hours before you go to bed.

- Some herbs have a mild sleep-inducing effect. Research about them is difficult because they contain a mix of a great many chemicals whose concentration varies a lot. Best known and studied is valerian. Others are chamomile, lavender, passion-flower and hop. One should be cautious when using extracts of these plants because most often very little is known about their toxicity. The classic tumbler of hot milk seems to have some proven effect. The explanation given is that it provides Tryptophan, which is needed for the production of Serotonin, which induces calmness and sleepiness.

- Caffeine messes up your normal sleep cycle. So if you have a sleep problem, eliminate all stimulant drinks from 6-8 hours before bedtime.

- Unless you work in shifts, expose yourself to bright dawn-like light in the morning and soft dusk-like light in the evening.

- Move about during the day as much as possible. If only your brain is tired, but not your body, it will be more difficult to fall asleep and to sleep healthily. Take the stairs instead of the elevator, walk over to talk to people instead of mailing

them, take a walk in your lunch break and bike to work if possible.
- Do not work out less than 2-3 hours before bedtime in order to give your body time to metabolize the activity hormones like adrenalin and to cool down.
- Enjoy sex. Making love can be very exciting, but when we have really good sex, especially with a partner with whom we have a special bond, our body also releases several relaxing and tranquilizing hormones, so that after the climax you will sleep well.
- Avoid heavy or late meals. Late means less than 2-3 hours before bedtime.
- Keep your pets out of the bedroom and prevent them from waking you up.
- Don't give up smoking if you are a smoker. Although it will be better for your sleep, you can only manage one addiction at a time. Prioritize your sleep and then tackle the smoking.
- Put a notebook next to your bed to write down any fantastic ideas or worries you might have. Use a pen with a tiny little LED-light in it so as not to wake up your partner. On the other hand, you could also just trust the work your archiving brain does while sleeping. If you get enough sleep, your brain will take care of the idea.
- If you have trouble falling asleep or if you wake up too early, learn a brief relaxation exercise from a practical pragmatic professional, who does not try to sell you many sessions to teach you all kinds of relaxation-related stuff like yoga and meditation. It is a fact that meditation improves sleep, but you do not need to take the long road via meditation to improve your sleep, unless you'd love to learn it.
- If you like to play around with gadgets, researchers at the University of Washington developed a free app called "ShutEye" that might help you to get back to healthy sleeping habits[14].

BE CAREFUL WITH NAPS

If you feel like you need a nap, it usually means that you don't sleep enough at night. With enough sleep at night you will be able to stay alert for a full day without more than one cup of coffee at breakfast and one after lunch and without a nap. Hence, a nap is a partial solution but it is also a signal that you don't sleep enough. If you are fully rested, you don't need a nap.

A nap is perfect for the rest of your body to physically recuperate but it is not sufficient for your terrific archiving brain to do its work because it needs many breaks and real sleep[15]. The research about the effect of a nap on our cognitive functioning after a lack of sleep is not totally clear because it varies with the amount of sleep debt and the length of the nap.

A nap of more than 20 minutes often results in so-called "sleep inertia", a period of lower alertness and performance. It seems that a 10-15 minute nap, eight hours after waking up, is most effective[16], better for your alertness and better than an active break[17]. Eight hours because the normal dip in body temperature and alertness after lunch is not only related to the intake of food. Even without eating, our biological clock causes a dip in alertness about eight hours after you woke up. Hence, when you feel the dip, that's the right time to have a nap if you need one, but no longer than 20 minutes.

If you don't fall asleep easily you should avoid napping. Taking a nap, especially if you do it later than eight hours after waking up, might upset your biological clock, stimulate you to work later at night and make falling asleep more difficult.

USE THE LIMITATIONS OF YOUR REFLECTING BRAIN TO FALL (BACK) ASLEEP INSTEAD OF THINKING AND WORRYING

A frequent complaint from the people in my workshops about stress is that they have trouble falling asleep because they start thinking and worrying, mostly about work.

As I described in Sections 1 and 2, our reflecting brain can only deal with one thought and its context at a time. This limitation has an advantage when thinking about work prevents you from sleeping. Since you can only think about one thing at a time, the remedy is simple: think about something else, something boring, something relaxing, that does not keep you awake. The old advice that you should count sheep is basically correct: while you are counting sheep you cannot think or worry about anything else.

I use simple, boring, monotonous mantras that I keep repeating to myself, like "sleeping is more important now... sleeping is more important now..." If you ever learned meditation, use your mantra.

If you learned relaxation exercises where in your imagination you had to tense and relax your muscles or where you had to go back to a scene where you were beautifully relaxed, use that method.

If you wake up in the middle of the night or too early, try to tether on to your last dream, try to remember your dream and continue with that story. Some people invent a dream, a story, sometimes a little erotic, to make it easier to stay with it.

In short, think about anything that is not going to keep you awake.

LEARN TO MANAGE YOUR JETLAG

Wise managers, professionals and politicians never make important decisions after arriving with jetlag, unless you can travel so comfortably that you can stay in your own time zone and everybody else adapts to your time on arrival.

If your stay is shorter than three days, do nothing, stay in your original home-rhythm as much as possible. If your stay is longer, there are quite a few things you can do to diminish the impact of jetlag. Below are details of what research suggests you should do to avoid jetlag[18].

The week before the trip:
- Leave fully rested. In other words, get enough sleep or, even better, build up a little sleep reserve. Avoid any sleep-debt before leaving, for example by badly planning your packing so that you miss out on sleep before you have even left. This makes jetlag worse!
- Try to shift your biological clock by adapting your bedtime and exposure to bright light for a few days before you go to your destination:
    Westward: go to bed 1-2 hours later, bright light in the evening.
    Eastward: go to bed 1-2 hours earlier (it is often easier when you take incremental steps of half an hour), get up earlier and bright light in the morning.
- Since your activities may not allow you to follow the ideal

light/dark schedule, dark sunglasses can be a helpful compromise. Since this might be unsafe while driving, you can use the pilot's solution: amber "blue blocking" glasses that block the blue wavelength. Why blocking blue is the most important part is explained in Section 2.
- For a quick solution, go to Jet Lag Rooster http://www.jetlagrooster.com/about, fill in your departure and arrival information and you'll get a simple instruction sheet about how to manage light and dark.

During the flight:
- After boarding: set your clock to the time at your destination.
- Drink more water than usual to avoid dehydration. Good hydration helps to set the body temperature.
- Avoid alcohol and caffeinated drinks.
- Take Melatonin if the time of your flight fits with the instructions below.
- Take a (low dose of) a very short-acting sleeping pill, at least six hours before arrival, to sleep in the plane when it's night at your destination. Don't bother with food and movies; setting your biological clock is more important.
- Use earplugs or a noise cancellation headset to sleep. Simple, cheap, wax earplugs turn out to be the best to block out most wavelengths. Before you buy expensive noise cancellation headphones, have a look at http://www.noisehelp.com/noise-protection.html and http://www.audiocheck.net/earplugreviews_index.php .

At your destination:
- Adjust yourself immediately to the local schedule, unless your stay is very short. Sunlight, meals and activity will help reset your biological clock.
    Westward: Look for bright light in the evening.
    Eastward: look for bright light in the morning.
- Some scholars think that if we travel more than eight time zones, our biological clock may confuse dawn and dusk and therefore advise
    Westward: the first two days avoid bright light 2-3 hours before dusk. After that look for bright light in the evening.

Eastward: the first two days avoid bright light for the first 2-3 hours after dawn. After that look for bright light in the morning.
- If you did not sleep enough during the trip, adapt to the local schedule anyway and take short (!) naps of no more than 20 minutes when you feel sleepy. Longer naps will make it more difficult for your clock to adjust.
- Take 3-5 mg of Melatonin for a few days
  Westward: during the second half of the night.
  Eastward: at bedtime.
- If needed, take a sleeping pill for the first few nights. Do not take them for more than three nights! They are more addictive than most people realize.
- Avoid caffeine in the afternoon.
- One nightcap might help falling asleep; more alcohol may mess up the resetting of your clock.

COPE BETTER WITH SHIFT WORK
Very often, the main things one can do to minimize the impact of shift work are beyond the control of the workers themselves: setting a regular, predictable schedule and limiting overtime. If the shifts change, then they should forward rotate, with sufficient breaks, permission to take a short nap when feeling really sleepy, enough days between shifts to adapt etc... These aspects belong to the employers' responsibility. Employers have more than enough economic and safety reasons to organize work in such a way that their workers' biological clocks are disrupted as little as possible. There are plenty of things they can do[19] once they have understood how heavy the negative impact of shift work can be because the human being is just not made for this kind of work. (Some of this advice is also useful for parents with a young baby.)

Since even a little better synchronization of your biological clock can make a big difference[20], employees should use light and dark to reset their biological clock. Looking for exposure to bright light as much possible during their scheduled work time, which for them is "daytime", and as little light as possible during their time off, which is their "night time", for example by wearing dark glasses when commuting and keeping home as dark as possible, especially the bathroom and the bedroom. Use a light-blocking lining in your curtains or cover the windows with aluminum foil or black plastic. If wearing dark sunglasses in your "night time" is not a good idea, for example because you need to drive, you can use amber blue-blocking "pilot" glasses that block out the blue wavelength.

Make the bedroom as soundproof as possible with heavy curtains (that also block light better) on the windows and doors and ask family members to keep as quiet as possible and to use headphones for the radio and TV. It might even be useful to explain to your neighbors that you have to sleep during the day. Use wax earplugs. It may take some time to get used to them but they can make a big difference. Unplug the phone and put your mobile phone in another room. Buy a very loud alarm clock so that you don't have to worry about waking up on time. Alarm clocks with a bright light that gradually increases, mimicking dawn, and starting the alarm after that, may help. Keep your bedroom cool.

Given that one of the most frequent complaints of shift workers are intestinal problems, you should eat light and healthy food at work and especially just before you go to bed. If at work you only can get fried food or food high in fat and spices, bring your own healthy meal with plenty of vegetables (enough roughage will prevent many troubles) and snacks such as fruit.

Avoid caffeine, alcohol, heavy meals and smoking because they undermine the quality of your sleep.

For an excellent review on the sleep-related problems of shift work and countermeasures, take a look at the review by Smith and Eastman[21]. You can find practical tips adapted for the different types of shift work (fast rotating, slow rotating or permanent night shifts) on the www.bupa.au website[22].

2.4 CHAINBREAKER 4: MANAGE YOUR STRESS WELL

Short stress, even high stress, can be a stimulus for your intellectual productivity. Think about how concentrated, efficient and creative you can be trying to meet a deadline. Under stress you may feel the signs that your body is being optimally mobilized for action, your mind is working at full capacity, your senses are sharper, and you are maximally concentrated. On the other hand, just like always being connected or multitasking, stress that is too high or that lasts too long ruins your intellectual performance: negative stress is the most important frequent reason why smart people do stupid things.

In my national bestseller "Stress: Friend and Foe" you can find everything you always wanted to know but never dared to ask about stress, not only about what stress is but also about how to restore your stress-balance and manage your stress better, to unchain the best of your brain.

Here I want to briefly focus your attention on just three aspects of stress-management, all of which are related to improving your intellectual productivity.

How to eliminate the continuous background stress.

How you can improve your resilience.

Why you should take your early warning signals seriously and act on them.

ELIMINATE YOUR CHRONIC BACKGROUND STRESS: BECOME A RIGHT-TASKER

Chronic background stress can be caused by many different things, including constantly dealing with e-mail. Starting your day by answering e-mails and then answering them at every spare moment during the rest of the day is exhausting for your reflecting brain. As I described in Section 2, we are not talking about energy in a vague metaphorical sense but in its literal sense. All these mini- or micro-email decisions add up and as a result you literally have no brainpower left to make good rational decisions. This is especially the case if, like most participants in my workshops and lectures, you don't take regular breaks and you skip lunch altogether. Don't forget: stress is summative, meaning that many little stresses and hassles end up having the same impact as one big stressful event. Moreover, stress is not only a question of the amount of stress but also its duration. Long, chronic low levels of stress can be more detrimental than one big challenge.

When you become a right-tasker, i.e. someone who doesn't constantly switch tasks and instead focuses on one task for an undisturbed period of time, you will experience a very significant drop in your negative stress.

IMPROVE YOUR RESILIENCE

The harder you pull a bow, the faster and further the arrow goes. How hard you can pull the bow depends on the resilience, the elasticity of the bow. Hence, the most interesting question is "How can I improve my resilience?" rather than "How can I lower the demands on me?". I prefer to use the word stress-resilience rather than stress-resistance because resistance is too static and rigid, whereas resilience is more dynamic. Of course it is often important to lower the workload, but many demands are an unavoidable part of work or life and even necessary to grow and develop. Therefore there is a lot to gain from increasing your resilience.

There is a part of your personal resilience for which you are not responsible. This part is the result of hereditary, biological and physical factors such as genetic make-up, problems incurred during pregnancy and childbirth, childhood illnesses, the quality

THE HARDER YOU PULL THE BOW

THE FASTER THE ARROW
HITS THE TARGET!

of care you received from your parents or educators and early physical and emotional experiences. They determine your limits and your potential for dealing with stress situations in a healthy and creative way. A piano cannot be played like a violin and a Mozart concerto cannot be played on a toy piano, but in the right context even a toy flute can play a vital role in a symphony and sound very good. Since there is nothing you can do about these factors, it makes no sense to worry about them. Instead you should concentrate on the many great things you can do, that are within your own sphere of control and responsibility.

You are definitely responsible for the personal part of your resilience. The level of your coping abilities can be constantly raised. Some of the major influences have their impact through the way you appraise your environment and your place in it. You should be aware of the way your thinking automatisms, your appraisal, are the basis of many of your emotional and behavioral responses in stress situations. Ideally you should have a method to undo these thoughts if they are undermining your resilience. Examples of basic attitudes that have a big impact on your resilience are: seeing change as an opportunity to grow and develop, the basic feeling of having a significant influence on your own life, commitment to your role at work and home, having clear priorities in life, and having clear and realistic goals.

Some of the influences have to do with your lifestyle. Don't forget that your brain is nothing but a part of your body. The ancient Romans already knew this: "mens sana in corpore sano", "a healthy mind in a healthy body". For sustained optimal intellectual productivity, you need a healthy body. Therefore you need things like good insight into the stress process, not smoking at all, keeping an eye on your weight, eating healthily, sleeping well, not depending on pep pills, lots of caffeine or tranquillizers, being satisfied with your job, having a sense of humor, knowing and practicing good relaxation techniques, moderate alcohol intake and managing deadlines with care. These are all explained in "Stress: Friend and Foe".

Probably the most important influence on your resilience is having good social support. Literally hundreds of research publications clearly show that your resilience depends very much on your "network of social support". This creates two interesting paradoxes:

- The more egoistic you are, the more you should invest in the people around you because good social relations are the best thing you can do to improve your own resilience.
- The less time you have for others because you are so busy and stressed, the more time you should invest in others.

The paradox is that under stress, professionals should increase their social contact for optimal resilience, whereas in fact most often they neglect it even more than usual. They also do the same with other factors that increase their resilience such as sleep, healthy eating habits, physical exercise etc... At stressful times when they need to be most resilient, they disregard these resilience-boosting factors the most.

FOREWARNED IS FOREARMED: SIGNS, SIGNALS AND ALARM SIGNALS

To cope well with your stress you need to know what your own personal early-warning stress-signals are and take action when you experience them.

When you are under stress, you will experience the signs of it. In stress situations not only can your body react vigorously, but stress also has an influence on your psychological functions and your behavior. Stress can give you a real kick as your body is perfectly prepared for action: your muscles work more efficiently, your heart is stimulated, you have greater stamina, better resistance to pain, more efficient breathing, improved immunity, your intestine slows down to save energy, and more energy is used more efficiently. If you are doing brainwork under stress, your brain is working at full capacity: you are more alert, better concentrated, more creative etc...

When stress risks turning into negative stress, these normal signs turn into more unpleasant signals. None of them is harmful or alarming as such. They are most often normal and temporary symptoms. You can easily ignore these stress symptoms or interpret them as a sign that you are functioning at or just beyond the peak of your capacities. You really do not need to bother about them too much. Even beyond your peak, you can still perform perfectly well.

However, these normal signs become important signals if you have many of them or if they do not cease when the stress situation is over but bother you constantly or very regularly. Then the negative stress has become a problem. It is wise to take these signals seriously and try to find out what they are warning you about. Taking negative stress signals seriously can often prevent more serious alarm symptoms, which are beyond the scope of this book.

RESTORE YOUR STRESS-BALANCE

To restore your stress-balance, the most important interventions come down to lowering the demands and increasing or improving your resources. However, you are your own most important resource, therefore, taking good care of yourself and your resilience is paramount. You should also restore or improve your social support network and your feeling of having an influence on matters. Since healthy stress is interval stress, you should start or restore taking regular breaks to relax and recuperate mentally and physically. The greater your stress, the longer these intervals need to be. Last but not least, you should be aware that your stress-balance is a subjective one and that in the end your appraisal of the situation, your appraisal of the demands, your resources, your social support and your influence will make the difference between negative stress and positive stress.

All these aspects of coping better with stress, with lots of practical advice, tips and tricks, are explained in my book; "Stress: Friend and Foe" available at www.brainchains.org.

MANAGE YOUR LOCAL STRESS BEFORE IT CAUSES GENERAL STRESS

You can prevent trouble AND pain in your hands, arms, shoulders, neck, back and head by paying attention to your posture and the ergonomics while you use your computer, tablet and smartphone. The big challenge is that you have to apply effort and willpower to prevent RSI before you develop any problems. Nothing reminds you of the importance of posture and breaks until... it's too late. Therefore, at the very least take action as soon as you have the very first light symptoms because once you have RSI it can be extremely handicapping and very difficult to cure. This becomes even more important when you are over 50 because a lot of the soft tissues, like ligaments and tendons, lose their elasticity with age.

The easiest, simplest, most neglected and most important remedy against many of these stress nuisances and problems is taking regular breaks. If like me, you tend to forget time when working, use one of the many timer apps like http://free-count-down-timer.com/ to remind you to take regular breaks.

While ergonomics are often taken care of in many companies, people often neglect them when they work at home, even though a basic healthy design of your workplace at home is not expensive. You can find the essentials of ergonomics on the web or in the booklet that came with your computer, but which most likely you never looked at[23]. For a wealth of information go to http://www.ccohs.ca/oshanswers/ergonomics/office/, read the article by Michael Sonne ao[24] or have a look at their "Rapid office strain assessment" (ROSA)[25]. This is about the use of a professional desk. The ergonomics of using laptops, tablets and smartphones are also well known but are almost always totally neglected by users[26]. So here are a few hints and recommendations:

- Do not look down at your phone, screen or keyboard for a long time. Think about how your neck works like pliers with long handles so that you do not underestimate the force on your neck and especially the intervertebral disks when you are bending for a long time.
- As I wrote in Section 2, for the sake of your back, shoulders, neck and head, don't use your laptop on your lap for a prolonged time! To reduce the strain, first of all, find a way to raise your screen. If there is no table available, put anything, a box, your briefcase... under your laptop. Put the screen at the angle that requires you to bend your neck as little as possible. If you regularly use your laptop to work at a table or desk, use a separate keyboard (they have become dirt cheap) and use a box or stand to raise the screen as much as possible to eye level. If your laptop has a small screen for portability, invest in a much bigger separate screen, the largest you can afford to use with your laptop at home or at work. Tablets are gadgets, not tools for prolonged work. If you want to keep the advantages of your tablet and do real work with it, invest in a stand, a separate screen, keyboard and mouse.
- To minimize tension, the back of your head and your upper back should be in the same plane as much as possible. This

will result in a posture that looks like the heads of soldiers standing at "attention", with their chins pointing forward. It is the position of your neck when you try to walk with a book on the top of your head. Your shoulders should feel relaxed. If they're not, adjust your position or take a break. Sometimes this is not the most comfortable position for your eyes as it is usually somewhat higher. So you'll have to find a compromise[27].

- Place your screen straight in front of you, at arm's length, with your eyes at the height of about the middle of the screen or a little higher. To find the most comfortable position for your neck, sit straight and move your head backwards and forwards, gradually decreasing the movement until you find the most comfortable position of your head. Then, adapt the height of your screen, small or large, so that you can look at it from that position.
- Don't slouch and avoid the "tablet hunchback" or "laptop hunchback" look. With the top of your head, your neck, lower back and sit bones aligned along the same perpendicular line, your upper body is an a neutral position, demanding the least from muscles and tendons. This is the tension our body can perfectly handle, except when it is rather immobile for a long period of time. The more you depart from this line, the more tension you create. If your upper legs are below horizontal, put your feet on a footrest, book, folder or whatever you have to hand and find support for your lower back.
- Hold your phone up when you text, e-mail or game, instead of looking down. You should be able to look at your screen by gazing down without bending your neck.
- One of the most important things you can do for your neck, if you work a lot on your computer is to learn to touch-type, then you can type without looking at your keyboard. Of course you will also gain a massive amount of time because it is so much faster than typing with two fingers. The return on investment makes this a no brainer. Still, when doing research for this book I realized how sloppy my own typing had become, so I improved my typing with "tipp10", a free open-access typing tutor[28].

- Once you can touch-type you will never have to work with a bent neck again. You can invest in a big screen where you have all your digital information next to the text you are working on and put any paper texts you need on a holder at the height of your screen.
- If you have to write a lot, use voice recognition. I started setting up Dragon[29], but I have not yet had the time to go through the learning curve. Once this book is finished, I'll give it another try. There is a simple voice to text dictation app for Apple products and a cheap Dragon notes for Windows tablets and Windows7.
- Train the muscles of your neck, upper back and shoulders by doing movements that go beyond the very limited and repetitive use when you work at a screen. I like Pilates exercises[30], but there are many more to find on the www. If you have pain in your neck, ask a physiotherapist to teach you exercises to strengthen the deep neck muscles.
- There is also something like stress on the eyes. My comfort increased a lot the day I bought a good pair of prescription computer glasses. As a result I squint a lot less. As I described in the second section, when you work on a screen you blink less and less efficiently, causing dry eyes. Therefore avoid squinting and keep blinking.
- In almost every computer program, you can increase the size of the fonts. Always do this to a comfortable size. Of course this is difficult on your smartphone, which is one more reason to limit its use.

2.5 SAVE A BRAIN AND A LIFE, MAYBE YOUR OWN: NEVER EVER USE YOUR PHONE OR OTHER ICT WHILE DRIVING

As far as using your phone while driving is concerned, the solution is crystal clear, simple and imperative: **never ever use your phone or any ICT while driving**. There is nothing else to add. Of course you should avoid distracted driving in general, but given the omnipresence of the phone you will avoid many accidents by not using your phone while driving. Before you read this book you could claim ignorance, but now you know better.

After going through all this research I totally stopped using my phone while driving and I became much more attentive to other sources of distraction. When I call a person on her mobile, I also ask "Are you driving?" When the person is driving, I say, "Call me when you have arrived or parked" or "When can I call you?" and I hang up straight away. I would hate it if I heard the sound of a crash while I was calling a friend or a client.

If you don't dare to disconnect your phone altogether, put it on voicemail and totally out of reach. You are never more than 15 or 30 minutes away from a place where you can park after you heard that somebody was calling you. You can change the intro to your voicemail, explaining in a friendly manner for example that you want to give everybody your full attention and drive safely and that you will therefore not pick up your phone while holding a conversation or while driving.

At the beginning of my own conversion and detox, I had to completely shut off my phone because any phone sound or buzz distracted me and made me nervous. It took quite some time, but now I stay perfectly relaxed when my phone sounds, I don't touch it and I park at the first convenience to answer my voicemail.

For its "Txtng & Drivng...It Can Wait" campaign, AT&T developed an app called DriveMode (www.att.com/drivemode), which, when downloaded and activated, automatically sends a customizable reply to incoming texts – notifying the sender that the user is driving and unable to respond. The auto-response is similar to an "out-of-office" e-mail alert[31]. Of course the weak link is the person who has to activate the app. Therefore a better solution is an application that automatically turns off your phone when you start driving. If you are convinced about the danger but can't control your addiction of being connected, use software like DriveScribe, iZup , Cellcontrol (also works with non-smartphones), tXtBlocker and SafeCell, all of which can help you drive safely. These services use your phone's GPS to determine if you are driving and then disable your cell phone until you stop the car. They reply with a message telling the caller that you are driving. If you phone while driving anyway, a message can also be sent to another person such as your change-buddy (see the paragraph about changing habits below) or a parent to blow the whistle on you.

2.6 A BRAINGAIN BEYOND YOUR CONTROL: BRAIN-FRIENDLY OFFICES

At the end of the day, there is not much you can do about an office design that undermines productivity, except try to influence the top of your organization to do something about it or join together with colleagues to increase the pressure. To help you convince others, I have turned an original chapter of this book into a booklet available for free on my website, www.brainchains.org. You may distribute and copy it as much as you want, as a whole or in parts, the only condition being that you mention that the information came from *"Brain-Hostile Open Offices: The Fifth BrainChain"* by Theo Compernolle MD., PhD at www.brainchains. org.

HOW TO COPE WITH A BRAINWORK-KILLING OFFICE AT WORK

Here a few examples of tools that people improvised when they needed to concentrate on high value-added, difficult brainwork in their open office.

If you belong to Generation Y, you may not be interested because you love the lively, animated and entertaining atmosphere of an open office. You may be convinced that it does not hinder your intellectual productivity and creativity. However, think twice, because as I described in Section 1 all the research proves you totally wrong.

- Make a movable cubicle or dividing wall from cardboard with some acoustic "egg box" foam on the outside, ideally after discussing the idea with the people around you and inviting them to join your effort to improve intellectual productivity and reduce exhaustion.
- Put up a DO NOT DISTURB sign, or a more friendly "Please do not disturb now. I will be totally available for you at 11am".
- If you want to buy earplugs or headsets, have a look at the different characteristics of solutions going from ultra-cheap earplugs to very expensive headphones at http://www.noisehelp.com/noise-protection.html and http://www.audiocheck.net/earplugreviews_index.php, where I learned that some cheap wax-cotton earplugs are the best solution to block all noise and that passive noise-isolating ear canal

headphones too are good for blocking any type of noise, not just the low-frequency drone of an airplane that one can eliminate with more expensive noise-cancellation headphones.

Too many employees think about these options but don't dare to use them because they fear it will be considered anti-social. The interesting thing is that when I push my audiences to openly discuss this with their peers, they usually find out that many, if not most, of them suffer from noise pollution, but don't dare use headphones. They then collude and start using them as a group. It's also worth noting that headsets have the additional advantage that they give a clear signal: "Do not disturb!"

- For some people masking noises like "white noise", "pink noise" or "grey noise" helps them to concentrate by masking other background noises[32]. Some people put it on their headphones. Others are angry enough to put it on their speakers in their cubicle... if they still have the luxury of a cubicle.

  - However, it is very difficult to get masking-noise right because the frequencies as we consciously perceive them have a complicated relationship with the frequencies at the source. Experiments have been done with white noise, pink noise and grey noise. The evidence suggests that grey noise most closely matches the way our ear deals with the different frequencies.

  - Secondly, the effect of masking noise also depends on the quality of our hearing. Older people whose hearing has naturally deteriorated with age or young people who have ruined their hearing with an overdose of decibels from earphones or loudspeakers at festivals need a different masking sound than people with perfect hearing.

  - A third problem with masking sound is that its usefulness depends on the loudness of the sound being masked. This changes all the time, alternating with silent periods. Hence a level of masking-noise that is useful when there is a lot of office noise itself becomes an annoyance when the office is quiet. As a result, systems that adapt to the level of office noise are being developed.

  - And last but not least, there are also important individual psychological differences. Introverts perform better than extroverts when there is no background noise or music at all. In general both perform worse with office noises, but the introverts more so than the extraverts[33]. Some extraverts do even better with some distraction noise than without, especially when the task is boring[34]. Some introverts can't work at all with masking-noises.

- If you want to experiment yourself with masking-noise, try it out at http://mynoise.net/NoiseMachines/whiteNoise-Generator.php developed by Dr. Ir. Stéphane Pigeon; a signal processing engineer Here you can even make your own custom-made masking-noise based on the quality of your hearing and the noise in your working environment. If you find a good masking-noise, you can put it on your headphones or speakers.
- In any case, the conclusion is that masking-noise is certainly no panacea for resolving the acoustic problems of a badly designed office.

– Make a big effort to refurbish the office.

The only real solution of course is convincing your employer of how counterproductive your offices are. Blaming your manager is useless because she is also rather powerless, even though she might enjoy a better office. It is much better to make her, and as many people as possible, join your effort to improve the office.

The best moment to do this of course is as soon as you hear the very first rumors of a new office being built so that you can try to avoid your company out of ignorance building another one that kills brainwork.

But it is also worthwhile banding together with as many people as possible to have your existing office refurbished in such a way that it is less counterproductive or stressful. Maybe the HR manager, SHE manager, workers council or company physician can join too.

As a starter, you could send my free booklet on the issue, as a whole or in parts, to managers and executives. There's no need to worry about copyright as long as you mention the source as: *"Brain-Hostile Open Offices: The Fifth BrainChain" by Theo Compernolle MD., PhD. www.brainchains.org*

If approaching the managers responsible for your office directly doesn't work, you can also try a more subversive approach by "forgetting" copies near photocopiers, coffee machines or water coolers or by adding it "by accident" as an attachment to an e-mail sent to many large groups of employees. Just be creative.

If that doesn't work, you have three choices:

- Look for another job in a more brainworker-friendly office.
- Accept the office as it is with the lower intellectual performance or the higher stress and exhaustion, if possible with some of the makeshift personal improvements I mentioned above.
- Organize a revolt of the brainworkers, like the manual workers of the first industrial revolution did when they revolted against their unhealthy working environments and managed to change them.

AVOID REFLECTION KILLERS AT HOME TOO

Given the chance, more and more brainworkers avoid the brain-hostile office by working at home. Sadly this is not only because this flexible work has other advantages but also because many modern offices are so totally unfit for difficult or complex intellectual work that people try to avoid them as much as possible.

When you work from home, don't forget: home is a soft emotional, relational culture, while work is a hard, contractual one. At home, you don't have bosses, contracts, appointments, calendars, bonuses and sanctions. If there are no clear boundaries, if you mix both domains without making deliberate choices, the "hard" work will always win in terms of time and the "soft" home will interfere emotionally. This is most evident in my work with families with a family business[35].

It is important to pay attention to the way you organize yourself when working from home. In the beginning of this "new way of working" movement, the most intelligent companies made a real effort to help and advise their employees on how to set up proper home offices. Now working at home has become so "normal" that many companies don't even think about assisting their flexible workforce in organizing work at home. Here are just a few ideas:

- Do not try to combine household, family and work; everything will suffer. Remember that the switching costs are the highest when you switch tasks from very different domains like work and home. You know the solution: Batch-process and keep very strict boundaries between the domains.

- When you work from home, family, friends, children, pets and acquaintances will often not consider this real work and will think you can be disturbed at any time. Explain the situation to them, set strict rules and clear boundaries (in the first place for yourself) and stick to them.

- Work in a home office or office corner with the fewest possible disturbances, in the quietest room with a nice view. You will probably spend many hours there. Be creative. Think attic, garden shed, tool shed or part of the garage (you are more important than your car). Avoid your bedroom because having your office there might spoil your sleep.

- Pamper yourself, invest in it: look at a specialist office store. Don't underestimate the impact that the quality of your working environment has on the quality of your work, your focus, your stress and your happiness. Get a proper desk and an excellent ergonomic chair and the biggest computer screen you can afford. You will spend many hours there, so make it comfortable. Read the chapter about Local Stress, where I explain that once you have experienced pain because of bad ergonomics at home, it's sometimes too late and so you should think hard about ergonomics before you feel the strain. At home too, masking-noise may help if you are disturbed by the noise around you.

- Keep to a time schedule. Set time for e-mail, phone calls, household chores and breaks. The secret to your intellectual productivity, at home as in the office, is the batch-processing that I described above. Most important of all, earmark undisturbed focus time to work on important tasks without any interruptions, with your e-mail, phones and the doorbell switched off.

- Above all, postpone all social media and web surfing until after your work for the day is done. Do not use them at all as a break to relax. They are so addictive that again and again you will spend much more time on them than you planned, especially because at home there is no longer any social control on the hours you spend online, while at work you might

avoid being caught spending too much time with social media or web surfing. It's better to use going online as a reward for a day of really hard and focused work... if you have nothing healthier to relax with.
- Get dressed for work as the quality of your work will be better than if you stay in your pajamas or jogging outfit.
- By the way, no matter whether or not you are working in the living room, get the TV out of your view and off. Good intellectual work is incompatible with TV. If you think you are an exception, you are totally wrong and you clearly did not read the first section of this book.

2.7 BRAINGAIN SUPPORT: HOW TO TURN BAD HABITS INTO GOOD HABITS

The first step to change a habit is to be really convinced the habit is wrong. Convincing is what I tried to do in the first sections. Since I didn't think I would persuade you with just my opinion on the matter, I spent five years delving deep into the research in the hope of winning you over with convincing scientific facts. Once you are convinced, you will have to help your long-term goal-oriented reflecting brain to beat your very short-term, reactive reflex brain. It's the battle between your internal adult and your internal child, the latter striving for instant gratification without considering the long-term consequences.

HABIT FORMATION: FRIEND AND FOE OF YOUR INTELLECTUAL PRODUCTIVITY

There are different degrees of difficulty controlling your connectivity, multitasking and lack of breaks and sleep: it may be a bad habit, a very bad habit or an addiction.

As I described in Section 2, habit formation is a very powerful mechanism that is extremely useful for freeing our reflecting brain from routine tasks. If habit formation didn't exist, we would for example not even be able to think while we were writing. As a result of intensive training in primary school, writing became a habit that frees up our reflecting brain for thinking.

On the other hand, this mechanism is so good that once a habit is developed it can be very difficult to undo it. Even if you haven't ridden a bike for many years, the moment you get back on a bike, the habit kicks in. It is impossible to unlearn habits like walking, riding a bike, reading, writing etc... It is as if the habit is hibernating in our brain and wakes up as soon as it is needed or triggered. It is also especially difficult to undo a habit if it triggers rewarding chemicals in our brain, which might even turn it into an addiction.

If it is a bad habit, then you should tackle it like a diet: the goal is not to stop connectivity and multitasking altogether, but to keep it productive and healthy. I am certain that some of the tips and tricks in this section will help you.

If it is an addiction to the rewarding chemicals in your brain, you will need all of the tricks and tools you can find and probably even specialized help to stop it. Undoing the habit will be extremely frustrating and you will come up with all kinds of rationalizations for not doing so. The first step is to admit that you are addicted. We have learned from research about "Alcoholics Anonymous" that this admission is a necessary first step to overcome the problem.

When the serial entrepreneur Nicholas Holland, was once in an exotic country with very little bandwidth, he got very irritated because of the many unimportant e-mails that were blocking him from getting to the important ones. This worked like an epiphany. He suddenly realized how much time he spent e-mailing and once he was back home he totally disconnected from all e-mail while he looked for other solutions[36].

You are probably not in a position to do this, but as you have seen from the examples in the chapter about taming the e-mail Frankenstein, and as you will see in more examples of professionals that I will give you, many other people have successfully managed to take measures that were rather drastic at their level too.

WARNING: CHANGING YOUR HABIT WILL AT FIRST CAUSE MORE STRESS AND MAKE YOU LESS EFFICIENT

A perfect understanding of the ways you ruin the best of your brainwork and a great motivation for changing your bad habits may actually make things worse at the start. The problem is that up until now you could claim ignorance. You behaved incompetently, but you didn't know any better. If you keep screwing up the best of your brain after reading this book, you will still be behaving incompetently, but now you will know it, and that feels (much) worse than before.

What's more, unchaining your brain will feel awful in the beginning because all kinds of more or less neurotic motivations will no longer be satisfied, like needing to feeling important or indispensable, wanting to be in control, wanting to please, career anxiety etc...

Very often, in the first stage of changing your habit, you will also be less efficient instead of more efficient. Like a golfer who learns a new swing or an office worker who gets much better software, you are on a learning curve. This asks for a lot of motivation and energy... until the new behavior becomes a new productive habit, a quite automatic, soft-wired shortcut in your reflex brain. At that point it will only need a little energy and motivation to keep it going because it has become natural and spontaneous. You now do it without thinking. You have become an unconsciously competent expert and your reflex brain may even have developed a few new helpful soft-wired shortcuts, better routines.

There is one exception to this laborious process of developing new skills, what the Germans call the "Aha-Erlebnis". Such an "aha-experience", or eye-opener, gives us a sudden unexpected insight, an epiphany[37], which can be so strong that it changes our behavior at once. If this already happened to you while you were reading the second section of this book, then that's great, if not, read on.

SET THE STAGE

TRUST OTHERS AND DELEGATE

Many professionals receive way too many e-mails because they don't delegate or share well. The widely hated over-controlling micromanagers usually have the biggest overflowing inboxes. But this is also true for professionals who are not managers. They lack confidence in themselves and trust in others. Sometimes they are even scared of the idea that things can go very well without them. They want to feel indispensable and needed. The way they manage their work in the end makes them indispensable, but at a very high cost to themselves, their colleagues and the company. No tips, tricks or tools in the world can stop their e-mail overload unless they start trusting others, develop confidence in themselves and change the underlying drivers of their behavior.

I once coached a 40-year-old country manager of a major global ICT-company. He was referred because of an HR manager's suspicion that he was getting close to burn-out. In the first session he complained about the daily avalanche of e-mails he had to process and that he considered to be the cause of never being able to finish his work. The main weakness in his 360 feedback, however, was about micromanaging and not delegating or empowering.

In the coaching we decided to focus first on delegating, empowerment and the underlying lack of confidence in himself and trust in others. The interesting result was that after a very significant initial increase in stress, his symptoms of burnout disappeared without giving any specific attention to his stress-management in a strict sense. The big surprise, however, was that the number of e-mails he received dwindled to one-third (!) of what they had been before without any specific interventions to reduce them. His greater trust and reduced micro-management resulted in people sending him less cover my back e-mails at every little step or for every little initiative they took. With some additional tips and tricks for handling his e-mail it was further reduced to one-fifth. Had he not changed his basic attitude, none of these e-mail reduction tactics would have worked because they simply wouldn't have been acceptable to him.

LOOK YOUR PROCRASTINATION IN THE FACE

Each time you go online, ask yourself: "What important, less pleasant work am I trying to put off?" E-mail is the ideal escape for procrastinators who avoid their highest priorities. Procrastination is not the subject of this book, but following some of my basic rules and applying some of the tools and tricks will help.

It may also be that your work really gives you little real pleasure, so you escape to the fun and kicks of being connected. In that case there are two strategies:

1 Find out what your sources of pleasure are and do the Pareto-pleasure reflection I described earlier on.
2 If that doesn't work, look for another job that will give you more pleasure. The risk is that with only the fun of being connected, your work will never be fulfilling.

WILLPOWER IS NECESSARY TO START, BUT NOT SUFFICIENT TO PERSIST AND SUCCEED

Kicking a strong habit demands a lot of willpower. As I explained in Section 2, resisting the continuous temptations that are all the time within arm's reach or in your pocket, one click away, is more exhausting than you think. Therefore you have to organize yourself in a way that decreases the temptations as much as possible. When as a smoker you try to quit the habit, you should not walk around with a packet of cigarettes in your pocket. When you try to diet you should not keep your cupboards, pockets and purse full of chocolate. When you learn to disconnect, you should not always have your phone at arm's length.

As I described before, I experienced this myself just after I bought my first smartphone. Very soon I was checking my e-mails and messages all the time. When I realized how counterproductive this was, I learned to resist the urge to look at my mails all the time, but I was almost continuously aware of the fact that I was resisting this temptation. Being a stress expert I realized that resisting the urge caused a low level of continuous stress. This temptation and tension totally disappeared after I reprogrammed my phone so that I only could get to my mails with four clicks and especially when I was brave enough to totally switch off my phone on a regular basis, knowing that it takes 50 seconds to start it up, input the pin code etc... At the time I didn't yet know that spending these tiny little bits of willpower to resist checking my phone had a negative impact on my willpower, thinking and decision making. Only later, when I was writing this book, did I discover the research about the biological limits of our willpower, thinking power and decision-making power.

Once she realized how counterproductive it was to be connected all the time, one of my clients started using one side of her desk to be connected and then moved to the opposite side to disconnect and do the more difficult brainwork, with her back towards her laptop lid and her phone left on silent on the other side too. Although she can easily turn her computer around, she doesn't. The obstacle she created was just enough for her to change her habit. When she has a conversation with somebody, she no longer does so from behind her desk, but sitting in front of it, with of course all the sounds of connecting tools disabled.

So, don't count on your (strong) motivation alone. You will always need willpower in the beginning, but you can make it easier by changing the habit or by replacing one habit with another. Willpower diminishes several times during the day and you will succumb in such a dip, especially when you become tired at the end of the workday. Below are a few things that may help you to reach your goal with less willpower.

KNOWLEDGE, TOOLS AND TRICKS TO CHANGE A (VERY) BAD HABIT

A hundred years ago a growing group of psychologists distanced themselves from the unscientific, non-researchable myths of psychoanalysis and started empirical research on the ways people learn and unlearn behavior. They named it "Behavior Modification". In the beginning they over-focused on modifying the behavior itself; later they also studied ways to change the thinking and feelings that accompany behavior. They produced tens of thousands of research publications, resulting in a wealth of scientific knowledge about the most efficient ways to change behavior. In the process the name was changed to "Applied Behavior Analysis".

THE ABC MODEL AND THE ABC DIARY

The ABC model is the simplest model and one that is still very useful for understanding, learning and changing habits. ABC stands for **A**ntecedent, **B**ehavior, **C**onsequence. Sometimes this is described as Trigger, Behavior/Habit, Reward.

To cut a long story short: When we want to change our habits, we should look carefully at what exactly elicits this behavior and what the reward is. Then, you can change, eliminate or avoid the trigger or the reward or both. Or you can also keep the trigger and the reward and change the behavior they apply to.

The ABC analysis

A good way to start when you want to eliminate a strong bad habit is to keep a diary, not with many words but rather in Twitter style.

Each time the habit occurs, you immediately write down the circumstances in which it happened, what you did and what the result was.

TRIGGER/SITUATION THOUGHTS	HABIT DEGREE: SCORE 1-10	CONSEQUENCE

Often you might gain even better cues or insights if you include your thinking as part of the antecedents, or in a separate column. This way you might discover a few thoughts that seem logical, but don't in fact have any rational base.

Recently while I was doing some developmental coaching with a CFO, as an aside he complained that under stress he was eating too many candy bars from the vending machines that were all over the office. When stressed he easily gained up to 20kg (44 pounds). He lost almost all of these with little effort during his vacations. His ABC analysis looked like the one in the next table.

TRIGGER/ SITUATION/ STIMULUS ANTECEDENTS	THINKING FEELING	DOING: HABIT DEGREE: SCORE 1-10	CONSEQUENCES
...	...	...	...
Tension in my neck and wrist	I'm bored and fed up	Got 2 candy bars	Got energy More concentrated Felt Guilty
Lost con-centration	Need calories	2 candy bars Kept chit-chatting for 20 minutes	Back in office in good mood

Analyzing and discussing a dozen A, B and C inputs in his diary, he discovered that his craving for sweets was an early warning signal that his stress-balance was out of balance (=trigger) and that he needed to restore regular breaks. This helped him significantly but... did not change his sweet tooth. Therefore we looked at the reward side. He found several: sugar that gave him a quick boost, getting away from his computer when he was no longer really concentrated or even bored, and meeting people. This also explained why keeping fruit in his office to eat instead of going for an unhealthy snack had not worked. The calorie boost in itself was insufficient as a reward. Instead he decided to bring fruit every day and put it as a snack for everybody on the reception desk. Then, whenever he felt the craving for sweets, he would get away from his computer (=reward), out of his office (=reward), walk through the office (meeting people = reward) and walk down three floors (reward= physical activity), get the fruit (eliminate craving for sweet =reward), walk back (reward= physical activity) and continue working (reward= much more concentrated). An unexpected bonus was that after a few weeks the company put free fruit baskets for everybody near the vending machines.

One of my coachees discovered that feeling a little bit depressed or unhappy was the most important trigger for going online. For another, it was feeling bored. These of course were more difficult triggers. First of all because, as I described in Section 2, going online stimulates the pleasures centers in our brain, so that any activity that produces less dopamine in our brain, like doing some necessary and important reflection, becomes less exciting. Secondly, because the feelings of boredom, depression and unhappiness can be the withdrawal symptoms of addiction. Going online stimulates the dopamine you need to counteract the withdrawal symptoms... keeping the vicious cycle going.

Online → dopamine → feeling good/excited → returning
to difficult brainwork → drop in dopamine → withdrawal
symptoms: unhappy, less energetic, bored → going online → ...

You can use this method to better understand when and why you connect. In the example (next page), after a few entries, a coachee became aware of some of the negative consequences of his behavior. This happens rather often: keeping the diary creates a distance that makes you a better, more objective observer of your own behavior.

After the ABC analysis, with or without an ABC diary, you decide if you will just replace one behavior by a better alternative and keep the triggers and reward intact, or if you will change the triggers or

TRIGGER/ SITUATION	THINKING FEELING	DOING: HABIT DEGREE: SCORE 1-10	CONSEQUENCE
...	...	...	...
Waiting in meeting room for director to arrive	Bored. Did not feel like chit-chatting. So many e-mails to do	Did e-mails on phone.	Got some e-mails done. Not feeling bored. Looking back: kind of isolated from team. Maybe should have joined the small talk.
Meeting: director discussing with Fred does not listen to Fred who had to repeat his point	Bored	Did some e-mail kind of stealthily	Got rid of many irrelevant e-mails. Maybe I should have helped Fred to get his good point across

rewards too. Bear in mind that your goal is to turn the new behavior into a new habit as quickly as possible so that you no longer have to use just your willpower.

CHANGING THE B OF ABC

Often, replacing a bad habit with another good or better one, while keeping all the triggers and rewards intact, is easier than just stopping a habit. If you do not replace the unwanted habit with a wanted one, the pull of the old one will be much harder.

In the case of our candy bar addict above, he could have left everything else as it was, just taking an apple with him and eating it at the same pantry where he used to eat his candy.

CHANGING THE A OF ABC

In the chapter about BrainChain #1, I described the experiment of Pavlov with his dogs and how triggers, totally unrelated to food, got them drooling. Therefore it is important to find out whether your bad habit has become a Pavlov reaction. Did it become unknowingly linked with a particular stimulus, trigger, situation or environment? Just being in that particular situation or environment can trigger your habit or trigger the feeling that in turn triggers your habit.

In the example of our candy bar addict, it certainly helped him a lot to eat his snack at the reception desk and not near the vending machine, given the risk that at the vending machine there were many Pavlovian stimuli to trigger his bad habit of eating candy bars.

On the other hand, you don't always have to find out exactly which stimulus triggers your bad habit of, for example, interrupting your important reflective work to look at your phone.

You can turn the Pavlovian conditioning to your advantage not only by avoiding triggers that "force" you to connect, but also by developing stimuli for reflection. Ideally you could have different rooms for connecting and for reflecting. But, since this is often not realistic, you can also make getting into reflection mode easier by little rituals like solemnly starting the app that disconnects you from the Internet, setting a timer, disconnecting your phone or giving it to an assistant or colleague, putting a 'Do not disturb' sign on your door or on the wall of your cubicle etc. After you have done this several times, you will develop a Pavlov reflex that puts your brain in brainwork mode, as soon as you go into the other room, hang up the 'Do not disturb' sign etc...

One example was the manager I mentioned above, who only connected and multitasked when she was sitting behind her desk, but who moved to the opposite side of her desk to do thinking work or to have a real conversation. Going through this one-minute ritual got her brain disconnected and in single-tasking mode.

Another professional only connected when he was in his cubicle. When he needed to do important or difficult thinking work, he went to a quiet room without a computer, leaving his phone with a colleague.

The same method will also help you with other BrainChaining behavior. When you have a sleeping problem, your bedroom should only be used for sleeping (and sex) and nothing else, certainly not for working. You should only work in your (home) office, never in your bedroom and certainly never in bed. In this way simply entering your bedroom and getting into bed becomes an exclusive and much more powerful Pavlovian trigger for sleeping.

CHANGING THE C OF ABC

If you want to change the consequences or reward, you might want to use the powerful Premack's Principle[38]. This is a well-researched method that parents all over the world have used for eons: "If you eat at least two spoonfuls of spinach, you will get a dessert". The principle is that if a low probability/desirability behavior is systematically followed by a high probability/desirability behavior, the less likely behavior will become more likely.

Replace the spinach by "disconnecting to reflect" and the dessert by "going on the Internet", and you get the idea. If you are addicted to your smartphone, only look at it after you have disconnected for more important work for 15 minutes. Then you slowly increase the time you stay disconnected before you can get the reward.

The most beautiful thing that can then happen is that the new behavior becomes so rewarding by itself that you no longer need an additional reward. In many cases the biggest reward for people is regularly getting into the flow of a task, becoming much more efficient and getting home earlier.

The success of any action plan depends 90% on the follow-up and follow-through. Below you can find a few more examples of easy practical tools, tips and tricks I have learned during several decades of working in psychotherapy and later in workshops and coaching with professionals to increase the chances of success The more difficult it is to change your habit, the more of these tools you should use.

USE SELF-REWARDS AND PUNISHMENTS
One tool that many coachees and participants in workshops often laugh at when I introduce the idea is to punish or reward yourself.

Usually they think it is childish or something more for training a dog... until they discover it really makes a difference.

Come up with creative rewards and punishments, bearing in mind that the rewards and punishments will have to be very serious since you are probably more addicted than you think. This sounds ridiculous but a century of research on behavior change has taught us that it really makes a difference.

For example, you can put a sum of money in a piggy bank every day you succeed with your plan. You then buy something you would never have otherwise dared buying. Each time you fail, you put the same amount of money in another piggy bank which you will donate to a charity whose ideology, religion or political orientation you... don't like at all.

With self-rewards and self-punishments you intervene in the c part of the ABC chain. Therefore your self-rewards and self-punishments shouldn't be peanuts. You need to choose ones that really weigh heavy on the balance. As long as the old habit is more immediately rewarding than the new habit you want to develop, you will not change. It is also important that rewards and punishment follow the behavior as closely as possible; the reward shouldn't come in half a year or a month, but every day.

Not something like 'if I do well I will buy this expensive briefcase', but rather 'every day I reach my score I get a token and when I have 60 of them I will buy the expensive briefcase'.

Not something like 'for every minute I go beyond the allotted e-mail time I will pay a fine of $1'. Make it instead $5 or any sum that you really find to be punishing.

Not something like, 'for every day I keep my promise, I will put $1 in a piggy bank to buy some excellent wine, wine I would otherwise never buy', but for every day I succeed I will put in $25 or whatever sum you consider at least a little over the top.

When one of my clients was discussing the idea of punishment/ reward with his wife, she suggested that for every successful day she would give him a token and for 50 tokens she would give him a very nice single malt whiskey for his collection, while for every day he did not succeed she would earn a token and for five tokens he would go to a movie of her choice with her.

This example illustrates how you can create a win-win situation by punishing yourself with something you don't do enough, in this case going to the movies with his wife. Another example would be for every minute you go over the time you allotted for batch-processing your e-mails, you add five minutes to the block you scheduled for important intellectual work. Or every time you do your e-mails outside the allotted time, you telephone two people instead of sending them an e-mail, or you play for 15 more minutes with your son, or you jog one extra mile or...

But you can also use clear-cut unrelated punishments: every time I let my old habit take over I will not drink any alcohol at night or I will put an amount of money in a piggy bank (money only works when the sum is really significant) to give to charity.

After deciding that he would put money aside for a charity every time he broke the new rules, one of my clients, a devout catholic, discovered that the punishment didn't work because every mistake was good for his beloved charity. Therefore we changed the contract and he decided to donate the same amount of money to a charity whose work he kind of appreciated, but whose ideology he did not like at all.

KEEP A LOG
A simple but efficient tool is to keep a log. Every time you let yourself be distracted while doing important work, you note a hash sign and go on. For many people it helps if they put the result on a graph because it tells you how you are doing at a glance.

You can also let technology help you. Joe Hruska and his team developed a great tool "Rescuetime" (https://www.rescuetime.com/) that as automatically as possible keeps track of the way you spend your time and gives you a productivity score based on the standards you have set for yourself.

FIVE MINUTES OF REFLECTION
A very simple yet very efficient little tool that can make a big difference is that whatever approach you use, it is always a good idea to take just five minutes every evening to reflect on your action plan. Most people find they remember to do this if they link this moment of reflection to a specific place. For example, if you commute, start the reflection after you're on the highway just past the first service station, or on the train after passing a particular station.

You must do this daily because the closer the feedback to the behavior the faster you will change. Moreover, if you do it the same day, it is much easier to correct it before the bad habit really takes over again. If the habit is to behave differently with people, you can most often still undo what you did if you do so within 24 hours.

For example if during the last 5 minutes you realize that you sent an e-mail about something that you should actually have discussed in person, if you correct this the next day, it is very easy to go to that person and say "Sorry, I sent you that mail about that very important issue, but I think we should have a real conversation about it instead of mailing back and forth". The longer you wait to correct it, the more difficult it becomes.

GET A BUDDY
A pet topic I developed while coaching more than a hundred professionals is: if you want to change, get a buddy. This is most often the most powerful intervention you can do to change.

Share your action plan with a person you trust and empower this person to correct you immediately if she catches you in the act of succumbing to the old habit. The minimum you expect from a buddy is that she just regularly reminds you about what you promised yourself. In many cases, however, that person can become a kind of peer coach, inspiring and supporting you to succeed.

You can also empower your buddy to decide if you earned your reward or punishment or not. If you are a manager, you can also engage a team member.

An executive of a family business wanted to unlearn his bad habit of quickly doing a few e-mails when he was waiting for other people to arrive instead of engaging in small talk He kept slipping back into the old habit until he got a colleague and team member involved. He asked them to rub their hands discreetly whenever they caught him in the act. This secret signal meant: close your phone and talk to us.

At home you can make this fun by involving not only your spouse, but also your children and letting them decide about punishments and rewards when you are on your screen instead of with them. You'll be surprised by the creative ideas even a 6-year-old can have to help you.

INVOLVE OTHERS IN YOUR ENDEAVOR

On top of having a buddy, you can involve many more people in your endeavor.

If you are leading a team or part of a team, you can make the team co-responsible. "Every time a phone rings or buzzes in our meeting the culprit will pay for a bottle of champagne". "Every time anybody does anything other than taking notes on his tablet, he will put $30 in the piggy bank that we will use to pay for our annual dinner".

You should explain to as many people as possible what you are trying to achieve and ask for their help. For example, make it clear to your colleagues that you do not want to be disturbed. Explain the why and how. Try to convince as many people as possible to do the same. For example: If you have your own office, close your door and put a small whiteboard on it with "Please do not disturb. I will be available for you at x o'clock". Or you can do as one of my clients did, adding an explanation: "I really need some time for thorough reflection. Please do not disturb. I will be all yours at 11:00". Another one used me as an explanation: "Theo told us to disconnect to reflect. That is what I'm doing until 4 o'clock". Don't let all kinds of politically correct or misunderstood ideas about "open-door policy" stop you. "Open door" is an attitude that has nothing to do with your door actually being open or not. We all know managers whose door is always open but who never have time to listen or who have a closed-door attitude.

One of my clients working in one of those intellectual productivity killing open offices resolved the problem by making a foldable carton screen that she put around her desk to create a kind of a cubicle. On the carton was a cartoon with the text "Brain at work. Please do not disturb till x o'clock". She also put on a pair of excellent noise-cancelling headphones with her favorite music. She explained this to her colleagues. People laughed at her in the beginning, then many people from outside her office heard about the cartoon, which gave her a chance to explain her plan, and gradually more and more people followed her example.

Do the same with your e-mail: use the out of office tool all the time. Make a few different messages. Use humor. Explain why you do this. Blame me or this book.

In a company where many bright young people had to work in an awful noisy open office, a group of them started bringing motorcycle helmets to work, which they put on their head as a sign of not wanting to be disturbed. At the same time it was a message to management that their working environment was lousy. Interestingly enough management did not react until more and more clients complained that the background noise in that office ruined their conference calls with these employees. Believe it or not, as a result the ignorant management installed... telephone booths in the corners... which of course were always taken by employees trying to do difficult brainwork.

On the other hand this is of course a perfect example of how utterly ignorant, callous and stupid managers can sometimes be about the negative impact of the work environment on brainworkers' intellectual productivity. Sometimes the only solution is to revolt! Be daring and creative.

USE REMINDERS

It is difficult to underestimate the usefulness of reminders. When I first suggest that people do this they often think it is kind of stupid, but they always discover that it really makes a difference.

Just things like a sticker on your phone or desktop, or a screensaver with a picture is a secret metaphor for the message "Really nothing better to do?" It could be a little statue on your desk, a poster on the wall, a drawing done by your child...

A partner in a law firm decided to stop phoning while driving but always forgot to disconnect her phone when getting in her car. Once the phone started ringing, she could not stop herself from taking the call. She then asked her daughter to make a small drawing to remind her. On the sticker the daughter made a lovely drawing of a pink princess with a mobile phone with "Mommy, please think about us". When her much younger brother heard about this he also made a cartoonish drawing of a gruesome dinosaur attacking the car of his mom. With these two stickers on the dashboard she no longer forgets to turn off her phone.

A simple reminder can be to use an app to remind you to log off when the time for your batch of work is finished. You can set a timer (such as http://free-countdown-timer.com/) at the start of every batch of work you start with. It is most important to do this systematically when you log on because almost everybody spends more time online than planned or even than they think they do.

LET TECHNOLOGY HELP YOU

So many people must have experienced the extreme difficulty of disconnecting and stopping multitasking that it has given birth to an interesting niche market of applications to help you with this. If you want to know how you really spend your time you can use a program like Manictime (http://www.manictime.com/) to automatically keep track. Even better is "Rescuetime"(https://www.rescuetime.com/). This program not only keeps track of how you spend your time but, following your own goals and wishes, it also calculates your productivity and your efficiency and shows you your progress at a glance. You can then reward and punish yourself accordingly. You can even share the results with your buddy or buddies, or turn it into a competition. The App can also block access to the sites that are your time-wasters and alert you when your productivity drops below a level you have chosen. As a bonus, if you have to keep track of your hours for billing purposes it can do that too.

If you are really afraid of missing very important e-mails, e.g. from your boss or key client, you can let "awayfind"[39] send you a message on your mobile whenever an e-mail comes in from an important person, so that you can be more relaxed about not checking your e-mails every 5 minutes.

You can also make your own "time out" rule that automatically replies to all e-mails with a message saying that you will only be able to read your e-mails at certain times, but that people can call or text your private mobile phone in case of emergency. For Gmail there is a gadget that does exactly that automatically: "Inbox-pause" http://inboxpause.com/.

If the only thing you need is to be forcefully prevented from connecting to your big timewasters like social media and news sites, LeechBlock®, Freedom® and Anti-Social® will help you by disconnecting. If you are addicted and you want to interrupt your real work for a little shot of your dope before the set time, you will have to reboot your computer and fully experience the humiliating confrontation with the fact that you are a real addict and probably need professional help if you ever want to become productive again.

GET ANOTHER JOB

Sometimes a professional has a stalking boss who expects 24/7 availability or a company culture where e-mail has got totally out of hand. If you have a boss or a company that demands that you are always connected and respond to e-mails within 10 minutes, open the discussion, start converting as many people as possible, spread the summary of this book everywhere... don't accept this counterproductive brain abuse any longer. REVOLT or change boss or company as soon as you can. It is impossible to become as intellectually productive as you would like in a company that propagates brain killers.

There is a caveat. In my experience this complaint about the company is often not real or at least exaggerated; it is merely used as an excuse by an addicted employee. In many situations, employees and managers who "broke rank" and started managing their e-mail in a healthy and efficient way attracted followers, applause and envy.

If you are not addicted, but you hate your job and are therefore always looking online for excitement, fun and distraction, get another job in or outside your company. Life is too short to drink bad wine.

3 BRAINGAINS AT THE "WE" LEVEL

The WE level is what people and teams can do together to improve their intellectual productivity.

The most important service brainworkers can do for each other is to respect each other's privacy by not interrupting the concentration of others with unwanted contact, noise and... e-mail. To the extent that ignorance about multitasking and always being connected plays a role, you can also help others by disseminating this information, putting the reduction of hyperconnectivity and multitasking on the agenda of your regular meetings, and if necessary banding together to make it a higher priority in your company or your part of it.

If you know each other better and more personally, you can help each other by reminding the multitaskers and especially the hypertaskers of the disservice they are doing to themselves and the team, and by helping and supporting them to develop healthier and more efficient ways of dealing with the continuous overflow of information.

Below are just a few suggestions and typical examples.

3.1 CHAINBREAKER 1: RESPECT AND SUPPORT PEOPLE WHO REGULARLY DISCONNECT

If you ever tried to modify ingrained inefficient personal or company habits, you know how difficult it can be to do. So you should respect and support your colleagues who try to be more productive by not being connected all the time everywhere, by not responding to e-mails within a few minutes and by processing their work in batches while eliminating distractions. People who take regular breaks are more productive and more creative than people who stay glued behind their desks or who hurry from one meeting to the next without any brain-breaks. You should not only respect their way of working but follow their example.

People who do not manage to improve their own intellectual performance have a tendency to laugh at 'Do not disturb' signs, make nasty comments when others take a break, ridicule the use of headphones or call them anti-social, and become angry when they don't get an immediate response to a question that has been sitting in their huge badly managed inbox for a week and that suddenly became urgent. They need your pity and help.

It might be frustrating for you if you want to ask something and your colleague has a 'Do no disturb' sign on her door or cubicle wall. In such a case, you should respect and support their effort, even if you are frustrated because you haven't yet succeeded in becoming more efficient yourself. Above all, if you are their manager, you should be the very first to respect these endeavors and see this lack of immediate response as a very short time loss for yourself, with a big gain in the end, which is your gain too.

3.2 CHAINBREAKER 2: COLLABORATE TO ENHANCE EACH OTHER'S RIGHT-TASKING

You get the best results of right-tasking when you collaborate with others. This can be starting the discussion about the subject with everybody in your team or office, putting the subject on the agenda of regular team meetings, brainstorming together to find creative solutions or just asking colleagues to answer your phone while you are batch-processing.

An executive who attended a workshop shared the story with his three management assistants. The three ladies, who were sharing an office, then took the idea a step further amongst themselves. They were so often disturbed, often for minor issues, that this had a negative impact on the quality of the minutes and reports they had to write, the events they had to plan, the information they had to scout for and on their stress-balance. They therefore decided amongst themselves that one of them would always be free to do the more difficult and complex work undisturbed – or to have a relaxing break –

while the other two would take all her phone calls and regularly look at her e-mails to see if there was anything really urgent. At first the board members were surprised that "their own" assistant was no longer always available, but they learned to appreciate and respect this new way of working, not the least because the quality and even the speed of the work improved and the atmosphere in the office became more relaxed and congenial, with fewer complaints about stress.

3.3 CHAINBREAKER 3: FIGHT FRANKENMAIL TOGETHER

In many companies a major productivity killer is irrelevant e-mail. If you really want to tame the e-mail Frankenstein, you need each other's help. As we saw in the second section, the main cause of the continuous e-mail diarrhea is the asymmetric relationship between the sender and the receiver. The sender has the power and the receiver is the victim. The million-dollar (literally) question is how can we discipline the senders and empower the receivers. The really structural solutions can only be realized at a company level, but what everybody can start doing are simple things that make a big difference. If lots of people start doing them, they become part of the company culture or at least the culture of your department. The change of the corporate e-mail culture can also be bottom-up.

- First of all, just write fewer e-mails. Ask yourself: If the e-mail system were down, would I print this and fax or send paper copies to all these people or call them? If the answer is "No", why the heck do you e-mail it?
- Keep your e-mails short and to the point, not forgetting to clearly define the action you expect and by when. Put the latter in the subject line.
- Make the subject line as relevant as possible and add a message about the action expected and its urgency, for example "please respond this week" or "fyi: no response needed etc...". You don't even have to type this. With a macro you can add these standard sentences with two keystrokes. "No response needed" is a clear message to all the people who think they have to respond to every e-mail, sparing you lots of irrelevant e-mail.

- Use the phone when there is a need for two-way communication.
- Stop using cc-mail. Your mail either is important for the other person or it is not... unless you are a little neurotic (or your company is) and you always want to cover your back.
- Do not send to groups unless you are convinced all those people really need to respond to your e-mail. If you do not expect a response, put everybody in BCC, so that when people do a "Reply to all", their mail is only sent to you and the people you have put in the TO field.
- Do not use "Reply to all" unless it really makes sense that all those people read your answer. The bad "Reply to all" habit causes an ever-increasing avalanche of e-mails. If you really need to send an e-mail to a group of people, at least put them in BCC, which makes "Reply to all" impossible. In some companies the "Reply to all" function has even been eliminated from the system.
- NB: When you do not use cc-mail, group-mail or "Reply to all" (or only very sparingly), you will also eliminate a lot of irrelevant replies. It's a clear win-win.
- By the way, you should never give negative feedback or other bad news by e-mail, unless you are just callous or do not have the social skills to have difficult conversations with people. Certainly never follow the example of managers who cold-heartedly fire people by e-mail. These should be executed.
- Moreover, never ever e-mail something that you do not want to become public or that you do not want to read in the newspaper mentioning you as its source. In the past two months two of my client companies fired a very senior person for misbehavior that came to light as the result of an e-mail that ended up in the wrong hands. Instead of the long paragraphs about confidentiality that some companies put below the signatures, I added one line on mine: "When you reply, please remember that e-mail is as confidential as an open postcard. If your information is confidential, please fax". Fifteen years ago I was thinking about e-mail mistakenly going wrong. Thanks to Snowden, everybody knows that the privacy of an e-mail is literally as good as a postcard.

- If you have a manager who expects you to always stay connected and to always respond immediately, explain politely that this is counterproductive, give him this book and if this does not help, band together with your colleagues to politely ask for a different approach and if that does not help, revolt against this counterproductive stalking and take it to a higher level. Executives responsible for HR and SHE might be interested to organize a companywide improvement of the e-mail culture. There are many specialized consultants and trainers who can help you as a department or a company.

3.4 CHAINBREAKER 4: CONVINCE PEOPLE OF THE DANGERS OF PHONING WHILE DRIVING

Since reading Section 2, you will hopefully have radically stopped using your phone while driving and will have explained to your colleagues and managers how dangerous it is to phone while driving. It is important to explain the situation to them, firstly because they should know that they will no longer be able to reach you while you are driving and secondly because you might convince them to do the same and become a phone-teetotaler while driving.

By the way, stop the call immediately when you become aware that your colleague is calling while driving. I think you would feel awful if all of a sudden you heard the sound of a crash and then silence while you were on the phone.

Try to convince as many people as possible about the risks of using a phone while driving. The more people stop doing it, the better for everybody. Eventually it might even become a company policy.

3.5 CHAINBREAKER 5: GIVE AS MUCH SOCIAL SUPPORT AS YOU CAN...FOR YOUR OWN BENEFIT

Given how important the positive impact of social support is on our stress-balance, giving practical support and emotional support and creating a mutually supportive team, department and company should always be a top priority for everybody, managers and employees alike. Investing in such a supportive atmosphere is the best thing you can do for your own stress-balance.

Elaborating on this very important subject would require a whole chapter if not a book, so I'll leave it there and hope that you work in a company where this is self-evident. If not, start with yourself, your team and your colleagues.

3.6 CHAINBREAKER 6: BAND TOGETHER AGAINST BADLY DESIGNED OPEN OFFICES

As I explained in Section 2, I want this book to be about things you can do yourself to improve the quantity and quality of your brain-work. Given that your office is beyond your individual control, I turned my chapter about bad offices – originally planned to be part of this book – into a separate booklet, *"Brain-Hostile Open Offices: The Fifth BrainChain"* (you can download it for free from www.brainchains.org). This booklet aims to help you prevent bad open offices being built or to improve existing ones as much as possible, for example by banding together with others to improve privacy and focus or to ask for improvements to the existing situation or to be heard in the planning phase for new offices.

4 BRAINGAINS AT THE "THEY" LEVEL: ALL THE ABOVE AND...

The THEY level is the responsibility of managers and leaders in organizations. They should be the very first to know what brainworkers need to be their most productive. THEY are the ones who play the biggest role in realizing the synergy between ICT and brainwork. They set the example, they define the ICT culture, they set the expectations. They should put the ICT policies, rules and culture on the agenda. Of course if they are not convinced, if they are constantly ruining their own intellectual performance, if they don't take time to reflect, to have real conversations and discussions, to do some thorough reading, they will never succeed in creating an optimally intellectually productive team, department or company. If they suffer from the delusion that they are the exceptional champions of multitasking, they will spread the disease and ruin the intellectual productivity of many others.

4.1 CHAINBREAKER 1: STIMULATE YOUR PROFESSIONALS TO REGULARLY DISCONNECT AND DO THE SAME

The First Commandment to increase intellectual productivity in your organization is very simple: do not expect your employees to always be connected and encourage them to disconnect to do intellectual work (for their reflecting brain) and to relax (for their archiving brain)!

As I explained extensively in the second section of this book, one of the most efficient ways to ruin the intellectual productivity of brainworkers is to expect them to always be connected and to respond to e-mails within minutes. You have invested so much capital in hiring the best and the brightest. Why would you want to ruin their intellectual productivity?

Most important: disconnect yourselves when you have off-site meetings. Totally disconnect to get in your strategic helicopter vision and to escape the executive grasshopper view I described in BrainChain #1.

4.2 CHAINBREAKER 2: PREVENT MULTITASKING AND TASK-SWITCHING, INCLUDING ON THE SHOP FLOOR

The Second Commandment to increase intellectual productivity in your organization is more difficult: weed out multitasking wherever it is taking root. Multitasking, be it serial or simultaneous multitasking, is hopelessly inefficient. Period. It is certainly not a solution if you want to do more with fewer people. If you expect people to respond to your e-mails within minutes rather than within 24 hours, you force them to switch tasks all the time, making them inefficient.

If you reorganize work in such a way that fewer people get more tasks, and they try to resolve the multiple priorities by multitasking you will need more people not fewer to do the same job or let the others exhaust themselves. Also bear in mind that forced multitasking is even more inefficient than the multitasking people freely choose to do, which is already bad enough. Hence managers should try to eliminate multitasking when they organize work, the workflow, projects etc... not only in the office, but also on the shop floor.

Hence, you should inform and educate your employees about this fact and be on the lookout for any situation where it can be and should be avoided. Many companies improved their productivity, safety and profit with methodologies like Six Sigma, Quality circles, Lean production, etc... Since multitasking it is so extremely counterproductive, why not use one of these methodologies that your company is already good at to reduce multitasking?

By the way, bear in mind that many programs like "Lean", used to doing more with fewer people, do not realize their potential because they increase multitasking as managers are not aware of the detrimental impact of multitasking on productivity.

Collaborating for many years with DuPont-deNemours made me very aware of safety issues. This sensitivity about the danger of multitasking on the shop floor was further heightened when, in another company, I did the post-traumatic stress debriefing after a horrible accident with a forklift truck. The workers who were near the accident were in shock and others were traumatized and had flashbacks of horror stories they went through in the army or at work.

If you are a professional with the slightest responsibility for safety, don't wait for an accident like that to get your attention about the safety risks of multitasking on the shop floor. I hope the massive amount of research I presented about the danger of using a phone while driving convinced you to quickly do something about the distraction caused by phones, Walkie-Talkies and touch-screens, which too many workers use or are even obliged to use in the workplace. Don't wait for an accident. Knowing that the risks increase between four times (for phoning) and 23 times (for texting), look at all driving situations where the distraction is built into the system. Think, for example, about the screens with which forklift-truck drivers and delivery-truck drivers have to interact and the combination of ignorance and extreme time pressure that makes them do this while driving. For trucks there is hardware and software that automatically disconnects all electronic distracters and freezes the screen as soon as the truck starts driving.

A worker on the phone or Walkie-Talkie while walking on the shop floor has the same high risk as a pedestrian on the phone in a busy town street. The use of cell phones should be forbidden on the shop floor or restricted to offices, special phone zones and rest areas.

Bearing this research in mind, you should go beyond this and look at all operational actions where the electronic distraction is not only too easily allowed but even built into the system. I am thinking for example about a maintenance worker whose Walkie-Talkie started talking while he was changing a heavy spare part, which almost fell out of his hands when he tried to answer. I am also thinking about an operator who badly hurt his chin when he bumped into a box while on the phone or another person who

forgot a step in the start-up of the process because at that moment he was summoned by his Walkie-Talkie to help a colleague. You might also think about the high-speed train conductor in Barcelona who caused an accident costing dozens of lives, while he was on the phone with his head office.

Not being aware of the negative impact of multitasking, managers sometimes organize and structure work for their employees in such a way that they are obliged to multitask or task-hop. Multitasking is only possible for a very limited number of routine tasks. Beyond that, multitasking becomes counterproductive. Hence when you set up a production line, for example, you should keep in mind that critical tasks should be organized to avoid multitasking and that routine tasks be planned in a way that avoids multitasking when things happen that are no longer routine. This is even more important when safety is at stake.

After a workshop about stress management, a plant manager asked for help because in a brand new plant they had built, one they were very proud of, they kept having (near-)accidents and production incidents, way past what they considered the normal learning curve.

When I visited the plant I discovered that the average stress was not the problem but the fact that the work was organized in a way where the operators had to multitask several very repetitive routines. Just like a cook having many pots on the stove, it was the kind of behavior that with some training can be handed over to the reflex brain and done on automatic pilot. The new way of organizing seemed to work well and, to some extent, the operators even liked the task-hopping until... something happened that wasn't part of the routine and that needed some reflection. Then the operators couldn't handle it anymore.

The multitasking was so tightly organized that there wasn't enough slack to handle the unexpected. Since in the new workflow every operator was managing his own production "island", they couldn't ask for help from a colleague either. The only safe solution was to stop the process, which they did not like to do because that slowed down the production for many colleagues, which impacted their pay. So they muddled through the unexpected with negative consequences for the production quality, stress and safety. Under pressure they found dangerous solutions, like blocking the sensors that stopped a cutting machine when the protective cover was opened so that they could tighten the knives without stopping the process.

BARCO Electronics resolved this kind of problem with "Butterflies", operators who rotate doing non-urgent, non-dangerous maintenance work that they can drop immediately when they get a call from a colleague who has to deal with something unexpected. Instead of trying to do two things at the same time, the operator can continue with his task, while the butterfly takes over the unexpected or vice versa.

An excellent example is how the nurses at the Kaiser Foundation hospital found simple and inexpensive solutions to avoid multi-tasking and other distractions while administering medication. Don't think: "I don't work in a hospital". Read on. This project is a best-practice case that has inspired many COOs, SHE managers and plant managers in my groups. Imagine what 50% fewer errors and a 15% increase in speed could mean for you and your business!

Realizing that multitasking is not a good idea while administering 22,000 medications a month, and knowing that about a third of all medication errors happen at distribution, a Kaiser hospital developed an anti-multitasking routine. The results were fast and excellent. There were several aspects to it but the main one was a medicine-handling procedure that eliminated distraction as much as possible. The most important elements were:

- *Effective signage: The nurses have to put on a very visible fluorescent sash or vest whenever they administer medication, and red tape or paint on the floor delineates a "sacred zone" in front of the medicine cupboard. Nobody is allowed to disturb them while they are wearing the sash or standing in the red zone painted in front of the medicine cabinet.*
- *Evidence-based strategies borrowed from the airline industry: "In the airlines, pilots have a 'sacred zone' when going through pre-flight checks and aren't to be disturbed. We implemented the same thing," says Melody Navarro[40].*
- *A simple short protocol: a standard medication administration protocol checklist for improving focus and reducing distractions.*
- *Empowerment: The nurses are empowered to speak up for themselves to discourage unwanted interruptions.*
- *Strong leadership and management principles.*

The result of single-tasking: A 50% decrease in interruptions led to 47% fewer errors and 15% faster distribution!! [41] No wonder that in the Netherlands most hospitals are introducing this approach too.

If these nurses can do this, you can do it in your business! Invent your own "sash", "red zone" or "sacred zone".

4.3 CHAINBREAKER 3: DRASTICALLY REDUCE E-MAIL WHILE IMPROVING ITS USE

What amazes me again and again when I am consulting and coaching for other reasons is that although e-mail takes up such an unbelievable and increasing amount of employees' time and causes so much frustration and drop in productivity, its use is almost never openly and thoroughly discussed. Nobody seems to know what is exactly expected from them in terms of e-mailing. There are no explicit rules, no code of practice about what are business critical e-mails, how fast one should respond, how many people can be in cc, when do you put people in cc, how to use groups, does one need to read e-mail during the weekend and vacations etc... etc... So people start guessing and propagate myths, often based on exceptional or stupid expectations from one or another manager or executive. Isn't it just crazy that the use of one of the most important and most time-consuming tools in the modern workplace is not assessed, measured or even discussed or regulated, even in companies that do this for the use of company pencils, paperclips and where you may park your car? As a result, a lot of useless e-mail is generated, ever increasing the information overload.

There are good financial reasons to put the use of ICT on the agenda. The CFO of a consulting company of 500 people calculated that just ONE hour less per day on e-mail would yield $2 million a year!

Another reason is that more and more employees no longer accept this abuse of having to always be connected with work. According to USA Today[42], the number of lawsuits filed by employees claiming unfair overtime is up 32% since 2008. The major reason for the increase? E-mail on devices like smartphones intruding into their personal time[43]. Moreover, most employees are not paid for the many hours they work via their continuous connection. I couldn't find the details of this survey to check what this means in absolute numbers, but it is an interesting idea. In times of recession, as a company, you can get away with murder, but once the recession is over and especially if you need highly qualified people doing high-level intellectual work, they will look for a healthier place to work, a place that allows a better balance between work and the rest of their lives.

Since people spend between 20% and 70% of their time on e-mail, do whatever you can to reduce e-mail traffic and to improve the way it is used. It puzzles me that many companies develop very efficient methods, lean production and Six Sigma for example, to increase efficiency, reduce waste etc... but they never apply the same rigorous methodologies to eradicate this increasingly counterproductive, wasteful use of ICT. I only found one example of a global financial institution where a Six Sigma project reduced mass mailings from 400 to 100 annually[44]. Please drop me a line at theo@BrainChains.org if you know of more examples.

Corporate e-mail reduction and internal communication improvement are not my expertise. There are hundreds of consultants and trainers who can help you to vastly reduce the e-mails sent, if they concentrate first of all on the employees in their role as senders of e-mail. For a few examples, see the paragraph on e-mail in the chapter on BrainGains at the WE level. The most important intervention, however, is that executives first and then managers set a good example.

There is low-hanging fruit with a great ROI that will drastically reduce the continuing productivity-destroying avalanche of e-mails. If you are a manager, and certainly if you are an executive, you will increase the productivity of the brainworkers in your company enormously if you create a rule about the email-response time for the whole company. If you set a rule that e-mails have to be answered within 24 hours and that people should call each other for anything more urgent than that, this means that people need only two batches a day to answer all their e-mails. With such a simple rule the gains in productivity will be massive. Nothing you can imagine on a strategic level will ever have such a huge return on investment.

As I mentioned above, eliminate "Reply to all" function and even the "group" function in your mail system. This will also restore the balance between the senders (perpetrators) and the receivers (the victims) of internal spam, who of course constantly take turns in these roles.

A word of warning: tackling problems with e-mail very often unearths more general problems with communication in a company. I am convinced that there is a correlation between the amount of time employees spend online and the lack of overall quality of the general communication in a company. The worse the overall in-company communication, the more unimportant or even irrelevant e-mail is produced, the more time is lost on it, the more important work is interrupted and the more frustrated people are.

In the end, to be efficient you also need to have a close look at your company-wide culture, not just the communication culture. If, for example, your company or your department is low on trust and handles mistakes and failures badly, you will have thousands of unnecessary cover-my-back e-mails being sent unnecessarily to large groups of people.

If as a manager or executive you use e-mail to explain how important something is, to inspire people, to improve trust, to improve relations, to give complex difficult information, feedback or instructions, to give nuances or to address sensitive subjects, to explain the context, to get commitment... you will need many e-mails that many people will forward to many more... and you will achieve absolutely nothing, zilch, naught, zero, nada because these are exactly the kinds of communication you can only do in a real conversation with real people and not at all with e-mail.

This seems like the right place to repeat the classic joke, which reflects the awful reality in too many companies. Do the test for your own company or department. Do it as a team exercise in a break or an ice-breaker to start a discussion about the communication and e-mail culture.

At each step, estimate the % and then use that figure to calculate a new overall percentage, as indicated in the table.

The scenario: Two months ago a business unit manager sent an enthusing, diligently crafted e-mail with a summary of the new strategy to his 500 employees.

What % of people actually **read** it?	....% = score 1
Of those who did, how many really **understood** the message?	...% of score 1 = score 2
Of those who did understand, how many took it really **seriously**?	...% of score 2 = score 3
Of those who did take it seriously, how many can still **repeat** the essence of the message now?	...% of score 3 = score 4
Of those who did remember, how many were **enthusiastic**?	...% of score 4 = score 5
Of those who were enthusiastic, how many **adapted their behavior...** at least a little?	...% of score 5 = ...????

In one of my client companies, the CEO decided that all electronic business contacts were forbidden on Saturday. Initially he wanted to include Sundays too, but too many employees wanted to check their e-mails on Sunday evening to prepare for the week ahead. In many books and articles you will find more examples of so-called enlightened companies who have made arrangements for their employees to have an email-free half-day or even full-day, with some also introducing email-free weekends or at least Saturdays. This is a good idea IF it is embedded in a healthy work, communication and e-mail culture, with room for disconnecting and having real conversations and where the e-mail diarrhea has already been stopped. More often than not, however, these initiatives are ridiculous because they don't change the intellectual productivity-ruining hyperconnectivity the rest of the week, or the abuse of e-mail and the poor communication in general. Don't expect your brainworkers to function much better than at 60% of their potential if you release their BrainChains a few hours a week and keep them shackled for the rest of their time.

Other companies let their employees freewheel on their own pet subjects for 10% or even 20% of their time. However, if during their freewheeling time they are still connected and working hard to find solutions related to their job, they miss the idling time the brain needs to be really creative, to have breakthrough ideas or to have really creative conversations. What's more, if their regular workload is too heavy, it will continuously attract their thoughts as a magnet and bring them back to their nearby reality and away from creative detachment.

> **Don't expect your brainworkers to function much better than at 60% of their potential if you release their BrainChains a few hours a week and keep them shackled for the rest of their time at work and home.**

The new solution propagated by consultants is the social media type communication platform that IT companies are touting and pushing for organizations to use rather than e-mail as a more efficient communication tool. As I wrote in the second section: If employees check their Chatter, Yammer, Jive etc... 50 times a day as they do with their e-mails, the gain in intellectual productivity will be marginal, zero or negative, because they will still be inefficient, hyper-connected, hyper-distracted multitaskers and task-hoppers. Their productivity might even be worse than before because the social media are very addictive attention grabbers, which now call for attention all the time not only via smartphones, but also via smart-watches and smart-rings.

If your basic culture and communication culture are fairly good, you might try a few experiments already done by other companies:

- Setting a rule that e-mails need to be answered on average within 24 hours, no faster.
- Stop stalking employees after hours. Explicit statements that the company does not expect employees to check their e-mails in the evenings and weekends. (Difficult for companies working in different time zones, but that is no excuse for all the others.)
- Dividing time into "quiet time" and "interactive time".
- Introduce email-free days and discourage the use of e-mails during the weekends.
- Vacations without e-mails. Daimler is organizing itself so that when professionals go on vacation, their e-mail is forwarded to a colleague and they return to a basically empty inbox. This looks like a good example to follow and to expand on so that professionals can regularly disconnect during the week too.
- Quiet Time and no-email days where people disconnect (Intel)[45].
- Training people about coping more efficiently with their inbox.
- Training people in "sending etiquette": the use of proper subject lines, brevity etc...
- Disabling the "Reply to all" function from the e-mail program.
- Disabling the "group contact" function from the e-mail program.
- Requiring the sender to add an Importance and Urgency score to all the subject lines of all their e-mails...

4.4 CHAINBREAKER 4: FIGHT AT ALL LEVELS TO BAN THE USE OF PHONES WHILE DRIVING

As you saw in Section 2, a special and heavily researched dangerous case of connectedness and multitasking is using your phone while driving. There is only one possible conclusion for any company that cares about its people: discourage or even forbid it if you can. If you're looking for a wealth of research, free didactic materials and policies to launch a "no phone while driving" campaign, go to one of the sites mentioned in the bibliography[46]. You can find an excellent "Cell phone Policy Kit" for employers at http://www.nsc.org/safety_road/Distracted_Driving/Pages/EmployerPolicies.aspx

The most frequent counter-argument managers have is that using the phone while driving is more productive because otherwise driving is just lost time.

The answer is clear and simple: this is not true. We learn from the surveys of the National Safety Council that 90% of people who organize themselves so that they can stop using the phone while driving discover that there is no change in productivity, even for sales people. Moreover, they are less stressed when they arrive! Sometimes the resistance comes from unexpected quarters. In one of the global companies I collaborate with, the safety and plant managers are totally convinced about the danger for their operators of always being connected and multitasking, and they are eliminating these distractions more and more, in more and more regions. When they started tackling the issue of unsafe driving, the most resistance came from... the HR department fearing nobody would want to work for a company that forbids the use of a phone while driving!

What's more, providing your employees with cars that have hands-free sets installed makes you co-responsible for their distracted driving. If you don't agree with this ethical/moral point of view, just wait a little until more and more states and countries will allow police, insurance companies and lawyers to check after an accident if people were using their phone. Lawyers suing your company as being co-responsible also have the solid scientific information I gave you in this book and they will win their cases.

More and more companies that really believe in their values, or that just want to avoid lawsuits, forbid their employees from using their phone while driving, even on hands-free sets! In 150 companies on the Forbes 500 list, **20% enforce a total ban**!

At the end of the 1990s Shell discovered a significant increase in fatal accidents due to phoning while driving. In 2002 they banned hand-held phones while driving. In 2005 they also forbade hands-free and texting/sms and enforced it in more and more countries more and more strictly, even to the point that the penalty was being fired. The company also made it part of a more general project for safe driving habits for the company as a whole as well as its suppliers and partners. Between 2008 and 2011 this resulted in a 57% drop in road accidents[47].

As a responsible employer, you should act now and not wait for the telecom and car companies to equip their hardware with software that prevents drivers from using their phones while driving. Since at any time about 10% of drivers are using their in-car ICT, these companies will never forgo the nice profits they make on these distracting tools unless they are forced to; they're certainly not going to do so just for ethical reasons.

Modern cars are equipped with great computers that give the driver lots of distracting information while driving. They call the stuff enhancements, although they make distraction worse. The most unintentionally cynical one I ever read was from a company that called its product a "Killer Application". Moreover, the computer screens are located in a spot on the middle console that take the driver's eyes off the road. These accessories are becoming an important source of profit, so you can't ask the industry not to install them or make it impossible to access them while driving.

As a responsible and safety-aware company, you shouldn't wait for the government either. If you remember how long it took the government to enforce wearing life-saving seat belts in the USA, you can't wait for them to make driving safer by enforcing a no-phone policy. The phone policy in the USA is now where it was with the use of safety belts in 1981. After 15 years of education about safety belts, only 14% of Americans were wearing them. During the next 15 years, education combined with state safety belt laws increased the usage rate to 61%. In the last 15 years, high-visibility enforcement campaigns, combined with more and better belt laws, have increased the usage rate to 84%.[48]

For you, the managers, I want to repeat that if you don't act, the insurance companies and lawyers will "help" you as well as your company! Coca-Cola paid $21 million because an employee caused an accident while discussing business on the phone... hands-free![49] I hope Thomas J. Henry, one of the plaintiff's attorneys, sends the necessary shivers down your spine to spur you to action: "From the time I took the Coca-Cola driver's testimony and obtained the company's inadequate cell phone driving policy, I knew we had a corporate giant with a huge safety problem on our hands"[50].

Hence, the major influence will probably come from lawyers and courts. More and more lawyers are suing and winning cases against drivers who caused accidents while using their phones, especially in Anglo-Saxon countries with their extremely high compensation verdicts. As a result, insurance companies started significantly reducing the insurance premium for drivers who install phone-blocking hardware and increasing the premium significantly whenever a driver causes an accident while being on the phone. They also lower the premium of companies who have a "no phone while driving" policy. The Nationwide insurance company has said that its customers who sign up for the call-blocking service from Aegis Mobility would be eligible for a discount of around 5% off their annual premium.

In any case, if as a company you are serious about the safety of your employees, you should not wait for the government but do it yourself. You can start with recommendations for your employees, or you can even set and enforce rules (as Shell and more and more other companies do).

Maybe ICT can help you to protect your workers. Sam Grobert[51] wrote about software like iZup, Cellcontrol and Aegis Mobility, similar to the apps individuals can use, that allow companies to place restrictions on phones based on the phone's GPS signal, data from the car itself or from nearby cellphone towers. Any incoming calls are then routed to voicemail or a message explaining that the phone's owner is driving. Exceptions can be made for certain numbers. Passengers in cars can override such systems, but in many cases doing so automatically sends an e-mail message to the account administrator alerting them that the cellphone is being used while driving. Community Coffee, a coffee roaster and distributor based in Baton Rouge, Louisiana, has had such a ban on its 400 trucks. It uses ObEdge from Cellcontrol, which the company says has helped reduce its accident rate by 30%.

4.5 CHAINBREAKER 5: DRASTICALLY ELIMINATE ICT FROM MEETINGS AND ELIMINATE BACK-TO-BACK MEETINGS

For meetings the solution is very simple. If people's presence is necessary, then they should not be half-present with their fractured attention and the use of ICT should be forbidden. Instead of losing so much time by being half-present, they should not be invited to the meeting or only be called in for the subjects they are needed for.

Without ICT your meetings will be much more efficient, shorter and more creative. If team members are badly organized or addicted to being connected, schedule regular ICT breaks. You should have a break anyway when you move from physical to social subjects (explained in Section 1).

Start the meeting with some small talk to give the participants who ran straight from another meeting a brain-break, to oil the meeting and to make it more efficient. Do not allow participants to miss this first part of the meeting.

You should at all costs avoid going from one meeting to another without a brain-break or filling these breaks with e-mails. You will be more successful if you include your manager, the president of the meeting and the other participants or your team members in your endeavor of never planning meetings back to back. It is management's responsibility to turn this into a company policy. Why not change the shared calendar in such a way that it becomes impossible to schedule back-to-back meetings?

Here's an example from Google to illustrate the main point:

"When I was at Google, I attended lots of meetings in which others had their laptops open. It wasn't that these people didn't care about what was being said. It's just that they had lots of other things to do, and juggling several tasks at once seemed like a good idea. It wasn't.

Soon it became clear that many people were missing important stuff in meetings. They weren't paying attention to what was going on around them because their brains were otherwise occupied. So the information shared in meetings never had a chance to break into their short-term memory banks.

Fairly soon, it became clear that having laptops open in meetings was lowering productivity instead of raising it. So we declared some meetings no-laptop zones.

Of course, this created an unintended consequence. When people thought they had something more important to deal with, they simply left the meeting. While this was distracting for the others in the meeting, at least it was a more effective use of the escapees' attention." Douglas Merrill[52]

4.6 CHAINBREAKER 6: BUILD BRAINWORK-FRIENDLY OFFICES, RESOLVING THE FOCUS-CONTACT DILEMMA

Except for people doing routine work and some Millennials who do not know what sustained attention and concentration are, most employees hate open offices. If for you as a manager, their dissatisfaction is not a good reason for action, the drop in intellectual productivity should motivate you.

In an audience of a hundred professionals, mostly engineers, at a top high-tech global company, the audience's guess was that their open offices lowered their own intellectual productivity by 40% (median). For most of them the most frustrating counterproductive factor was that in the office they made more mistakes, compared to working undisturbed, which then took even more time to correct. As became evident in my research too, these very high-level professionals have to escape from their office to be really productive!!! Many do their best reflecting at home, in the car, in the train or even in a coffee shop, not by choice, but because their office is totally unfit for high-level brainwork.

What was even more surprising is that since they had been working in open offices, the spontaneous communication had decreased (!) compared with the time when they had individual offices or cubicles in the old building. The two most important reasons were that they did not want to bother their colleagues in the room when having a conversation with one of them and that they missed the privacy to discuss subjects freely.

You don't need to be a super-brain to understand that the daily loss for the company of 50% of these expensive professionals working at 60% of their potential is much higher than whatever profit was made when these open offices were built. It's just penny wise, pound foolish. In my small booklet *"Brain-Hostile Open Offices: The Fifth BrainChain"* (free at www.brainchains.org), I give a few suggestions about what you can and should do to improve the working environment to increase people's intellectual productivity and wellbeing.

4.7 CHAINBREAKER 7: MANAGE THEIR STRESS WELL

The figure beside explains at a glance how you can improve the stress-balance of your employees, summarized in six questions.

1 Are my demands realistic?
2 Do I give my employees the resources they need to realize my demands?
3 Do I provide enough practical and emotional social support for my demands to be met?
4 Are my employees able to have an influence that matters on these demands?
5 Do they have enough time to recuperate and relax?
6 Last but not least, how does my management style impact their view about this balance?

I elaborate on this in detail in my book "Stress: Friend and Foe: Managing stress at home and at work".

DO NOT OVER-DEMAND

As a manager, you can stimulate your employees, enhance their performance and in the right circumstances even over-stretch them once in a while to go beyond their usual limits. Well-defined, attainable and feasible goal-setting is a major aspect of stress-management. The workload will only become too heavy when the work is too often too much, too difficult, too dangerous, too boringly easy or too monotonous.

But workload is not just a question of objective workload. Some jobs weigh heavier than others. For example, being responsible for people has a greater impact on the stress-balance than being responsible for money or machines. Engineers, lawyers and econ-

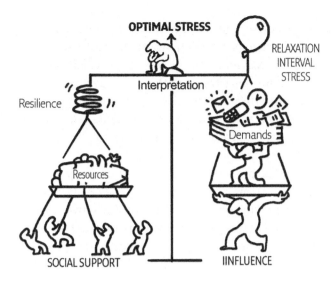

OPTIMAL STRESS

RELAXATION
INTERVAL
STRESS

Interpretation

Resilience

Demands

Resources

SOCIAL SUPPORT

IINFLUENCE

omists are trained primarily to deal with things, numbers, words and money, with 'hardware'. This is the choice they made, probably back in secondary school. In a position of management, they have to deal with other human beings, with 'peopleware' and all that entails in emotions, irrational behavior, intuition, relations and so on. They did not opt for this when they embarked on their engineering courses; they have learned little or nothing about it and have scarcely had any training in it. This responsibility will consequently weigh more heavily on their shoulders. Besides this, managers who are responsible for people experience more serious role-conflict and role-ambiguity than those who are only responsible for material affairs.

The best way to know how much workload people can carry is to regularly discuss it with them. In these conversations you should keep in mind that the workload a person can cope with depends on the five other elements of the stress-balance. Hence, it is often possible to restore the stress-balance even without diminishing the demands.

PROVIDE THE NECESSARY RESOURCES

Paul, one of the mangers in a team I coached, said: "If I've understood you well, a manager cleans the shit so that his people can do a terrific job". This one sentence cannot be improved by a long paragraph. Indeed your main responsibility is to provide your people with the company culture, the tools, the infrastructure, the finances and the people necessary to do their job very well... and get out of their way. A manager is a service-provider who provides his team and his department with what they need to do a terrific job. There are still a few dinosaurs around who think that the people are in their service, but these are dying out because brainworkers and especially the highly-skilled and creative ones don't accept this demotivating attitude any more.

If you still have one of these dinosaurs in your company, you should look after them, make pictures and movies, so that when the race has completely died out you still have a few souvenirs and a nice picture to hang in the hall to show to visitors and new employees "... and this is the last dinosaur we had in our company, who till his last day thought people were in his service instead of the other way around...".

PROVIDE AMPLE SUPPORT

There is a lot of very convincing research showing that a social context perceived as supportive has a decidedly favorable influence on the way an individual handles stress. Social support builds up resilience; its absence leads to diseases (physical ones as well) and delays recovery. An employee who feels well supported can cope with more stress than a similarly competent employee who does not have, or does not feel he has, such support. In a work situation, social support means first and foremost: support from the boss, which is YOU.

Your support is largely practical, providing the advice and resources needed to do a terrific job, but you should also provide emotional support, for example recognition, encouragement and reinforcement. Emotions are the drivers of people's intellectual productivity. Positive ones like passion and enthusiasm will enhance it, negative ones like demotivation, anxiety and fear will put the brakes on it. Like it or not, you will have to manage emotions for optimal intellectual productivity. When you are managing people, never forget that management by reinforcement and support is tens of times more efficient than management by punishment and critical comments. A 3:1 ratio of positive versus negative feedback is the minimum; 5:1 is optimal.

A major ingredient of support is giving your employees all the credit for success. Too many managers undermine the resilience of their subordinates by stealing their success and delegating the blame. If you want your employees to be highly productive, take the blame and delegate the success. Paul sums this up as: "The best-kept secret in people management is: Take the shit and delegate the success". But usually it is the other way around.

After support from the boss, support and solidarity among colleagues is a second cornerstone of productivity, so you should do what you can to improve the esprit de corps amongst your staff. Creating this collaborative, supportive environment is first and foremost your responsibility. Some managers like to play Machiavellian games with their subordinates, incite one against the other, igniting competition all the time. This may work in the (very) short term, but it will destroy trust and intellectual productivity in the long term and especially in times of stress.

To a large extent our resilience depends on the support we get from our family and friends. An employee who feels well supported at home can cope with more stress than a similarly competent employee who does not have, or does not feel he has, such support. A company making demands that harm the family relationships of its employees, for example by requiring them to be connected all the time, harms itself.

MAKE THEIR WORK CONTROLLABLE AND PREDICTABLE

Having an influence that matters is of the utmost importance in coping with stress situations. Stress easily turns into negative stress when we have the impression that we have no influence on a situation that we must cope with.

Give your people room, freedom and possibilities to have an influence that matters for them, upon you and upon their own work and immediate work environment. The first and most important step here is to LISTEN to them. If people feel really listened to, this will give them the minimum feeling of influence they need to be resilient and productive. If the boss then once in a while does what they suggest and gives them the credit for it, this will of course boost their feeling of having an influence that matters. The chief complaint I hear about from managers at all levels is: "They (above us) just don't listen to us". The powerless feeling this causes is detrimental to their productivity and wellbeing.

Managers are so often better at talking and at selling their own ideas than listening to those below them. They have hypertrophied mouths and atrophied ears. Not only did they fail to learn that the best way to convince somebody is to listen 80% and to talk 20% of the time, but they don't seem to realize how much stress this provokes and how many terrific ideas they never hear. In the hands of bad managers, e-mail has made this worse. It has become an overused megaphone to speak to, instead of speak with, people.

The second most important way to respond to this very basic need of people to have an influence that matters is not to micromanage. Micromanagement is the ideal method to ruin the intellectual productivity of professionals. Discuss what they should do and why, but as a general rule, leave it to them to decide how, unless they ask for your advice.

PROVIDE TIME FOR RELAXATION AND RECUPERATION

We are perfectly built to deal with stress, even high levels of stress, if there is frequently enough room for relaxation, for recuperation. So not only is the workload in itself important, but the possibilities for time out are just as important. Especially in companies under stress, management should take care of their workers' daily possibilities and opportunities for relaxation and recuperation: breaks, time for meals, and avoiding undermining your people's recuperation at home due to excessive overtime, travelling, evening and weekend work.

BEWARE OF THEIR EARLY WARNING SIGNALS

Stress-resistant managers in particular should beware and heed the signals of their people. The more stress-sensitive employees can serve as stress-sensors for the group. They will signal, earlier than others, that the team has passed its peak. They are as important to the team as the security bolt to a machine, the canaries to miners or as the fuse to an electrical installation. Throwing out the canaries is a recipe for disaster later.

BEWARE: YOUR LEADERSHIP STYLE INFLUENCES ALL THE ABOVE

As I explained in BrainChain #3, most of what you consider stress situations are neither good nor bad in themselves; it's your think-

STRESS IS IN THE MIND OF THE BEHOLDER

AT WORK THE MAJOR INFLUENCE IS

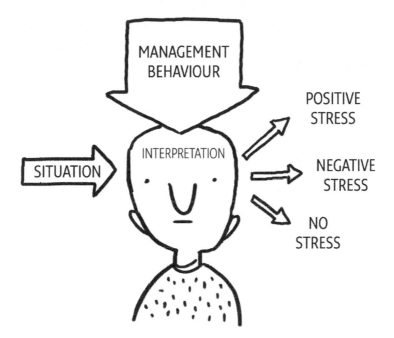

ing that makes them so. Different people can judge one and the same stress situation as irrelevant, a threat, a challenge, a danger, aggression or a pleasure. Consequently, their response to it will be different: indifference, fear, anxiety, fleeing, fighting, depression, apathy, joy, etc.

For a manager it is important to know that your leadership style has the most important impact on the way your employees appraise their work situation.

Whatever your company is or is not doing, you as a manager always have the choice of implementing good stress-management for the people you are responsible for, and you should analyze your own management style from that point of view. Your good stress-management is one of the cornerstones of their intellectual productivity and it is by far the one that is based on the most, the best research.

CONCLUSION

1 IN A NUTSHELL

To be optimally intellectually productive and creative as a professional, you should be in charge of your ICT, not the other way around. You need to counter the seduction, stickiness and addiction that the ICT companies create and increase every day to keep you eyeballing their ads and giving them your personal information all the time and everywhere. You may enjoy this process as a consumer, but as a professional you need to break the Brain-Chains that are built into their systems in order to unleash your brain potential and use ICT to enhance the abilities of your brain instead of letting them ruin your brainwork.

1.1 THE FUNDAMENTAL AND FASCINATING SCIENTIFIC FACTS ARE SIMPLE:

1 Our reflecting brain cannot multitask; it can only manage one task at a time.
2 When we try to multitask, our reflecting brain has to switch continuously
3 Each switch, even paying attention to the tiniest distraction, lowers our concentration, attention, memory... efficiency and productivity.
4 Our conscious, slow, easily tiring, fragile yet sophisticated, human reflecting brain needs to be managed well. Otherwise our unconscious, very fast, untiring, robust, primitive and bestial reflex brain will make too many wrong, important decisions.
5 Our archiving brain competes with our reflecting brain for the same "processor time" and therefore it needs ample breaks and sleep.
6 Always being connected causes a chronic unrelenting background stress.

7 Negative stress, even at a low level when it's chronic, undermines the best of our reflecting brain: abstract thinking,

logical thinking, analytical thinking, synthesis, creative thinking, empathic thinking etc. etc... It also causes local problems such as muscle and joint pain and undermines our physical abilities and health.

8 Using any kind of ICT while driving increases the risk of an accident 9 to 23 times.

9 Most open offices are brainwork-hostile and have a detrimental impact on intellectual productivity and health.

1.2 THE MOST IMPORTANT SOLUTIONS ARE JUST AS SIMPLE, ALTHOUGH SIMPLE DOES NOT MEAN EASY TO APPLY:

1 Disconnect to reflect

2 Don't multitask but right-task: eliminate as many switches as possible – that is a great many more than you think!

   A Batch-process important work as well as chores and especially when dealing with e-mails.

   B Disconnect to get the optimal performance and productivity with every batch: eliminate all possible distractions and interruptions while you work on a batch (you can do much more than you think).

3 Disconnect to have regular breaks: micro-breaks, mini-breaks, long breaks and sufficient sleep.

   A This will give your tiring reflecting brain time to recuperate and to be strong enough to rein in your untiring reflex brain.

   B It will also give your archiving brain a chance to file the billions of bits and bytes of information and to find in your long-term memory the ideas your reflecting brain needs to make good, well thought through, creative and wise decisions.

   C And it will give your whole body in general, and your joints and muscles in particular, a chance to relax and recuperate. Remember: healthy stress is interval stress.

4 Save a life, maybe your own, by NEVER using your phone or other ICT while driving.

5 Avoid doing any brainwork, except routine work, in open offices: collaborate, conspire or revolt to change them, to get rid of them or to avoid new ones being built.

2 IN THREE RULES

Once you get to the core of the matter, there are only three commandments to become much more productive:

Rule Number 1: Ruthlessly and radically reduce switches

Rule Number 2: Disconnect to reflect

Rule Number 3: Disconnect to relax

RULE 1
REDUCE TASK-SWITCHES

RULE 2
DISCONNECT TO REFLECT

RULE 3
DISCONNECT TO RELAX

3 IN A POEM

To summarize "BrainChains" in a very different way, let me conclude by paraphrasing an old English poem[1].

RECAPTURE YOUR TIME TO UNCHAIN YOUR BRAIN
Recapture time to **reflect**; it's the foundation of your
   intellectual performance and wisdom.
Recapture time to **disconnect**; it's the essential condition
   for reflection.
Recapture time to **focus**; it's the only remedy against
   shallow scatterbrained brainwork.
Recapture time to **right-task**; it's the royal road to greater
   intellectual performance.
Recapture time to **batch-process**; it's the only way to be
   intellectually productive.
Recapture time to **pause**; it's requisite for your archiving
   brain to store, recombine and find information.
Recapture time to **relax**; it's indispensable to stay healthy
   and sharp in challenging, stressful times.
Recapture time to **sleep**; it's a great source of insight,
   creativity, health and happiness.
Recapture time to **read**; it's essential, if it is thorough,
   to prepare and train your brain.
Recapture time to **have real conversations**; it's an
   opportunity to create new joint meanings and to connect
   with real people.
Recapture time to **give people undivided attention**;
   it is the greatest gift at work and at home.
Recapture time to **love and be loved**, it is the keystone of
   happiness and resilience: yours and theirs.
Recapture time to **drive without a phone**; it might save
   a body or a life, maybe your own.
Recapture time to **fight brain-hostile offices**; it's imperative
   to stop this brain-hostile trend.
Recapture time to **laugh**; it's good for your health ;-)
Recapture time to **dream**; it's what your future is made of.

AFTERWORD

- **The trigger and motivation to write this book:
  my clients and my curiosity**

The original idea for this book came from the challenges and questions of the many managers, executives and professionals in my lectures, training, coaching and consulting sessions. They complained about always having to be connected, feeling stalked by their work, the lack of time for reflection, RSI and meetings where people are more involved with ICT than with the discussion.

They asked about safety aspects of always being connected and a lot about stress. They talked about the good old days before e-mail and some bragged about how good they were at multitasking. I also observed them glued to their screens in meetings, immediately reconnecting after a course, all the time interrupting conversations to react to their phones, and using their smartphones at concerts, at dinner parties, on vacation at the beach, even in the toilet.

When I was coaching them their use of ICT was an obstacle to personal development, establishing a better life balance and efficient stress management. I observed how the ICT in their pocket or handbag constantly pulled executives down to an operational level and prevented them from thinking and acting at the strategic level that was their principal responsibility.

At one point I started to worry that they were unknowingly ruining their intellectual productivity by the way they were using their great ICT. And as I mentioned in the book, I was also baffled by how my own first smartphone briefly ruined my own brainwork.

Then a telecoms company asked me to do a keynote speech for their most important clients. When they asked me to talk about my core specialty, "Stress", I responded with a challenge and said, "That's easy and I would love to do it, but would you, who sell 'connectedness', dare to let me give a keynote about the disadvantages of always being connected?". The reaction of the B2B manager was: "Whoa... I'll have to check with the CEO". I'm happy to say that the CEO came back with a yes and I started to delve into the research about the subject to prepare for the presentation. I quickly discovered that my hunch was correct, and in fact that the situation was even worse than I thought and the area better researched than I had expected. The presentation was a success, I am still working with this company and in the process I became utterly hooked by the subject and ended up scanning and reading about 600 scientific publications and writing this book.

I should perhaps note that I didn't originally set out to write such a long book. Initially I summarized the practical advice for my coaching and teaching sessions in a handout of a few pages. I then discovered that this advice often went nowhere because managers and other professionals have no clue about how their most important tool, their brain, works and so they didn't understand the reasoning behind my advice. So I added a few pages to explain some basic knowledge about the brain on which my advice was based. I also added the subject to my talks, teaching and training about stress management, and I discovered that the story hit the bull's-eye. The interest as well as the appreciation was awesome.

Since so many participants wanted to read more about the subject I looked for books to recommend, but couldn't find what I wanted. I therefore decided to postpone writing the book I had already started on, "Corporate Brain Disorder", in order to write this one first.

· **The core idea: how to better use ICT by taking into account the strenghts and weaknesses of our brain**

The crux of the problem is not our great ICT tools, but the way we use them. We don't use them as professional creators and processors of information but as mere consumers.

Hearing and observing how professionals use their ICT, I

realized that professionals were falling into a trap made by technological companies that spend billions on the design of software to seduce billions of customers *to consume information*. They invent *gadgets and apps* to keep the users glued to their screens, connected all the time and everywhere, continuously eyeballing ads and giving away as much personal information as possible.

Your job as a professional, however, is not to consume, but *to create and process information, knowledge and insights* for your company and your own development.

The first and most important tool to do this is your brain. Therefore, you should know the basic manual for your brain and especially your reflecting brain. The second most important tool is having real conversations. The third tool is ICT. However, if you use the very sticky and addictive ICT, which have been developed to consume information, in order to produce professional information, then you are like Linus, of the Peanuts cartoons, who thinks he can play Beethoven on a toy piano.

It was a dilemma for Microsoft and one that they dealt with by adapting Windows to the needs of billions of swiping gadget consumers, while frustrating millions of professionals who need the equivalent of a Steinway piano to process information at a truly professional level, without distractions. Professionals need software developed for them – large screens, good keyboards, mice and good ergonomics – so that they can do their knowledge work for many hours a day, ideally in a brain-friendly office, without ruining their neck, thumbs, wrists, shoulders and back.

Halfway through writing this book, I became so upset by the research I was discovering that my working title became "How we unknowingly f*** up our intellectual productivity by always being connected and multitasking".

Let me be painfully transparent and share a personal anecdote. After a long trip to China for work and pleasure, I fell back into the trap of multitasking myself! What's more, it took a whole month before I pulled myself together again (!). This was a forceful reminder of the power of these BrainChains. Once I returned to batch-processing, I once again became much more efficient, my backlog quickly disappeared, I experienced less stress, I was more creative, I went deeper into the articles I screened and read, I regularly got into the "flow" forgetting time and everything around me while I was working, my file with notes of things to do "when I have time" became bigger and bigger and in the end I just threw it away, I had more time for my family, I had more fun and joy...

- **My challenge: scientifically grounded while simple and useful**

In writing this book I was confronted with two dilemmas. The first was that I wanted to write a book that is very easy to read and understand AND at the same time is based on lots of good peer-reviewed scholarly research. The second was to stimulate you to truly understand the basic knowledge about your brain and the BrainChains before doing anything AND at the same time to inspire you with the practical solutions that other people have already found so that you can further learn by doing.

I ended up screening more than 600 scientific publications and studying more than 400. I have the advantage that I am a medical doctor, a neuropsychiatrist and a psychotherapist and that I spent the greater part of my career in universities. This allows me to understand and evaluate a wide range of articles on subjects including medicine, neurology, biology, physiology and psychology. I am very grateful to the TIASNIMBAS business school for allowing me to keep using their electronic library so that I had instant access to the full-text articles.

My next task was to translate all the scientific jargon into terms that are easy to understand for lay people. Doing my homework, I often burned the midnight oil to do what Steve Jobs describes so beautifully, and which is why I quote him again: "If you read Apple's first brochure, the headline was 'Simplicity is the Ultimate Sophistication.' What we meant by that was that when you first attack a problem it seems really simple because you don't understand it. Then when you start to really understand it, you come up with these very complicated solutions because it's really hairy. Most people stop there. But a few people keep burning the midnight oil and finally understand the underlying principles of the problem and come up with an elegantly simple solution for it. But very few people go the distance to get there".

I burned the midnight oil to study all the research and then I burned the midnight oil again to turn this knowledge into an easy text. This was not a chore for me because curiosity and making science simple and useful in order to pass it on to others are two of my main professional drivers.

I already knew from my other books that writing a simple text that everybody can easily understand needs more work than writing a scholarly text full of jargon: easy reading is hard writing. To reach this goal in a non-native language I asked Anna Jenkinson, a writer, editor and native English speaker, to turn my simple English into simple real English. After reading the book I'm sure you'll agree that she did an excellent job.

This goal of simplicity and readability led to a compromise for the layout of the notes. To write this book I stand on the shoulders of so many bright and creative colleagues. I wanted to mention the names of all the researchers who invested so much knowledge, creativity, time and energy in their research. Putting their names in the text or in footnotes, however, meant that the text was no longer easy-to-read because there are simply too many. It also turned out to be impossible for an eBook. I therefore put their work in endnotes, even though this makes the layout, with all the little endnote numbers, less clean than I ideally would have liked. To make the long list of articles easily searchable and available for everybody, I have put it on the Internet at www.brainchains.org.

The second challenge was to let you understand your brain so well that you can find and develop your own creative solutions. In a way I would have preferred not to include a section with practical solutions at all, to let you invent your own based on the knowledge you have gained. On the other hand we can also learn a lot by doing, following very practical tips or learning from the tools and tricks used by other people.

My solution was to divide the book into three parts. The first section explains how our thinking brain works and why we should protect our reflecting brain. In the second section, "BrainChains", I explain how we unknowingly chain our brain. I clarify the "what" and "why" and invite you to think about "how" you can apply the ideas in your situation. In the third section "How to unchain your brain" I describe lots of practical tips and tricks that have helped other people before, not necessarily for you to copy, but to inspire you to find your own creative custom-made solutions.

Please share your own solutions and challenges at the forum on www.brainchains.org.

- **Why a free booklet on the Fifth BrainChain:**
  Brain-Hostile Open Offices?

Every single time I dealt with the subject of intellectual productivity in workshops or lectures, except when they were executives, a group of participants complained that one of the major factors undermining their brainwork was the badly designed open offices they have to work in.

This stimulated me to delve into the research on open offices. The results more than support their complaints: Most offices are totally unfit for brainwork because they make reflection very stressful and, perplexingly, often even impossible.

The goal of this book, however, is to address issues that you can change yourself or in collaboration with others. For most people, doing something about a badly designed office is not within their control. There is not much they can do about it unless they get together and revolt or demand changes.

The complaints as well as the research, however, were so convincing that I felt I could not leave it out completely. I therefore only make a brief reference to it in this book and instead turned the chapter into a separate free booklet "The Fifth BrainChain", available to download for free at www.brainchains.org. You can use it to fight for improvements or disseminate it more subversively to make others aware of the problem. It has no copyright; you just need to acknowledge the source as "Brain Hostile Offices. The Fifth BrainChain that ruins your intellectual productivity". Theo Compernolle. www.brainchains.org.

- **Warning. The next challenge is yours: simple is not**
  necessarily easy.

Easy to read and easy to understand does not mean easy to apply. Very simple advice can be very difficult to apply. However, if you do follow through, increased efficiency and effectiveness are guaranteed and if you stop using ICT while driving, it might save a life, maybe your own.

If you have any questions, suggestions, ideas, experiences, tips or best practices for the next edition of this book, please let me know at www.BrainChains.org or theo@BrainChains.org

I wish you every success in increasing your efficiency and, as a result, experiencing more joy at work and at home.

Good luck!

Theo Compernolle

REFERENCES

PREFACE

1   Arthur Schopenhauer: On Noise.
1851. translation by T. Bailey Saunders.
http://www.noisehelp.com/schopen-
hauer-quotes.html see also ttp://www.
schopenhauervereinigung.com/articles/
arthur-schopenhauer-on-noise/
2   The Brain's Last Stand. Stephen
Levvy. May 1997, Newsweek. http://
www.academicchess.org/Focus/Deep-
Blue/newsbrain.shtml
3   The Chess Master and the Computer. Garry Kasparov. The New York
Review of Books. February 11, 2010.
http://www.nybooks.com/articles/
archives/2010/feb/11/the-chess-master-
and-the-computer/
4   The Chess Master and the Computer. Garry Kasparov. The New York
Review of Books. February 11, 2010.
http://www.nybooks.com/articles/
archives/2010/feb/11/the-chess-master-
and-the-computer/

SECTION 1

1   http://www.gse.upenn.edu/press-
room/press-releases/2013/12/penn-gse-
study-shows-moocs-have-relatively-
few-active-users-only-few-persisti
2   "After Setbacks, Online Courses Are
Rethought". Tamar Lewin. New York
Times. December 10, 2013
3   "Over bevlogen, enthousiasmerend
en inspirerend onderwijs" (About pas-
sionate, enthusing and inspiring teaching). Theo Compernolle in "Van jonge

mensen, de dingen die gaan en komen"
Theo Doreleijers. 2013. Uitg. Vrije Universiteit Amsterdam.
4   Targeting Glia Cells: Novel Perspectives for the Treatment of Neuro-psychi-
atric Diseases. B. Di Benedetto and
R. Rupprecht; Current Neuropharmacology, 2013, 11, 2
5   Nonlinear dendritic integration of
sensory and motor input during an
active sensing task. Ning-long Xu, Mark
T. Harnett, Stephen R. Williams, Daniel
Huber, Daniel H. O'Connor, Karel Svo-
boda& Jeffrey C. Magee; Nature 492,
247-251 (13 December 2012)
Dendrites. Yuh-Nung Jan and Lily Yeh
Jan. Genes & Dev. 2001. 15: 2627-2641
DENDRITIC COMPUTATION. Michael
London and Michael Häusser. Annual
Review of Neuroscience. Vol. 28: 503-
532
Active dendrites: colorful wings of the
mysterious butterflies, Daniel Johnston,
Rishikesh Narayanan, Trends in Neuro-
sciences, Volume 31, Issue 6, June 2008,
pp. 309-316
Dendritic spikes enhance stimulus
selectivity in cortical neurons in vivo.
Spencer L. Smith, Ikuko T. Smith, Tiago
Branco & Michael Häusser. Nature.
Letter 27 October 2013
Orientation and Direction Selectivity
of Synaptic Inputs in Visual Cortical
Neurons: A Diversity of Combinations
Produces Spike Tuning, Cyril Monier,
Frédéric Chavane, Pierre Baudot, Lyle J
Graham, Yves Frégnac, Neuron, Volume

37, Issue 4, 20 February 2003, pp. 663-680
Wave Propagation Along Spiny Dendrites. Paul C. BressloffWaves. Neural Media. Lecture Notes on Mathematical Modelling in the Life Sciences 2014, pp. 101-136

6 Machine, heal thyself, Build yourself a brain, Paul Marks,New Scientist. February 16, 2013

7 Paul Marks, Computer that heals itself uses nature's randomness to work, New Scientist, Volume 217, Issue 2904, 16 February 2013, p. 21,

8 SpiNNaker: A 1-W 18-Core System-on-Chip for Massively-Parallel Neural Network Simulation. S.B. Painkras, E.; Plana, L.A.; Garside, J.; Temple, S.; Galluppi, F.; Patterson, C.; Lester, D.R.; Brown, A.D.; Furber, Solid-State Circuits, IEEE Journal of, Issue Date: Aug. 2013, http://ieeexplore.ieee.org/xpls/icp.jsp?arnumber=6515159
Power analysis of large-scale, real-time neural networks on SpiNNaker. Evangelos Stromatias, Francesco Galluppi, Cameron Patterson and Steve Furber. 2013. neuromorphs.net . https://www.neuromorphs.net/nm/raw-attachment/wiki/2013/uns13/Power_analysis_of_large_scale_real_time_neural_networks_on_SpiNNaker.pdf
Improving the Interconnection Network of a Brain Simulator. Jonathan Heathcote. 2013 http://jhnet.co.uk/misc/phdFirstYearReport.pdf
SpiNNaker: A 1-W 18-Core System-on-Chip for Massively-Parallel Neural Network Simulation. Painkras, E.; Plana, L.A.; Garside, J.; Temple, S.; Galluppi, F.; Patterson, C.; Lester, D.R.; Brown, A.D.; Furber, S.B. Solid-State Circuits, IEEE Journal of, Issue Date: Aug. 2013

9 Large-scale brain networks in affective and social neuroscience: towards an integrative functional architecture of the brain, Lisa Feldman Barrett, Ajay Bhaskar Satpute, Current Opinion in Neurobiology, Volume 23, Issue 3, June 2013, pp. 361-372
A functional architecture of the human brain: emerging insights from the science of emotion. K.A. Lindquist,

T.D. Wager, H. Kober, E. Bliss-Moreau, L.F. Barrett. Trends in Cognitive Sciences, November 2012, Vol. 16, No. 11 533
Clarify Brain Affective Processing Without Necessarily Clarifying Emotions. Peter Walla and Jaak Panksepp. Novel Frontiers of Advanced Neuroimaging 2013. Chapter 6

10 Dynamics of Hippocampal Neurogenesis in Adult Humans, Kirsty L. Spalding, Olaf Bergmann, Kanar Alkass, Samuel Bernard, Mehran Salehpour, Hagen B. Huttner, Emil Boström, Isabelle Westerlund, Céline Vial, Bruce A. Buchholz, Göran Possnert, Deborah C. Mash, Henrik Druid, Jonas Frisén, Cell, Volume 153, Issue 6, 6 June 2013, pp. 1219-1227

11 For a great review of the state of affairs of this techology and its discoveries, have a look at the recent volume 80, Neuroimage 15 October 2013. "Mapping the Connectome"
Introduction to the NeuroImage Special Issue "Mapping the Connectome", Steve Smith, NeuroImage, Volume 80, 15 October 2013, p. 1,
Functional interactions between intrinsic brain activity and behavior, Sepideh Sadaghiani, Andreas Kleinschmidt, NeuroImage, Volume 80, 15 October 2013, pp. 379-386
What we can and cannot tell about the wiring of the human brain, Richard E. Passingham, NeuroImage, Volume 80, 15 October 2013, pp. 14-17,
Function in the human connectome: Task-fMRI and individual differences in behavior, Deanna M. Barch, and many others, NeuroImage, Volume 80, 15 October 2013, pp. 169-189,
Dynamic functional connectivity: Promise, issues, and interpretations, Deanna M. Barch, and many others, NeuroImage, Volume 80, 15 October 2013, pp. 360-378,

12 For an excellent review: Dual-Processing Accounts of Reasoning, Judgment, and Social Cognition. Jonathan St. B. T. Evans. Annual Review of Psychology. 2007/2008 Vol. 59: 255-278
An evaluation of dual-process theories of reasoning. MAGDA OSMAN. Psycho-

nomic Bulletin & Review. Volume 11, Number 6 (2004), 988-1010 2004. https://qmro.qmul.ac.uk/xmlui/bitstream/handle/123456789/151/Evaluation%20of%20dual%20process%20theories.pdf?sequence=8 Explaining modulation of reasoning by belief. Goel, V. and Dolan, R.J. (2003) Cognition 87, B11–B22

13   Stress: Vriend en Vijand. T. Compernolle Uitgeverij Lannoo Belgium. 2012. 14th edition.
Stress: Friend and Foe. New 4th totally updated edition planned for the beginning of 2015. A few copies left at www.brainchains.com

14   Control of goal-directed and stimulus driven attention in the brain. Corbetta, M , & Shulman, G. L. (2002). Nature Reviews Neuroscience, 3, 201–215.

15   Thinking fast and slow. Daniel Kahneman. Penguin Books. 2012

16   Ramscar, M., Hendrix, P., Shaoul, C., Milin, P., & Baayen, H. (2014). The Myth of Cognitive Decline: Non-Linear Dynamics of Lifelong Learning. Topics in cognitive science.

17   The human brain is intrinsically organized into dynamic, anticorrelated functional networks. Fox MD, Snyder AZ, Vincent JL, Corbetta M, Van Essen DC, Raichle ME. Proc Natl Acad Sci U S A. 2005 Jul 5; 102(27):9673-8.
Functional connectivity in the resting brain: a network analysis of the default mode hypothesis. Greicius MD, Krasnow B, Reiss AL, Menon V. Proc Natl Acad Sci U S A. 2003 Jan 7; 100(1):253-8. Default network connectivity during a working memory task. Bluhm RL, Clark CR, McFarlane AC, Moores KA, Shaw ME, Lanius RA. Hum Brain Mapp. 2011 Jul; 32(7):1029-35. Epub 2010 Jul 20.

18   Individual Differences and the Belief Bias Effect: Mental Models, Logical Necessity, and Abstract Reasoning. Donna Torrens. Thinking & Reasoning. Volume 5, Issue 1, 1999. pp. 1-28
More evidence for a dual-process model of conditional reasoning. Henry Markovits, Hugues Lortie Forgues and Marie-Laurence Brunet. MEMORY & COGNI-TION. Volume 40, Number 5 (2012), 736-747

19   General intellectual ability. Mithen, Steven. In Steven W. Gangestad & Jeffrey A. Simpson (eds.), The Evolution of Mind: Fundamental Questions and Controversies. 2006a. pp. 319-324. New York: The Guilford Press.

20   Divided Representation of Concurrent Goals in the Human Frontal Lobes. Sylvain Charron, Etienne Koechlin. Science 16 April 2010:Vol. 328 no. 5976 pp. 360-363
http://www.sciencemag.org/content/328/5976/360/F3.expansion.html

21   Control of Attention Shifts between Vision and Audition in Human Cortex. Sarah Shomstein and Steven Yantis. The Journal of Neuroscience, November 24, 2004 • 24(47):10702–10706

22   Visual attention is a single, integrated resource. Alexander Pastukhov . Laura Fischer,Jochen Braun. Vision. Research. Volume 49, Issue 10, 2 June 2009, pp. 1166–1173

23   Divided Representation of Concurrent Goals in the Human Frontal Lobes. Sylvain Charron, Etienne Koechlin. Science 16 April 2010: Vol. 328 no. 5976 pp. 360-363
http://www.sciencemag.org/content/328/5976/360/F3.expansion.html
Is dual-task slowing instruction dependent? By Levy, Jonathan; Pashler, Harold. Journal of Experimental Psychology: Human Perception and Performance, Vol 27(4), Aug 2001, 862-869.

24   Rene Marois, a neuroscientist at Vanderbilt University. Quoted in http://www.npr.org/templates/story/story.php?storyId=126018694

25   Understanding email interaction increases organizational productivity. T Jackson. Ray Dawson. Darren Wilson. Communications of the ACM - Program compaction CACM Volume 46 Issue 8, August 2003. pp. 80-84 . http://citeseerx.ist.psu.edu/viewdoc/download?doi=10.1.1.5.8860&rep=rep1&type=pdf

26   eg Rogers and Monsell 1995, Rubinstein and co 2001

27   A computational theory of executive cognitive processes and multiple-task

performance: Part i. Basic mechanisms. Meyer, David E.; Kieras, David E. Psychological Review, Vol 104(1), Jan 1997, 3-65.

28 Juggling on a high wire: Multitasking effects on performance. Rachel F. Adlera,Raquel Benbunan-Fich. International Journal of Human-Computer Studies. Volume 70, Issue 2, February 2012, pp. 156–168

Investigating the effects of computer mediated interruptions: An analysis of task characteristics and interruption frequency on financial performance. K. Asli Basoglu, Mark A. Fuller,John T. Sweeney. International Journal of Accounting Information Systems. Volume 10, Issue 4, December 2009, pp. 177–189

29 Executive Control of Cognitive Processes in Task Switching. Rubinstein, J. S., Meyer, D. E. & Evans, J. E. (2001). Journal of Experimental Psychology: Human Perception and Performance, 27, 763-797.Task switching and the measurement of "switch costs". Glenn Wylie, Alan Allport. Psychological Research. August 2000, Volume 63, Issue 3-4, pp. 212-233

An integrated model of cognitive control in task switching. Altmann, Erik M.; Gray, Wayne D. Psychological Review, Vol 115(3), Jul 2008, 602-639

The cost of a voluntary task switch, CM Arrington, G Logan, Psychological Science September 2004 vol. 15 no. 9 610-615

The role of inner speech in task switching: A dual-task investigation. MJ Emerson, Akira Miyake, Journal of Memory and Language, 2003. 48(1):148

The effects of attentional load on saccadic task switching, Jason L. Chan, Joseph F. X. DeSouza, Experimental Brain Research, June 2013, Volume 227, Issue 3, pp. 301-309

Burnout and impaired cognitive functioning: The role of executive control in the performance of cognitive tasks, Stefan Diestela, Marlen Cosmar & Klaus-Helmut Schmidt. Work & Stress: An International Journal of Work, Health & Organisations.Volume 27, Issue 2, 2013 pp. 164-180

Self-interruptions in discretionary multitasking, Rachel F. Adler, Raquel Benbunan-Fich, Computers in Human Behavior, Volume 29, Issue 4, July 2013, pp. 1441-1449

MRI reveals reciprocal inhibition between social and physical cognitive domains, Anthony I. Jack, Abigail J. Dawson, Katelyn L. Begany, Regina L. Leckie, Kevin P. Barry, Angela H. Ciccia, Abraham Z. Snyder, NeuroImage, Volume 66, 1 February 2013, pp. 385-401

30 Voluntary Task Switching: Chasing the Elusive Homunculus. Arrington, Catherine M.; Logan, Gordon D. Journal of Experimental Psychology: Learning, Memory, and Cognition, Vol 31(4), Jul 2005, 683-702.

31 Understanding email interaction increases organizational productivity. T Jackson. Ray Dawson. Darren Wilson. Communications of the ACM - Program compaction CACM Volume 46 Issue 8, August 2003. pp. 80-84 . http://citeseerx.ist.psu.edu/viewdoc/download?doi=10.1.1.5.8860&rep=rep1&type=pdf

32 Allport, Styles, & Hsieh, 1994; Meiran, 1996; Rogers & Monsell, 1995 Juggling on a high wire: Multitasking effects on performance. Rachel F. Adlera,Raquel Benbunan-Fich. International Journal of Human-Computer Studies. Volume 70, Issue 2, February 2012, pp. 156-168

33 Florian Waszak, Bernhard Hommel, Alan Allport, Task-switching and long-term priming: Role of episodic stimulus-task bindings in task-shift costs, Cognitive Psychology, Volume 46, Issue 4, June 2003, pp. 361-413, Task switching, Trends in Cognitive Sciences, Stephen Monsell, Volume 7, Issue 3, March 2003, pp. 134-140, http://matt.colorado.edu/teaching/highcog/fall8/m3.pdf

34 Task-switching: Positive and negative priming of task-set. Allport, Alan; Wylie, Glenn Humphreys, Glyn W. (Ed); Duncan, John (Ed); Treisman, Anne (Ed), (1999). Attention, space, and action: Studies in cognitive neuroscience, pp. 273-296.

Task-Set Inertia, Attitude Accessibility,

and Compatibility-Order Effects: New Evidence for a Task-Set Switching Account of the Implicit Association Test Effect. Karl Christoph KlauerPers Soc Psychol Bull February 2005 vol. 31 no. 2 208-217

Inhibition, interference, and conflict in task switching, Russell E. Costa, Frances J. Friedrich, Psychonomic Bulletin & Review, December 2012, Volume 19, Issue 6, pp. 1193-1201

Neural substrates of cognitive switching and inhibition in a face processing task, Camille Piguet, Virginie Sterpenich, Martin Desseilles, Yann Cojan, Gilles Bertschy, Patrik Vuilleumier, NeuroImage, Volume 82, 15 November 2013, pp. 489-499

The role of inhibition in task switching: A review. Iring Koch, Miriam Gade, Stefanie Schuch, Andrea M. Philipp, Psychonomic Bulletin & Review, February 2010, Volume 17, Issue 1, pp. 1-14. http://download.springer.com/static/pdf/871/art%253A10.3758%252FPBR.17.1.1.pdf?auth66=1382011321_165db4d3f17d4383dce8638d6be473c5&ext=.pdf

35 Concurrent task effects on memory retrieval. Doug Rohrer, Harold E. Pashler. Psychonomic Bulletin & Review. March 2003, Volume 10, Issue 1, pp. 96-103

36 Divided Representation of Concurrent Goals in the Human Frontal Lobes. Sylvain Charron,Etienne Koechlin. Science 16 April 2010:Vol. 328 no. 5976 pp. 360-363

37 Mayr, U. & Kliegl, R. (2000); Oulasvirta, A and Saariluoma, P. The laptop and the lecture: The effects of multitasking in learning environments. Helene Hembrooke and Geri Gay.Journal of Computing in Higher Education. Volume 15, Number 1. 2003

38 Strategic modulation of response inhibition in task-switching. Kai Robin Grzyb and Ronald Hübner. Front Psychol. 2013; 4: 545. http://www.ncbi.nlm.nih.gov/pmc/articles/PMC3749430/

The effects of attentional load on saccadic task switching. Jason L. Chan, Joseph F. X. DeSouza. Experimental Brain Research. June 2013, Volume 227, Issue 3, pp. 301-309

The effects of attentional load on saccadic task switching. Jason L. Chan, Joseph F. X. DeSouza. Experimental Brain Research. June 2013, Volume 227, Issue 3, pp. 301-309

39 Modulation of competing memory systems by distraction. Karin Foerde, Barbara J. Knowlton, and Russell A. Poldrack. PNAS . PNAS August 1, 2006 vol. 103 no. 31 11778-11783

40 Enhanced Media Multitasking: The restorative cognitive effects of temporarily escaping the multitasking mindset. Jordan McCarthy. Thesis submission for the degree of master of arts in Communication. Stanford University. June 7, 2013 http://comm.stanford.edu/wp-content/uploads/2013/01/JordanMcCarthyMAThesis.pdf

41 fMRI reveals reciprocal inhibition between social and physical cognitive domains, Anthony I. Jack, Abigail J. Dawson, Katelyn L. Begany, Regina L. Leckie, Kevin P. Barry, Angela H. Ciccia, Abraham Z. Snyder, NeuroImage, Volume 66, 1 February 2013, pp. 385-401

42 Are women better than men at multi-tasking? Gijsbert Stoet, Daryl B O'Connor, Mark Conner, Keith R Laws. BMC Psychology. October 2013, 1:18

Gender differences in multitasking reflect spatial ability. Mäntylä, T (2013). Psychological Science, 24, 514-520.

Multitasking. Buser, T, & Peter, N (2012). Experimental Economics, 15, 641-655.

Revisiting the gender gap in time-use patterns: multitasking and wellbeing among mothers and fathers in dual-earner families. Offer S, & Schneider, B (2011). American Sociological Review, 76(6), 809-833.

A deeper look at gender difference in multitasking: gender-specific mechanism of cognitive control. In Fifth international conference on natural computation (pp. 13-17). Washington: IEEE Computer Society.

Gender differences in the relationship between long employment hours and multitasking. Sayer, LC (2007). In BA

Rubin (Ed.), Workplace Temporalities (Research in the Sociology of Work) (pp. 403–435). Amsterdam: Elsevier. Task switching: interplay of reconfiguration and interference control. Vandierendonck, A, Liefooghe, B, Verbruggen F (2010). Psychological Bulletin, 136(4), 601–626.

43 Who Multi-Tasks and Why? Multi-Tasking Ability, Perceived Multi-Tasking Ability, Impulsivity, and Sensation Seeking. Sanbonmatsu DM, Strayer DL, Medeiros-Ward N, Watson JM (2013) PLoS ONE 8(1): e54402.

44 Cognitive control in media multitaskers. Eyal Ophir, Clifford Nass, Anthony D. Wagner. PNAS September 15, 2009 vol. 106 no. 37 15583-15587 Interview Clifford Nass. PBS Frontline. http://www.pbs.org/wgbh/pages/frontline/digitalnation/interviews/nass.html
Who Multi-Tasks and Why? Multi-Tasking Ability, Perceived Multi-Tasking Ability, Impulsivity, and Sensation Seeking. Sanbonmatsu DM, Strayer DL, Medeiros-Ward N, Watson JM (2013) PLoS ONE 8(1): e54402.

45 Interview Clifford Nass. PBS Frontline. http://www.pbs.org/wgbh/pages/frontline/digitalnation/interviews/nass.html

46 http://news.stanford.edu/news/2009/august24/multitask-research-study-082409.html

47 Supertaskers: Profiles in extraordinary multitasking ability. Jason M. Watson and David L. Strayer. Psychonomic Bulletin & Review. 2010, 17 (4), 479-485

48 Distracted driving in elderly and middle-aged drivers. Kelsey R. Thompson et al. Accident Analysis & Prevention. Volume 45, March 2012, pp. 711–717

49 Aging and dual-task performance: A meta-analysis.Verhaeghen, Paul; Steitz, David W.; Sliwinski, Martin J.; Cerella, John. Psychology and Aging, Vol 18(3), Sep 2003, 443-460.
Distracted driving in elderly and middle-aged drivers. Kelsey R. Thompson et al. Accident Analysis & Prevention. Volume 45, March 2012, pp. 711–717

Deficit in switching between functional brain networks underlies the impact of multitasking on working memory in older adults. Wesley C. Clapp, Michael T. Rubens,Jasdeep Sabharwal, and Adam Gazzaley. PNAS April 26, 2011 vol. 108. http://www.pnas.org/content/108/17/7212.full.pdf+html
Training effects on dual-task performance: Are there age-related differences in plasticity of attentional control? Bherer, Louis; Kramer, Arthur F.; Peterson, Matthew S.; Colcombe, Stanley; Erickson, Kirk; Becic, Ensar. Psychology and Aging, Vol 20(4), Dec 2005, 695-709. http://www.brams.umontreal.ca/cours/files/PSY-6022A2006/LBherer/Lectures/Bherer%20et%20al_2005.pdf

50 Interview BDW 11 April 2013 p. 6

51 Terry Judd, Making sense of multitasking: The role of Facebook, Computers & Education, Volume 70, January 2014, pp. 194-202

52 GENERATION M2. Media in the Lives of 8- to 18-Year-Olds. Victoria J. Rideout, M.A.Ulla G. Foehr, Ph.D.and Donald F. Roberts, Ph.D.A Kaiser Family Foundation Study. JANUARY 2010. http://myweb.wwu.edu/karlberg/444/readings/GenM2.pdf
See also: Teens and mobile phones. Lenhart, A., Ling, R., Campbell, S., & Purcell, K. (2010). Washington, DC: Pew Internet and American Life Project. http://pewinternet.org/Reports/2010/Teens-and-Mobile-Phones.aspx

53 BMRB International (British Market Research Bureaux). (2004) 'Increasing Screen Time [quoted in DOES NOT COMPUTE. Screen Technology in Early Years Education. Aric Sigman. Original not found]
is Leading to Inactivity of 11-15s'. Youth TGI Study.

54 An Empirical Examination of the Educational Impact of Text Message-Induced Task Switching in the Classroom: Educational Implications and Strategies to Enhance LearningIn addition. Larry D. Rosen, Alex F. Lim, L. Mark Carrier, and Nancy A. Cheever. Psicología Educativa. Vol. 17, n.º 2, 2011 - pp. 163-177

55 http://www.oivo.be Denise Van den Broeck 2010
56 Getting plugged in: An overview of Internet addiction. Caroline Flisher. Journal of Paediatrics and Child Health. Volume 46, Issue 10, pp. 557-559, October 2010
57 The choice to text and drive in younger drivers: Behavior may shape attitude. Paul Atchley, Stephanie Atwood,Aaron Boulton. Accident Analysis & Prevention. Volume 43, Issue 1, January 2011, pp. 134-142
58 College students' prevalence and perceptions of text messaging while driving. Marissa A. Harrison. Accident Analysis & Prevention. Volume 43, Issue 4, July 2011, pp. 1516-1520
59 Adriana Bianchi and Dr. James G. Phillips. CyberPsychology & Behavior. February 2005, 8(1): 39-51.
60 Digital natives. Sue Bennett. 2012 University of Wollongong Bennett, S. (2012). Digital natives. In Z. Yan (Eds.), Encyclopedia of Cyber Behavior. Volume 1 (pp. 212-219). United States. IGI Global.
Digital natives: where is the evidence? Helsper, Ellen Johanna, Eynon, Rebecca. British Educational Research Journal. Jun2010, Vol. 36 Issue 3, pp. 503-520
The 'digital natives' debate: A critical review of the evidence. S Bennett. British journal of educational technology : the journal of the National Council for Educational Technology 2008. 0007-1013. 39(5):775
Digital natives: where is the evidence? Helsper, Ellen Johanna, Eynon, Rebecca. British Educational Research Journal. Jun2010, Vol. 36 Issue 3, pp. 503-520
61 Getting plugged in: An overview of Internet addiction. Caroline Flisher. Journal of Paediatrics and Child Health. Volume 46, Issue 10, pp. 557-559, October 2010
62 The effect of multitasking on the grade performance of business students. Y Ellis. Research in Higher Education Journal. 2010. 1941-3432. 8:1
No A 4 U:the relationship between multitasking and academic performance, Computers & Education, Reynol Junco, Shelia R. Cotten, No A 4 U: TVolume 59, Issue 2, September 2012, pp. 505-514,
Facebook and texting made me do it: Media-induced task-switching while studying, Larry D. Rosen, L. Mark Carrier, Nancy A. Cheever, Computers in Human Behavior, Volume 29, Issue 3, May 2013, pp. 948-958,
In-class multitasking and academic performance, Reynol Junco, Computers in Human Behavior, Volume 28, Issue 6, November 2012, pp. 2236-2243
Female College Students' Media Use and Academic Outcomes. Results From a Longitudinal Cohort Study. Jennifer L. Walsh. Robyn L. Fielder. Kate B. Carey. Michael P. Carey. Emerging Adulthood March 26, 2013
No A 4 U: The relationship between multitasking and academic performance. Reynol Juncoa, Shelia R. Cotten. Computers & Education. Volume 59, Issue 2, September 2012, pp. 505-514
The Wired Generation: Academic and Social Outcomes of Electronic Media Use Among University Students. Wade C. Jacobsen, B.S., and Renata Forste, Ph.D. CYBERPSYCHOLOGY, BEHAVIOR, AND SOCIAL NETWORKING. Volume 14, Number 5, 2011
Facebook and texting made me do it: Media-induced task-switching while studying, Larry D. Rosen, L. Mark Carrier, Nancy A. Cheever, Computers in Human Behavior, Volume 29, Issue 3, May 2013, pp. 948-958,
Electronic Media Use, Reading, and Academic Distractibility in College Youth. Laura E. Levine, Ph.D., Bradley M. Waite, Ph.D., And Laura L. Bowman, Ph.D. Cyberpsychology & Behavior. Volume 10, Number 4, 2007
The laptop and the lecture: The effects of multitasking in learning environments. Helene Hembrooke and Geri Gay. Journal of Computing in Higher Education. Volume 15, Number 1. 2003
In-class laptop use and its effects on student learning. Carrie B. Fried.Computers & Education. Volume 50, Issue 3, April 2008, pp. 906-914.
Facebook® and academic performance.

Paul A. Kirschner,Aryn C. Karpinski. Computers in Human Behavior. Volume 26, Issue 6, November 2010, pp. 1237-1245
Too much face and not enough books: The relationship between multiple indices of Facebook use and academic performance.Reynol Junco. Computers in Human Behavior. Volume 28, Issue 1, January 2012, pp. 187-198
Distracted: Academic Performance Differences Between Teen Users and Non-Users of MySpace and Other Communication Technology. Tamyra A. PIERCE, Roberto VACA, 2000.
The Wired Generation: Academic and Social Outcomes of Electronic Media Use Among University Students. Wade C. Jacobsen, B.S., and Renata Forste, Ph.D. cyberpsychology, behavior, and social networking. Volume 14, Number 5, 2011
Generation M. Media in the Lives of 8- to 18-Year-Olds. Victoria J. Rideout, M.A.Ulla G. Foehr, Ph.D.and Donald F. Roberts, Ph.D.A Kaiser Family Foundation Study. January 2010. http://myweb.wwu.edu/karlberg/444/readings/GenM2.pdf
Electronic Media Use, Reading, and Academic Distractibility in College Youth. Laura E. Levine, Ph.D., Bradley M. Waite, Ph.D., And Laura L. Bowman, Ph.D. Cyberpsychology & Behavior. Volume 10, Number 4, 2007
Influence of Social Media on the Academic Performance of the Undergraduate Students of Kogi . State University, Anyigba, Nigeria. Ezekiel S. Asemah, Ruth A. Okpanachi, Leo O.N. Edegoh. Research on Humanities and Social Sciences. Vol 3, No 12 (2013)
63   The effect of multitasking on the grade performance of business students. Y Ellis, B Daniels, A Jauregui - Research in Higher Education Journal, 2010 - w.aabri.com
Distracted: Academic Performance Differences Between Teen Users and Non-Users of MySpace and Other Communication Technology. Tamyra A. Pierce. http://www.iiisci.org/journal/CV$/sci/pdfs/E214BL.pdf
The Laptop and the Lecture:The Effects of Multitasking in Learning Environments. Helene Hembrooke and Geri Gay. Journal of Computing in Higher Education. Fall 2003, Vol. 15(1)
64   Laptop und Internet im Hörsaal? Wirkungen und Wirkungsmechanismen für evidenzbasierte Lehre. M Spitzer, Nervenheilkunde 32 (2013): 805-812.
65   Distracted: Academic Performance Differences Between Teen Users and Non-Users of MySpace. and Other Communication Technology. Tamyra A. PIERCE.http://www.iiisci.org/journal/CV$/sci/pdfs/E214BL.pdf
66   Digital Distractions in the Classroom: Student Classroom Use of Digital Devices for Non-Class Related Purposes. Bernard McCoy, Journal of Media Education, October 15, 2013.
67   Do Action Video Games Improve Perception and Cognition? Walter R. Boot, Daniel P. Blakely, and Daniel J. Simons.Front Psychol. 2011; 2: 226. Pauline L. Baniqued, Hyunkyu Lee, Michelle W. Voss, Chandramallika Basak, Joshua D. Selling points: What cognitive abilities are tapped by casual video games?, Cosman, Shanna DeSouza, Joan Severson, Timothy A. Salthouse, Arthur F. Kramer, Acta Psychologica, Volume 142, Issue 1, January 2013, pp. 74-86,
68   Media use, face-to-face communication, media multitasking, and social well-being among 8- to 12-year-old girls. By Pea, Roy; Nass, Clifford; Meheula, Lyn; Rance, Marcus; Kumar, Aman; Bamford, Holden; Nass, Matthew; Simha, Aneesh; Stillerman, Benjamin; Yang, Steven; Zhou, Michael. Developmental Psychology, Vol 48(2), Mar 2012, 327-336.
69   http://news.stanford.edu/news/2012/january/tweenage-girls-multitasking-012512.html
70   Wasting Time Is New Divide in Digital Era. Matt Richtel. International Herald Tribune. 29 may 2012 (sources not checked)
71   GENERATION M. Media in the Lives of 8- to 18-Year-Olds. Victoria J. Rideout, M.A.Ulla G. Foehr, Ph.D.and Donald F. Roberts, Ph.D.A Kaiser Family Founda-

tion Study. January 2010. http://myweb.wwu.edu/karlberg/444/readings/GenM2.pdf

72 At least five a week: Evidence on the impact of physical activity and its relationship to health. A report from the Chief Medical Officer. UK Department of Health http://www.dh.gov.uk/prod_consum_dh/groups/dh_digitalassets/@dh/@en/documents/digitalasset/dh_4080984.pdf

73 The influence of writing practice on letter recognition in preschool children: A comparison between handwriting and typing, Marieke Longcamp, Marie-Thérèse Zerbato-Poudou, Jean-Luc Velay, Acta Psychologica, Volume 119, Issue 1, May 2005, pp. 67-79,
Contribution de la motricité graphique à la reconnaissance visuelle des lettres, M. Longcamp, A. Lagarrigue, J.-L. Velay, Psychologie Française, Volume 55, Issue 2, June 2010, pp. 181-194,
Handwriting versus Typewriting: Behavioural and Cerebral Consequences in Letter Recognition, Jean-Luc Velay, Marieke Longcamp (2012), Chapter 4.00.07 in Mark Torrance, Denis Alamargot, Montserrat Castelló, Franck Ganier, Otto Kruse, Anne Mangen, Liliana Tolchinsky, Luuk van Waes (ed.) Learning to Write Effectively: Current Trends in European Research
The Haptics of Writing: Cross-Disciplinary Explorations of the Impact of Writing Technologies on the Cognitive-Sensorimotor Processes Involved in Writing, Anne Mangen, Jean-Luc Velay (2012), Chapter 4.00.16 in Mark Torrance, Denis Alamargot, Montserrat Castelló, Franck Ganier, Otto Kruse, Anne Mangen, Liliana Tolchinsky, Luuk van Waes (ed.) Learning to Write Effectively: Current Trends in European Research (Studies in Writing, Volume 25), Emerald Group Publishing Limited, pp.405-407
Learning through Hand- or Typewriting Influences Visual Recognition of New Graphic Shapes: Behavioral and Functional Imaging Evidence
Marieke Longcamp, Céline Boucard, Jean-Claude Gilhodes, Jean-Luc Anton, Muriel Roth, Bruno Nazarian, and Jean-Luc Velay. Journal of Cognitive Neuroscience. May 2008, Vol. 20, No. 5, pp. 802-815
Digitizing Literacy: Reflections on the Haptics of Writing, Advances, Anne Mangen and Jean-Luc Velay (2010). in Haptics, Mehrdad Hosseini Zadeh (Ed.), ISBN: 978-953-307-093-3, InTech, DOI: 10.5772/8710. Available from: http://www.intechopen.com/books/advances-in-haptics/digitizing-literacy-reflections-on-the-haptics-of-writing
The science of Handwriting. Keim, Brandon. Scientific American Mind, Sep/Oct2013, Vol. 24 Issue 4, pp. 54-59

74 Thinking fast and slow. Daniel Kahneman. Penguin Books. 2012
Thinking fast and slow. Daniel Kahneman. Penguin Books. 2012

75 Mueller, P. A., & Oppenheimer, D. M. (in press). The pen is mightier than the keyboard: Advantages of longhand over laptop note-taking. Psychological Science

76 Your Phone vs. Your Heart. Barbara L. Fredrickson. New York Times: March 23, 2013. Research not yet published at this point.

77 http://www.nytimes.com/2011/10/23/technology/at-waldorf-school-in-silicon-valley-technology-can-wait.html? r=1

78 http://dotcomplicated.co/content/2013/10/introducing-dot/

79 How attention partitions itself during simultaneous message presentations. Lori Bergen, Tom Grimes and Deborah Potter. Human Communication Research vol. 31 (2005) nr. 3, p. 311

80 The laptop and the lecture: The effects of multitasking in learning environments. Helene Hembrooke and Geri Gay. Journal of Computing in Higher Education vol. 15 (2003) nr. 1, p. 46

81 Examining the Affects of Student Multitasking with Laptops during the Lecture. Kraushaar, James M.; Novak, David C.. Journal of Information Systems Education, v21 n2 pp. 241-251, 2010

82 Getting plugged in: An overview of Internet addiction. Caroline Flisher. Journal of Paediatrics and Child Health.

Volume 46, Issue 10, pp. 557-559, October 2010

83 Do Learners Really Know Best? Paul A. Kirschner & Jeroen J.G. van Merriënboer. Urban Legends in Education.Educational Psychologist. Volume 48, Issue 3, 2013

84 Visual voodoo: the biological impact of watching TV. Aric Sigman. Biologist Volume 54 Number 1, February 2007. http://aricsigman.com/IMAGES/VisualVoodoo.pdf

85 Sedentary Behaviour and Obesity: Review of the Current Scientific Evidence. Stuart Biddle(Chair. The Sedentary Behaviour and Obesity Expert Working Group. UK Department of Health. March 26, 2010

86 TVs in the bedrooms of children: Does it impact health and behavior? Susan B. Sissona et al. Preventive Medicine. Volume 52, Issue 2, 1 February 2011, pp. 104-108

87 Behavioral Correlates of Television Viewing in Primary School Children Elif Özmert, Müge Toyran, Kadriye Yurdakök, Arch Pediatr Adolesc Med. 2002;156:910-914. http://archpedi.ama-assn.org/cgi/content/full/156/9/910

88 Early Television Exposure and Subsequent Attentional Problems in Children. Pediatrics, 113(4) 708-13 http://www.pediatricsdigest.mobi/content/113/4/708.full

89 Infant Media Exposure and Toddler Development. Suzy Tomopoulos, et al. Arch Pediatr Adolesc Med. 2010;164(12): 1105-1111. http://archpedi.ama-assn.org/cgi/content/abstract/164/12/1105

90 Does watching TV make us happy? Bruno S. Frey. Christine Benesch, Alois Stutzer.Journal of Economic Psychology. 2007. http://www.wwz.unibas.ch/fileadmin/wwz/redaktion/Forum/Publikationen/2007/Stutzer_TV.pdf

91 Williams TM, Joy LA, Kimball M. The impact of television: natural experiment involving three communities. Symposium presented at the meeting of the Canadian Psychological Association, Vancouver, British Columbia, 1977. [quoted in Arch Pediatr Adolesc Med. 2002. Original not found]

92 TVs in the bedrooms of children: Does it impact health and behavior? Susan B. Sissona et al. Preventive Medicine. Volume 52, Issue 2, 1 February 2011, pp. 104-108 Zero to Six: Electronic Media in the Lives of Infants, Toddlers and Preschoolers. http://eric.ed.gov/PDFS/ED482302.pdf Digital Childhood: Electronic Media and Technology Use Among Infants, Toddlers, and Preschoolers. Elizabeth A. Vandewater et al. Pediatrics Vol. 119 No. 5 May 1, 2007. http://www.pediatricsdigest.mobi/content/119/5/e1006.full

93 Thinking fast and slow. Daniel Kahneman. Pinguin Books. 2012

94 Dan Ariely. Predictably Irrational, Harper Collins. 2008.

95 Thinking fast and slow. Daniel Kahneman. Pinguin Books. 2012

96 Kahneman, D., & Tversky, A. (1979). Prospect theory: An analysis of decision under risk. Econometrica: Journal of the Econometric Society, 263-291. http://www.princeton.edu/~kahneman/docs/Publications/prospect_theory.pdf

97 Thinking fast and slow. Daniel Kahneman. Pinguin Books. 2012

98 Dan Ariely. Predictably Irrational, Harper Collins. 2008.

99 Over breinblinddoeken en ezelsbreinbrugjes die ons brengen waar we niet willen zijn. Theo Compernolle. Marketing Jaarboek. pp. 52-61. Pimms NV. 2011.

100 http://en.wikipedia.org/wiki/List_of_cognitive_biases

101 http://lesswrong.com/lw/a8k/ambiguity_in_cognitive_bias_names_a_refresher/

102 http://www.farnamstreetblog.com/mental-models/

103 Thinking fast and slow. Daniel Kahneman. Pinguin Books. 2012

104 Honesty requires time (and lack of justifications). Shaul Shalv, Ori Eldar and Yoella Bereby-Meyer.Forthcoming in Psychological Science 2012. http://www.erim.eur.nl/portal/page/portal/ERIM/Content_Area/Documents/Shalvi%20et%20al_Honesty%20requires%20time_PS.pdf

105 http://www.aomonline.org/aom.asp?ID=251&page_ID=224&pr_id=453

106 Predictability Modulates Human Brain Response to Reward. Gregory S. Berns, Samuel M. McClure, Giuseppe Pagnoni, and P. Read Montague. The Journal of Neuroscience, 15 April 2001, 21(8): 2793-2798

107 Experienced surgeons can do more than one thing at a time: effect of distraction on performance of a simple laparoscopic and cognitive task by experienced and novice surgeons. K. E. Hsu, F.-Y. Man Æ R. A. Gizicki, L. S. Feldman Æ G. M. Fried. Surg Endosc (2008) 22:196-201

108 Habit and Nonhabit Systems for Unconscious and Conscious Behavior: Implications for Multitasking. John Lisman and Eliezer J. Sternberg. Journal of Cognitive Neuroscience 2013 25:2, 273-283

109 Talks to Teachers on Psychology: And to Students on Some of Life's Ideals. William James (1899) in: Google Books. http://books.google.nl/books?id= w-GNZHwQxEUC&printsec=frontcover &dq=James,+W.,+1899.+Talksto+Teacher son+Psychology.&hl=en&sa=X&ei=1LYo UdCXGcW9oQXAk4DwCg&redir_ esc=y#v=onepage&q&f=false

110 A Critical Review of Habit Learning and the Basal Ganglia. Carol A. Seger and Brian J. Spiering. Front Syst Neurosci. 2011; 5: 66.
Cortical andIk informer nog eens her en der. basal ganglia contributions to habit learning and automaticity.Ashby FG, Turner BO, Horvitz JC. Trends Cogn Sci. 2010 May;14(5):208-15.
Using optogenetics to study habits, Kyle S. Smith, Ann M. Graybiel, Brain Research, Available online 10 January 2013,http://www.sciencedirect.com/ science/article/pii/S0006899313000516

111 Steve Jobs. The making of Macintosh - An Interview with The Macintosh Design Team (Byte. Feb, 1984. p. 60) for a facsimile of the original article: http:// blog.modernmechanix.com/2008/06/ 09/the-making-of-macintosh-an-intervi ew-with-the-macintosh-design-team/

112 Conditions for Intuitive Expertise. A Failure to Disagree. Daniel Kahneman and Gary Klein.American Psychologist, Vol 64(6), Sep 2009, 515-526

113 Conditions for Intuitive Expertise. A Failure to Disagree. Daniel Kahneman and Gary Klein.American Psychologist, Vol 64(6), Sep 2009, 515-526

114 The effects of stress and desire for control on superstitious behavior. Keinan, G. (2002). Personality and Social Psychology Bulletin, 28, 102-108

115 Skinner, B.F. (1948). Superstition in the pigeon. Journal of Experimental Psychology, 38, 168-172.

116 Bijgeloof in de sport. Peter De Wannemaeker. 1984. Katholieke Universiteit Leuven.

117 Souza, André L., and Cristine H. Legare. "Priming randomness increases the evaluation of ritual efficacy."

118 Wright, P., & Erdal, K.J. (2008). Sport superstition as a function of skill level and task difficulty. Journal of Sport Behavior, 31(2), 187-199.

119 Burger, J., & Lynn, A.L. (2005). Superstitious behaviour among American and Japanese professional baseball players. Basic and Applied Social Psychology, 27(1), 71-76.

120 Rudski, J.M., & Edwards, A. (2007). Malinowski goes to college: Factors influencing students' use of ritual and superstition. The Journal of General Psychology, 134(4), 389-403.

121 Interesting research with a good review:
Contemplation and Conversation: Subtle Influences on Moral Decision Making. Brian C. Gunia, Long Wang, Li Huang, Jiunwen Wang and J. Keith Murnighan. ACAD MANAGE J February 1, 2012 vol. 55 no. 1 13-33

122 The Morning Morality Effect. The Influence of Time of Day on Unethical Behavior. Maryam Kouchaki. Isaac H. Smith. Psychological Science October 28, 2013

123 Compliant Sinners, Obstinate Saints: How Power and Self-Focus Determine the Effectiveness of Social Influences in Ethical Decision Making. Marko Pitesa. Stefan Thau. Academy of Management Journal. 56, 3 (2013) 635-

658. http://hal.archives-ouvertes.fr/docs/00/81/46/14/PDF/pitesa_thau_amj_2013.pdf
Contemplation and Conversation: Subtle Influences on Moral Decision Making. Brian C. Gunia, Long Wang, Li Huang, Jiunwen Wang and J. Keith Murnighan. ACAD MANAGE J February 1, 2012 vol. 55 no. 1 13-33
Read more on this in my little manual on "Pain in the ass managers" that you can freely download at www.compernolle.com

124 https://docs.google.com/file/d/1r90VtnEhL82LJZJJKpizLmVCfKiqiP25UuS-dQn6bTWI/edit?pli=1 or go to www.compernolle.com and click on free texts to download.

125 Carefrontation is a word I invented to express that in real conversations we need a combination of caring and confronting. Confronting without caring will easily hurt. If too much caring stands in the way of confronting this leads to stagnation.

126 Over breinblinddoeken en ezelsbreinbrugjes die ons brengen waar we niet willen zijn. Theo Compernolle. Marketing Jaarboek. pag. 52-61. Pimms NV. 2011.

127 Large-scale brain networks in affective and social neuroscience: towards an integrative functional architecture of the brain, Lisa Feldman Barrett, Ajay Bhaskar Satpute, Current Opinion in Neurobiology, Volume 23, Issue 3, June 2013, pp. 361-372
The brain basis of emotion: a meta-analytic review. K.A. Lindquist, T.D. Wager, H. Kober, E. Bliss-Moreau, L.F. Barrett. Behav Brain Sci, 35 (2012), pp. 121-143
A functional architecture of the human brain: emerging insights from the science of emotion. K.A. Lindquist, T.D. Wager, H. Kober, E. Bliss-Moreau, L.F. Barrett. Trends in Cognitive Sciences, November 2012, Vol. 16, No. 11 533
Comment: The Appraising Brain: Towards a Neuro-Cognitive Model of Appraisal Processes in Emotion. Tobias Brosch, David Sander. Emotion Review April 2013 vol. 5 no. 2 163-168

On the Causal Role of Appraisal in Emotion. Agnes Moors. 2013 5: 132 Emotion Review
Identifying Emotions on the Basis of Neural Activation. Kassam KS, Markey AR, Cherkassky VL, Loewenstein G, Just MA. PLoS ONE 8(6): e66032. (2013)
Clarify Brain Affective Processing Without Necessarily Clarifying Emotions. Peter Walla and Jaak Panksepp. Novel Frontiers of Advanced Neuroimaging 2013. Chapter 6
http://cdn.intechopen.com/pdfs/41876/InTech-Neuroimaging_helps_to_clarify_brain_affective_processing_without_necessarily_clarifying_emotions.pdf
On the Causal Role of Appraisal in Emotion. Agnes Moors. Emotion Review April 2013 vol. 5 no. 2 132-140 +++.
Appraisal Theories of Emotion: State of the Art and Future Development. Agnes Moors, Phoebe C. Ellsworth, Klaus R. Scherer and Nico H. Frijda. 2013 5: 119 Emotion Review
Neuroscience of affect: brain mechanisms of pleasure and displeasure, Kent C Berridge, Morten L Kringelbach, Current Opinion in Neurobiology, Volume 23, Issue 3, June 2013, pp. 294-303

128 Control of goal-directed and stimulus-driven attention in the brain. Corbetta, M., & Shulman, G. L. (2002). Nature Reviews Neuroscience, 3, 201-215.
Anxiety and Cognitive Performance: Attentional Control Theory, Michael W. Eysenck et al., 7 Emotion 336, 338 (2007).
Anxiety, processing efficiency, and cognitive performance.Derakshan, Nazanin, and Michael W. Eysenck. European Psychologist 14.2 (2009): 168-176.
Anxiety and Performance: The Disparate Roles of Prefrontal Subregions Under Maintained Psychological Stress." Takizawa, Ryu, et al. Cerebral Cortex (2013).
Portrait of the angry decision maker: how appraisal tendencies shape anger's influence on cognition. Jennifer S. Lerner1, Larissa Z. Tiedens. Journal of Behavioral Decision Making. Special

Issue: The Role of Affect in Decision Making. Volume 19, Issue 2, pp. 115-137, April 200

129 The Mirror Mechanism as Neurophysiological Basis for Action and Intention Understanding. Leonardo Fogassi, Giacomo Rizzolatti. in: Is Science Compatible with Free Will? Suarez, Antoine; Adams, Peter (Eds.) 2013, pp. 117-134

130 'Like me': a foundation for social cognition. Andrew N. Meltzoff. Developmental Science. Volume 10, Issue 1, pp. 126-134, January 2007

Foundations for a New Science of Learning. Andrew N. Meltzoff, Patricia K. Kuhl, Javier Movellan Terrence J. Sejnowski. Science 17 July 2009: Vol. 325 no. 5938 pp. 284-288

Observing complex action sequences: The role of the fronto-parietal mirror neuron system, Istvan Molnar-Szakacs, Jonas Kaplan, Patricia M. Greenfield, Marco Iacoboni, NeuroImage, Volume 33, Issue 3, 15 November 2006, pp. 923-935

131 Neural Substrates of Social Emotion Regulation: A fMRI Study on Imitation and Expressive Suppression to Dynamic Facial Signals. Pascal Vrticka, Samanta Simioni, Eleonora Fornari, Myriam Schluep, Patrik Vuilleumier, and David Sander. Front Psychol. 2013; 4: 95. http://www.ncbi.nlm.nih.gov/pmc/articles/PMC3582997/

132 Getting a grip on other minds: Mirror neurons, intention understanding, and cognitive empathy. Jonas T. Kaplan. Social Neuroscience. Volume 1, Issue 3-4, 2006

The Mirror Mechanism as Neurophysiological Basis for Action and Intention Understanding. Leonardo Fogassi, Giacomo Rizzolatti in: Is Science Compatible with Free Will? Suarez, Antoine; Adams, Peter (Eds.) 2013, pp 117-134

Mirror Neurons, Evolution, and Eco-Empathy. Gary Olson. SpringerBriefs in Political Science Volume 10, 2013, pp. 21-30

How from action-mirroring to intention-ascription? Pierre Jacob. Consciousness and Cognition. http://www.sciencedirect.com/science/article/pii/

S1053810013000287?

133 Unconscious cerebral initiative and the role of conscious will in voluntary action.

Libet, B. (1985). Behavioral and Brain Sciences. , 8, 529-539.

On Habit Learning in Neuroscience and Free Will. Javier Bernácer, José Manuel Giménez-Amaya. Chapter 12 In: Is Science Compatible with Free Will? 2013, pp. 177-193

Does the brain "initiate" freely willed processes? A philosophy of science critique of Libet-type experiments and their interpretation. Hans Radder & Gerben Meynen. Theory Psychology February 2013 vol. 23 no. 1, pp. 3-21

134 Much later this was still true in some cultures: Read "Indian Boyhood" by Charles Eastman.

135 The World Is Flat: A Brief History of the Twenty-First Century.Thomas Friedman; Farrar, Straus and Giroux, 2005

136 The full quote is:
"If you read the Apple's first brochure, the headline was 'Simplicity is the Ultimate Sophistication.'
What we meant by that was that when you first attack a problem it seems really simple because you don't understand it. Then when you start to really understand it, you come up with these very complicated solutions because it's really hairy. Most people stop there.
But a few people keep burning the midnight oil and finally understand the underlying principles of the problem and come up with an elegantly simple solution for it. But very few people go the distance to get there" — Steve Jobs. The making of Macintosh - An Interview with The Macintosh Design Team (Byte. Feb, 1984. p. 60) for a facsimile of the original article: http://blog.modernmechanix.com/2008/06/09/the-making-of-macintosh-an-interview-with-the-macintosh-design-team/

137 A comparison of the influence of electronic books and paper books on reading comprehension, eye fatigue, and perception,Hanho Jeong, (2012) "Electronic Library, Vol. 30 Iss: 3, pp.390 - 408

Reading from an LCD monitor versus

paper: Teenagers' reading performance. Hak Joon Kim, Joan Kim. Computers in Human Behavior. Volume 28, Issue 5, September 2012, pp. 1816–1828 http://consortiacademia.org/index.php/ijrset/article/view/170

Taking readingcomprehension exams on screen or on paper? A metacognitive analysis of learning texts under time pressure Rakefet Ackerman, , Tirza Lauterman. Computers in Human Behavior. Volume 28, Issue 5, September 2012, pp. 1816–1828

Usability evaluation of E-books. Yen-Yu Kanga,Mao-Jiun J. Wangb,Rungtai LincDisplays. Volume 30, Issue 2, April 2009, pp. 49-52. Comprehension and workload differences for VDT and paper-based reading. Daniel K Mayes,Valerie K Sims,Jefferson M Koonce. International Journal of Industrial Ergonomics. Volume 28, Issue 6, December 2001, pp. 367-378

138 http://www.nea.gov/research/ToRead.pdf and

139 Technology and adolescents: Perspectives on the things to come. Raul L. Katz, Max Felix, Madlen Gubernick. Education and Information Technologies. May 2013. http://link.springer.com/article/10.1007/s10639-013-9258-8#page-2

Generation M2: Media in the Lives of 8- to 18-Year-Olds. Rideout, Victoria J.; Foehr, Ulla G.; Roberts, Donald F. Henry J. Kaiser Family Foundation. 2010. http://www.eric.ed.gov/PDFS/ED527859.pdf

140 Reading Literary Fiction Improves Theory of Mind. David Comer Kidd and Emanuele Castano. Science. 373 (2013)

141 http://www.ted.com/talks/richard_branson_s_life_at_30_000_feet.html

142 Au choc des idées jaillit la lumière

143 http://www.philosophie-management.com/docs/Arts_of_the_wise_leader_-_Ledoux__Strom_-_SPES_Forum_-_2010_04_23.pdf

144 Who Multi-Tasks and Why? Multi-Tasking Ability, Perceived Multi-Tasking Ability, Impulsivity, and Sensation Seeking. Sanbonmatsu DM, Strayer DL, Medeiros-Ward N, Watson JM (2013) PLoS ONE 8(1): e54402

145 Nathan Zeldes, IT Principal Engineer, in a study of 2,300 employees at Intel.

146 Victor M. González and Gloria Mark Timespace in the workplace: Dealing with interruptions. Proceedings of CHI 95, ACM Press (1995), 262-263.

147 Basex 2005

148 Touch and personality: Extraversion predicts somatosensory brain response, Michael Schaefer, Hans-Jochen Heinze, Michael Rotte, NeuroImage, Volume 62, Issue 1, 1 August 2012, pp. 432-438

Do extraverts process social stimuli differently from introverts? Inna Fishman, Rowena Ng, Ursula Bellugi. Cognitive Neuroscience. Vol. 2, Iss. 2, 2011

Extraversion Is Linked to Volume of the Orbitofrontal Cortex and Amygdala. Cremers H, van Tol M-J, Roelofs K, Aleman A, Zitman FG, et al. (2011) PLoS ONE 6(12)

Personality similarity in twins reared apart and together.Tellegen, Auke; Lykken, David T.; Bouchard, Thomas J.; Wilcox, Kimerly J.; Segal, Nancy L.; Rich, Stephen. Journal of Personality and Social Psychology, Vol 54(6), Jun 1988, 1031-1039.

Exploring personality through test construction: Development of the Multidimensional Personality Questionnaire. Tellegen, A., & Waller, N. G. (2008). In G. J.Boyle, G.Matthews, & D. H.Saklofske, Handbook of Personality Theory and Testing, Vol. II, Personality Measurement and Assessment (pp. 261-292). Thousand Oaks, CA

Age changes in personality traits and their heritabilities during the adult years: evidence from Australian twin registry samples, J.C Loehlin, N.G Martin, Personality and Individual Differences, Volume 30, Issue 7, May 2001, pp. 1147-1160,

149 Cognitive control in media multitaskers. Eyal Ophir, Clifford Nass, Anthony D. Wagner. PNAS September 15, 2009 vol. 106 no. 37 15583-15587

http://news.stanford.edu/news/2009/august24/multitask-research-study-082409.html

150 Personality Processes: Mechanisms by Which Personality Traits "Get Outside the Skin". Sarah E. HampsonAnnual Review of Psychology. Vol. 63: 315-339, 2012.

151 The Moderating Effect of Extraversion-Introversion Differences on Group Idea Generation Performance J. H. Jung, Younghwa Lee, Rex Karsten. Small Group Research February 2012 vol. 43 no. 1 30-49

152 Would introverts be better off if they acted more like extraverts? Exploring emotional and cognitive consequences of counterdispositional behavior.Zelenski, John M.; Santoro, Maya S.; Whelan, Deanna C. Emotion, Vol 12(2), Apr 201

153 The Language of Extraversion: Extraverted People Talk More Abstractly, Introverts Are More Concrete. Camiel J. Beukeboom, Martin Tanis, Ivar E. Vermeulen, Journal of Language and Social Psychology October 5, 2012

SECTION 2

1 For a review: http://i3pod.com/wp-content/uploads/2011/04/Revisiting-the-Swiss-Cheese-Modek-EEC-note-2006-13.pdf

2 http://www.jumio.com/2013/07/americans-cant-put-down-their-smartphones-even-during-sex/

3 The Promise and Peril of Hyperconnectivity for Organizations and Societies John Fredette, Revital Marom, Kurt Steinert, and Louis Witters (Alcatel-Lucent) "The Global Information Technology Report" World Economic Forum 2012. Chapter 1.10 p. 113

4 Pew Research Center's Internet & American Life Project. March 19, 2012. http://wwww.pewinternet.com/~/media/Files/Reports/2012/PIP_Teens_Smartphones_and_Texting.pdf

5 http://pewinternet.org/Commentary/2012/February/Pew-Internet-Mobile.aspx

6 http://www.webmd.com/mental-health/features/when-technology-addiction-takes-over-your-life

7 http://www.jumio.com/2013/07/americans-cant-put-down-their-smartphones-even-during-sex/

8 Zo ga je om met je zakelijke smartphone. Marieke van Twillert. Intermediair 10-11-2011. http://www.intermediair.nl/artikel/persberichten/202778/56-ergert-zich-aan-smartphonegebruik-collega.html

9 Ubiquitous Blackberry: The New Overtime Liability, The; Barbu, Maria L. 5 Liberty U. L. Rev. 47 (2010-2011) Blackberrys and the Fair Labor Standards Act: Does a Wireless Ball and Chain Entitle White-Collar Workers to Overtime Compensation? A M Rothe. Saint Louis University law journal. 54, no. 2, (2010): 709-738 Ellen Wulfhorst,BlackBerrys, Blogs Create Overtime Work Disputes,USA TODAY,June 25, 2008, http://www.usatoday.com/tech/products/2008-06-25-blackberry-blogs-overtime-pay_N.htm

10 The Effects of Interruptions on Task Performance, Annoyance, and Anxiety in the User Interface. Brian P. Bailey, Joseph A. Konstan, and John V. Carlis Investigating the effects of computer mediated interruptions: An analysis of task characteristics and interruption frequency on financial performance. K. Asli Basoglu, Mark A. Fuller,John T. Sweeney. International Journal of Accounting Information Systems. Volume 10, Issue 4, December 2009, pp. 177-189 Costly Cell Phones: The Impact of Cell Phone Rings on Academic Performance. Christian M. Enda, Shaye Worthmana, Mary Bridget Mathewsa & Katharina Wetteraua. Teaching of Psychology. Volume 37, Issue 1, 2009 Entirely irrelevant distractors can capture and captivate attention. Sophie Forster Nilli Lavie. Psychon Bull Rev. 2011 December; 18(6): 1064-1070. Failures to ignore entirely irrelevant distractors: the role of load. Forster S, Lavie N. Journal of Experimental Psychology. Applied [2008, 14(1):73-83]

Tan, Mark Khai Shean and Richardson, Alex, "Please Do Not Disturb: Managing Interruptions And Task Complexity" (2011). PACIS 2011 Proceedings. Paper 187.

11   Tan, Mark Khai Shean and Richardson, Alex, "Please Do Not Disturb: Managing Interruptions And Task Complexity" (2011). PACIS 2011 Proceedings. Paper 187.

12   Instant Messaging: Effects of Relevance and Timing. Mary Czerwinski, Edward Cutrell and Eric Horvitz. Microsoft Research. marycz@microsoft.com

13   Cyber-Serfdom. Thomas L. Friedman. New York Times. January 30, 2001

14   Investigating the effects of computer mediated interruptions: An analysis of task characteristics and interruption frequency on financial performance. K. Asli Basoglu, Mark A. Fuller,John T. Sweeney. International Journal of Accounting Information Systems. Volume 10, Issue 4, December 2009, pp. 177–18

15   Association of Interruptions With an Increased Risk and Severity of Medication Administration Errors. Johanna I. Westbrook,Amanda Woods, Marilyn I. Rob, William T. M. Dunsmuir, Richard O. Day. Arch Intern Med. 2010;170(8):683-690.

16   The cost of interrupted work: more speed and stress. Gloria Mark, Daniela Gudith, Ulrich Klocke. CHI '08 Proceedings of the twenty-sixth annual SIGCHI conference on Human factors in computing systems. pp. 107-110. ACM New York 2008

17   Arthur Schopenhauer: On Noise. 1851 translation by T. Bailey Saunders. ttp://www.schopenhauervereinigung.com/articles/arthur-schopenhauer-on-noise/ Also at http://www.noisehelp.com/schopenhauer-quotes.html

18   Conard, Maureen A. and Marsh, Robert M., "Single And Multiple Interruptions Increase Task Performance Time, But Don't Affect Stress, Pressure or Flow" (2010). WCOB Working Papers. Paper 1. http://digitalcommons.sacredheart.edu/wcob_wp/1

19   Distinct mechanisms for the impact of distraction and interruption on working memory in aging. Wesley C. Clapp,Adam Gazzaley. Neurobiology of Aging. Volume 33, Issue 1, January 2012, pp. 134–148

20   The Effects of Interruptions, Task Complexity, and Information Presentation on Computer-Supported Decision-Making Performance. Cheri Speier. Decision Sciences. Volume 34 Number 4. 2003

Juggling on a high wire: Multitasking effects on performance. Rachel F. Adlera,Raquel Benbunan-Fich. International Journal of Human-Computer Studies. Volume 70, Issue 2, February 2012, pp. 156–168

21   Basex 2011

22   Extraneous factors in judicial decisions. Shai Danzigera, Jonathan Levavb, Liora Avnaim-Pesso. Proceedings of the National Academy of Sciences of the United States of America. April 26, 2011 vol. 108 no. 17 6889-6892

23   Making choices impairs subsequent self-control: A limited-resource account of decision making, self-regulation, and active initiative.Vohs, Kathleen D.; Baumeister, Roy F.; Schmeichel, Brandon J.; Twenge, Jean M.; Nelson, Noelle M.; Tice, Dianne M. Journal of Personality and Social Psychology, Vol 94(5), May 2008, 883-898

Self-control: limited resources and extensive benefits. Jessica Alquist, Roy F. Baumeister.Wiley Interdisciplinary Reviews: Cognitive Science. Volume 3, Issue 3, pp. 419-423, May/June 2012

24   Motivation, personal beliefs, and limited resources all contribute to self-control.. Kathleen D. Vohs,Roy F. Baumeister, Brandon J. Schmeichel Journal of Experimental Social PsychologyVolume 48, Issue 4, July 2012, pp. 943-947

25   Stress and open-office noise. Evans, Gary W.; Johnson, Dana. Journal of Applied Psychology, Vol 85(5), Oct 2000, 779-783.

26   Self-control relies on glucose as a limited energy source: Willpower is more than a metaphor. Gailliot, Matthew T.; Baumeister, Roy F.; DeWall, C. Nathan; Maner, Jon K.; Plant, E. Ashby; Tice, Dianne M.; Brewer,

Lauren E.; Schmeichel, Brandon J. Journal of Personality and Social Psychology, Vol 92(2), Feb 2007, 325-336
27   Self-Control Without a "Self"? Common Self-Control Processes in Humans and Dogs Holly C. Miller, Kristina F. Pattison, C. Nathan DeWall, Rebecca Rayburn-Reeves and Thomas R. Zentall. Psychological Science April 2010 vol. 21 no. 4 534-538
28   Cognitive neuroscience of self-regulation failure. Todd F. Heatherton, Dylan D. Wagner, Trends in Cognitive Sciences, Volume 15, Issue 3, March 2011, pp. 132-139
Dietary Restraint Violations Influence Reward Responses in Nucleus Accumbens and Amygdala
Kathryn E. Demos, William M. Kelley, and Todd F. Heatherton. Journal of Cognitive Neuroscience. August 2011, Vol. 23, No. 8, pp. 1952-1963
29   The Morning Morality Effect. The Influence of Time of Day on Unethical Behavior. Maryam Kouchaki. Isaac H. Smith. Psychological Science October 28, 2013
30   http://www.linkedin.com/today/post/article/20130402091536-204068115 things-i-carry-smart-phone-i-prefer-a-brilliant-assistant
31   http://www.jumio.com/2013/07/americans-cant-put-down-their-smart-phones-even-during-sex/
32   McCann Advertising company campaign for "Macquarie Dictionary" http://www.mccann.com.au/project/phubbing-a-word-is-born/ http://www.youtube.com/watch?v=ZSOfuUYCV_o
33   Can you connect with me now? How the presence of mobile communication technology influences face-to-face conversation quality. Andrew K. Przybylski and Netta Weinstein. Journal of Social and Personal Relationships July 19, 2012
34   Emberson L and Goldstein M., "Overheard Cell-Phone Conversations: When Less Speech is More Distracting," Psychological Science.
The effect of speech and speech intelligibility on task performance. N. Venetjokia, A. Kaarlela-Tuomaalaa, E. Keskinenb & V. Hongistoa. Ergonomics.

Volume 49, Issue 11, 2006
35   Indicative research, not very scientific, done amongst clients of the Gazelle trade-in company. Consumers Crave iPhone® More Than Facebook, Sex, According to Gazelle. www.prnewswire.com/news-releases/consumers-crave-iphone-more-than-facebook-sex-according-to-gazelle-159430685.html
36   Stress: Friend and Foe. Theo Compernolle. Synergo.
37   The Machine Zone: This Is Where You Go When You Just Can't Stop Looking at Pictures on Facebook. What an anthropologist's examination of Vegas slot machines reveals about the hours we spend on social networks. ALEXIS C. MADRIGALJUL. The Atlantic. 31 2013
38   http://pewinternet.org/Commentary/2012/February/Pew-Internet-Mobile.aspx
39   http://www.webmd.com/mental-health/features/when-technology-addiction-takes-over-your-life
40   Critical review. The Cell Phone in the Twenty-First Century:A Risk for Addiction or a Necessary Tool? Xavier Carbonell, Ursula Oberst, Marta Beranuy. Principles of Addiction, First Edition, 2013, 901-909. http://site.blanquerna.url.edu/condesa/wp-content/uploads/2013/07/The-Cell-Phone-in-the-Twenty-First-Century.pdf
41   Prevalence of internet addiction in the general population: results from a German population-based survey. Kai W. Müller, Heide Glaesmer, Elmar Brähler, Klaus Woelfling, Manfred E. Beutel. Behaviour & Information Technology
Adolescent Internet Addiction: Testing the Association Between Self-Esteem, the Perception of Internet Attributes, and Preference for Online Social Interactions. Giulia Fioravanti, Ph.D., Davide De`ttore, Ph.D., and Silvia Casale, Ph.D. Cyberpsychology, Behavior, and Social Networking. Volume 15, Number 6, 2012
Behavioral Addictions: An Overview. Reef Karim D.O. & Priya Chaudhri Ph.D. Journal of Psychoactive Drugs.Volume 44, Issue 1, pp. 5-17 2012
Confirmation of the Three-Factor Model

of Problematic. Internet Use on Off-Line Adolescent and Adult Samples. Beatrix Koronczai, M.A and others. Cyberpsychology, Behavior, and Social Networking. Volume 14, Number 11, p. 657, 2011
Internet Over-Users' Psychological Profiles: A Behavior Sampling Analysis on Internet Addiction. Leo Sang-Min Whang, Ph.D.,1 Sujin Lee, Ph.D.,2 and Geunyoung Chang, M.A.1. Cyberpsychology & Behavior Volume 6, Number 2, 2003
Modification in the Proposed Diagnostic Criteria for Internet Addiction. Keith W. Beard, Psy.D., and Eve M. Wolf, Ph.D. Cyberpsychology & Behavior Volume 4, Number 3, 2001
An Outcome Evaluation Study on Internet Addiction. Seher Ozcan. Sahin Gokcearslan AWERProcedia Information. Technology & Computer Science. [Online]. 2013, 3, pp. 790-795. Available from: http://www.worldeducation-center.org/index.php/P-ITCS P. http://www.world-education-center.org/index.php/P-ITCS/article/view/1849/1637
42   Adolescent Internet Addiction: Testing the Association Between Self-Esteem, the Perception of Internet Attributes, and Preference for Online Social Interactions. Giulia Fioravanti, Ph.D., Davide De`ttore, Ph.D., and Silvia Casale, Ph.D. Cyberpsychology, Behavior, and Social Networking. Volume 15, Number 6, 2012
43   Should DSM-V Designate "Internet Addiction" a Mental Disorder? Ronald Pies, MD. Psychiatry (Edgmont). 2009 February; 6(2): 31-37. http://www.ncbi.nlm.nih.gov/pmc/articles/PMC2719452/
44   For the original text: http://psychclassics.yorku.ca/Pavlov/
45   Another example are the many cognitive biases and heuristics that makes us predictably irrational (Predictably Irrational, Ariely D., Harper Collins 2008), but which were very helpful for the caveman to survive in a word were fast reactions were more important for survival than thorough reflection. (Over breinblinddoeken en ezelsbreinbrugjes. Theo Compernolle. Marketing Jaarboek. pp. 52-61.

Pimms NV. 2011.) See also: Adaptive memory: Ancestral priorities and the mnemonic. value of survival processing. James S. Nairne , Josefa N.S. Pandeirada. Cognitive Psychology 61 (2010) 1–22
46   "A Pace Not Dictated by Electrons": An Empirical Study of Work Without Email. Gloria J. Mark, Stephen Voida, Armand V. Cardello. Proceedings of CHI 2012
47   The effect of cognitive style and curiosity on information task multitasking. Angela Manyangara Elaine G. Toms 10 Proceeding of the third symposium on Information interaction in context. ACM New York, NY, USA 2010
The Effect of Repeated Exposure to Unpredictable Reward on Dopamine Neuroplasticity. Sarah Ann Mathewson. Department of Psychology - Master theses. http://hdl.handle.net/1807/18915
Novelty Seekers and Drug Abusers Tap Same Brain Reward System, Animal Studies Show. By Robert Mathias. http://archives.drugabuse.gov/nida_notes/nnvol1on4/Novelty.html
Novelty Seekers and Drug Abusers Tap Same Brain Reward System, Animal Studies Show. By Robert Mathias. 2009 January 14. http://archives.drugabuse.gov/nida_notes/nnvol1on4/Novelty.html
48   http://www.intersperience.com/news_more.asp?news_id=39
49   A nation addicted to smartphones http://media.ofcom.org.uk/2011/08/04/a-nation-addicted-to-smartphones/
50   Tim Locke, Nasty Bugs Lurking on Your Cell Phone http://www.medscape.com/viewarticle/751569
51   Turel, Ofir; Serenko, Alexander; and Bontis, Nick, "Blackberry Addiction: Symptoms and Outcomes" (2008). AMCIS 2008 Proceedings. Paper 73. http://aisel.aisnet.org/amcis2008/73
The psychological roots of overconsumption. N. Hagens.in Fleeing Vesuvius.R. Douthwaite, G Fallon and R Heinberg p 339
(the title of this chapter is misleading. It's a very readable text on addiction)
Internet addiction: a 21st century epidemic? Dimitri A Christakis. BMC Medi-

cine 2010, 8:61. or ttp://www.biomed-central.com/1741-7015/8/61 Glücksspiel- und Internetsucht. Review und Forschungsagenda.K. Wölfling, M. Bühler, T. Leménager, C. Mörsen and K. Mann. Der Nervenarzt. Volume 80, Number 9, 1030-1039, Treatment of internet addiction. Huang XQ, Li MC, Tao R. Curr Psychiatry Rep. 2010 Oct;12(5):462-70. "Overcoming Email Addiction: Understanding the 'Leave Me Alone!'Approach" Gupta, Ashish; Sharda, Ramesh; and Greve, Robert A., (2009). AMCIS 2009 Proceedings. Paper 128. http://aisel.aisnet.org/amcis2009/128 Should DSM-V Designate "Internet Addiction" a Mental Disorder?, Ronald Pies. Psychiatry (Edgmont). 2009 February; 6(2): 31-37. The Role of Internet User Characteristics and Motives in Explaining Three Dimensions of Internet Addiction. Junghyun Kim,Paul M. Haridakis, Journal of Computer Mediated Communication. Volume 14, Issue 4, pp. 988-1015, July 2009 Flisher, C. (2010), Getting plugged in: An overview of Internet addiction. Journal of Paediatrics and Child Health, 46: 557-559

52   'Liking' and 'wanting' food rewards: brain substrates and roles in eating disorders. Berridge, K.C.,. Physiology & Behavior, 97(5), 537 550, 2009. Building a neuroscience of pleasure and well-being. Psychology of Well-Being: Theory Research and Practice. Berridge, K.C. & Kringelbach, M.L. http://www.psywb.com/content/1/1/3 , 2011.

53   Opioids for hedonic experience and dopamine to get ready for it. M. Flavia Barbano and Martine Cador. PSYCHOPHARMACOLOGY. Volume 191, Number 3 (2007), 497-506

54   Positive Reinforcement Produced By Electrical Stimulation Of Septal Area And Other Regions Of Rat Brain. Olds, James; Milner, Peter . Journal Of Comparative And Physiological Psychology, Vol 47(6), Dec 1954, 419-427

55   Later research showed that we don't have one pleasure centre, but a complex of many interconnected reward systems in our brain and that dopamine plays many roles. It also stimulates activity, sociability, curiosity and the search for novelty.

56   The Machine Zone: This Is Where You Go When You Just Can't Stop Looking at Pictures on Facebook What an anthropologist's examination of Vegas slot machines reveals about the hours we spend on social networks ALEXIS C. MADRIGAL The Atlantic. JUL 31 2013

57   For Impatient Web Users, an Eye Blink Is Just Too Long to Wait By STEVE LOHR The New York Times. February 29, 2012

58   Predictability Modulates Human Brain Response to Reward. Gregory S. Berns, Samuel M. McClure, Giuseppe Pagnoni, and P. Read Montague. The Journal of Neuroscience, 15 April 2001, 21(8): 2793-2798

59   The psychological roots of overconsumption. N. Hagens.in Fleeing Vesuvius.R. Douthwaite, G Fallon and R Heinberg p 339. (the title of this chapter is misleading. It's a very readable text on addiction) Operant Sensation Seeking Engages Similar Neural Substrates to Operant Drug Seeking in C57 Mice. Christopher M Olsen and Danny G Winder. Neuropsychopharmacology. 2009 June; 34(7): 1685-1694. Neural Differentiation of Expected Reward and Risk in Human Subcortical Structures Kerstin Preuschoff, Peter Bossaerts, and Steven R. Quartz. Neuron. Volume 51, Issue 3, 3 August 2006, pp. 381-390 The Neurobiology and Genetics of Impulse Control Disorders: Relationships to Drug Addictions Judson A. Brewer, MD PhD and Marc N. Potenza, MD PhD Biochem Pharmacol. 2008 January 1; 75(1): 63-75. Effects of dopamine depletion in reward seeking behavior M. Pessiglione and L Tremblay In Jean-Claude Dreher, Handbook of reward and decision making 2009 Elsevier Inc. p 271

481

60 Stress: Friend and Foe. Theo Compernolle. Synergo/Lannoo

61 Influences of socioeconomic status, social network, and competence on subjective well-being in later life: A meta-analysis. Pinquart, Martin; Sörensen, Silvia. Psychology and Aging, Vol 15(2), Jun 2000, 187-224

Stress, social support, and the buffering hypothesis.Cohen, Sheldon; Wills, Thomas A.

Psychological Bulletin, Vol 98(2), Sep 1985, 310-357

Sense of community belonging and health in Canada: A regional analysis. Kitchen, P., Williams, A., & Chowhan, J. (2012). Social indicators research, 107(1), 103-126.

How Groups Affect Our Health and Well-Being: The Path from Theory to Policy. Jetten, J., Haslam, C., Haslam, S. A., Dingle, G., & Jones, J. M. (2014). Social Issues and Policy Review, 8(1), 103-130.

Cross-cultural adaptation of Hispanic youth: a study of communication patterns, functional fitness, and psychological health. McKay-Semmler, K., & Kim, Y. Y. (2014). Communication Monographs, (ahead-of-print), 1-24.

A brief social-belonging intervention improves academic and health outcomes of minority students. Walton, G. M., & Cohen, G. L. (2011). Science, 331(6023), 1447-1451.

62 How does online social networking enhance life satisfaction? The relationships among online supportive interaction, affect, perceived social support, sense of community, and life satisfaction, Hyun Jung Oh, Elif Ozkaya, Robert LaRose, Computers in Human Behavior, Volume 30, January 2014, pp. 69-78

63 Targeting college students on Facebook? How to stop wasting your money. Hemant Sashittala,Rajendran Sriramachandramurthyb,Monica Hodisa. Business Horizons. June 2012

64 Envy on Facebook: A Hidden Threat to Users' Life Satisfaction? H Krasnova, H Wenninger, T Widjaja and Peter Buxmann. 11th International Conference on Wirtschaftsinformatik, 27th February -

01st March 2013, Leipzig, Germany. http://karynemlira.com/wp-content/uploads/2013/01/Envy-on-Facebook_A-Hidden-Threat-to-Users%E2%80%99-Life.pdf

Status Anxiety. Alain de Botton. 2004 Hamish Hamilton..

65 Cyberpsychology, Behavior, and Social Networking. Hui-Tzu Grace Chou and Nicholas Edge. February 2012, 15(2): 117-121. doi:10.1089/cyber.2011.0324.

The Impact of Social Media on Children, Adolescents, and--Clinical Report Gwenn Schurgin O'Keeffe, Kathleen Clarke-Pearson Pediatrics. 28 March 2011 Pediatrics http://pediatrics.aap-publications.org/content/early/2011/03/28/peds.2011-0054.full.pdf+html

66 Facebook Use Predicts Declines in Subjective Well-Being in Young Adults. Ethan Kross, Philippe Verduyn, Emre Demiralp, Jiyoung Park, David Seungjae Lee, Natalie Lin, Holly Shablack, John Jonides, Oscar Ybarra. 2013. PLoS ONE 8(8): e69841. doi:10.1371/journal.pone.0069841

67 The World Is Flat: A Brief History of the Twenty-First Century.Thomas Friedman; Farrar, Straus and Giroux, 2005

68 Getting plugged in: An overview of Internet addiction. Caroline Flisher. Journal of Paediatrics and Child Health. Volume 46, Issue 10, pp. 557-559, October 2010

69 Managing mobile multitasking: the culture of iPhones on stanford campus. Morgan G. Ames. cscw '13 Proceedings of the 2013 conference on Computer supported cooperative work. pp. 1487-1498 . http://delivery.acm.org/10.1145/2450000/2441945/p1487-ames.pdf?ip=137.56.81.143&id=2441945&acc=ACTIVE%20SERVICE&key=C2716FEBFA981EF1DADB8F2F3426481F339C1C9BAE845449&CFID=240362957&CFTOKEN=33442562&__acm__=1377108098_4a1290acc120374cec76d396a4b5397a

70 Why do I keep interrupting myself?: environment, habit and self-interruption.Laura Dabbish, Victor M. Gonzále, Gloria Mark. Proceedings of the 2011 annual conference on Human factors in computing systems. ACM New York, NY, USA ©2011 On the need for attention-aware systems: Measuring effects of interruption on task performance, error rate, and affective state. Brian P. Bailey, Joseph A. Konstan. Computers in Human Behavior Volume 22, Issue 4, July 2006, pp. 685–708 Reducing the disruptive effects of interruption: A cognitive framework for analysing the costs and benefits of intervention strategies.Deborah A. Boehm-Davis, Roger Remington Accident Analysis & Prevention. Volume 41, Issue 5, September 2009, pp. 1124–1129 The effects of interruptions on task performance, annoyance, and anxiety in the user interface. Brian P Bailey, Joseph A Konstan, John V Carlis. Proceedings of INTERACT (2001). Volume: 1, Publisher: Citeseer, pp. 593-601 "Constant, constant, multi-tasking craziness": managing multiple working spheres. Victor M. Gonzále, Gloria Mark. Proceedings of the SIGCHI conference on Human factors in computing systems. ACM New York, NY, USA ©2004

71   Corporate Brain Disorder. Theo Compernolle. 1999. Conference "The New Millennium" TIAS Business School. Tilburg. https://sites.google.com/site/compernolleconsulting3/books--tools-and-video-s/artcles-to-download

72   Multitasking. Buser, T, & Peter, N (2012). Experimental Economics, 15, 641-655.

73   DRIVER DISTRACTION IN COMMERCIAL VEHICLE OPERATIONS. Rebecca L. Olson, Richard J. Hanowski, Jeffrey S. Hickman, and Joseph Bocanegra. 2009. U.S. Department of Transportation . http://www.fmcsa.dot.gov/facts-research/research-technology/report/FMCSA-RRR-09-042.pdf

74   Hanging on the telephone: Mobile phone use patterns among UK-based business travellers on work-related journeys. Donald Hislop. Transportation Research Part F: Traffic Psychology and Behaviour. Volume 15, Issue 2, March 2012, pp. 101–110

75   see for example William Horrey ao. or Ann Mccartt ao.

76   Time allocation and task juggling. D Coviello, A Ichino, N Persico - 2011. http://home.business.utah.edu/finmh/persico.pdf

77   The relation of strength of stimulus to rapidity of habit formation. R.M. Yerkes, J.D. Dodson. J Comp Neurol Psychol, 18 (1908), pp. 459-482 Revolutionizing product development. Quantum leaps in speed, efficiency, and quality. Wheelwright, SC, Clark, KB, Free Press 1992/2011. p. 91 Investigating the effects of computer mediated interruptions: An analysis of task characteristics and interruption frequency on financial performance. K. Asli Basoglu, Mark A. Fuller,John T. Sweeney. International Journal of Accounting Information Systems. Volume 10, Issue 4, December 2009, pp. 177-189 Juggling on a high wire: Multitasking effects on performance. Rachel F. Adler, Raquel Benbunan-Fich. International Journal of Human-Computer Studies. Volume 70, Issue 2, February 2012, pp. 156-168

78   Stress: Vriend en Vijand. Uitgeverij Lannoo Belgium. 2012. 14th edition.

79   Quoted from my book "Stress: Friend and Foe" References of that book at www.compernolle.com Free texts to download.

80   Stress: Vriend en Vijand. Uitgeverij Lannoo Belgium. 2012. 14th edition.

81   "A Pace Not Dictated by Electrons":An Empirical Study of Work Without Email. Gloria J. Mark, Stephen Voida, Armand V. Cardello. Proceedings of CHI 2012

82   The cost of interrupted work: more speed and stress. Gloria Mark. Proceedings of the twenty-sixth annual SIGCHI conference on Human factors in computing systems. ACM New York, NY, USA ©2008

83   Switching on and off ... : Does smartphone use obstruct the possibility to engage in recovery activities? Daantje Derksa, Lieke L. ten Brummelhuis, Dino Zecica & Arnold B. Bakker.

European Journal of Work and Organizational Psychology. 23 dec 2010
84 Stress and open-office noise. Evans, Gary W.; Johnson, Dana. Journal of Applied Psychology, Vol 85(5), Oct 2000, 779-783.
85 Daily computer usage correlated with undergraduate students' musculoskeletal symptoms. C.-H. Chang, B.C. Amick III, C.C. Menendez, J.N. Katz, P.W. Johnson, M. Robertson, J.T. Dennerlein. Am. J. Ind. Med., 50 (2007), pp. 481-488
Undergraduate college students' upper extremity symptoms and functional limitations related to computer use: a replication study. M. Jenkins, C.C. Menéndez, B.C. Amick III, J. Tullar, N. Hupert, M.M. Robertson, J.N. KatzWork, 28 (2007), pp. 231-238
A prospective study of computer users: I. Study design and incidence of musculoskeletal symptoms and disorders. F. Gerr, M. Marcus, C. Ensor, D. Kleinbaum, S. Cohen, A. Edwards, E. Gentry, D.J. Ortiz, C. Monteilh. Am. J. Ind. Med., 41 (2002), pp. 221-235
Daily computer usage correlated with undergraduate students' musculoskeletal symptoms. Che-hsu (Joe) Chang PT, MS, Benjamin C. Amick III PhD, Cammie Chaumont Menendez MPH, MS, Jeffrey N. Katz MD, MS, Peter W. Johnson PhD, Michelle Robertson PhD, CPE, Jack Tigh Dennerlein PhD,American Journal of Industrial Medicine. Volume 50, Issue 6, pp. 481-488, June 2007
86 A comparison of the influence of electronic books and paper books on reading comprehension, eye fatigue, and perception,Hanho Jeong, (2012) "Electronic Library, Vol. 30 Iss: 3, pp. 390-408
Reading from an LCD monitor versus paper: Teenagers' reading performance. Hak Joon Kim, Joan Kim. Computers in Human Behavior. Volume 28, Issue 5, September 2012, pp. 1816-1828
http://consortiacademia.org/index.php/ijrset/article/view/170
Taking readingcomprehension exams on screen or on paper? A metacognitive analysis of learning texts under time pressure

Rakefet Ackerman, , Tirza Lauterman. Computers in Human Behavior. Volume 28, Issue 5, September 2012, pp. 1816-1828
Usability evaluation of E-books. Yen-Yu Kanga,Mao-Jiun J. Wangb,Rungtai LincDisplays. Volume 30, Issue 2, April 2009, pp. 49-52. Comprehension and workload differences for VDT and paper-based reading. Daniel K Mayes,Valerie K Sims,Jefferson M Koonce. International Journal of Industrial Ergonomics. Volume 28, Issue 6, December 2001, pp. 367-378
87 Psychophysiological Patterns During Cell Phone Text Messaging: A Preliminary Study. I-Mei Lin, Erik Peper. Applied Psychophysiology and Biofeedback. March 2009, Volume 34, Issue 1, pp 53-57
Musculoskeletal symptoms among mobile hand-held device users and their relationship to device use: a preliminary study in a canadian university population. S. Berolo, R.P. Wells, B.C. Amick 3rd. Appl. Ergon., 42 (2) (2010), pp. 371-378
Musculoskeletal symptoms among mobile hand-held device users and their relationship to device use: A preliminary study in a Canadian university population, Sophia Berolo, Richard P. Wells, Benjamin C. Amick III, Applied Ergonomics, Volume 42, Issue 2, January 2011, Pages 371-378
Self-reported neck symptoms and use of personal computers, laptops and cell phones among Finns aged 18-65. Leena Korpinenab, Rauno Pääkkönenc Fabriziomaria Gobbad . Ergonomics. Volume 56, Issue 7, 2013. pages 1134-1146
88 Psychophysiological Patterns During Cell Phone Text Messaging: A Preliminary Study. I-Mei Lin, Erik Peper. Applied Psychophysiology and Biofeedback. March 2009, Volume 34, Issue 1, pp. 53-57
Musculoskeletal symptoms among mobile hand-held device users and their relationship to device use: a preliminary study in a canadian university population. S. Berolo, R.P. Wells, B.C. Amick 3rd. Appl. Ergon., 42 (2) (2010), pp. 371-378

Musculoskeletal symptoms among mobile hand-held device users and their relationship to device use: A preliminary study in a Canadian university population, Sophia Berolo, Richard P. Wells, Benjamin C. Amick III, Applied Ergonomics, Volume 42, Issue 2, January 2011, pp. 371-378

Self-reported neck symptoms and use of personal computers, laptops and cell phones among Finns aged 18-65. Leena Korpinenab, Rauno Pääkkönenc Fabriziomaria Gobbad . Ergonomics. Volume 56, Issue 7, 2013. pp. 1134-1146

89 http://www.forbes.com/sites/nextavenue/2013/06/07/how-texting-can-give-you-a-permanent-pain-in-the-neck/

90 Cervicogenic headache: Clinical presentation, diagnostic criteria, and differential diagnosis. Fabio Antonaci MD, PhD, Torbjorn A. Fredriksen MD, PhD, Ottar Sjaastad MD, PhD. Current Pain and Headache Reports. 2001, Volume 5, Issue 4, pp. 387-392

Cervicogenic headache: an assessment of the evidence on clinical diagnosis, invasive tests, and treatment, Nikolai Bogduk, Jayantilal Govind, The Lancet Neurology, Volume 8, Issue 10, October 2009, pp. 959-968

Musculoskeletal physical outcome measures in individuals with tension-type headache: A scoping review. Jacques Abboud, Andrée-Anne Marchand, Karin Sorra, Martin Descarreaux. Cephalalgia June 26, 2013

Reinvestigation of the dysfunction in neck and shoulder girdle muscles as the reason of cervicogenic headache among office workers. Juliusz Huber, Przemysław Lisiński, Agnieszka Polowczyk.Disability and Rehabilitation. May 2013, Vol. 35, No. 10 , pp. 793-802

Review Cervicogenic headache: an assessment of the evidence on clinical diagnosis, invasive tests, and treatment. Bogduk N, Govind J. Lancet Neurol. 2009 Oct; 8(10):959-68.

Review Cervicogenic headache: anatomic basis and pathophysiologic mechanisms. Bogduk N. Curr Pain Headache Rep. 2001 Aug; 5(4):382-6.

Review Cervicogenic headaches: a critical review. Haldeman S, Dagenais S. Spine J. 2001 Jan-Feb; 1(1):31-46

91 Dry Eyes and Video Display Terminals. Kazuo Tsubota, M.D. Katsu Nakamori, Ph.D. N Engl J Med 1993; 328:584February 25, 1993. http://www.nejm.org/doi/full/10.1056/NEJM199302253280817

Eye blink frequency during different computer tasks quantified by electrooculography. J. H. Skotte, J. K. Nøjgaard, L. V. Jørgensen, K. B. Christensen, G. Sjøgaard. European Journal of Applied Physiology. January 2007, Volume 99, Issue 2, pp 113-119

Blink Rate, Incomplete Blinks and Computer Vision Syndrome. Portello, Joan K.; Rosenfield, Mark; Chu, Christina A. Optometry & Vision Science: May 2013 - Volume 90 - Issue 5 - pp. 482-487

92 Iam very happy with my " Pluggable®"

93 Posture, muscle activity and muscle fatigue in prolonged VDT work at different screen height settings. Jan Seghers, Arnaud Jochem & Arthur Spaepen. Ergonomics. Volume 46, Issue 7, 2000. pp. 714-730

Development and evaluation of an office ergonomic risk checklist: ROSA - Rapid office strain assessment,Michael Sonne, Dino L. Villalta, David M. Andrews, Applied Ergonomics, Volume 43, Issue 1, January 2012, pp. 98-108

Assessing Posture While Typing on Portable Computing Devices in Traditional Work Environments and at Home. Abigail J. Werth Kari Babski-Reeves, Ph.D., CPEProceedings of the Human Factors and Ergonomics Society Annual Meeting September 2012 vol. 56 no. 1 1258-1262

An ergonomics training program for student notebook computer users: Preliminary outcomes of a six-year cohort study. Karen Jacobs and others. Journal of Prevention, Assessment and Rehabilitation. Volume - Volume 44. Issue - 2 -221/230

Wrist and shoulder posture and muscle activity during touch-screen tablet use: Effects of usage configuration, tablet type, and interacting hand. Justin G. Young , Matthieu B. Trudeau, Dan Odell, Kim Marinelli, Jack T. DennerleinJournal of Prevention, Assessment and Rehabilitation (pre-press: http://iospress.metapress.com/content/w12751t54x304550/)

94 Osteoarthritis of the thumb carpometacarpal joint in women and occupational risk factors: a case–control study. L. Fontana, S. Neel, J.-M. Claise, S. Ughetto, P. Catilina. J. Hand Surg. Am., 32 (2007), pp. 459-465

Texting tenosynovitis. E.F. Storr, F.O. De Vere Beavis, M.D. Stringer. N. Z. Med. J., 120 (1267) (2007), p. 2868

"Texting" tendinitis. R.J. Menz. Med. J. Aust., 182 (6) (2005), p. 308

Excessive texting in pathophysiology of first carpometacarpal joint arthritis. Z. Ming, S. Pietikainen, O. Hanninen. Pathophysiology, 13 (4) (2006), pp. 269-270

Musculoskeletal symptoms among mobile hand-held device users and their relationship to device use: A preliminary study in a Canadian university population, Sophia Berolo, Richard P. Wells, Benjamin C. Amick III, Applied Ergonomics, Volume 42, Issue 2, January 2011, pp. 371-378

95 Accuracy and feasibility of using an electrogoniometer for measuring simple thumb movements. Per Jonsson, Peter W. Johnsonb & Mats Hagberga. Ergonomics. Volume 50, Issue 5, 2007. pp. 647-659

96 Thumbs up and down. Erin Walkinshaw. Canadian Medical Association Journal. August 9, 2011 vol. 183 no. 11 E711-E712. http://www.cmaj.ca/content/183/11/E711.short

Risk factors and clinical features of text message injuries. Deepak Sharan and Ajeesh PS.Tiasnimbas1Work 41 (2012) 1145-1148 .http://iospress.metapress.com/content/a465852l10826319/full-text.pdf

97 Live from Apple's iPhone OS 4 event!Joshua Topolsky. Apr 8th 2010. http://www.engadget.com/2010/04/08/live-from-apples-iphone-os-4-event/

98 On Touch Screens, Rest Your Finger by Using a Stylus. David Pogue. The New York Times. August 1, 2012

99 Sleep Loss and Fatigue in Residency Training. A Reappraisal. Sigrid Veasey. JAMA. 2002;288(9):1116-1124

Patterns of performance degradation and restoration during sleep restriction and subsequent recovery:a sleep dose-response study. Gregory Belenky, et al. J. Sleep Res. (2003) 12, 1-12

Too Little Sleep: The New Performance Killer. By Margaret Heffernan BNET February 10, 2011

Effect of Reducing Interns' Weekly Work Hours on Sleep and Attentional Failures. Steven W. Lockley, et al. New England J of Medecine. October 28, 2004

Extended Work Shifts and the Risk of Motor Vehicle Crashes among Interns. Laura K. Barge et al.New England J of Medecine. January 13, 2005

Effects of Health Care Provider Work Hours and Sleep Deprivation on Safety and Performance. Lockley, Steven W. et al.Joint Commission Journal on Quality and Patient Safety, Volume 33, Supplement 1, November 2007 , pp. 7-18(12)

Transport and industrial safety, how are they affected by sleepiness and sleep restriction? Pierre Philip, Torbjorn Åkerstedt. Sleep Medicine Reviews. Volume 10, Issue 5, October 2006, pp. 347-356

Suppression of sleepiness and melatonin by bright light exposure during breaks in night work. T. Akerstedt, G. Kecklund, S.E. Johansson. Shift work and mortality. A. Lowden, T. Åkerstedt, R. Wibomhronobiol Int, 21 (6) (2004), pp. 1055-1061.

Trends in the risk of accidents and injuries and their implications for models of fatigue and performance. S. Folkard, T. Åkerstedt. Aviat Space Environ Med, 75 (3) (2004), pp. A161-A167

Sleep on the night shift: 24-hour EEG monitoring of spontaneous sleep/wake behavior. L. Torsvall, T. Åkerstedt, K. Gillander, A. Knutsson. Psychophysiology, 26 (3) (1989), pp. 352-358

A prospective study of fatal occupational accidents—relationship to sleeping difficulties and occupational factors. T. Åkerstedt, P. Fredlund, M. Gillberg, B. Jansson. J Sleep Res, 11 (2002), pp. 69-71

Mortality associated with sleep duration and insomnia. D.F. Kripke, L. Garfinkel, D.L. Wingard, M.R. Klauber, M.R. Marler. Arch Gen Psychiatr, 59 (2002), pp. 131–136
The impact of sleep deprivation on decision making: A review. Harrison, Yvonne; Horne, James A. Journal of Experimental Psychology: Applied, Vol 6(3), Sep 2000
Junior doctors' extended work hours and the effects on their performance: the Irish case. Fiona Flinn and claire Armstrong. Int J Qual Health Care (2011) 23 (2): 210-217.
Sleeping brain, learning brain. The role of sleep for memory systems. Peigneux, Philippe et al. Neuroreport:21 December 2001 - Volume 12 - Issue 18 - pp. A111-A124
Immune, inflammatory and cardiovascular consequences of sleep restriction and recovery. Brice Faraut,Karim Zouaoui Boudjeltia,Luc Vanhamme, Myriam Kerkhofs. Sleep Medicine Reviews. Volume 16, Issue 2, April 2012, pp. 137–149
A brief afternoon nap following nocturnal sleep restriction: Which nap duration is most recuperative? Brooks, A.a,Lack, L. Sleep. Volume 29, Issue 6, 1 June 2006, pp. 831-840
100 Short Sleep Duration Among Workers – United States, 2010. Center for Disease Control and Prevention. April 27, 2012 / 61(16);281-285. http://www.cdc.gov/mmwr/pdf/wk/mm6116.pdf
101 Sleep duration and mortality: a systematic review and meta-analysis. Gallicchio, L. and Kalesan, B. (2009), Journal of Sleep Research, 18: 148-158
Sleep duration predicts cardiovascular outcomes: a systematic review and meta-analysis of prospective studies. Francesco P. Cappuccio and others. European Heart Journal (2011) 32, 1484-1492.
102 Too Little Sleep: The New Performance Killer. By Margaret Heffernan BNET february 10, 2011
103 The cumulative cost of additional wakefulness: dose-response effects on neurobehavioral functions and sleep

physiology from chronic sleep restriction and total sleep deprivation. H.P. Van Dongen, G. Maislin et al.Sleep, 26 (2) (2003), pp. 117–126
For a good discussion of the issues: Sleep duration and chronic sleep debt: Are 6 hours enough? Mathias Basner. Biological Psychology. Volume 87, Issue 1, April 2011, pp. 15–16.
104 Uncovering Residual Effects of Chronic Sleep Loss on Human Performance.Daniel A. Cohen and others. Sci Transl Med. 2010 January 13; 2(14)
The Cumulative Cost of Additional Wakefulness: Dose-Response Effects on Neurobehavioral Functions and Sleep Physiology From Chronic Sleep Restriction and Total Sleep Deprivation. Hans P.A. Van Dongen,and others. web2.med.upenn.edu/uep/user_documents/VanDongen_etal_Sleep_26_2_2003.pdf
105 Too Little Sleep: The New Performance Killer. By Margaret Heffernan | February 10, 2011 http://www.cbsnews.com/8301 505125_162-44341161/too-little-sleep-the-new-performance-killer/?tag=mncol;lst;1
106 Sleep and emotions: A focus on insomnia, Chiara Baglioni, Kai Spiegelhalder, Caterina Lombardo, Dieter Riemann, Sleep Medicine Reviews, Volume 14, Issue 4, August 2010, pp. 227-238
Effects of dietary caffeine on mood when rested and sleep restricted. Jack E. James, M. Elizabeth Gregg. Human Psychopharmacology: Clinical and Experimental. Volume 19, Issue 5, pp. 333-341, July 2004
107 Withdrawal Syndrome after the Double-Blind Cessation of Caffeine Consumption. Kenneth Silverman, Ph.D., Suzette M. Evans, Ph.D., Eric C. Strain, M.D., and Roland R. Griffiths, Ph.D.N Engl J Med 1992; 327:1109-1114
Sleep and emotions: A focus on insomnia, Chiara Baglioni, Kai Spiegelhalder, Caterina Lombardo, Dieter Riemann, Sleep Medicine Reviews, Volume 14, Issue 4, August 2010, pp. 227-238
108 Stop, That and One Hundred Other Sleep Scales. Colin M Shapiro, Azmeh Shahid, Kate Wilkinson. Springer. 2012

109 The emotional brain and sleep: an intimate relationship. Vandekerckhove, M., & Cluydts, R. (2010). Sleep medicine reviews, 14(4), 219-226.
Sleep and emotions: A focus on insomnia, Chiara Baglioni, Kai Spiegelhalder, Caterina Lombardo, Dieter Riemann, Sleep Medicine Reviews, Volume 14, Issue 4, August 2010, pp. 227-238
The relationship between depressive symptoms among female workers and job stress and sleep quality. Cho, H. S., Kim, Y. W., Park, H. W., Lee, K. H., Jeong, B. G., Kang, Y. S., & Park, K. S. (2013). Annals of Occupational and Environmental Medicine, 25(1), 12.
Sleep disorders and depression: brief review of the literature, case report, and nonpharmacologic interventions for depression. Luca, A., Luca, M., & Calandra, C. (2013). Clinical interventions in aging, 8, 1033.
Neuroscience-driven discovery and development of sleep therapeutics, M. Dresler, V.I. Spoormaker, P. Beitinger, M. Czisch, M. Kimura, A. Steiger, F. Holsboer, Pharmacology & Therapeutics, Available online 1 November 2013, ISSN 0163-7258
110 Stress: Friend and Foe. Theo Compernolle. Synergo Publishing. Available at www.brainchains.org
Stress: Vriend en Vijand. Uitgeverij Lannoo Belgium. 2012. 14th edition.
111 http://www.cdc.gov/features/dssleep/index.html#References
112 TNS research in March 2009. It surveyed 2,500 managers*- equally split across the UK, Germany, USA, Japan and The Netherlands http://www.newscenter.philips.com/about/news/press/20090518_sleep.page
113 http://www.cdc.gov/features/dssleep/index.html#References
Schoenborn CA, Adams PF. Health behaviors of adults: United States, 2005-2007. National Center for Health Statistics. Vital Health Stat 10(245). 2010.
Youth Risk Behavior Surveillance—United States, Centers for disease control and prevention. 2009. MMWR 2010;59:SS-5.
114 http://www.bls.gov/tus/charts/sleep.htm

115 Short Sleep Duration Among Workers – United States, 2010. Center for Disease Control and Prevention. April 27, 2012 / 61(16);281-285. http://www.cdc.gov/mmwr/pdf/wk/mm6116.pdf
Longer Work Days Leave Americans Nodding Off On the Job. National Sleep Foundation - Information on Sleep Health and Safety. 2008. http://www.sleepfoundation.org/article/press-release/longer-work-days-leave-americans-nodding-the-job
2011 National Survey of the Sleep Foundation. http://www.sleepfoundation.org/sites/default/files/sleepinamericapoll/SIAP_2011_Summary_of_Findings.pdf
Social Jetlag and Obesity. Till Roenneberg, Karla V. Allebrandt, Martha Merrow, Céline Vetter. Current Biology - 22 May 2012 (Vol. 22, Issue 10, pp. 939-943)
116 http://www.newscenter.philips.com/about/news/press/20090518_sleep.page
117 2011 National Survey of the Sleep Foundation. http://www.sleepfoundation.org/sites/default/files/sleepinamericapoll/SIAP_2011_Summary_of_Findings.pdf
118 Effects of sleep deprivation on cognition. Killgore WD. Prog Brain Res. 2010;185:105-29.
A meta-analysis of the impact of short-term sleep deprivation on cognitive variables. Lim, Julian; Dinges, David F. Psychological Bulletin, Vol 136(3), May 2010
Impairment of Attentional Networks after 1 Night of Sleep Deprivation. D. Tomasi, R.L. Wang, F. Telang, V. Boronikolas, M.C. Jayne, G.-J. Wang, J.S. Fowler, and N.D. Volkow. Cereb Cortex. 2009 January; 19(1): 233-240.
Neuroscience-driven discovery and development of sleep therapeutics, M. Dresler, V.I. Spoormaker, P. Beitinger, M. Czisch, M. Kimura, A. Steiger, F. Holsboer, Pharmacology & Therapeutics, Available online 1 November 2013, ISSN 0163-7258
119 Control of Sleep and Wakefulness. Ritchie E. Brown, Radhika Basheer, James T. McKenna, Robert E. Strecker,

and Robert W. McCarley. Physiol Rev July 1, 2012 vol. 92 no. 3 1087-1187

120 The cumulative cost of additional wakefulness: dose-response effects on neurobehavioral functions and sleep physiology from chronic sleep restriction and total sleep deprivation. Van Dongen HP, Maislin G, Mullington JM, Dinges DF. Sleep. 2003 Mar 15;26(2):117-26.

121 Invited Review: Integration of human sleep-wake regulation and circadian rhythmicity. Derk-Jan Dijk and Steven W. Lockley. Journal of Applied Physiology February 1, 2002 vol. 92 no. 2 852-862. http://www.jappl.org/content/92/2/852.full

122 Excellent review: MAMMALIAN CIRCADIAN BIOLOGY: Elucidating Genome-Wide Levels of Temporal Organization. Phillip L. Lowrey and Joseph S. Takahashi. Annu. Rev. Genomics Hum. Genet. 2004. 5:407-41
Clock genes in mammalian peripheral tissues. Aurélio Balsalobre. Cell and Tissue Research. July 2002, Volume 309, Issue 1, pp. 193-199
Circadian clock in cell culture: I. Oscillation of melatonin release from dissociated chick pineal cells in flow-through microcarrier culture. LM Robertson and JS Takahashi. The Journal of Neuroscience, 1 January 1988, 8(1). 12-21;
The circadian clock: pacemaker and tumour suppressor. Loning Fu & Cheng Chi Lee. Nature Reviews Cancer 3, 350-361 (May 2003)
Analysis of the molecular pathophysiology of sleep disorders relevant to a disturbed biological clock. Takashi Ebisawa. Mol Genet Genomics (2013) 288:185-193
Circadian Disruption Leads to Insulin Resistance and Obesity, Shu-qun Shi, Tasneem S. Ansari, Owen P. McGuinness, David H. Wasserman, Carl Hirschie Johnson, Current Biology, Volume 23, Issue 5, 4 March 2013, pp. 372-381,

123 Stability of melatonin and temperature as circadian phase markers and their relation to sleep in humans. S. Benloucif, M. J. Guico, K. J. Reid, L. F. Wolfe, M. L'Hermite-Balériaux and P. C.

Zee. J. Biol.Rhythms 20:178-188.

124 Effects of acutely displaced sleep on testosterone. J. Axelsson, M. Ingre, T. Akerstedt, U. Holmback. J. Clin. Endocrinol. Metab., 90 (8) (2005), pp. 4530-4535

125 Evening exposure to a light-emitting diodes (LED)-backlit computer screen affects circadian physiology and cognitive performance, Christian Cajochen, Sylvia Frey1, Doreen Anders, Jakub Späti1, Matthias Bues, Achim Pross, Ralph Mager, Anna Wirz-Justice1, and Oliver Stefani. Journal of Applied Physiology May 1, 2011 vol. 110 no. 5 1432-1438

126 Entrainment of the human circadian system by light. Duffy JF, Wright KP., Jr, J Biol Rhythms. 2005;20:326-38

127 A Novel Human Opsin in the Inner Retina. Ignacio Provencio et al. The Journal of Neuroscience, 15 January 2000, 20(2): 600-605;
Action Spectrum for Melatonin Regulation in Humans: Evidence for a Novel Circadian Photoreceptor C. Brainard et al. The Journal of Neuroscience, 15 August 2001, 21(16): 6405-6412;
High sensitivity of the human circadian melatonin rhythm to resetting by short wavelength light. Lockley SW, Brainard GC, Czeisler CA. J Clin Endocrinol Metab. 2003;88:4502-5.
Melanopsin: an exciting photopigment, Mark W. Hankins, Stuart N. Peirson, Russell G. Foster, Trends in Neurosciences, Volume 31, Issue 1, January 2008, pp. 27-36
Photoreceptors and Circadian Clocks, S.N. Peirson, R.G. Foster, In: Editor-in-Chief: Larry R. Squire, Editor(s)-in-Chief, Encyclopedia of Neuroscience, Academic Press, Oxford, 2009, pp. 669-676, http://www.sciencedirect.com/science/article/pii/B9780080450469016028)
Diverse types of ganglion cell photoreceptors in the mammalian retina, Andrea Sand, Tiffany M. Schmidt, Paulo Kofuji, Progress in Retinal and Eye Research, Volume 31, Issue 4, July 2012, pp. 287-302, http://www.sciencedirect.com/science/article/pii/S1350946212000171
Everything you want to know about

colour temperature and the Kelvin see http://www.handprint.com/HP/WCL/color12.html
When and Why Colors Change Their Appearance. http://www.uni-bielefeld.de/lili/kumu/farbenlehre-kueppers/en/funktionsprinzip_des_sehens/wann_und_warum_farben_ihr_aussehen_veraendern.html
For the analysis of the wavelenghth of a few lcd screens go to http://www.displaymate.com/Spectra_4.html
128 The relationship between media use in the bedroom, sleep habits and symptoms of insomnia. Geir Scott Brunborg, Rune Aune Mentzoni, Helge Molde, Helga Myrseth, Knut Joachim Mår Skouverøe, Bjørn Bjorvatn, Ståle Pallesen. Journal of Sleep Research. Volume 20, Issue 4, pp. 569-575, December 2011
Blue light improves cognitive performance. Lehrl S, Gerstmeyer K, Jacob JH, Frieling H, Henkel AW, Meyrer R, Wiltfang J, Kornhuber J, Bleich S.J Neural Transm. 2007;114(4):457-60
Evening exposure to a light-emitting diodes (LED)-backlit computer screen affects circadian physiology and cognitive performance. Christian Cajochen, Sylvia Frey1, Doreen Anders, Jakub Späti, Matthias Bues, Achim Pross, Ralph Mager3, Anna Wirz-Justice1, and Oliver Stefani. Journal of Applied Physiology May 1, 2011 vol. 110 no. 5 1432-1438
Light level and duration of exposure determine the impact of self-luminous tablets on melatonin suppression. Brittany Wood, Mark S. Rea, Barbara Plitnick, Mariana G. Figueiro. Applied Ergonomics, Available online 31 July 2012
Can light make us bright? Effects of light on cognition and sleep. Chellappa SL, Gordijn MC, Cajochen C. Progress in Brain Research. 2011(190):119-133.
Exposure to room light before bedtime suppresses melatonin onset and shortens melatonin duration in humans. Gooley JJ, Chamberlain K, Smith KA, et al. Journal of Clinical Endocrinology and Metabolism. 2011;96(3):E463-472.
Daytime light exposure dynamically enhances brain responses. Vandewalle G, Balteau E, Phillips C, et al. Current

Biology. 2006;16(16):1616-1621.
129 Evening exposure to a light-emitting diodes (LED)-backlit computer screen affects circadian physiology and cognitive performance, Christian Cajochen, Sylvia Frey1, Doreen Anders, Jakub Späti1, Matthias Bues, Achim Pross, Ralph Mager, Anna Wirz-Justice1, and Oliver Stefani. Journal of Applied Physiology May 1, 2011 vol. 110 no. 5 1432-1438
Light level and duration of exposure determine the impact of self-luminous tablets on melatonin suppression,Brittany Wood, Mark S. Rea, Barbara Plitnick, Mariana G. Figueiro, In press: Applied Ergonomics, Available online 31 July 2012 http://www.sciencedirect.com/science/article/pii/S0003687012001159
Non-Visual Effects of Light on Melatonin, Alertness and Cognitive Performance: Can Blue-Enriched Light Keep Us Alert? Sarah Laxhmi Chellappa,Roland Steiner,Peter Blattner, Peter Oelhafen, Thomas Götz, and Christian Cajochen. PLoS One. 2011; 6(1)
Photons, clocks, and consciousness. Brainard GC, Hanifin JP.J Biol Rhythms. 2005 Aug;20(4):314-25.
Alerting effects of light, Christian Cajochen, Sleep Medicine Reviews, Volume 11, Issue 6, December 2007, pp. 453-464,
130 2011 National Survey of the Sleep Foundation. http://www.sleepfoundation.org/sites/default/files/sleepinamericapoll/SIAP_2011_Summary_of_Findings.pdf
131 Identifying some determinants of "jet lag" and its symptoms: A study of athletes and other travellers. Waterhouse, J.; Edwards, B.; Nevill, A.; Carvalho, S.; Atkinson, G.; Buckley, P.; Reilly, T.; Godfrey, R.; Ramsay, R. (2002). British journal of sports medicine 36 (1): 54-60.
Excellent review: Jet lag: trends and coping strategies. Jim Waterhouse, Thomas Reilly, Greg Atkinson, Ben Edwards. Lancet 2007; 369: 1117-29
Haimov I, Arendt J. The prevention and treatment of jet lag. Sleep Med Rev 1999; 3: 229-40.
132 Work and rest sleep schedules of

227 European truck drivers, P Philip, J Taillard, D Léger, K Diefenbach, T Akerstedt, B Bioulac, C Guilleminault, Sleep Medicine, Volume 3, Issue 6, November 2002, pp. 507-511

133 Social Jetlag and Obesity. Till Roenneberg, Karla V. Allebrandt, Martha Merrow, Céline Vetter. Current Biology - 22 May 2012 (Vol. 22, Issue 10, pp. 939-943)

134 Circadian Rhythm Sleep Disorders: Part I, Basic Principles, Shift Work and Jet Lag Disorders. An American Academy of Sleep Medicine Review. Sleep. Robert L Sack, MD, Dennis Auckley, MD, R. Robert Auger, MD, Mary A. Carskadon, PhD, Kenneth P. Wright, Jr, PhD, Michael V. Vitiello, PhD, and Irina V. Zhdanova, MD. Sleep. 2007 . November 1; 30(11): 1460-1483.
Shift Work Disorder: Overview and Diagnosis. Thomas Roth, PhD. Brief report.J Clin Psychiatry 2012;73. http://www.psychiatrist.com/briefreports/series-1/BR2/index.asp
Shift Work Disorder in Nurses - Assessment, Prevalence and Related Health Problems. Flo E, Pallesen S, Magerøy N, Moen BE, Grønli J, et al. (2012) PLoS ONE 7(4)
Circadian Phase, Sleepiness, and Light Exposure Assessment in Night Workers With and Without. Valentina Gumenyuk, Thomas Roth, and Christopher L. Drake, 6Chronobiology International 2012 29:7, 928-936

135 IN-DEPTH REVIEW: SHIFT WORK: Shift work, safety and productivity, Simon Folkard and Philip Tucker. Occup Med (Lond) (2003) 53 (2): 95-101.

136 Junior doctors' extended work hours and the effects on their performance: the Irish case. Fiona Flinn and claire Armstrong. Int J Qual Health Care (2011) 23 (2): 210-217.
Remarks by dr. Chuck czeisler, sleep specialist with harvard medical school. http://wakeupdoctor.org/index.php?option=com_content&view=article&id=54&itemid=55
Effect of Reducing Interns' Weekly Work Hours on Sleep and Attentional Failures Steven W. Lockley, and many others., N

Engl J Med 2004; 351:1829-1837

137 Effect of Reducing Interns' Weekly Work Hours on Sleep and Attentional Failures Steven W. Lockley, and many others., N Engl J Med 2004; 351:1829-1837

138 Extended Work Shifts and the Risk of Motor Vehicle Crashes among Interns. Laura K. Barge et al.New England J of Medecine. January 13, 2005
Effects of Health Care Provider Work Hours and Sleep Deprivation on Safety and Performance. Lockley, Steven W. et al.Joint Commission Journal on Quality and Patient Safety, Volume 33, Supplement 1, November 2007 , pp. 7-18(12)

139 Effect of Reducing Interns' Weekly Work Hours on Sleep and Attentional Failures. Steven W. Lockley, et al. New England J of Medecine. October 28, 2004

140 T. Akerstedt, G. Kecklund, S.E. Johansson. Shift work and mortality. Chronobiol Int, 21 (6) (2004), pp. 1055-1061

141 Trends in the risk of accidents and injuries and their implications for models of fatigue and performance. S. Folkard, T. Åkerstedt. Aviat Space Environ Med, 75 (3) (2004), pp. A161-A167
Sleep on the night shift: 24-hour EEG monitoring of spontaneous sleep/wake behavior. L. Torsvall, T. Åkerstedt, K. Gillander, A. Knutsson. Psychophysiology, 26 (3) (1989), pp. 352-358
A prospective study of fatal occupational accidents—relationship to sleeping difficulties and occupational factors. T. Åkerstedt, P. Fredlund, M. Gillberg, B. Jansson. J Sleep Res, 11 (2002), pp. 69-71

142 Suppression of sleepiness and melatonin by bright light exposure during breaks in night work. T. Akerstedt, G. Kecklund, S.E. Johansson. Shift work and mortality. A. Lowden, T. Åkerstedt, R. Wibomhronobiol Int, 21 (6) (2004), pp. 1055-1061..

143 Transport and industrial safety, how are they affected by sleepiness and sleep restriction? Pierre Philip, Torbjorn Åkerstedt. Sleep Medicine Reviews. Volume 10, Issue 5, October 2006, pp. 347-356

144 Excellent review: The impact of

daylight saving time on sleep and related behaviours. Harrison, Y. (2013). Sleep medicine reviews.Volume 17, Issue 4, August 2013, pp. 285-292

Individual response to the end of Daylight Saving Time is largely dependent on habitual sleep duration. Biological Rhythm Research, 44(3), 391-401.Harrison, Y. (2013).

Changing to daylight saving time cuts into sleep and increases workplace injuries. Barnes, C. M., & Wagner, D. T. (2009). Journal of applied psychology, 94(5), 1305.

Daytime sleepiness during transition into daylight saving time in adolescents: Are owls higher at risk?, Anne-Marie Schneider, Christoph Randler, Sleep Medicine, Volume 10, Issue 9, October 2009, pp. 1047-1050

Work and rest sleep schedules of 227 European truck drivers, P Philip, J Taillard, D Léger, K Diefenbach, T Akerstedt, B Bioulac, C Guilleminault, Sleep Medicine, Volume 3, Issue 6, November 2002, pp. 507-511

About time: Daylight Saving Time transition and individual well-being, Yiannis Kountouris, Kyriaki Remoundou, Economics Letters, Volume 122, Issue 1, January 2014, pp. 100-103

Sullivan, J. M., & Flannagan, M. J. (2002). The role of ambient light level in fatal crashes: inferences from daylight saving time transitions. Accident Analysis & Prevention, 34(4), 487-498.

Only abstract available: Coren, S. (1996). Accidental death and the shift to daylight savings time. Perceptual and motor skills, 83(3), 921-922

145 Sleep Restriction Suppresses Neurogenesis Induced by Hippocampus-Dependent Learning Ilana S. Hairston and others. AJP - JN Physiol December 2005 vol. 94 no. 6 4224-4233

146 The emotional brain and sleep: an intimate relationship. Vandekerckhove, M., & Cluydts, R. (2010). Sleep medicine reviews, 14(4), 219-226.

Sleep and emotions: A focus on insomnia, Chiara Baglioni, Kai Spiegelhalder, Caterina Lombardo, Dieter Riemann, Sleep Medicine Reviews, Volume 14, Issue 4, August 2010, pp. 227-238

The relationship between depressive symptoms among female workers and job stress and sleep quality. Cho, H. S., Kim, Y. W., Park, H. W., Lee, K. H., Jeong, B. G., Kang, Y. S., & Park, K. S. (2013). Annals of Occupational and Environmental Medicine, 25(1), 12.

Sleep disorders and depression: brief review of the literature, case report, and nonpharmacologic interventions for depression. Luca, A., Luca, M., & Calandra, C. (2013). Clinical interventions in aging, 8, 1033.

Neuroscience-driven discovery and development of sleep therapeutics, M. Dresler, V.I. Spoormaker, P. Beitinger, M. Czisch, M. Kimura, A. Steiger, F. Holsboer, Pharmacology & Therapeutics, Available online 1 November 2013, ISSN 0163-7258

The relationship between depressive symptoms among female workers and job stress and sleep quality. Cho, H. S., Kim, Y. W., Park, H. W., Lee, K. H., Jeong, B. G., Kang, Y. S., & Park, K. S. (2013). Annals of Occupational and Environmental Medicine, 25(1), 12.

147 For a really excellent scientific review about what is going on in the brain read: CONTROL OF SLEEP AND WAKEFULNESS. Ritchie E. Brown, Radhika Basheer, James T. McKenna, Robert E. Strecker, and Robert W. McCarley. Physiol Rev 92: 1087-1187, 2012

148 The emotional brain and sleep: an intimate relationship. Vandekerckhove, M., & Cluydts, R. (2010). Sleep medicine reviews, 14(4), 219-226.

Sleep and emotions: A focus on insomnia, Chiara Baglioni, Kai Spiegelhalder, Caterina Lombardo, Dieter Riemann, Sleep Medicine Reviews, Volume 14, Issue 4, August 2010, pp. 227-238

The relationship between depressive symptoms among female workers and job stress and sleep quality. Cho, H. S., Kim, Y. W., Park, H. W., Lee, K. H., Jeong, B. G., Kang, Y. S., & Park, K. S. (2013). Annals of Occupational and Environmental Medicine, 25(1), 12.

Sleep disorders and depression: brief review of the literature, case report, and nonpharmacologic interventions for depression. Luca, A., Luca, M., & Calandra, C. (2013). Clinical interventions in aging, 8, 1033.

Neuroscience-driven discovery and development of sleep therapeutics, M. Dresler, V.I. Spoormaker, P. Beitinger, M. Czisch, M. Kimura, A. Steiger, F. Holsboer, Pharmacology & Therapeutics, Available online 1 November 2013, ISSN 0163-7258

The relationship between depressive symptoms among female workers and job stress and sleep quality. Cho, H. S., Kim, Y. W., Park, H. W., Lee, K. H., Jeong, B. G., Kang, Y. S., & Park, K. S. (2013). Annals of Occupational and Environmental Medicine, 25(1), 12.

Calandra, C. (2013). Clinical interventions in aging, 8, 1033.

149 Sleep-dependent memory consolidation and reconsolidation. Robert Stickgold, Matthew P. Walker. Sleep Medicine 8 (2007) 331-343

150 The role of sleep in cognition and emotion. Walker, M. P. (2009). Annals of the New York Academy of Sciences, 1156(1), 168-197

151 The emotional brain and sleep: an intimate relationship. Vandekerckhove, M., & Cluydts, R. (2010). Sleep medicine reviews, 14(4), 219-226.

Sleep and emotions: A focus on insomnia, Chiara Baglioni, Kai Spiegelhalder, Caterina Lombardo, Dieter Riemann, Sleep Medicine Reviews, Volume 14, Issue 4, August 2010, pp. 227-238

The relationship between depressive symptoms among female workers and job stress and sleep quality. Cho, H. S., Kim, Y. W., Park, H. W., Lee, K. H., Jeong, B. G., Kang, Y. S., & Park, K. S. (2013). Annals of Occupational and Environmental Medicine, 25(1), 12.

Sleep disorders and depression: brief review of the literature, case report, and nonpharmacologic interventions for depression. Luca, A., Luca, M., & Calandra, C. (2013). Clinical interventions in aging, 8, 1033.

Neuroscience-driven discovery and

development of sleep therapeutics, M. Dresler, V.I. Spoormaker, P. Beitinger, M. Czisch, M. Kimura, A. Steiger, F. Holsboer, Pharmacology & Therapeutics, Available online 1 November 2013, ISSN 0163-7258

The relationship between depressive symptoms among female workers and job stress and sleep quality. Cho, H. S., Kim, Y. W., Park, H. W., Lee, K. H., Jeong, B. G., Kang, Y. S., & Park, K. S. (2013). Annals of Occupational and Environmental Medicine, 25(1), 12.

Sleep disorders and depression: brief review of the literature, case report, and nonpharmacologic interventions for depression. Luca, A., Luca, M., & Calandra, C. (2013). Clinical interventions in aging, 8, 1033.

Neuroscience-driven discovery and development of sleep therapeutics, M. Dresler, V.I. Spoormaker, P. Beitinger, M. Czisch, M. Kimura, A. Steiger, F. Holsboer, Pharmacology & Therapeutics, Available online 1 November 2013, ISSN 0163-7258

Quantitative genetic research on sleep: A review of normal sleep, sleep disturbances and associated emotional, behavioural, and health-related difficulties, Sleep Medicine Reviews, Nicola L. Barclay, Alice M. Gregory, Volume 17, Issue 1, February 2013, pp. 29-40,

Sleep deprivation reduces perceived emotional intelligence and constructive thinking skills. W.D. Killgore, E.T. Kahn-Greene, E.L. Lipizzi, R.A. Newman, G.H. Kamimori, T.J. Balkin Sleep Med, 9 (2008), pp. 517-526

The effects of 53 hours of sleep deprivation on moral judgment. W.D. Killgore, D.B. Killgore, L.M. Day, C. Li, G.H. Kamimori, T.J. Balkin. Sleep, 30 (2007), pp. 345-352

Sleep and emotions: A focus on insomnia, Chiara Baglioni, Kai Spiegelhalder, Caterina Lombardo, Dieter Riemann, Sleep Medicine Reviews, Volume 14, Issue 4, August 2010, pp. 227-238

152 Overnight therapy? The role of sleep in emotional brain processing. Walker, Matthew P.; van der Helm, Els. Psychological Bulletin, Vol 135(5), Sep 2009, 731-748

153 Why REM sleep? Jim Horne, Clues beyond the laboratory in a more challenging world, Biological Psychology, Volume 92, Issue 2, February 2013, pp. 152-168

154 Prefrontal atrophy, disrupted NREM slow waves and impaired hippocampal-dependent memory in aging. Bryce A Mander and others. Nature Neuroscience. 16,357-364.(2013)

155 Wake deterioration and sleep restoration of human learning, Bryce A. Mander, Sangeetha Santhanam, Jared M. Saletin, Matthew P. Walker, Current Biology, Volume 21, Issue 5, 8 March 2011, pp. 183-184,

156 Wake deterioration and sleep restoration of human learning, Bryce A. Mander, Sangeetha Santhanam, Jared M. Saletin, Matthew P. Walker, Current Biology, Volume 21, Issue 5, 8 March 2011, pp. R183-R184.

157 Sleep Restriction Suppresses Neurogenesis Induced by Hippocampus-Dependent Learning. Ilana S. Hairston1, Milton T. M. Little, Michael D. Scanlon, Monique T. Barakat, Theo D. Palmer, Robert M. Sapolsky, and H. Craig Heller. AJP - JN Physiol December 2005 vol. 94 no. 6 4224-4233

158 For a review: The impact of sleep deprivation on decision making: A review. Harrison, Yvonne; Horne, James A. Journal of Experimental Psychology: Applied, Vol 6(3), Sep 2000
Neuroscience-driven discovery and development of sleep therapeutics, M. Dresler, V.I. Spoormaker, P. Beitinger, M. Czisch, M. Kimura, A. Steiger, F. Holsboer, Pharmacology & Therapeutics, Available online 1 November 2013, ISSN 0163-7258
Sleep inspires insight. Ullrich Wagner, Steffen Gais, Hilde Haider, Rolf Verleger & Jan Born. Letters to Nature. Nature 427, 352-355 (2004)
http://www.cogsci.ucsd.edu/~chiba/SleepInsightWagnerNature04.pdf
Memory Consolidation during Sleep: Interactive Effects of Sleep Stages and HPA Regulation, Ullrich Wagner & Jan Born, Stress 28, 2838 (2008).
Sleep and Student Performance at School, Howard Taras & William Potts-Datema, J. Sch. Health 248, 248254 (2005)
Human Relational Memory Requires Time and Sleep, Jeffrey M. Ellenbogen et al., Proceedings Natl. Acad. Science 7723, 77237728 (2007).
University students and the "all nighter". Pamela V. Thacher, Sleep Med. 16, 24 (2008)
Sleep Schedules and Daytime Functioning in Adolescents, R. Wolfson & Mary A. Carskadon, Child Dev. 875, 884 (1998)
Sleep Deprivation Reduces Perceived Emotional Intelligence and Constructive Thinking Skills, William D. S. Killgore et al., Sleep Med. 517, 523 (2008)
"Multi-Tasking: The Effects of Interacting With Technology On Learning In A Real-Time Classroom Lecture" Zivcakova, Lucia, (2011). Theses and Dissertations (Comprehensive). Paper 1038.

159 The impact of sleep deprivation on decision making: A review. Harrison, Yvonne; Horne, James A. Journal of Experimental Psychology: Applied, Vol 6(3), Sep 2000

160 The impact of sleep deprivation on decision making: A review. Harrison, Yvonne; Horne, James A. Journal of Experimental Psychology: Applied, Vol 6(3), Sep 2000

161 The influence of sleep quality, sleep duration and sleepiness on school performance in children and adolescents: A meta-analytic review, Julia F. Dewald, Anne M. Meijer, Frans J. Oort, Gerard A. Kerkhof, Susan M. Bögels, Sleep Medicine Reviews, Volume 14, Issue 3, June 2010, pp. 179-189
The association between sleep spindles and IQ in healthy school-age children, Reut Gruber, Merrill S. Wise, Sonia Frenette, Bärbel Knäuper, Alice Boom, Laura Fontil, Julie Carrier, International Journal of Psychophysiology, Volume 89, Issue 2, August 2013, pp. 229-240,

162 The impact of sleep deprivation on decision making: A review. Harrison, Yvonne; Horne, James A. Journal of Experimental Psychology: Applied, Vol 6(3), Sep 2000

163 The impact of sleep deprivation on decision making: A review. Harrison, Yvonne; Horne, James A. Journal of Experimental Psychology: Applied, Vol 6(3), Sep 2000

164 www.thedailyshow.com/watch/thu-september-20-2007/bill-clinton-pt--2?videoId=103116

165 The human emotional brain without sleep — a prefrontal amygdala disconnect, Seung-Schik Yoo, Ninad Gujar, Peter Hu, Ferenc A. Jolesz, Matthew P. Walker, Current Biology, Volume 17, Issue 20, 23 October 2007, pp. R877-R878

166 Sleep and emotions: Bidirectional links and underlying mechanisms, Michal Kahn, Gal Sheppes, Avi Sadeh, International Journal of Psychophysiology, Volume 89, Issue 2, August 2013, pp. 218-228
Quantitative genetic research on sleep: A review of normal sleep, sleep disturbances and associated emotional, behavioural, and health-related difficulties, Sleep Medicine Reviews, Nicola L. Barclay, Alice M. Gregory, Volume 17, Issue 1, February 2013, pp. 29-40,
Sleep deprivation reduces perceived emotional intelligence and constructive thinking skills. W.D. Killgore, E.T. Kahn-Greene, E.L. Lipizzi, R.A. Newman, G.H. Kamimori, T.J. Balkin Sleep Med, 9 (2008), pp. 517-526
The effects of 53 hours of sleep deprivation on moral judgment. W.D. Killgore, D.B. Killgore, L.M. Day, C. Li, G.H. Kamimori, T.J. Balkin. Sleep, 30 (2007), pp. 345-352
Sleep and emotions: A focus on insomnia, Chiara Baglioni, Kai Spiegelhalder, Caterina Lombardo, Dieter Riemann, Sleep Medicine Reviews, Volume 14, Issue 4, August 2010, pp. 227-238

167 A role for REM sleep in recalibrating the sensitivity of the human brain to specific emotions. Gujar, N., McDonald, S. A., Nishida, M., & Walker, M. P. (2011). Cerebral Cortex, 21(1), 115-123.
Sleep deprivation impairs the accurate recognition of human emotions. van der Helm E; Gujar N; Walker MP. SLEEP 2010;33(3):335-342.

168 The memory function of sleep. Susanne Diekelmann & Jan Born. Nature Reviews Neuroscience 11, 114-126 (February 2010)

169 A deficit in the ability to form new human memories without sleep. Seung-Schik Yoo, Peter T Hu, Ninad Gujar, Ferenc A Jolesz & Matthew P Walker. Nature Neuroscience 10, 385 - 392 (2007)

170 Motor memory consolidation in sleep shapes more effective neuronal representations.Fischer S, Nitschke MF, Melchert UH, Erdmann C, Born J. J Neurosci. 2005 Dec 7;25(49):11248-55.
Sleep inspires insight.Wagner U, Gais S, Haider H, Verleger R, Born J. Nature. 2004 Jan 22;427(6972):352-5.
Sleeping brain, learning brain. The role of sleep for memory systems. Peigneux, Philippe et al. Neuroreport:21 December 2001, Volume 12, Issue 18, pp A111-A124

171 Ultradian and asymmetric rhythms of hemispheric processing speed. Iskra-Golec I, Smith L. (2006). Chronobiol. Int. 23:1229-1239.
Cognitive efficiency and circadian typologies: a diurnal study, Personality and Individual Differences, Vincenzo Natale, Antonella Alzani, PierCarla Cicogna, Volume 35, Issue 5, October 2003, pp. 1089-1105,

172 Circadian Typology. A Comprehensive Review. Ana Adan,Simon N. Archer,Maria Paz Hidalgo,Lee Di Milia,Vincenzo Natale,Christoph Randler. Chronobiology International, 29(9): 1153-1175, (2012)

173 Harvard Medical School: http://healthysleep.med.harvard.edu/healthy/matters/consequences/sleep-performance-and-public-safety

174 2011 National Survey of the Sleep Foundation. http://www.sleepfoundation.org/sites/default/files/sleepinamericapoll/SIAP_2011_Summary_of_Findings.pdf
Sleep, Performance, and Public Safety. Harvard Medical School. http://healthysleep.med.harvard.edu/healthy/matters/consequences/sleep-performance-and-public-safety

175 Robert Koch Institute http://www.rki.de/cln_162/nn_216470/EN/Content/Health Reporting/GBEDownloadsT/

schlafstoerung,templateId=raw,property =publicationFile.pdf/schlafstoerung. pdf

176 Sleep-Deprived Young Drivers and the Risk for Crash: The DRIVE Prospective Cohort Study. Martiniuk AC, Senserrick T, Lo S, et al. JAMA Pediatr. 2013;167(7):647-655.

177 Sleep-Deprived Young Drivers and the Risk for Crash: The DRIVE Prospective Cohort Study. Martiniuk AC, Senserrick T, Lo S, et al. JAMA Pediatr. 2013;167(7):647-655.

178 Fatigue Risk Management in the Workplace. ACOEM Presidential Task Force on Fatigue Risk Management:; Lerman, Steven E. MD, MPH; Eskin, Evamaria MD, MPH; Flower, David J. MBBS, MD; George, Eugenia C. MD; Gerson, Benjamin MD; Hartenbaum, Natalie MD, MPH; Hursh, Steven R. PhD; Moore-Ede, Martin MD, PhD. ournal of Occupational & Environmental Medicine: February 2012 - Volume 54 - Issue 2 - p 231-258. http://journals.lww. com/joem/Fulltext/2012/02000/Fatigue_Risk_Management_in_the_ Workplace.17.aspx

179 Fatigue among Clinicians and the Safety of Patients. David M. Gaba, M.D., and Steven K. Howard, M.D. N Engl J Med 2002; 347:1249-1255October 17, 2002

Impact of Fatigue on Performance in Registered Nurses: Data Mining and Implications for Practice. Kalyan S. Pasupathy, Linsey M. Barker. (2012) Journal for Healthcare Quality 34:5, 22-30

Sleep Disorders, Health, and Safety in Police Officers. S.F. Jones. Yearbook of Pulmonary Disease 2012, 204-206

The occupational impact of sleep quality and insomnia symptoms, Erica R. Kucharczyk, Kevin Morgan, Andrew P. Hall, Sleep Medicine Reviews, Available online 7 March 2012

Sleep Quality and Motor Vehicle Crashes in Adolescents. Fabio Pizza, M.D.,Sara Contardi, M.D.,Alessandro Baldi Antognini, Ph.D.,Maroussa Zagoraiou, Ph.D.,Matteo Borrotti,Barbara Mostacci, M.D.,Susanna Mondini, M.D., and Fabio

Cirignotta, M.D. Clin Sleep Med. 2010 February 15; 6(1): 41-45.

Sleep, sleepiness and motor vehicle accidents: a national survey.Gander PH, Marshall NS, Harris RB, Reid P.Aust N Z J Public Health. 2005 Feb;29(1):16-21.

Immune, inflammatory and cardiovascular consequences of sleep restriction and recovery.Faraut B, Boudjeltia KZ, Vanhamme L, Kerkhofs M.Sleep Med Rev. 2012 Apr;16(2):137-49. Epub 2011 Aug 10.

A case-crossover study of sleep and work hours and the risk of road traffic accidents. Valent F; Di Bartolomeo S; Marchetti R; Sbrojavacca R; Barbone F. SLEEP 2010;33(3):349-354.

Drowsy Driving. The Road Safety Monitor 2004. Traffic Injury Research Foundation. Canada. 2004. http://www.tirf. ca/publications/PDF_publications/ RSM_Drowsy_Driving_2004.pdf

Insufficient sleep impairs driving performance and cognitive function, Seiko Miyata, Akiko Noda, Norio Ozaki, Yuki Hara, Makoto Minoshima, Kunihiro Iwamoto, Masahiro Takahashi, Tetsuya Iidaka, Yasuo Koike, Neuroscience Letters, Volume 469, Issue 2, 22 January 2010, pp. 229-233

Risk Factors for the Injury Severity of Fatigue-Related Traffic Accidents. Lian Zhen Wang, Yu Long Pei, Bo Tong Liu. 2012, Advanced Engineering Forum, 5, 61

Sleepiness/fatigue and distraction/ inattention as factors for fatal versus nonfatal commercial motor vehicle driver injuries.Bunn, T. L.; Slavova, S.; Struttmann, T. W. & Browning, S. R. (2005). Accident Analysis & Prevention, 37(5), 862-869

Hazard perception in novice and experienced drivers: The effects of sleepiness, Simon S. Smith, Mark S. Horswill, Brooke Chambers, Mark Wetton, Accident Analysis & Prevention, Volume 41, Issue 4, July 2009, pp. 729-733,

Fatigue Risk Management in the Workplace. ACOEM Presidential Task Force on Fatigue Risk Management:; Lerman, Steven E. MD eo; Journal of Occupational & Environmental Medicine: Feb-

ruary 2012 - Volume 54 - Issue 2 - pp. 231-258
Young drivers' perceptions of culpability of sleep-deprived versus drinking drivers, Lela Rankin Williams, David R. Davies, Kris Thiele, Judith R. Davidson, Alistair W. MacLean, Journal of Safety Research, Volume 43, Issue 2, April 2012, pp. 115-122

180 The occupational impact of sleep quality and insomnia symptoms, Erica R. Kucharczyk, Kevin Morgan, Andrew P. Hall, Sleep Medicine Reviews, Available online 7 March 2012
A Meta-Analysis of the Impact of Short-Term Sleep Deprivation on Cognitive VariablesJulian Lim and David F. Dinges. Psychol Bull. 2010 May; 136(3): 375-389.

181 Mortality associated with sleep duration and insomnia. D.F. Kripke, L. Garfinkel, D.L. Wingard, M.R. Klauber, M.R. Marler. Arch Gen Psychiatr, 59 (2002), pp. 131-136

182 Cerebral Arterial Pulsation Drives Paravascular CSF-Interstitial Fluid Exchange in the Murine Brain. Jeffrey J. Iliff. The Journal of Neuroscience, 13 November 2013, 33(46): 18190-18199
Sleep Drives Metabolite Clearance from the Adult Brain. Lulu Xie and others. Science 18 October 2013: Vol. 342 no. 6156 pp. 373 377
Self-reported Sleep and β-Amyloid Deposition in Community-Dwelling Older Adults. JAMA Neurol. Adam P. Spira and others. Published online October 21, 2013
Amyloid-β Dynamics Are Regulated by Orexin and the Sleep-Wake Cycle. Jae-Eun Kang and others. Science 13 November 2009: Vol. 326 no. 5955 pp
Garbage Truck of the Brain. Maiken Nedergaard. Science 28 June 2013: Vol. 340 no. 6140 pp. 1529-1530
Sleep Drives Metabolite Clearance from the Adult Brain. Lulu Xie, et al. , Science. 342 (2013)
http://www.sciencemag.org/content/342/6156/373.full.pdf

183 Acute Sleep Deprivation Enhances the Brain's Response to Hedonic Food Stimuli: An fMRI Study. Christian Benedict*, Samantha J. Brooks*, Owen G.

O'Daly, Markus S. Almèn, Arvid Morell, Karin Åberg, Malin Gingnell, Bernd Schultes, Manfred Hallschmid, Jan-Erik Broman, Elna-Marie Larsson and Helgi B. Schiöth The Journal of Clinical Endocrinology & Metabolism March 1, 2012 vol. 97 no. 3 E443-E447
Lifestyle determinants of the drive to eat: a meta-analysis. Colin Daniel Chapman, Christian Benedict, Samantha Jane Brooks, and Helgi Birgir Schiöth. Am J Clin Nutr September 2012 vol. 96 no. 3 492-497
Social Jetlag and Obesity. Till Roennebery, Karla V. Allebrandt, Martha Merrow, Céline Vetter. Current Biology - 22 May 2012 (Vol. 22, Issue 10, pp. 939-943)
Acute partial sleep deprivation increases food intake in healthy men.. Brondel L, Romer MA,Nougues PM, Touyarou P, Davenne. Am J Clin Nutr 91:1550-1559.

184 Is Sleep Duration Associated With Childhood Obesity? A Systematic Review and Meta-analysis.Chen, X., Beydoun, M. A. and Wang, Y. (2008), Obesity, 16: 265-274

185 Daytime sleepiness affects prefrontal regulation of food intake. William D.S. Killgore, Zachary J. Schwab, Mareen Weber, Maia Kipman, Sophie R. DelDonno, Melissa R. Weiner, Scott L. Rauch. NeuroImage 71 (2013) 216-223

186 Medecine: sleep it off. Helen Pearson. Nature 443, 261-263 (21 September 2006) http://www.nature.com/nature/journal/v443/n7109/full/443261a.html
Acute Sleep Deprivation Enhances the Brain's Response to Hedonic Food Stimuli: An fMRI Study. Christian Benedict, Samantha J. Brooks,Owen G. O'Daly, Markus S. Almen,Arvid Morell, Karin Åberg, Malin Gingnell, Bernd Schultes, Manfred Hallschmid, Jan-Erik Broman, Elna-Marie Larsson, and Helgi B. Schioth. J Clin Endocrinol Metab 97/3 March 2012
Sleep restriction leads to increased activation of brain regions sensitive to food stimuli. Marie-Pierre St-Onge, Andrew McReynolds, Zalak B Trivedi, Amy L Roberts, Melissa Sy, and Joy Hirsch. Am J Clin Nutr April 2012
Short sleep duration increases energy

intakes but does not change energy expenditure in normal-weight individuals. Marie-Pierre St-Onge ao. Am J Clin Nutr August 2011 vol. 94 no. 2 410-416
Short sleep duration as a possible cause of obesity: critical analysis of the epidemiological evidence. L. S. Nielsen†, K. V. Danielsen†, T. I. A. Sørensen. Obesity Reviews.Volume 12, Issue 2, pp. 78-92, February 2011
Short Sleep Duration is Associated with Reduced Leptin Levels and Increased Adiposity: Results from the Québec Family Study. Chaput, J.-P., Després, J.-P., Bouchard, C. and Tremblay, A. (2007), Obesity, 15: 253-261.
187 How Sleep Loss Adds To Weight Gain. Anahad O'connor. New York Times August 6, 2013
188 Short sleep duration associated with a higher prevalence of metabolic syndrome in an apparently healthy population. Preventive Medicine, Available online 27 July 2012. http://www.sciencedirect.com/science/article/pii/S0091743512003234
189 Sleep and antibody response to hepatitis B vaccination. Prather AA; Hall M; Fury JM; Ross DC; Muldoon MF; Cohen S; Marsland AL. SLEEP. 2012;35(8):1063-1069
Sleep and immune function. Luciana Besedovsky&Tanja Lange&Jan Born. Invited review.Eur J Physiol (2012) 463:121-137
190 For an excellent review: Sleep and immune function. Luciana Besedovsky, Tanja Lange ,and Jan Born. Pflugers Arch. 2012 January; 463(1): 121-137.
A Prospective Study of Sleep Duration and Pneumonia Risk in Women Sanjay R. Patel, Atul Malhotra, Xiang Gao,Frank B. Hu, Mark I. Neuman, and Wafaie W. Fawzi,Sleep. 2012 January 1; 35(1): 97-101.
191 Sleep Habits and Susceptibility to the Common Cold.Sheldon Cohen ao. Arch Intern Med. 2009 January 12; 169(1): 62-67
192 Sleep duration and endometrial cancer risk. Cancer Causes and Control-Susan R. Sturgeon, Nicole Luisi, Raji Balasubramanian and Katherine W.

Reeves.Volume 23, Number 4 (2012), 547-553
Circadian Disruption, Sleep Loss, and Prostate Cancer Risk: A Systematic Review of Epidemiologic Studies Cancer Epidemiol Biomarkers Prev July 2012 21:1002-1011;
Association of sleep duration and breast cancer OncotypeDX recurrence score. Cheryl L. Thompson and Li Li. Breast Cancer Research and Treatment. Volume 134, Number 3 (2012), 1291-1295
Non-apnea sleep disorders will increase subsequent liver cancer risk - A nationwide population-based cohort study. Ji-An Liang, Li-Min Sun, Chih-Hsin Muo, Fung-Chang Sung,Shih-Ni Chang. Sleep Medicine. Volume 13, Issue 7, August 2012, pp. 869-874
Recommendations for the prevention of breast cancer in shift workers. Kneginja Richter, Jens Acker, Nikola Kamcev, Stojan Bajraktarov, Anja Piehl and Guenter Niklewski. The EPMA Journal. Volume 2, Number 4 (2011), 351-356
Sleep disturbance, cytokines, and fatigue in women with ovariancancer. Lauren Clevenger ao. Brain, Behavior, and Immunity. Volume 26, Issue 7, October 2012, pp. 1037-1044
IARC Monographs Programme http://www.iarc.fr/en/media-centre/pr/2007/pr180.html
193 Association between habitual sleep duration and blood pressure and clinical implications: A systematic review. Elizabeth Dean and others. Blood Pressure. February 2012, Vol. 21, No. 1 , pp. 45-57
194 Short and long sleep duration are associated with prevalent cardiovascular disease in Australian adults. Magee, Christopher A., et al.Journal of sleep research 21.4 (2012): 441-447.
Sleep duration and sleep quality in relation to 12-year cardiovascular disease incidence: the MORGEN study. Hoevenaar-Blom MP, Spijkerman AM, Kromhout D, van den Berg JF, Verschuren WM. Sleep. 2011 Nov 1;34(11):1487-92
Immune, inflammatory and cardiovascular consequences of sleep restriction and recovery. Brice Faraut,Karim

Zouaoui Boudjeltia,Luc Vanhamme, Myriam Kerkhofs. Sleep Medicine Reviews. Volume 16, Issue 2, April 2012, pp. 137-149

195 Headache and sleep, Sleep Medicine Reviews, Andrea Alberti, Volume 10, Issue 6, December 2006, pp. 431-437 Melatonin, the pineal gland and their implications for headache disorders. MFP Peres. Cephalalgia June 2005 vol. 25 no. 6 403-411

196 Beauty sleep: experimental study on the perceived health. and attractiveness of sleep deprived people John Axelsson. British Medial Journal oct 2010;341:c6614

197 Chronic Insomnia as a Risk Factor for Developing Anxiety and Depression. Dag Neckelmann, MD, PhD,Amstein Mykletun, PhD, and Alv A. Dahl, MD, PhD. Sleep. 2007 July 1; 30(7): 873-880. Prevalence, Course, and Comorbidity of Insomnia and Depression in Young Adults. Daniel J. Buysse, MD,Jules Angst, MD,Alex Gamma, PhD, Vladeta Ajdacic, PhD, Dominique Eich, MD, and Wulf Rössler, MA, MD. Sleep. 2008 April 1; 31(4): 473-480. Insomnia in Young Men and Subsequent Depression. The Johns Hopkins Precursors Study. Patricia P. Chang Daniel E. Ford Lucy A. Mead Lisa Cooper-Patrick1, and Michael J. Klag. Am. J. Epidemiol. (1997) 146 (2): 105-114.

198 Earlier Parental Set Bedtimes as a Protective Factor Against Depression and Suicidal Ideation. James E. Gangwisch. Sleep. Volume 33, Issue 01. 2012

199 Influences of early shift work on the diurnal cortisol rhythm, mood and sleep: Within-subject variation in male airline pilots, Sophie Bostock, Andrew Steptoe, Psychoneuroendocrinology, Available online 9 August 2012

200 The association of testosterone, sleep, and sexual function in men and women, Monica L. Andersen, Tathiana F. Alvarenga, Renata Mazaro-Costa, Helena C. Hachul, Sergio Tufik, Brain Research, Volume 1416, 6 October 2011, pp. 80-104 Sleep deprivation lowers reactive aggression and testosterone in men, Kimberly A. Cote, Cheryl M. McCormick, Shawn, N. Geniole, Ryan P. Renn, Stacey D. MacAulay, Biological Psychology, Available online 6 October 2012. http://www.sciencedirect.com/science/article/pii/S0301051112002037 The association of testosterone, sleep, and sexual function in men and women,Monica L. Andersen, Tathiana F. Alvarenga, Renata Mazaro-Costa, Helena C. Hachul, Sergio Tufik, Brain Research, Volume 1416, 6 October 2011, pp. 80-104, ISSN 0006-8993, 10.1016/j.brainres.2011.07.060. http://www.sciencedirect.com/science/article/pii/S0006899311014302

201 Daytime sleepiness during transition into daylight saving time in adolescents: Are owls higher at risk?, Anne-Marie Schneider, Christoph Randler, Sleep Medicine, Volume 10, Issue 9, October 2009, pp. 1047-1050

202 For an excellent review see: Functional consequences of inadequate sleep in adolescents: A systematic review, Tamar Shochat, Mairav Cohen-Zion, Orna Tzischinsky, Sleep Medicine Reviews, Available online 24 June 2013, ISSN 1087-0792 For an excellent review see: Sleep, cognition, and behavioral problems in school-age children: a century of research meta-analyzed. R.G. Astill, K.B. Van der Heijden, M.H. Van Ijzendoorn, E.J. Van Someren. Psychological Bulletin, 138 (2012), pp. 1109-1138 Sleep, cognition, and behavioral problems in school-age children: A century of research meta-analyzed. Astill, R. G., Van der Heijden, K. B., Van IJzendoorn, M. H., & Van Someren, E. J. (2012).Psychological bulletin, 138(6), 1109. In search of lost sleep: secular trends in the sleep time of school-aged children and adolescents. Matricciani, L., Olds, T., & Petkov, J. (2012). Sleep medicine reviews, 16(3), 203-211. Pathways to adolescent health sleep regulation and behavior. Journal of Adolescent Health, 31 (2002), pp. 175-184 Sleep and emotions: Bidirectional links and underlying mechanisms, Michal Kahn, Gal Sheppes, Avi Sadeh, Interna-

tional Journal of Psychophysiology, Volume 89, Issue 2, August 2013, pp. 218-228
Adolescent sleep patterns: biological, social, and psychological influences. M.A. Carskadon, C. Acebo
Regulation of sleepiness in adolescents: update, insights, and speculation. Sleep, 25 (2002), pp. 606-614
The sleepy adolescent: causes and consequences of sleepiness in teens. Moore, M. and Meltzer, L. J. Paediatr. Respir. Rev., 2008, 9: 114-120.
203 The influence of sleep quality, sleep duration and sleepiness on school performance in children and adolescents: A meta-analytic review, Julia F. Dewald, Anne M. Meijer, Frans J. Oort, Gerard A. Kerkhof, Susan M. Bögels, Sleep Medicine Reviews, Volume 14, Issue 3, June 2010, pp. 179-189
The association between sleep spindles and IQ in healthy school-age children, Reut Gruber, Merrill S. Wise, Sonia Frenette, Bärbel Knäauper, Alice Boom, Laura Fontil, Julie Carrier, International Journal of Psychophysiology, Volume 89, Issue 2, August 2013, pp. 229-240,
204 Recent worldwide sleep patterns and problems during adolescence: a review and meta-analysis of age, region, and sleep. M. Gradisar, G. Gardner, H. Dohnt, Sleep Med, 12 (2011), pp. 110-118
Weekend catch-up sleep is independently associated with suicide attempts and self-injury in Korean adolescents. Kang, S. G., Lee, Y. J., Kim, S. J., Lim, W., Lee, H. J., Park, Y. M., ... & Hong, J. P. (2013). Comprehensive psychiatry. Available online 22 October 2013
Functional consequences of inadequate sleep in adolescents: A systematic review, Tamar Shochat, Mairav Cohen-Zion, Orna Tzischinsky, Sleep Medicine Reviews, Available online 24 June 2013, ISSN 1087-0792
205 Pathways to adolescent health sleep regulation and behavior. Ronald E Dahl, Daniel S Lewin. Journal of Adolescent Health. Volume 31, Issue 6, Supplement, December 2002, pp. 175-184
Sleep deprivation may be undermining teen health. SIRI CARPENTER. Monitor on psychology. Volume 32, No. 9 October 2001. http://www.mjsd.k12.wi.us/mhs/depts/socialstudies/Kelly/documents/sleepteen.pdf
Understanding adolescent's sleep patterns and school performance: a critical appraisal. Amy R Wolfson Mary A Carskadon. Sleep Medicine Reviews. Volume 7, Issue 6, 2003, pp. 491-506
Sleep duration and overweight/obesity in children: Review and implications for pediatric nursing. Liu, J., Zhang, A. and Li, L. (2012), Journal for Specialists in Pediatric Nursing.
206 Reut Gruber, Rachelle Laviolette, Paolo Deluca, Eva Monson, Kim Cornish, Julie Carrier, Short sleep duration is associated with poor performance on IQ measures in healthy school-age children, Sleep Medicine, Volume 11, Issue 3, March 2010, pp. 289-294, ISSN 1389-9457, 10.1016/j.sleep.2009.09.007.
Sadeh, A., Gruber, R. and Raviv, A. (2003), The Effects of Sleep Restriction and Extension on School-Age Children: What a Difference an Hour Makes. Child Development, 74: 444-455.
207 Recent worldwide sleep patterns and problems during adolescence: a review and meta-analysis of age, region, and sleep. M. Gradisar, G. Gardner, H. Dohnt, Sleep Med, 12 (2011), pp. 110-118
In search of lost sleep: secular trends in the sleep time of school-aged children and adolescents. Matricciani, L., Olds, T., & Petkov, J. (2012). Sleep medicine reviews, 16(3), 203-211.
The Chronic Sleep Reduction Questionnaire (CSRQ): a cross-cultural comparison and validation in Dutch and Australian adolescents. Julia F. Dewald, Michelle A. Short, Michael Gradisar, Frans J. Oort, Anne Marie Meijer. Journal of Sleep Research.2012. http://dx.doi.org/10.1111/j.1365-2869.2012.00999.x
208 Stress: Friend and Foe. Theo Compernolle. Synergo 1999 / Lannoo 2011
209 Environmental Satisfaction in Open-Plan Environment: 2 Effect of Workstation Size. Charles, K. E.; Veitch, J.A. NRC Institute for Research in Construction; National Research Council Canada 2002. http://www.nrc-cnrc.gc.

ca/obj/irc/doc/pubs/ir/ir845/ir845.pdf
210 Office Type in Relation to Health, Well-Being, and Job Satisfaction Among Employees. Christina Bodin Danielsson and Lennart Bodin,Environment and Behavior 2008 40: 636
Also: http://eab.sagepub.com/content/40/5/636
211 Should Health Service Managers Embrace Open Plan Work Environments? Vinesh G. Oommen, Mike Knowles, Isabella Zhao. A Review Asia Pacific Journal of Health Management, Vol. 3, No. 2. (December 2008), pp. 37-43
212 G. Mylonas, J. Carstairs: Review chapter. Open Plan Office Environments: Rhetoric and Reality 2010 http://api.ning.com/files/3ZJ3t4b2xNN3HrWuGscREjmNhRwtnZKwtnD-JXjXXnoo_/OpenPlanOffices.pdf
213 Individual Flexibility in the Workplace A Spatial Perspective. S Värlander. Journal of Applied Behavioral Science, 2012 0021-8863. 48(1):33. http://jab.sagepub.com/content/48/1/33.full.pdf+html
214 Remaining afloat amid email deluge. Nick Bilton. International New York Times.januari 20. 2014. Page 14
215 "Constant, constant, multi-tasking craziness": managing multiple working spheres. Victor M. Gonzále, Gloria Mark. Proceedings of the SIGCHI conference on Human factors in computing systems. ACM New York, NY, USA ©2004
216 "You've Got E-Mail!" ... Shall I Deal With It Now? Electronic Mail From The Recipient's Perspective. Karen Renaud Judith Ramsay, Mario Hair . International Journal Of Human–Computer Interaction, 21(3), 313-332
217 E-mail as a source and symbol of stress. Barley, S., Myerson, D., and Grodel, S. Organization Science 22, 4 (2011), 887-906.
218 harris interactive Survey, 2010. Quoted in The definitive guide to taming the em@il monster. David Grossman. http://www.yourthoughtpartner.com/Portals/83405/pdf/taming%20the%20e-mail%20monster.pdf?hsCtaTracking=a6b8dec3-ccff-4202-

982e-d2363877ef01%7C6bd3eafd-bcb9-42b8-a463-2d1ef2bdg13e
219 Charles R. Stoner, Paul Stephens, Matthew K. McGowan, Connectivity and work dominance: Panacea or pariah?, Business Horizons, Volume 52, Issue 1, January–February 2009, pp. 67-78. http://www.sciencedirect.com/science/article/pii/S0007681308001298
220 Google's Chief Works to Trim a Bloated Ship. CLAIRE CAIN MILLER. The New York Times. November 9, 2011
221 Effects of e-mail addiction and interruptions on employees, Laura Marulanda-Carter, Thomas W. Jackson, (2012) Journal of Systems and Information Technology, Vol. 14 Iss: 1, pp.82 - 94
222 Toward taming the monster in electronic mail. Demiridjian, Z. S. (2005). The Journal of American Academy of Business, 7, 1-2.
223 "The social economy: Unlocking value and productivity through social technology" McKinsey Global Institute. 2012 http://www.mckinsey.com/-/media/McKinsey/dotcom/Insights%20and%20pubs/MGI/Research/Technology%20and%20Innovation/The%20social%20economy/MGI_The_social_economy_Full_report.ashx
224 The cost of e-mail within organizations. Jackson, Thomas W., Ray Dawson, and Darren Wilson. Strategies for eCommerce Success (2002): 307.
225 The cost of email within organizations. Jackson, Thomas W., Ray Dawson, and Darren Wilson. Strategies for eCommerce Success (2002): 307.
226 The effects of interruptions on task performance, annoyance, and anxiety in the user interface. Brian P Bailey, Joseph A Konstan, John V Carlis. Proceedings of INTERACT (2001). Volume: 1, Publisher: Citeseer, pp. 593-601
On the need for attention-aware systems: Measuring effects of interruption on task performance, error rate, and affective state. Brian P. Bailey, Joseph A. Konstan.Computers in Human Behavior Volume 22, Issue 4, July 2006, pp. 685-708
Reducing the disruptive effects of interruption: A cognitive framework for

analysing the costs and benefits of intervention strategies.Deborah A. Boehm-Davis, Roger Remington Accident Analysis & Prevention. Volume 41, Issue 5, September 2009, pp. 1124–1129

227 Understanding email interaction increases organizational productivity. T. Jackson, R. Dawson, D. Wilson Communications of the ACM, 46 (2003), pp. 80–84 http://dl.acm.org/citation.cfm?id=859673

228 "You've Got E-Mail!" ... Shall I Deal With It Now? Electronic Mail From The Recipient's Perspective. Karen Renaud Judith Ramsay, Mario Hair . International Journal Of Human–Computer Interaction, 21(3), 313–332

229 Email training significantly reduces email defects, International Journal of Information Management, Anthony Burgess, Thomas Jackson, Janet Edwards, Volume 25, Issue 1, February 2005, pp. 71-83

230 quoted by Jake Breeden in Tipping Sacred Cows. John Wiley & Sons 2013

231 "A Pace Not Dictated by Electrons': An Empirical Study of Work without E-Mail" Gloria Mark, Stephen Voida and Armand Cardello. https://students.ics.uci.edu/~svoida/uploads/Publications/Publications/markvoida-chi12.pdf

232 Driving While Distracted. Nationwide. 2008. http://www.nationwide.com/pdf/dwd-2008-survey-results.pdf? NWOSS=survey+2008&NWOSSPos=1 State of the Nation of cell phone distracted driving. http://www.nsc.org/safety_road/Distracted_Driving/Documents/State%20of%20the%20Nation.pdf www.nhtsa.gov/staticfiles/nti/pdf/811555.pdf

233 Promoting the Car Phone, Despite Risks. By Matt Richtel. New York Times. December 6, 2009

234 Drivers and Legislators Dismiss Cellphone Risks. Matt Richtel. New York Times. July 19, 2009

235 BlackBerry cuts made roads safer, police say. Awad Mustafa and Caline Malek "The National" UAE Oct 15, 2011 http://www.thenational.ae/news/uae-news/blackberry-cuts-made-roads-safer-police-say

236 http://www.nhtsa.gov/Research/Human+Factors/Naturalistic+driving+studies

237 Reducing Distracted Driving: Regulation and Education to Avert Traffic Injuries and Fatalities. Lawrence O. Gostin. Peter D. Jacobson. 303 JAMA 1419-1420 (2010) http://scholarship.law.georgetown.edu/facpub/380

238 A Comparison of the Cell Phone Driver and the Drunk Driver. David L. Strayer, Frank A. Drews and Dennis J. Crouch. Hum Factors 2006; 48; 381 http://www.psych.utah.edu/abclab/publications/distraction/Strayer(2006)%20-%20A%20comparison%20of%20the%20cell-phone%20driver%20and%20the%20drunk%20driver.pdf Engrossed in conversation: The impact of cell phones on simulated driving performance, Kristen E. Beede, Steven J. Kass, Accident Analysis & Prevention, Volume 38, Issue 2, March 2006, pp. 415-421 Driver Safety Impacts of Voice-to-Text Mobile Applications. Christine E. Yager. Proceedings of the Human Factors and Ergonomics Society Annual Meeting September 2013 vol. 57 no. 1 1869-1873

239 Influence of personal mobile phone ringing and usual intention to answer on driver error, Carol Holland, Versha Rathod, Accident Analysis & Prevention, Volume 50, January 2013, pp. 793-800

240 A Comparison of the Cell Phone Driver and the Drunk Driver. David L. Strayer, Frank A. Drews and Dennis J. Crouch. Hum Factors 2006; 48; 381 http://www.psych.utah.edu/abclab/publications/distraction/Strayer(2006)%20-%20A%20comparison%20of%20the%20cell-phone%20driver%20and%20the%20drunk%20driver.pdf See also: Driving whilst using in-vehicle information systems (IVIS): benchmarking the impairment to alcohol. Wynn, T., Richardson, J.H. and Stevens, A., 2013. Driving whilst using in-vehicle information systems (IVIS): benchmarking the impairment to alcohol. IN: Regan, M.A.,

Lee, J.D. and Victor, T.W. (eds.) Driver Distraction and Inattention Advances in Research and Countermeasures, Volume 1, pp. 253-275.

241 Passenger and cell phone conversations in simulated driving. Drews, Frank A.; Pasupathi, Monisha; Strayer, David L. Journal of Experimental Psychology: Applied, Vol 14(4)

Distracted driving in elderly and middle-aged drivers. Kelsey R. Thompson et al. Accident Analysis & Prevention. Volume 45, March 2012, pp. 711-717

Effects of cellular telephones on driving behaviour and crash risk: Results of meta-analysis. JK Caird, CT Scialfa... - 2004 - psych.ucalgary.ca http://www.psych.ucalgary.ca/pace/PCA-Lab/pdf/Final%20Report%20-%20Cell%20Phones.pdf

242 The Effects of Text Messaging During Dual-Task Driving Simulation on Cardiovascular and Respiratory Responses and Reaction Time Creators: Park, Andrew; Salsbury, Joshua; Corbett, Keira; Aiello, JenniferIssue Date:2013-01 The Ohio Journal of Science, v111, n2-5 (January, 2013), 42-44.

243 http://www.distraction.gov/content/get-the-facts/index.html Texting while driving: evaluation of glance distributions forFrequent/infrequent texters and keypad/touchpad texters .Siby samuel, alexander pollatsek, & donald fisher. Proceedings of the sixth international driving symposium on human factors in driver assessment, training and vehicle design. http://drivingassessment.uiowa.edu/sites/default/files/DA2011/Papers/061_SamuelPollatsek.pdf

VirginiaTech Transportation Institute. New data from VTTI provides insight into cell phone use and driving distraction. July 27, 2009.

Fernando A. Wilson and Jim P. Stimpson. Trends in Fatalities From Distracted Driving in the United States, 1999 to 2008. American Journal of Public Health: November 2010, Vol. 100, No. 11, pp. 2213-2219.!

244 The choice to text and drive in younger drivers: Behavior may shape attitude. Paul Atchley, Stephanie Atwood,Aaron Boulton. Accident Analysis & Prevention. Volume 43, Issue 1, January 2011, pp. 134-142

245 College students' prevalence and perceptions of text messaging while driving. Marissa A. Harrison. Accident Analysis & Prevention. Volume 43, Issue 4, July 2011, pp. 1516-1520

246 Adults and Cell Phone Distractions. Madden, M. & Rainie, L., Pew Internet & American Life Project, Pew Research Center (2010). http://pewinternet.org/Reports/2010/Cell-Phone-Distractions.aspx .

The effects of perception of risk and importance of answering and initiating a cellular phone call while driving.Erik Nelson,Paul Atchley,Todd D. Little. Accident Analysis & Prevention. Volume 41, Issue 3, May 2009, pp. 438-444

247 Effects of car-phone use and aggressive disposition during critical driving maneuvers. Lui, B.-S., Lee, Y.-H., 2005. Transportation Research: Part F 8,369-382.

Tison, J., Chaudhary, N., & Cosgrove, L. (2011, December). National phone survey on distracted driving attitudes and behaviors. (DOT HS 811 555). Washington, DC: National Highway Traffic Safety Administration. www.nhtsa.gov/static-files/nti/pdf/811555.pdf

248 Cognitive Distraction While Multitasking in the Automobile. David L. Strayer, Jason M. Watson, and Frank A. Drews, In Brian Ross, editor: The Psychology ofLearning and Motivation, Vol. 54, Burlington: Academic Press, 2011, pp. 29-58.

249 Inattentional Blindness in a Simulated Driving Task. Kellie D. Kennedy James P. Bliss Proceedings of the Human Factors and Ergonomics Society Annual Meeting September 2013 vol. 57 no. 1 1899-1903

250 Driver distraction: The effects of concurrent in-vehicle tasks, road environment complexity and age on driving performance. Tim Horberry, Janet Anderson, Michael A. Regana,Thomas J. Triggs,John Brown. Accident Analysis &

Prevention. Volume 38, Issue 1, January 2006, pp. 185–191

Distraction Effects of In-Vehicle Tasks Requiring Number and Text Entry Using Auto Alliance's Principle 2.1B Verification Procedure.Thomas A. Ranney ao. National Highway Traffic Safety Administration Vehicle Research and Test Center. http://www.distraction.gov/download/research-pdf/Distraction_Effects_of_In-Vehicle_Tasks_508.pdf

The effects of using a portable music player on simulated driving performance and task-sharing strategies Original Research Article. Kristie L. Young, Eve Mitsopoulos-Rubens, Christina M. Rudin-Brown, Michael G. Lenné. Applied Ergonomics, Volume 43, Issue 4, July 2012, pp. 738-746.

251 Speech-Based Interaction with In-Vehicle Computers: The Effect of Speech-Based E-Mail on Drivers' Attention to the Roadway John D. Lee Human Factors: The Journal of the Human Factors and Ergonomics Society Winter 2001 vol. 43 no. 4 631-640

Inattentional Blindness in a Simulated Driving Task. Kellie D. Kennedy James P. Bliss Proceedings of the Human Factors and Ergonomics Society Annual Meeting September 2013 vol. 57 no. 1 1899-1903

The Effects of Text Messaging During Dual-Task Driving Simulation on Cardiovascular and Respiratory Responses and Reaction Time Park, Andrew; Salsbury, Joshua; Corbett, Keira; Aiello, JenniferIssue Date:2013-01 The Ohio Journal of Science, v111, n2-5 (January, 2013), 42-44.

(only abstract) Driving whilst using in-vehicle information systems (IVIS): benchmarking the impairment to alcohol. Wynn, T., Richardson, J.H. and Stevens, A., 2013. Driving whilst using in-vehicle information systems (IVIS): benchmarking the impairment to alcohol. IN: Regan, M.A., Lee, J.D. and Victor, T.W. (eds.) Driver Distraction and Inattention. Advances in Research and Countermeasures, Volume 1, pp. 253-275.

(only abstract)Texting while driving: is speech-based texting less risky than handheld texting? Proceedings of the 5th International Conference on Automotive User Interfaces and Interactive Vehicular Applications Jibo He and others pp. 124-130 2013

Driver Safety Impacts of Voice-to-Text Mobile Applications. Christine E. Yager. Proceedings of the Human Factors and Ergonomics Society Annual Meeting September 2013 vol. 57 no. 1 1869-1873 (abstract only) Hands Free Texting While Driving - Is It Safer than Conventional Texting While Driving? Young, Kaysha

252 Control of Attention Shifts between Vision and Audition in Human Cortex. Sarah Shomstein and Steven Yantis. The Journal of Neuroscience, November 24, 2004 • 24(47):10702-10706

253 The crosstalk hypothesis: Why language interferes with driving. Bergen, Benjamin; Medeiros-Ward, Nathan; Wheeler, Kathryn; Drews, Frank; Strayer, David. Journal of Experimental Psychology: General, Vol 142(1), Feb 2013, 119-130

How Speech Modifies Visual Attention. Spence, I., Jia, A., Feng, J., Elserafi, J., & Zhao, Y. (2013). Applied Cognitive Psychology, 27(5), 633-643.

Effect of cellular telephone conversations and other potential interference on reaction time in a braking response. William Consiglio, Peter Driscoll, Matthew Witte, William P. Ber.Accident Analysis and Prevention 35 (2003) 495-500

254 Distracted Driving Among. Newly Licensed Teen. Drivers. March 2012. AAA Foundation/UNC Highway Safety Research Center . Arthur H. Goodwin. Robert D. Foss. Stephanie S. Harrell Natalie P. O'Brien. http://www.distraction.gov/download/DistractedDrivingAmongNewlyLicensedTeenDrivers.pdf

255 For a very recent review of the research got to Governors Highways Safety Association at http://www.ghsa.org/html/publications/pdf/sfdist11.pdf

256 www.nhtsa.gov/staticfiles/nti/pdf/811555.pdf

257 The 100-Car Naturalistic Driving Study, Phase II – Results of the 100-Car

Field Experiment. Dingus, T. A., ao. 2006.National Highway Traffic Safety Admin. (NHTSA). http://www.distraction.gov/research/PDF-Files/The-100-Car-Naturalistic-Driving-Study.pdf

258 The 100-Car Naturalistic Driving Study, Phase II - Results of the 100-Car Field Experiment. Dingus, T. A., ao. 2006.National Highway Traffic Safety Admin. (NHTSA). http://www.distraction.gov/research/PDF-Files/The-100-Car-Naturalistic-Driving-Study.pdf

259 Cognitive Distraction While Multitasking in the Automobile. David L. Strayer, Jason M. Watson, and Frank A. Drews. Psychology of Learning and Motivation, Volume 54 2011p 29-58 http://psych.utah.edu/lab/appliedcognition/publications/distractionmultitasking.pdf Measuring Cognitive Distraction in the Automobile. Strayer, David L. Cooper, Joel M. for AAA Foundation for Traffic Safety. 2013. https://www.aaafoundation.org/sites/default/files/Measuring-CognitiveDistractions.pdf http://trid.trb.org/view.aspx?id=1252566

260 Cell Phones and Driving: Review of Research. Anne T. McCartt, Laurie A. Hellinga, and Keli a. Braitman. Traffic Injury Prevention, 7:89-106, 2006 http://www.childinjurylaws.com/pdf/Cell%20Phones%20and%20Driving-%20Review%20of%20Research.pdf Effect of cellular telephone conversations and other potential interference on reaction time in a braking response. William Consiglio, Peter Driscoll, Matthew Witte, William P. Ber.Accident Analysis and Prevention 35 (2003) 495-500 How Speech Modifies Visual Attention. Spence, I., Jia, A., Feng, J., Elserafi, J., & Zhao, Y. (2013). Applied Cognitive Psychology, 27(5), 633-643. Speech-Based Interaction with In-Vehicle Computers: The Effect of Speech-Based E-Mail on Drivers' Attention to the Roadway John D. Lee Human Factors: The Journal of the Human Factors and Ergonomics Society Winter 2001 vol. 43 no. 4 631-640

261 Engrossed in conversation: The impact of cell phones on simulated driving performance. Kristen E. Beede,Steven J. Kass.Volume 38, Issue 2, March 2006, pp. 415-421

262 An on-road assessment of cognitive distraction: Impacts on drivers' visual behavior and braking performance. J. Harbluk et al. Accident Analysis and Prevention. Volume 39, 2007, p. 372. Examining the impact of cell phone conversations on driving using meta-analytic techniques. W. Horrey et al. Human Factors. Volume 48, Spring 2006, p. 196. Gorillas in our midst: sustained inattentional blindness for dynamic events. D. Simons and C. Chabris. Perception. Volume 28, 1999, p. 1059

263 (distance × sin10°)/sin85°

264 For interesting visual ones, just Google or Bing "Subjective Constancy"

265 David Strayer quoted in: Impactful Distraction. Talking while driving poses dangers that people seem unable to see. Nathan Seppa 12:15PM, August 9, 2013

266 A few examples http://www.youtube.com/watch?v=dCHdZxO4_tQ http://www.youtube.com/watch?v=PRPkRFAQBYU http://www.youtube.com/watch?v=HhbBXFw6dm4 http://www.youtube.com/watch?v=1Y_sdJKbIbo http://www.youtube.com/watch?v=umRXAkZ8Xoo

267 Cell Phone Use While Driving and Attributable Crash Risk. Annette Maciej,Manuela Nitsch, Mark Vollrath. Transportation Research Part F: Traffic Psychology and Behaviour. Volume 14, Issue 6, November 2011, pp. 512-524 Shut up i'm driving! is talking to an inconsiderate passenger the same as talking on a mobile telephone? Natasha Merat, A. Hamish Jamson, PROCEEDINGS of the Third International Driving Symposium on Human Factors in Driver Assessment, Training and Vehicle Design. 2005. http://drivingassessment.uiowa.edu/DA2005/PDF/63_Meratformat.pdf Cell Phones and Driving: Review of Research. Anne T. McCartt, Laurie A. Hellinga, and Keli a. Braitman. Traffic Injury Prevention, 7:89-106, 2006

http://www.childinjurylaws.com/pdf/
Cell%20Phones%20and%20Driv-
ing-%20Review%20of%20Research.pdf
268 Driver Reaction Time to Tactile and
Auditory Rear-End Collision Warnings
WhileTalking on a Cell Phone. Rayka
Mohebbi, Rob Gray and Hong Z.
Tan2009 51: 102Human Factors: The
Journal of the Human Factors and Ergo-
nomics Society
269 Passenger and cell phone conversa-
tions in simulated driving. Drews, F.A.,
Pasuppathi, M. and Strayer D.L. , Journal
of Experimental Psychology: Applied 14
(2008), 392–400.
The contribution of passengers versus
mobile phone use to motor vehicle
crashes resulting in hospital attendance
by the driver. Suzanne P McEvoy, Mark R
Stevenson,Mark Woodward. Accident
Analysis & Prevention. Volume 39, Issue
6, November 2007, pp. 1170–1176
Carrying Passengers as a Risk Factor for
Crashes Fatal to 16- and 17-Year-Old
Drivers. Li-Hui Chen, susan P.
Baker,Elisa R. Braver, Guohua Li. JAMA.
2000;283(12):1578-1582.
270 Cognitive Distraction While Multi-
tasking in the Automobile. Strayer,
Watson & Drews, Chapter two - The
Psychology of Learning and Motivation:
Advances in Research and Theory. Ed-
ited by Brian H. Ross. Volume 54, pp.
1-305 (2011)
Crundall, M. Bains, P. Chapman, G.
Underwood. Regulating conversation
during driving: a problem for mobile
phones. Transport Res. F, 8 (2005), pp.
197–211.
Passenger and cell phone conversations
in simulated driving.
Drews, Frank A.; Pasupathi, Monisha;
Strayer, David L.
Journal of Experimental Psychology:
Applied, Vol 14(4)
Regulating conversation during driving:
a problem for mobile telephones?
Crundall, D., Bains, M., Chapman, P.,
Underwood, G., 2005.Transp. Res., Part
F 8, 197–211. (research during real driv-
ing)
Distracted driving in elderly and middle-
aged drivers. Kelsey R. Thompson et al.
Accident Analysis & Prevention. Volume
45, March 2012, pp. 711–717
Effects of cellular telephones on driving
behaviour and crash risk: Results of
meta-analysis. JK Caird, CT Scialfa... -
2004 - psych.ucalgary.ca
http://www.psych.ucalgary.ca/pace/
PCA-Lab/pdf/Final%20Report%20-%20
Cell%20Phones.pdf
271 The Effects Of Acute Sleep Depriva-
tion On Selective Attention. Royan
Norton. British Journal Of Psychology.
Volume 61, Issue 2, pp. 157–161, May
1970
The Effects Of Early And Late Night
Partial Sleep Deprivation On Automatic
And Selective Attention: An Erp Study.
Zerouali Y, Jemel B, Godbout R. Brain
Res. 2010 Jan 13;1308:87-99. Doi:
10.1016/J.Brainres.2009.09.090. Epub
2009 Sep 30.
Sleep Deprivation Impairs Object-Selec-
tive Attention: A View From The Ventral
Visual Cortex.Lim J, Tan Jc, Parimal S,
Dinges Df, Chee Mw. Plos One. 2010 Feb
5;5(2):E9087. Doi: 10.1371/Journal.
Pone.0009087.
272 Objective and subjective measures
of sleepiness, and their associations
with on-road driving events in shift
workers. Ftouni, S., Sletten, T. L., Howard, M., Anderson, C., Lenné, M. G.,
Lockley, S. W., & Rajaratnam, S. M.
(2013). Journal of Sleep Research, 22(1),
58-69.
273 Road accidents caused by sleepy
drivers: Update of a Norwegian survey,
Ross Owen Phillips, Fridulv Sagberg,
Accident Analysis & Prevention, Volume
50, January 2013, pp. 138-146
Objective and subjective measures of
sleepiness, and their associations with
on road driving events in shift workers.
Ftouni, S., Sletten, T. L., Howard, M.,
Anderson, C., Lenné, M. G., Lockley, S.
W., & Rajaratnam, S. M. (2013). Journal
of Sleep Research, 22(1), 58-69.
Now you hear me, now you don't: eyelid
closures as an indicator of auditory task
disengagement. Ong, J. L., Asplund, C.
L., Chia, T. T. Y., & Chee, M. W. L. (2013).
Sleep, 36(12), 1867.
Driver performance in the moments

surrounding a microsleep, Linda Ng Boyle, Jon Tippin, Amit Paul, Matthew Rizzo, Transportation Research Part F: Traffic Psychology and Behaviour, Volume 11, Issue 2, March 2008, pp. 126-136
Driver performance in the moments surrounding a microsleep, Linda Ng Boyle, Jon Tippin, Amit Paul, Matthew Rizzo, Transportation Research Part F: Traffic Psychology and Behaviour, Volume 11, Issue 2, March 2008, pp. 126-136
Having to stop driving at night because of dangerous sleepiness-awareness, physiology and behaviour. Åkerstedt, T., Hallvig, D., Anund, A., Fors, C., Schwarz, J., & Kecklund, G. (2013). Journal of sleep research.
Driver sleepiness. J. A. Horne*, L. A. Reyner Journal of Sleep Research. Volume 4, Issue Supplement s2, pp. 23-29, December 1995
Specific sleepiness symptoms are indicators of performance impairment during sleep deprivation, Mark E. Howard, Melinda L. Jackson, David Berlowitz, Fergal O'Donoghue, Philip Swann, Justine Westlake, Vanessa Wilkinson, Rob J. Pierce, Accident Analysis & Prevention, Volume 62, January 2014, pp. 1 8
Half of drivers ignore basic advice to prevent deadly tiredness at the wheel 25th July 2013 http://www.directline.com/about_us/news_25072013.htm
274 The effect of caffeine on working memory load-related brain activation in middle-aged males, Elissa B. Klaassen, Renate H.M. de Groot, Elisabeth .T. Evers, Jan Snel, Enno C.I. Veerman, Antoon J.M. Ligtenberg, Jelle Jolles, Dick J. Veltman, Neuropharmacology, Volume 64, January 2013, pp. 160-167
Effects of caffeine on human behavior, A. Smith, Food and Chemical Toxicology, Volume 40, Issue 9, September 2002, pp. 1243-1255
Influence of caffeine on physiological and cognitive functions of humans. Shapkin, S. A. (2002). Human Physiology, 28(1), 128-133
Use of caffeinated substances and risk of crashes in long distance drivers of commercial vehicles: case-control study.

Sharwood, L. N., Elkington, J., Meuleners, L., Ivers, R., Boufous, S., & Stevenson, M. (2013). BMJ: British Medical Journal, 346.
Cognition enhancers between treating and doping the mind, Pharmacological Research, Cristina Lanni, Silvia C. Lenzken, Alessia Pascale, Igor Del Vecchio, Marco Racchi, Francesca Pistoia, Stefano Govoni, Volume 57, Issue 3, March 2008, pp. 196-213
Cognitive components of simulated driving performance: Sleep loss effects and predictors, M.L. Jackson, R.J. Croft, G.A. Kennedy, K. Owens, M.E. Howard, Accident Analysis & Prevention, Volume 50, January 2013, pp. 438-444.
Slow-release caffeine as a countermeasure to driver sleepiness induced by partial sleep deprivation. De Valck, E., & Cluydts, R. (2001). Journal of Sleep Research, 10(3), 203-209.
Sleep and daytime sleepiness, Timothy Roehrs, Thomas Roth, Caffeine: Sleep Medicine Reviews, Volume 12, Issue 2, April 2008, pp. 153-162
Is caffeine a cognitive enhancer?. Nehlig, A. (2010). Journal of Alzheimer's Disease, 20, 85-94.
Energy drink ingredients. Contribution of caffeine and taurine to performance outcomes, Amy Peacock, Frances Heritage Martin, Andrea Carr, Appetite, Volume 64, 1 May 2013, pp. 1-4
Caffeine antagonism of alcohol-induced driving impairment, Anthony Liguori, John H Robinson, Drug and Alcohol Dependence, Volume 63, Issue 2, 1 July 2001, pp. 123-129
Cognitive and mood improvements of caffeine in habitual consumers and habitual non-consumers of caffeine. Haskell, C. F., Kennedy, D. O., Wesnes, K. A., & Scholey, A. B. (2005). Psychopharmacology, 179(4), 813-825.
275 Cell phones change the way we walk, Eric M. Lamberg, Lisa M. Muratori, Gait & Posture, Volume 35, Issue 4, April 2012, pp. 688-690
The effects of personal music devices on pedestrian behaviour, Esther J. Walker, Sophie N. Lanthier, Evan F. Risko, Alan Kingstone, Safety Science, Volume 50,

Issue 1, January 2012, pp. 123-128
Did you see the unicycling clown? Inattentional blindness while walking and talking on a cell phone. Hyman, I. E., Boss, S. M., Wise, B. M., McKenzie, K. E., & Caggiano, J. M. (2010). Applied Cognitive Psychology, 24(5), 597-607.
Effects of listening to music, and of using a handheld and handsfree telephone on cycling behaviour, Dick de Waard, Koen Edlinger, Karel Brookhuis. Transportation Research Part F: Traffic Psychology and Behaviour, Volume 14, Issue 6, November 2011, pp. 626-637
Mobile telephones, distracted attention, and pedestrian safety, Jack Nasar, Peter Hecht, Richard Wener, Accident Analysis & Prevention, Volume 40, Issue 1, January 2008, pp. 69-75
The effects of mobile phone use on pedestrian crossing behaviour at signalised and unsignalised intersections, Julie Hatfield, Susanne Murphy, Accident Analysis & Prevention, Volume 39, Issue 1, January 2007, pp. 197-205
The cell phone effect on pedestrian fatalities, Peter D. Loeb, William A. Clarke, TTransportation Research Part E: Logistics and Transportation Review, Volume 45, Issue 1, January 2009, pp. 284-290
Distracted walking: Cell phones increase injury risk for college pedestrians, Despina Stavrinos, Katherine W. Byington, David C. Schwebel, Journal of Safety Research, Volume 42, Issue 2, April 2011, pp. 101-107
276 Did you see the unicycling clown? Inattentional blindness while walking and talking on a cell phone. Ira E. Hyman Jr, S. Matthew Boss, Breanne M. Wise, Kira E. McKenzie, Jenna M. Caggiano. Applied Cognitive Psychology. Volume 24, Issue 5, pp. 597-607, July 2010
277 Pedestrian injuries due to mobile phone use in public places, Jack L. Nasar, Derek Troyer, Accident Analysis & Prevention, Volume 57, August 2013, pp. 91-95. http://facweb.knowlton.ohio-state.edu/jnasar/crpinfo/research/AAP3092Accidents_Final2013.pdf
278 The choice to text and drive in younger drivers: Behavior may shape attitude. P. Atchley, S. Atwood and A. Boulton. Accident Analysis and Prevention. Volume 43, 2011, p. 134
279 U.S. Safety Board Urges Cellphone Ban for Drivers Matt Richtel December 14, 2011 New York Times
280 Mobile Device Use While Driving – United States and Seven European Countries in 2011. Weekly. March 15, 2013 / 62(10);177-182
281 http://www.iihs.org/laws/maptextingbans.aspx
282 http://www.iihs.org/laws/maphandheldcellbans.aspx
283 California Office of Traffic Safety: http://www.ots.ca.gov/Media_and_Research/Campaigns/Phone_in_Hand.asp High Visibility Enforcement Demonstration Programs in Connecticut and New York Reduce Hand-Held Phone Use. Linda Cosgrove, Neil Chaudhary, and Scott Roberts. NHTSA's Office of Behavioral Safety Research 2010. http://www.distraction.gov/download/research-pdf/High-Visibility-Enforcement-Demo.pdf
284 Use of Thumbs Confounds Use of Sense. Clyde Haberman. New York Times. September 1, 2009
285 Driving While Distracted. Nationwide. 2008. http://www.nationwide.com/pdf/dwd-2008-survey-results.pdf?NWOSS=survey+2008&NWOSSPos=1
286 U.S. Safety Board Urges Cellphone Ban for Drivers Matt Richtel December 14, 2011 New York Times
287 Hands-free tech still poses high risk for drivers. AAA wants tech companies to limit what their in-car, hands-free systems can do. Lucas Mearian. Computerworld. June 12, 2013. http://www.computerworld.com/s/article/9240003/Hands_free_tech_still_poses_high_risk_for_drivers
288 DRIVEN TO DISTRACTION. Drivers and Legislators Dismiss Cellphone Risks. Matt Richtel. New York Times: July 18, 2009
289 DRIVEN TO DISTRACTION. Drivers and Legislators Dismiss Cellphone Risks. Matt Richtel. New York Times: July 18, 2009
290 EDITORIAL. The Global Tobacco

Threat. NYT. February 19, 2008
Tobacco Firms' Strategy Limits Poorer
Nations' Smoking Laws. Sabrina Taver-
nise. NYT. December 13, 2013
291 DRIVEN TO DISTRACTION. Drivers
and Legislators Dismiss Cellphone
Risks. Matt Richtel. New York Times:
July 18, 2009
292 http://abcnews.go.com/US/aaron-
deveau-found-guilty-landmark-texting-
driving-case/story?id=16508694
293 http://www.riskmanagementmoni-
tor.com/coca-cola-hit-with-a-21-million-
distracted-driving-judgement/

SECTION 3

1 A field test of the quiet hour as a
time management technique, C.J. König,
M. Kleinmann, W. Höhmann, Revue
Européenne de Psychologie Appliquée/
European Review of Applied Psychology,
Volume 63, Issue 3, May 2013, pp. 137-
145,
2 quoted by Ina Fried http://news.
cnet.com/driven%20to%20distrac-
tion%20by%20technolo-
gy/2100-1022_3-5797028.html
3 A comparison of the influence of
electronic books and paper books on
reading comprehension, eye fatigue, and
perception,Hanho Jeong, (2012) "Electronic Library, Vol. 30 Iss: 3, pp. 390-408
Reading from an LCD monitor versus
paper: Teenagers' reading performance.
Hak Joon Kim, Joan Kim. Computers in
Human Behavior. Volume 28, Issue 5,
September 2012, pp. 1816-1828 http://
consortiacademia.org/index.php/ijrset/
article/view/170
Taking readingcomprehension exams on
screen or on paper? A metacognitive
analysis of learning texts under time
pressure
Rakefet Ackerman, , Tirza Lauterman.
Computers in Human Behavior. Volume
28, Issue 5, September 2012, pp. 1816-
1828
Usability evaluation of E-books. Yen-Yu
Kanga,Mao-Jiun J. Wangb,Rungtai
LincDisplays. Volume 30, Issue 2, April
2009, pp. 49-52
.Comprehension and workload differences for VDT and paper-based reading.
Daniel K Mayes,Valerie K Sims,Jefferson
M Koonce. International Journal of
Industrial Ergonomics. Volume 28, Issue
6, December 2001, pp. 367-378
4 Digital Detox: Not as easy as it
might weem. Matt Haber. New Yourk
Times july 9, 2013.
5 Email training significantly reduces
email defects, International Journal of
Information Management, Anthony
Burgess, Thomas Jackson, Janet Edwards, Volume 25, Issue 1, February
2005, pp. 71-83
6 Teresa Amabile and Steven Kramer
in HBR
7 Small Talk steigert die Meetingef-
fektivität. Joseph A. Allen und Dr. Nale
Lehmann-Willenbrock. Personal Quar-
terly 02/ 13.
8 http://www.awayfind.com/prod-
uct_tour.php
9 This, by the way, is an excellent
example of utterly stupid cost cutting in
companies, where managers are typing
their mail and memo's themselves with
one or two fingers or thumbs, while
secretaries could do a much better job,
in a fraction of the time, for much less
money and give the manager a cause less
for multitasking.
10 personal communication Loren
Frank at UCSF
11 Stress: Friend and Foe. Theo Compernolle. Synergo 1999 / Lannoo 2011
12 The Effects of Recovery Sleep after
One Workweek of Mild Sleep Restriction
on Interleukin-6 and Cortisol Secretion
and Daytime Sleepiness and Performance. Slobodanka Pejovic , Maria
Basta , Alexandros N Vgontzas , Ilia
Kritikou , Michele L. Shaffer , Marina
Tsaoussoglou , David Stiffler , Zacharias
Stefanakis , Edward O Bixler , George P
Chrousos. American Journal of Physiology - Endocrinology and Metabo-
lismPublished 13 August 2013. http://
ajpendo.physiology.org/content/ear-
ly/2013/08/07/ajpendo.00301.2013
13 http://stereopsis.com/flux/
14 ShutEye: Encouraging Awareness of
Healthy Sleep Recommendations with a
Mobile, Peripheral Display. Jared S

Bauer, Sunny Consolvo , Ben Greenstein, Jonathan O. Schooler , Eric Wu, Nathaniel F. Watson and Julie A. Kientz . Conference on Human Factors in Computing Systems, 2012. Full Paper at http://dub. washington.edu/djangosite/media/ papers/ShutEye.pdf or http://dub.washington.edu/pubs/301 App at https://play.google.com/store/ apps/details?id=com.shuteye

15   Horne, J. A. (2000, February10). Images of lost sleep. Nature, 403, 605-606 electroencephalogram of deep, non-dreaming sleep.

16   A brief afternoon nap following nocturnal sleep restriction: Which nap duration is most recuperative? Brooks, A.a,Lack, L. Sleep. Volume 29, Issue 6, 1 June 2006, pp. 831-840

17   Stop and revive? : the effectiveness of nap and active rest breaks for reducing driver sleepiness. Watling, Christopher Noel (2012) Masters by Research thesis, Queensland University of Technology.

18   Jet lag: trends and coping strategies, Jim Waterhouse, Thomas Reilly, Greg Atkinson, Ben Edwards, The Lancet, Volume 369, Issue 9567, 31 March-6 April 2007, pp. 1117-1129 Advancing circadian rhythms before eastward flight: a strategy to prevent or reduce Jet lag. Eastman CI,Gazda CJ, Burgess HJ,Crowley SJ,Fogg LF,Sleep 2005; 28:33-44. Jet Lag. Robert L. Sack, M.D. N Engl J Med 2010; 362:440-447 How to Trick Mother Nature into Letting You Fly Around or Stay Up All Night. Victoria L. Revell, Charmane I. Eastman, J Biol Rhythms August 2005 vol. 20 no. 4 353-365

19   IN-DEPTH REVIEW: SHIFT WORK. Preventive and compensatory measures for shift workers., Peter Knauth and Sonia Hornberger. Occupational Medicine 2003;53:109-116 Information and tips for employers from the New Zealand Government at: http:// www.osh.dol.govt.nz/order/catalogue/ shiftwork-fatigue2007.shtml

20   Shift Work Disorder: Clinical Assessment and Treatment Strategies.

Richard D. Simon, Jr. Brief report. .J Clin Psychiatry 2012;73. http://www.psychiatrist.com/briefreports/series-1/BR2/ index.asp

21   Shift work: health, performance and safety problems, traditional countermeasures, and innovative management strategies to reduce circadian misalignment. Mark R Smith, Charmane I Eastman. Nature and Science of Sleep 2012:4 111-132.

22   http://www.bupa.com.au/health-and-wellness/health-information/ az-health-information/sleep-and-shift-work#tips2

23   Posture, muscle activity and muscle fatigue in prolonged VDT work at different screen height settings. Jan Seghers, Arnaud Jochem & Arthur Spaepen. Ergonomics. Volume 46, Issue 7, 2000. pp. 714-730 Development and evaluation of an office ergonomic risk checklist: ROSA - Rapid office strain assessment,Michael Sonne, Dino L. Villalta, David M. Andrews, Applied Ergonomics, Volume 43, Issue 1, January 2012, pp. 98-108

24   Development and evaluation of an office ergonomic risk checklist: ROSA - Rapid office strain assessment,Michael Sonne, Dino L. Villalta, David M. Andrews, Applied Ergonomics, Volume 43, Issue 1, January 2012, pp. 98-108 http://leadergonomics.com/ROSA/ session/ROSA.pdf

25   For an explanation on the ROSA checklist go to http://ergo.human.cornell.edu/CUErgoTools/ROSA/ROSA%20 -%20Instructions%202011-2012.pdf For an example of the ROSA questionnaire go to http://ergo.human.cornell. edu/ahROSA.html

26   Assessing Posture While Typing on Portable Computing Devices in Traditional Work Environments and at Home. Abigail J. Werth Kari Babski-Reeves, Ph.D., CPEProceedings of the Human Factors and Ergonomics Society Annual Meeting September 2012 vol. 56 no. 1 1258-1262 An ergonomics training program for student notebook computer users: Preliminary outcomes of a six-year cohort

study. Karen Jacobs and others. Journal of Prevention, Assessment and Rehabilitation. Volume - Volume 44. Issue - 2 -221/230
Wrist and shoulder posture and muscle activity during touch-screen tablet use: Effects of usage configuration, tablet type, and interacting hand. Justin G. Young , Matthieu B. Trudeau, Dan Odell, Kim Marinelli, Jack T. DennerleinJournal of Prevention, Assessment and Rehabilitation (pre-press: http://iospress.metapress.com/content/w12751t54x304550/)
27 Subjects with chronic neck pain demonstrated a reduced ability to maintain an upright neutral posture when distracted by a computer task. Effect of Neck Exercise on Sitting Posture in Patients With Chronic Neck Pain. Deborah Falla, Gwendolen Jull, Trevor Russell, Bill Vicenzino and Paul Hodges. Physical Therapy April 2007 vol. 87 no. 4 408-417
Effects of Computer Monitor Viewing Angle and Related Factors on Strain, Carolyn M. Sommerich, Sharon M. B. Joines and Jennie P. Psihogios 2001 43: 39 Human Factors: The Journal of the Human Factors and Ergonomics Society
28 http://www.tipp10.com/cn/index/
29 http://www.nuance.com/dragon/index.htm
30 http://www.cbsnews.com/video/watch/?id=10187237n?tag=bnetdomain
31 http://www.att.com/gen/press-room?pid=20882&cdvn=news&newsarticleid=32644
32 Effects Of Five Speech Masking Sounds On Performance And Acoustic Satisfaction. Implications For Open-Plan Offices. Haapakangas, A.; Kankkunen, E.; Hongisto, V.; Virjonen, P.; Oliva, D.; Keskinen, E. Acta Acustica United With Acustica, Volume 97, Number 4, July/August 2011 , Pp. 641-655(15)
We Have Created This Collection Of Photographs Mainly To Serve As An Easy To Access Educational Resource. Contact Curator@Old-Picture.Com
33 Mental Performance In Noise: The Role Of Introversion, G. Belojevic, V. Slepcevic, B. Jakovljevic, Journal Of Environmental Psychology, Volume 21,

Issue 2, June 2001, pp. 209-213
Music While You Work: The Differential Distraction of Background Music on the Cognitive Test Performance of Introverts and Extraverts. Adrian Furnham* and Anna Bradley. Appl. Cognit. Psychol. 11: 445 (1997)
34 The Effect Of Background Music And Background Noise On The Task Performance Of Introverts And Extraverts
G Cassidy... - Psychology Of Music, 2007 Sagepublications
Music Is As Distracting As Noise: The Differential Distraction Of Background Music And Noise On The Cognitive Test Performance Of Introverts And Extraverts; A Furnham, L Strbac - Ergonomics, 2002 - Taylor & Francis
Work Efficiency And Personality: A Comparison Of Introverted And Extraverted Subjects Exposed To Conditions Of Distraction And Distortion Of Stimulus In A Learning Task; F. S. Morgensterna, R. J. Hodgsonb & L. LA; Ergonomics Volume 17, Issue 2, 1974 - Taylor & Francis
35 Succesgids Voor Families Met Een Bedrijf. Theo Compernolle. Lanno/Synergo. 2002
36 Inbox detox: A ceo's journey into a world without e-mail. April Wortham. Nashville Business Journal. Feb 4, 2011. http://www.bizjournals.com/nashville/print-edition/2011/02/04/inbox-detox-a-ceos-without-e-mail.html
37 The Aha! Moment. The Cognitive Neuroscience of Insight. John Kounios and Mark Beeman.Current Directions in Psychological Science 2009 18: 210. http://groups.psych.northwestern.edu/mbeeman/documents/CurrentDirxns_Kounios-Beeman_2009.pdf
38 Premack D. Toward empirical behavior laws. 1. positive reinforcement. Psychol Rev. 1959 Jul;66(4):219-233.
39 http://www.awayfind.com/product_tour.php
40 http://nursing.advanceweb.com/article/quality-time.aspx
41 Innovative Approaches to Reducing Nurses' Distractions During Medication Administration. Tess M. Pape, PhD,

MSN, BSN, RN, Denise M. Guerra, BSN, RN, Marguerite Muzquiz, MSN, RN, BC, John 6. Bryant, RN, BSN, Michelle Ingram, BSN, RN, Bonnie Schranner, MSN, RN, Armando Alcala, RN, Johanna Sharp, MSN, RN, Dawn Bishop, MSN, RN, Estella Carreno, RN, and Jesusita Welker, RN The Journal of Continuing Education in Nursing MayIJune 2005 . Vol36, No 3. http://citeseerx.ist.psu.edu/viewdoc/download?doi=10.1.1.80.1075&rep=rep1&type=pdf
Stop "knowledge creep". Pape, Tera (Theresa) PhD, RN, CNOR; Richards, Becky MA, BSN, RN. Nursing Management (Springhouse). Issue: Volume 41(2), February 2010, p 8–11

42 http://usatoday30.usatoday.com/money/jobcenter/workplace/story/2012-04-15/workers-sue-unpaid-overtime/54301774/1

43 http://blogs.hbr.org/bregman/2012/04/coping-with-email-overload.html?utm_source=feedburner&utm_medium=feed&utm_campaign=Feed%3A+harvardbusiness+%28HBR.org%29&utm_content=Google+Feed fetcher

44 http://www.instituteforpr.org/iprwp/wp-content/uploads/CoM_JPMorganChase.pdf

45 "Quiet Time" on track "No Email Day" is next!" "Quiet Time" pilot has launched! Zeldes, Nathan, IT@Intel Blog, 2007. Quoted by Uliana Popova Makarov in Networking or Not Working: A Model of Social Procrastination from Communication

46 http://www.nsc.org/safety_road/Distracted_Driving/Pages/Employer-Policies.aspx#.UCDTsqDcDgU
http://trafficsafety.org/dsww-2011-materials-now-available-for-free
http://www.distraction.gov/content/get-involved/employers.html

47 http://www.shell.com/global/environment-society/safety/road-safety/driving-safety-home.html

48 State of the Nation of cell phone distracted driving. The National Safety Council http://www.nsc.org/safety_road/Distracted_Driving/Documents/State%20of%20the%20Nation.pdf

49 Employees told to stay off phone while driving. Tanya Mohn. International Herald Tribune. May 29 2012. page 16.
Podcast with Mike Watson. Global road safety manager at Shell: http://www.shell.com/home/content/environment_society/safety/safety_podcast/ #subtitle_8

50 Quoted from the Risk Management Monitor: Morgan O'Rourke on May 14, 2012.
New York Times November 209=09

51 High-Tech Devices Help Drivers Put Down Phone. Sam Grobart. New York Times. 21 November 2009.

52 Douglas Merrill, Forbes 8/17/2012. http://www.forbes.com/sites/douglasmerrill/2012/08/17/why-multitasking-doesnt-work/

AFTERWORD

1 Inspired by an old English poem or prayer: Take time to work, it is the price of success., Take time to think, it is the source of power., Take time to play, it is the secret of perpetual youth., Take time to read, it is the foundation of wisdom., Take time to worship, it is the highway to reverence., Take time to be friendly, it is the road to happiness., Take time to dream- It is what the future is made of., Take time to dream, it is hitching your wagon to a star., Take time to love and be loved, it is the privilege of the gods., Take time to look around; it is too short a day to be selfish., Take time to laugh; it is the music of the soul., Take time to share, life is too short to be selfish

INDEX

NOTES

NOTES